The One-Day-at-a-Time
Low-Fat Cookbook

Sharon Sassaman Claessens

HPBooks

HPBooks

are published by The Berkley Publishing Group
200 Madison Avenue
New York, NY 10016

Copyright © 1996 by Sharon Claessens
Book design by Richard Oriolo
Cover photograph by Zeva Oelbaum
Cover design by James R. Harris

First edition: January 1996

Published simultaneously in Canada.

Library of Congress Cataloging-in-Publication Data

Claessens, Sharon Sassaman.
    The one-day-at-a-time low-fat cookbook / Sharon Sassaman
      Claessens.
      p.   cm.
    ISBN 1-55788-236-3
    1. Cookery.   2. Low-fat diet—Recipes.   I. Title.
    TX714.C523 1996
641.5′638—dc20   95-24043

Printed in the United States of America

10 9 8 7 6 5 4

Dedicated to Adam and to Anne,
and to you, the reader,
in the hope that this book will be
as much a gift to you in the reading
as it was to me in the writing.

Acknowledgments

My thanks to Kae Tienstra, who gave me encouragement and placed the proposal where it needed to go; to publisher John Duff at Berkley, who was attracted to my ideas and gave me the opportunity to go beyond the "concept" stage; to Terry Scott, who deciphered every word and arrow of my longhand to type a readable manuscript; to Jeanette Egan, who, with a good heart and good sense, edited the book with the best interests of the reader in mind; and to all the other people at The Berkley Publishing Group who helped make this book a reality.

I am also indebted to Dr. M. John Kennedy and the outstanding bone marrow transplant team at the Johns Hopkins University Hospital Oncology Center, Dr. Subhash Proothi and the terrific staff at Oncology Hematology of the Lehigh Valley, Dr. Victor Risch and the caring staff at the Morgan Cancer Center, and the friendly and responsive nurses at St. Luke's Outpatient Blood Clinic. In terms of emotional and spiritual support, I am grateful to my family, my friends and to the incredible women of the Fox Chase Breast Cancer Support Group and the honest and open sharing of members at the meetings of Artists Recovering through the Twelve Steps (ARTS) in Allentown, PA.

Introduction

How often do we hear promptings to eat more vegetables and grains, cut down on meats, eliminate most fats and cut back on sweets? What a huge undertaking it is to tackle our entire diet! Then, of course, we should exercise more, get enough sleep and, above all, RELAX!

Usually when we decide to change, we attempt to do it all at once. And when we inevitably fail, we give up. Good resolutions may last days or weeks, but most often end up broken. But it is possible to do for just one day something that would daunt us if we set out to do it "forever."

Anyone who has taken part in a twelve-step recovery group is already familiar with the one-day-at-a-time concept. These groups (including, but not limited to, Alcoholics Anonymous, Narcotics Anonymous, Overeaters Anonymous, Al-Anon, Artists Recovering through the Twelve Steps, Survivors of Incest Anonymous and Adult Children of Alcoholics) have helped millions of people to begin functioning as whole human beings.

As a cancer survivor, I have also learned to live one day at a time. After a mastectomy in 1985, I have faced several recurrences. Since then I have learned (or mostly, anyway) to take

nothing for granted. Each day is a gift. I've heard it said that once you've experienced cancer, you'll never view life the same way again. From my own point of view, cancer changed one thing drastically—my assumption that I would live a long life. But while I've lost an assumption, I've gained a perspective.

For example, as I was preparing myself for a bone marrow transplant in the summer of 1991, I ran into a man at a local mall who had been my first boyfriend when I was a teenager. Although I rarely encounter other friends who remained in my hometown after graduation, I bumped into John two or three times every year. As he chatted about how he had recognized me from a considerable distance by my curly red hair, I lifted up an edge of my wig and told him what I was up against. John never missed a beat, and cheerfully went on about his current activities, my son and small talk. I felt isolated by this casual conversation, knowing I was struggling for my life. I wanted to shake my friend and yell, "You know, I could die here." I did, however, successfully complete the bone marrow transplant.

That fall I was on my way to pick up my son after school when I saw a roadblock. Though I didn't know what was happening, I had the overwhelming feeling that I belonged there. As other cars turned off to detour, I approached the policeman to see if I could get through. I reluctantly followed his directive to turn away, but was so affected by my need to be present that I searched the newspaper the next day to see what had happened. It was John's fatal accident I had stumbled upon, a head-on collision that took his life. This man, with whom I had shared a connection for most of my life, a proverbial "picture of health," was gone. The person I had hoped to impress with the tenuousness of my own life had lost his. I was the one attending *his* funeral.

Every day any one of us can pick up a newspaper and read about a young person who climbed into his or her car or crossed the street and never made it home again. Heart attacks and strokes claim people in the prime of their lives. Even more unfortunately, some are victims of random violence.

We know, though we do not like to think about it, that some day we are going to die: "God, grant me the serenity to accept the things I cannot change . . ." But there are things we *can* do to reduce our risks of dying prematurely: ". . . and grant me the courage to change the things I can . . ." Yet sometimes it is difficult to know what it is we can control in our lives and what we can't: ". . . and the wisdom to know the difference." We can't control our genetic heritage or our early family life, but we can wear a seatbelt, eat less fat, reduce the stress in our lives, find contentment and pursue happiness.

Fat & Sodium

Diet, for example, is not the only factor in disease, but it is one that we can control. Four of the leading causes of death in the United States—heart disease, cancer, stroke and diabetes—are associated with diet. One of the

prime elements in all four of these diseases is fat, especially saturated fat. As a result, most health experts state that, over the age of two years, no more than 30 percent of our daily calories should come from total fat. A few foods can have more; most should have less.

The American Heart Association, the National Cancer Institute, the National Academy of Sciences and the American Health Foundation all endorse the 30 percent maximum for calories from fat, with some nutrition authorities urging that our diets be even lower in fat. Some nutrition experts also hold that our diets are too rich in animal foods—even low-fat products—and too meager in plant foods such as beans and grains. In fact, eating more fruits and vegetables is the most important dietary guideline for reducing cancer risk.

Sodium can be another health risk when consumed in excess. Because nearly 75 percent of the sodium consumed in the United States comes from processed foods, it can most easily be avoided by eating simple meals prepared at home, dishes you'll find in this book.

Alcohol & Other Risks

Alcohol-related illnesses and accidents also take their toll. We can support our own sobriety and that of friends and loved ones by being careful with what we cook and serve. For example, because they usually contain alcohol, the following ingredients are missing from the recipes in this book: flavoring extracts, nonstick cooking sprays, tamari soy sauce and the more obvious beer, wine and liqueurs. When alcohol is used in cooking, not all of the alcohol is cooked away—depending on the cooking method, a substantial amount of the alcohol remains.

Margarine has also been omitted in the recipe ingredients. Although many margarines begin as polyunsaturated oils, manufacturers mix the oils with hydrogen, so they will remain solid at room temperature. This process of hydrogenation creates saturated fats and trans fatty acids, which are unlike any naturally occurring fats. These trans fats are present, not just in margarine, but in chips, mixes, prepared baked goods and fried fast foods. According to Michael Jacobson of the Center for Science in the Public Interest "...trans fats are at least as bad as saturated fats," which have been shown to raise blood-cholesterol levels. If you do not wish to use the small amounts of butter called for, substitute olive or canola oil. To make your own alcohol-free nonstick cooking spray, pour olive or canola oil into a small pump spray bottle.

Smoking is another health risk, thought to account for up to one-third of all premature deaths. Clearly, there are areas where diet and behavioral changes can have significant impact on our well-being. What does that mean? Must we begin changing everything about our lives?

Actually, our lives are changing every day, whether we like it or not. As we move through our lives day by day, we don't have to just react. We can make some modest changes, too. We can adjust what we eat, how we manage stress, how we set priorities. Each of these small adjustments can add up to a big difference— not just in health, but in overall enjoyment of life. This cookbook is about learning to eat well and take good care of ourselves in a variety of ways, but at a measured pace. It is about changing the things that we can, making our lives better and avoiding some of the things that could make our lives shorter.

Throughout this cookbook, the focus will be on balance:

- a balance between foods that taste good and are good for our bodies
- a balance that avoids overindulgence or denial

- a balance of foods in season, when they are at their freshest, crispest and cheapest
- a balance of fiber, vitamins and minerals from foods we eat to provide us with the best possible health
- a balance between work and play, relationships and solitude, body and soul.

That balance, and a gentleness, is what this book is about. It's about treating ourselves well with food. Perhaps you, as I, have found many ways to punish yourself with food. Overeat, or indulge in something "bad," and writhe in guilt over the transgression. Diet and abstinence itself become the punishment, in the denial of even the simplest pleasures. Vacillating between the two extremes makes it impossible to find a balance, and assures that we will never feel good about ourselves.

This book isn't about spending exorbitant amounts of money on costly cuts of meats, expensive seafoods or exotic ingredients. It isn't about outlawing every ounce of fat from our diets. (Remember, moderation in *all* things, even moderation!) Rather, this book is about simple, balanced dishes that will enrich our bodies, tantalize our taste buds and please the eye. And simple, balanced lives that will bring us peace.

The Higher Power that moves all things has given us life and a certain amount of time on the earth. The time can be spent (like money) on things of lasting value or frittered away on nonessentials. I might choose to focus my life on accumulating things to impress people (who are probably too busy accumulating to notice me, anyway) or on finding ways to give back the really valuable gifts I've been given— humor, love, a talent for writing, a penchant for food. In giving back, we find ourselves becoming ever richer, though not in a way our calculators could reveal.

The One-Day-at-a-Time Low-Fat Cookbook is

about celebration, about conservation, relationships, and sharing. It is about taking
time for laughter. About being sober, but not
too serious. It is about being aware of today
and making the most of the amount of time
we're given. I hope this book inspires you to
take good care of yourself each day of your
life.

Nutritional Analysis

All recipes were analyzed using
Nutritionist III database program. If the
recipe lists a range for ingredients or number
of servings, the lower number was used for
analysis.

Percentage of Fat

The recommended percentage of calories from fat is 30 percent as the average for
the total diet. Some foods and even some
meals in a healthy diet may exceed this
amount without causing concern. What is
important is that the average diet is around
the recommended level of fat. As you plan
meals, balance higher fat-foods with nonfat
or low-fat dishes. Be aware that some recipes
seem to have a large percentage of fat, usually recipes whose ingredients are low in
total calories such as many salads or vegetable dishes. In these recipes even a small
amount of oil in the dressing or as seasoning
pushes the percentage of calories from fat
well above 30 percent.

Someone eating a 2000-calorie diet
should consume between 65 and 70 grams
of total fat on the average per day.

Eggs

All recipes use large eggs.

INSPIRATION: *This year I will make my New Year's resolutions positive. Not, "I won't do this, I won't do that," but steps I will take to bring my life into balance.*

Glazed Pork Roast with Cranberry-Apple Sauerkraut

Eating certain foods on the first day of the New Year will ensure a lucky year. So believe people in various cultures all over the world. In the south of the United States, the culinary talisman is the black-eyed pea. In Italy, it's lentils, and among the Pennsylvania Dutch, pork and sauerkraut. Pork, in fact, is prominent in many New Year's cuisines.

1 (1 1/2-pound) pork tenderloin
1 tablespoon medium unsulfured molasses
1 tablespoon honey
1 pound sauerkraut, drained and rinsed
2 tart apples, peeled, cored and chopped
1/4 cup chopped cranberries
1/2 cup apple juice
Apple slices for garnish
Parsley sprigs for garnish

Preheat oven to 300°F (150°C). Trim any fat from roast. Place in a shallow 12 × 9-inch casserole dish. Combine molasses and honey and spoon over roast. Roast 30 minutes, basting several times with pan juices.

Combine sauerkraut, chopped apples, cranberries and apple juice. Arrange sauerkraut mixture around pork and continue to roast 1 to 1 1/2 hours, or until internal temperature of the roast reaches 185°F (80°C). Stir sauerkraut mixture occasionally during cooking.

Place pork on a heated platter. Arrange sauerkraut around pork. Garnish platter with apple slices and parsley sprigs. *Makes 4 servings.*

PER SERVING: Cal 290 • Carbo 331 gm • Prot 32 gm • Total fat 5 gm • Sat fat 2 gm • Cal from fat 17% • Chol 99 mg

EDUCATION: Intention may be an important part of strengthening our immune system. Simply by choosing protein and zinc-rich foods such as pork, dark-meat turkey, or lamb, vitamin C–rich fruits and beta-carotene–rich vegetables, we send the message to our body that we want it to do well. At a time when science is learning ever more about the mind-body connection, we know that this is a powerful message, indeed.

INSPIRATION: *Taking good care of myself is a priority. Eating right is an important part of my life.*

Honey Apple Raisin Oatmeal

❧ Apples and raisins dress up plain oatmeal for a satisfying beginning to your day.

1¹/₂ cups water
²/₃ cup old-fashioned rolled oats
¹/₂ cup peeled, cored and chopped apples
¹/₄ cup raisins
2 teaspoons honey
¹/₂ teaspoon ground cinnamon
Skim milk

Combine water, oats, apples, raisins, honey and cinnamon in a small saucepan. Bring to a boil, reduce heat and simmer, partially covered, 3 to 4 minutes, until thick, stirring occasionally. Serve with skim milk.

To make in the microwave, combine all ingredients, except milk, in a medium bowl. Microwave on HIGH 2¹/₂ minutes. Stir and microwave an additional minute. Stir and serve with milk. *Makes 2 servings.*

PER SERVING WITHOUT MILK: Cal 289 • Carbo 57 gm • Prot 9 gm • Total fat 4 gm • Sat fat 0.7 gm • Cal from fat 12% • Chol 0 mg

EDUCATION: Start off the year, and every day, right—with breakfast! It's the most important meal of the day. Avoid a high-sugar breakfast, which can let you down mid-morning and tempt you to indulge in high-fat snacks.

INSPIRATION: *Providing good, nutritious meals for myself and those I care about is a conscious act of love.*

Pecan–Wild Rice Pilaf

❧ Often wild rice, the seed of a northern wetlands grass, is dried over a low fire after harvesting. Rinse before cooking to remove any smoky flavor.

1 small onion, chopped
¹/₂ tablespoon unsalted butter
¹/₃ cup chopped pecans
¹/₃ cup dried currants or raisins
¹/₄ teaspoon salt
¹/₂ teaspoon ground coriander
¹/₄ teaspoon ground cinnamon
¹/₈ teaspoon ground cardamom
1¹/₂ cups brown rice
¹/₂ cup wild rice
3³/₄ cups chicken broth
¹/₄ cup minced fresh parsley

Cook onion in butter in a large saucepan over medium heat, stirring frequently, until onion is translucent, 2 to 3 minutes. Stir in pecans, currants, salt, coriander, cinnamon and cardamom. Stir 1 minute.

Add brown rice, wild rice and broth. Bring to a boil, reduce heat to low, cover and simmer, without stirring, 40 to 45 minutes, until liquid is absorbed. Fluff with a fork while adding parsley.

Makes 6 servings.

PER SERVING: Cal 321 • Carbo 55 gm • Prot 10 gm • Total fat 7 gm • Sat fat 1 gm • Cal from fat 19% • Chol 2 mg

EDUCATION: Enjoying wild rice is a good example of treating yourself without being too extravagant. Wild rice expands to four times or more its volume when cooked, which helps keep its per-serving cost affordable. Combining it with less expensive brown rice (the grains cook in the same amount of time—roughly twice as long as white rice) is another way to enjoy wild rice economically.

INSPIRATION: *I am able and willing to devote time to quietude and self-nurturing today.*

Snow Moon Lobster Soup

 Widely used for cooking in Southeast Asia and the Pacific, coconut milk is as basic there as broth is in the United States. You won't find fresh coconut milk on grocer's shelves, but you can make your own.

 2 lobster tails, thawed
 ¹/₂ cup chopped onion
 1 tablespoon minced gingerroot or 1 teaspoon
   ground ginger
 ¹/₂ teaspoon ground red (cayenne) pepper
 ¹/₂ tablespoon canola oil
 5 cups chicken broth
 ¹/₃ cup basmati or other long-grain white rice
 1 tablespoon grated lime peel
 1 cup canned low-fat coconut milk or fresh
   coconut milk (see glossary)
 6 large mushrooms, thinly sliced
 1 tablespoon minced fresh cilantro or parsley
 2 tablespoons fresh lime juice
 Thinly sliced green onions for garnish

Remove lobster tails from shell, slice and set aside. Combine onion, gingerroot and cayenne in oil in a large saucepan over medium heat, and cook, stirring frequently, until onion is soft, 4 to 5 minutes. Add broth, rice and lime peel and bring to a boil. Reduce heat to low, cover and simmer 20 minutes, or until liquid is absorbed.

Add coconut milk, mushrooms and cilantro or parsley. Return to a boil, reduce heat to low and simmer 5 minutes. Add lobster and simmer 4 or 5 minutes or until lobster meat is firm and opaque. Stir in lime juice and serve, garnished with sliced green onions.   *Makes 6 servings.*

PER SERVING: Cal 188 • Carbo 3 gm • Prot 23 gm • Total fat 9 gm • Sat fat 3 gm • Cal from fat 43% • Chol 114 mg

EDUCATION: Reduce the amount of sodium in your diet. A significant amount of sodium is found in processed foods. Some canned soups, for example, contain more than half the recommended daily allotment of sodium in just one serving. Making your own soups with fresh ingredients is an enjoyable way to help keep sodium intake below 2,000 milligrams per day.

INSPIRATION: *It is meant for me to be happy, not to try to make myself happy with food.*

Winter's Best Fruit Compote

❧ This combination of fruit flavors creates a dish far tastier than any of its parts, alone. Serve as an accompaniment to chicken or pork, or serve as a dessert.

2 to 3 oranges
1/4 cup sugar
1 cup apple juice
2 cinnamon sticks
4 large tart green apples, peeled, cored and thinly sliced
2 Anjou or Bosc pears, peeled, cored and thinly sliced
1 cup pitted prunes, halved
1/2 cup dried apricot halves, quartered

Finely grate orange peel (do not include white portion of peel, which is bitter). Stir orange peel into sugar in a large saucepan. Squeeze oranges to get 1 cup juice. Add orange juice, apple juice and cinnamon sticks to sugar mixture. Over low heat, stir until sugar dissolves, then increase heat to medium and cook, uncovered, 5 minutes.

Add apples, pears, prunes and apricots. Return to a boil, stir, reduce heat to low, cover and simmer 20 minutes, until fruits are tender. Serve hot. *Makes 8 servings.*

PER SERVING: Cal 177 • Carbo 46 gm • Prot 1 gm • Total fat 0.5 gm • Sat fat 0.06 gm • Cal from fat 3% • Chol 0 mg

EDUCATION: Balance your system with fiber. When you eat a meal, insoluble fiber is the part that doesn't get digested. Found in the outer coverings of whole grains, in most fruits and vegetables (such as the apples here), these tough tissues resist dissolution by the enzymes and acids of our digestive systems. This residue is what gives the muscles of the intestinal tract something to work on. Fiber adds balance to your system by acting as a regulator, keeping things from moving either too fast or too slow. Increasing the proportion of these foods in your diet will benefit your digestive system and your general health.

INSPIRATION: *Choosing proper foods provides my body with the energy of life.*

Great Pacific Salmon Cakes

❧ Couscous can take the place of fresh bread crumbs in fish cakes, meat loaves and stuffings. Just rehydrate this tiny pasta, and it's ready to use.

1/4 cup chicken broth
3 tablespoons couscous
1 (14 3/4-ounce) can red salmon
1/2 cup finely grated carrot
2 tablespoons minced onion
1 tablespoon minced green bell pepper
1 egg, beaten
Lemon wedges for garnish
Parsley sprigs for garnish

Bring broth to a boil in a small saucepan over medium heat. Remove from heat, stir in couscous, cover and set aside for 5 minutes, until the liquid is absorbed.

Remove skin from salmon and discard. Flake salmon in a large bowl, crushing and stirring in bones. Stir in carrot, onion, bell pepper, egg and couscous. Form into 4 patties. Lightly butter a medium-size nonstick skillet over medium-low heat. Add patties and cook until browned on both sides, turning when first side is browned. Serve garnished with lemon wedges and parsley sprigs.   *Makes 4 servings.*

PER SERVING: Cal 194 • Carbo 6 gm • Prot 23 gm • Total fat 8 gm • Sat fat 2 gm • Cal from fat 37% • Chol 37 mg

EDUCATION: Substitute fish for meat that has more saturated fat. Although salmon is a high-fat fish, it can be included in a healthy, low-fat diet by balancing the fat intake by serving low-fat or nonfat side dishes such as steamed vegetables and rice. Since we hear bad news about fats all the time, it's a surprise to learn of fats that can be good for us. But such is the case with omega-3 fatty acids, found exclusively in fish, like the salmon above.

INSPIRATION: *I will be open today to the healing and renewing energy running through me.*

Morning Maple Couscous with Almonds

A new use for couscous: quick microwave breakfast with pizzazz!

2/3 cup water
2 tablespoons raisins
1 tablespoon slivered almonds, toasted
  (see glossary)
2 teaspoons pure maple syrup
1/4 teaspoon ground cinnamon
Dash of ground cardamom
Dash of salt
1/3 cup couscous
Skim milk

Place water, raisins, nuts, maple syrup, cinnamon, cardamom and salt in a large microwave-proof cereal bowl and microwave on HIGH 2 minutes, or until boiling, or bring to a boil in a small saucepan. Stir in couscous, cover and let stand 5 minutes. Serve with skim milk.   *Makes 1 serving.*

PER SERVING WITHOUT MILK: Cal 269 • Carbo 52 gm • Prot 7 gm • Total fat 5 gm • Sat fat 0.5 gm • Cal from fat 17% • Chol 0 mg

EDUCATION: Build a strong immune system with a healthy diet. Almonds are rich in vitamin E, a nutrient some researchers believe can help strengthen the immune system, and even reverse some of the effects of aging. The germ of whole wheat, sunflower seeds and peanuts are also good sources of vitamin E.

INSPIRATION: *My body, mind and spirit contain the wisdom and energy necessary for my healing.*

Savoy Cabbage with Tart Apples

🌿 Fancy Savoy cabbage is a nutritious side dish made with the added interest of tart red apples.

1 medium-size (about 1¹/₂ pounds)
    Savoy cabbage
2 small tart red apples
1 small red onion
1 tablespoon olive oil
¹/₄ cup chicken broth
1 tablespoon minced fresh parsley
¹/₈ teaspoon salt
Dash of freshly ground
    black pepper

Coarsely shred cabbage. Core and cut apples into thin slices. Peel and cut onion in half lengthwise, then thinly slice crosswise.

Cook onion in the oil in a large skillet over medium heat, stirring frequently, 4 to 5 minutes, until translucent. Add apples and cook, stirring frequently, 4 or 5 minutes, or until apples are firm-tender. Add cabbage and cook, stirring constantly, about 2 minutes or until cabbage is wilted.

Add broth, parsley, salt and pepper. Bring to a boil, reduce heat, cover and simmer 6 to 8 minutes or until cabbage is just tender.

Makes 4 servings.

PER SERVING: Cal 122 • Carbo 22 gm • Prot 3 gm • Total fat 4 gm • Sat fat 0.6 gm • Cal from fat 29% • Chol 0 mg

EDUCATION: Eat foods high in vitamin C daily. This vitamin, an important nutrient found in cabbage, is an essential building block of collagen—a tough, fibrous substance that cements cells together. Without collagen, wounds would not heal.

Cabbage should be stored in the refrigerator in a perforated plastic bag to retain its vitamin C content. Savoy cabbage will keep this way for about one week.

INSPIRATION: *Not wasting food benefits me, personally, then others. I can appreciate abundance more fully when I share.*

Home-on-the-Range Pinto Beans

🌿 Buy the bacon in small quantities at the butcher shop or in the deli section of your supermarket. That way there is no temptation with "leftovers," nor wasted food.

1 pound dried pinto beans
¹/₄ pound (4 thick slices) slab bacon
2 large onions, chopped
4 garlic cloves, minced
2 tablespoons chili powder
1 tablespoon dried oregano
2 teaspoons ground cumin
¹/₂ teaspoon salt
¹/₄ teaspoon freshly ground pepper
3 cups water
1 (15-ounce) can tomato sauce
2 tablespoons brown sugar
2 carrots, coarsely shredded
2¹/₂ cups brown rice
5 cups water
3 tablespoons minced fresh parsley

2 thin slices red onion, separated into rings
5 green onions, thinly sliced

Wash pintos and discard debris or moldy beans. Place beans in a large bowl, cover generously with water and soak overnight. (Or, use quick-soak method; see glossary.)

Cut bacon into 1-inch pieces. In a large, heavy saucepan, cook the bacon over medium-low heat until it is crisp and most of the fat is rendered. Remove bacon to a double layer of paper towels and press to remove additional fat. Strain drippings from pan into a small dish. Wash pan to remove cooked-on meat solids.

Using 1½ teaspoons of bacon drippings, cook onion over medium heat, stirring frequently, until onions are translucent, 4 to 5 minutes. Stir in garlic, chili, oregano, cumin, salt and pepper and cook, stirring, 1 minute. Add 3 cups water, stir well and bring to a boil. Cover, reduce heat and simmer beans 45 minutes, until tender but firm.

Add tomato sauce and brown sugar and return to a simmer. Cook slowly, uncovered, 40 minutes, stirring occasionally, until sauce thickens. Add carrots and cook 5 minutes more.

While beans are thickening, combine rice and 5 cups water in a medium-size saucepan and bring to a boil. Reduce heat, cover and steam rice on lowest heat 40 minutes, or until rice is tender and liquid absorbed. Stir in parsley just before serving.

To serve, have each person spoon some rice into a bowl, top with beans and garnish with onion rings and sliced green onions.

Makes 8 servings.

PER SERVING: Cal 367 • Carbo 72 gm • Prot 12 gm • Total fat 4 gm • Sat fat 1 gm • Cal from fat 9% • Chol 3 mg

EDUCATION: If you are adding more healthful beans to your diet, but eating them makes you uncomfortable because of the gas, try the soaking and cooking method in the glossary. This method decreases the amount of oligosaccharides, carbohydrates made up of simple sugar molecules, which ferment in the intestinal tract and cause gas.

INSPIRATION: *Being fully alive today is the great treasure that unfolds from within me.*

Spicy Turkey Sausage with Fennel Seeds

❧ If you like the taste of sausage, but need to cut back on fat, ground turkey breast offers a healthy substitute. A generous combination of herbs provides "sausage" flavor.

> *1 pound ground skinless turkey breast*
> *2 egg whites, lightly beaten*
> *¹/₂ cup fresh bread crumbs*
> *³/₄ teaspoon crumbled dried sage*
> *¹/₂ teaspoon ground coriander*
> *¹/₂ teaspoon fennel seeds*
> *¹/₄ teaspoon salt*
> *¹/₄ teaspoon dried marjoram*
> *¹/₄ teaspoon dried thyme*
> *¹/₄ teaspoon paprika*
> *¹/₄ teaspoon freshly ground black pepper*
> *Dash of freshly grated nutmeg*
> *Dash of ground red (cayenne) pepper*
> *Parsley sprigs for garnish*

Combine ground turkey, egg whites, bread crumbs, sage, coriander, fennel seeds, salt, marjoram, thyme, paprika, black pepper, nutmeg and hot pepper in a medium-size bowl. Form into 4 patties. Cook in a lightly oiled, medium-size nonstick skillet 3 to 4 minutes, until lightly browned. Turn and brown remaining sides until patties are cooked through. Serve garnished with parsley. *Makes 4 servings.*

PER SERVING: Cal 161 • Carbo 4 gm • Prot 28 gm • Total fat 3 gm • Sat fat 1 gm • Cal from fat 17% • Chol 58 mg

EDUCATION: Cutting down on salt is a healthy step. But when our taste buds are accustomed to a high-salt diet, foods might taste bland and uninteresting for a while. Fortunately, as we become more accustomed to lower salt content in foods, our taste buds begin to become more sensitive to delicate flavorings. Commercial sausages are generally high in sodium. By making your own flavorful turkey sausage you can not only cut down on sodium, but also avoid the nitrates and nitrites used as preservatives.

INSPIRATION: *By simplifying my life, I can reduce my frustrations and open up more fully to an inner feeling of peace.*

Chunky Applesauce with Raisins

❧ Serve as a side dish or dessert. Stir into cooked cereals for a morning treat, too. The apple peels add a rosy hue and fiber to the applesauce.

> *4 tart red apples, cored and quartered*
> *¹/₄ cup apple juice or cider*
> *2 tablespoons pure maple syrup*
> *1 tablespoon fresh lemon juice*
> *4 tart green apples, cored, peeled and coarsely*
>   *chopped*
> *¹/₃ cup raisins*
> *Dash of cinnamon*
> *Dash of freshly grated nutmeg*

Place red apples in a blender or food processor with apple juice, maple syrup and lemon juice. Process until apples are pureed, scraping down sides of container as needed.

Combine pureed apples with green apples, raisins and spices in a medium-size saucepan. Bring to a boil over medium heat, reduce heat to low, cover and simmer 15 to 20 minutes, until apples are tender. Serve hot or cold.

Makes 4 servings.

PER SERVING: Cal 151 • Carbo 39 gm • Prot 0.6 gm • Total fat 0.7 gm • Sat fat 0.1 gm • Cal from fat 4% • Chol 0 mg

EDUCATION: Look for a variety of ways to get your "apple a day." One is applesauce; another is a fresh crisp apple. Pack apples in your lunch or arrange in a bowl on your table or counter-top to make them convenient for snacking.

January 12

INSPIRATION: *The essence of my soul is powerful, adding its flavor to each portion of the world it touches.*

Sweet Potato–Butternut Soup with Saffron

With saffron, a little goes a long way. To release flavor from the saffron threads, oven roast for 3 minutes at 350°F (175°C) or steep untoasted strands in liquid from your recipe for 10 minutes before adding remaining ingredients. The liquid will absorb the saffron's color and flavor, which is then easily distributed throughout the dish.

4 cups chicken broth
¹/₂ teaspoon saffron threads
1 tablespoon unsalted butter
2¹/₂ cups sliced leeks (see glossary)
1 small onion, coarsely chopped
2 large garlic cloves, minced
¹/₂ teaspoon fresh ginger juice squeezed from 2 tablespoons grated gingerroot (see glossary)
3 cups peeled, seeded and cubed butternut squash
1¹/₂ cups peeled and cubed sweet potato
1 teaspoon brown sugar
¹/₄ teaspoon ground cinnamon
¹/₄ teaspoon salt
1 cup low-fat milk
2 tablespoons nonfat yogurt
¹/₂ teaspoon pure maple syrup

Heat 1 cup of the broth until hot, add saffron and let stand 10 minutes.

In a large saucepan or Dutch oven, melt butter over medium heat. Add leeks, onion, garlic and ginger juice. Stir over medium heat until leeks begin to soften, 4 to 5 minutes. Add the saffron-flavored broth to the leek mixture with remaining broth, squash, sweet potato, sugar, cinnamon and salt.

Cook, partially covered, over medium heat until squash and sweet potato are tender, 25 to 30 minutes. Transfer soup to a food processor or blender and puree. Add milk and return to pan to heat through before serving. Stir yogurt and maple syrup together. Drizzle a teaspoon of maple-flavored yogurt over each serving.

Makes 8 servings.

PER SERVING: Cal 121 • Carbo 22 gm • Prot 5 gm • Total fat 1 gm • Sat fat 0.7 gm • Cal from fat 7% • Chol 3 mg

EDUCATION: Eat hearty, making sure you get an adequate quantity, as you concentrate on high-fiber, low-fat foods. Cutting back too much on food intake alarms your bodily systems so calories are actually hoarded. Relax and make sure the calories come from complex carbohydrates, vegetables, lean poultry and fish and little fat. It actually makes it easier to stay trim.

INSPIRATION: *The slow creation of a meal can be a satisfying respite from my hectic life.*

Lamb Aushak (Afghan Ravioli)

Leek-filled ravioli with thickened yogurt and meat sauce is a traditional, tasty dish from Afghanistan.

> 3 cups low-fat yogurt
> 3 cups unbleached all-purpose flour
> $^1/_2$ teaspoon salt
> $^3/_4$ to 1 cup cold water
> 2 large leeks
> 3 teaspoons canola oil
> 1 large onion, finely chopped
> 1 pound lean ground lamb
> 1 teaspoon minced fresh garlic
> 1 teaspoon freshly ground black pepper
> $^1/_8$ teaspoon ground cinnamon
> $^1/_8$ teaspoon ground coriander
> 1 cup tomato juice
> 1 cup water
> 2 garlic cloves, minced
> $^1/_4$ teaspoon salt
> $^1/_2$ teaspoon crushed dried mint (optional)

Line a colander with 2 layers of cheesecloth and set over a large, shallow bowl. Ladle yogurt into the cheesecloth and allow it to drain about 1 hour.

In a food processor by thirds, combine flour, salt and $^3/_4$ cup cold water. Process until mixture forms a ball, adding additional teaspoons of water as needed. Or mix by hand in a bowl, kneading dough until smooth. Wrap in plastic and set aside.

Clean and finely chop leeks (see glossary). Microwave 2 minutes on HIGH, stir and microwave an additional 2 minutes to soften leeks, or steam over boiling water 4 or 5 minutes until softened. Allow to cool, then squeeze with your hands to remove water. Combine leeks with 2 teaspoons oil.

With the remaining oil, cook onion over medium heat in a large nonstick skillet until lightly browned, 6 to 7 minutes. Add meat, break up well, and brown. Drain off any fat from the pan. Add minced garlic, pepper, cinnamon and coriander. Stir 1 to 2 minutes. Add tomato juice and water, bring to a boil, reduce heat and simmer until liquid is evaporated, and meat is soft, about 45 minutes.

Divide dough into thirds. Roll out each piece on a floured surface until thin, about 1/16 inch thick. Cut out circles with a round cookie cutter 2 to 2$^1/_2$ inches in diameter, or cut dough in squares about the same size. Place a small spoonful of leeks on half the dough, moisten the edges, fold over dough and seal tightly. Place filled raviolis on a floured baking sheet and cover with waxed paper until all the raviolis are prepared.

Bring a large kettle of water to a boil. Drop half the raviolis into the water and cook 10 minutes, until dough is delicate and translucent. Stir garlic and salt into 2 cups drained yogurt. Spoon half the yogurt on an ovenproof platter and top with cooked raviolis. Keep in a warm oven while cooking remaining raviolis. Top with remaining yogurt, then meat sauce. Serve hot. *Makes 6 servings.*

PER SERVING: Cal 493 • Carbo 66 gm • Prot 34 gm • Total fat 9 gm • Sat fat 3 gm • Cal from fat 7% • Chol 70 mg

EDUCATION: Cut the fat in traditional recipes to combine their comforting, familiar flavors with a healthier outlook. Afghan meat dishes are traditionally high in fat. The recipe I found in Kabul for this dish calls for 1 cup vegetable oil to brown the onion and meat. This leaner adaptation maintains the exotic flavor and appearance of the original dish.

INSPIRATION: *My purpose today is simple—to feel good about myself.*

Oven-Baked Chicken with Vegetables

❧ While the meal bakes, you can catch up on your day. Serve with green beans or peas for color contrast and a crisp salad and crusty rolls for added texture.

1 (3½-pound) roasting chicken
6 medium-size potatoes, peeled and quartered
6 carrots, peeled and halved
1 small onion, quartered
1 tomato, peeled, quartered and seeded
About 2 cups chicken broth
⅛ teaspoon dried thyme
Dash of salt
Dash of paprika

Preheat oven to 350°F (175°C). Rinse chicken and remove giblets and any fat from body cavity. (You can freeze neck and giblets for future use in making soup or broth.) Fold wings under back and tie legs together with string.

In a large, ovenproof casserole or small roasting pan, place potatoes, carrots, onion, and tomato. Add just enough broth to nearly cover vegetables. Sprinkle with thyme. Place chicken on top of vegetables and sprinkle with salt and paprika.

Bake, uncovered, 1½ hours, or until chicken is tender. Serve vegetables, mashed slightly, with pan juices in place of butter.

Makes 6 servings.

PER SERVING: Cal 480 • Carbo 38 gm • Prot 44 gm • Total fat 16 gm • Sat fat 4 gm • Cal from fat 30% • Chol 125 mg

EDUCATION: Taking care of ourselves means giving poultry careful attention. Salmonella, often present on chicken, is a common cause of foodborne illness. However, it is easily destroyed, succumbing to temperatures as low as 140°F. Cooked just until the flesh is opaque, poultry is quite safe.

Danger comes if we spread bacteria from the chicken to work surfaces, utensils or other foods. To prevent this, gather all utensils, a wooden or plastic cutting board, and the pan or dish in which the chicken will be cooked. Prepare chicken without touching any other kitchen items, unless you wash your hands with soap and water. Immediately after the chicken is set to cooking, wash all utensils, work surfaces and your hands with soap and hot water. And never serve a marinade that has been used with raw poultry unless the marinade is first cooked.

INSPIRATION: Q. *What can you do if your microwave doesn't have a defrost setting? A. Turn to your higher power.*

Maple Acorn Squash with Apples & Walnuts

The microwave is perfect for quick-cooking winter squash, allowing its use as a convenient side dish or as a nutritious ingredient in other dishes.

1 acorn squash
1 tart apple, cored, peeled and diced
2 tablespoons apple cider or juice
2 teaspoons pure maple syrup
1 tablespoon chopped walnuts
1 teaspoon unsalted butter, softened
Dash of ground cinnamon
Dash of freshly grated nutmeg

To simplify cutting squash in half, first pierce squash through to the hollow center with a knife. Place in microwave and heat on HIGH 2 minutes to soften skin. Cut squash in half from stem to blossom end. Remove seeds and fibrous portion from cavities.

Place squash cut side up in an oval microwave-safe casserole dish. Add about ½ inch of water. Divide apple, cider or juice, maple syrup and walnuts between the 2 squash halves, placing ingredients in the hollow cavities. Spread the cut edges of the squash with the butter. Dust squash with cinnamon and nutmeg.

Microwave on HIGH 10 to 12 minutes, until the squash is tender when pierced with a fork. Not covering the squash gives an oven-baked flavor and appearance in less than one-fourth the cooking time.   *Makes 2 servings.*

PER SERVING: Cal 220 • Carbo 50 gm • Prot 3 gm • Total fat 4 gm • Sat fat 1 gm • Cal from fat 16% • Chol 4 mg

VARIATION

Squash can also be baked in a 350°F (175°C) oven 1 hour.

EDUCATION: Use kitchen tools such as the microwave to simplify food preparation so you have more time for other activities. The microwave is perfect for cooking vitamin- and fiber-rich winter vegetables such as squashes, potatoes and other root vegetables, so you can easily get more of these into your diet. A safety tip: piercing whole squash to the inner cavity prevents a buildup of steam which could cause the squash to explode even after it is removed from the oven. (You don't want to terrorize your pets with squash shrapnel!)

INSPIRATION: *Food cannot repair my emotional wounds, but, chosen properly, can help me to physically heal as I attend to the rest.*

Old-Fashioned Vegetable Soup

🌿 Served with whole-grain rolls and a salad, this delicious soup is a main course in itself.

1 cup Great Northern white beans
Water to cover
1/2 bay leaf
1/2 celery stalk and leaves
1 small onion, halved
1 1/2 pounds beef shin
1 teaspoon unbleached flour
1/2 tablespoon unsalted butter
1 1/2 cups chopped onion
2 large garlic cloves, minced
5 cups water
1 cup crushed tomatoes
1 teaspoon dried thyme, crumbled
3 carrots
2 potatoes
2 celery stalks
1 turnip
2 cups coarsely shredded cabbage
3 tablespoons minced fresh parsley

Pick over and rinse beans. Soak overnight in water in a large saucepan. Cover generously as they will nearly double in size, or use quick-soak method (see glossary). Drain beans. Cover with fresh water, add bay leaf, celery and small onion. Simmer beans, partially covered, until tender, 1 to 1 1/2 hours.

Lightly dust beef with flour. Melt butter in a Dutch oven or kettle and brown beef over medium heat, turning as needed. Remove beef and set aside. Add chopped onions to kettle and cook, stirring up bits of meat clinging to pan. When onions have begun to soften, add garlic. Cook 1 to 2 minutes. Return meat to kettle and add the 5 cups water, tomatoes and thyme. Simmer until beef is very tender, about 1 1/2 hours. Lift out meat and set aside to cool.

Slice carrots; peel and dice potatoes. Dice celery and turnip. Discard fat and bone from beef and shred meat into small pieces. Return meat to pot, add vegetables and cook 30 minutes. Add beans and parsley and heat through before serving. *Makes 6 servings.*

PER SERVING: Cal 227 • Carbo 30 gm • Prot 16 gm • Total fat 5 gm • Sat fat 2 gm • Cal from fat 21% • Chol 28 mg

EDUCATION: Eat more soups. It's hard to think of a better meal than soup. Some research shows that soup-eaters are more successful at losing weight and keeping a healthful weight balance. It may be that a hot soup, eaten slowly, helps the appetite adjust before the heavier main course, prompting us to eat less. Eating fast may mean we overdo it long before our bodies have had the chance to say, "Enough!"

INSPIRATION: *Today I will work on accepting my own and others' shortcomings.*

Joze's Sauerkraut & Potato Casserole

❧ In the south of the Netherlands, in an area called Limburg, a German influence flavors Dutch foods. A side dish features a layer of sauerkraut to flavor mashed potatoes in a hearty, stick-to-the-ribs, cold weather dish.

> 6 potatoes, peeled and cubed
> 1 pound sauerkraut, rinsed
> 1 large onion, chopped
> $^1/_2$ garlic clove, minced
> $^1/_3$ to $^1/_2$ cup hot skim milk
> 2 tablespoons nonfat yogurt
> 1 tablespoon butter
> $^1/_4$ teaspoon salt
> $^1/_8$ teaspoon freshly ground white pepper
> Dash of freshly grated nutmeg
> 1 tablespoon dried bread crumbs

Place potatoes in a large saucepan, cover generously with water and bring to a boil over medium heat. Reduce heat, cover and simmer 20 to 25 minutes, until potatoes are tender.

Meanwhile, place sauerkraut, onion and garlic in a large saucepan, cover generously with water, and bring to a boil over medium heat. Simmer 15 to 20 minutes, until the sauerkraut is tender. Drain and keep warm.

Preheat oven to 350°F (175°C). When potatoes are tender, drain and mash with hot milk, yogurt, butter, salt, pepper and nutmeg. Lightly butter a deep large casserole dish. Spread drained sauerkraut on the bottom of dish. Top with mashed potatoes and sprinkle with crumbs. Bake 15 to 20 minutes, until heated through. *Makes 6 servings.*

PER SERVING: Cal 170 • Carbo 34 gm • Prot 4 gm • Total fat 2 gm • Sat fat 1 gm • Cal from fat 10% • Chol 6 mg

EDUCATION: If you've decided to turn over a new leaf and started exercising, but feel nothing but total exhaustion, make sure you're getting enough potassium. Muscles release potassium into the bloodstream to avoid overheating, and from there potassium is excreted.

Fruit juice, bananas, carrots, broccoli, peanuts, potatoes, raisins, sunflower seeds and tuna are all good sources of potassium. Eating more of these foods can help ensure that exercising becomes and remains an enjoyable activity.

INSPIRATION: *Let me find the things I do best, and use them where they'll do me and the world the most good.*

Pineapple-Carrot Gelatin Salad

❧ This is a great winter salad because using canned fruit is a must. Fresh pineapple, or even frozen juice, contains bromelin, an enzyme that breaks down protein, which would prevent jelling.

> 1 (8-ounce) can crushed pineapple
> 1 lemon
> 1 envelope unflavored gelatin
> 1$^1/_2$ cups water
> 1 tablespoon sugar
> $^1/_3$ cup grated carrots

Pour crushed pineapple into a strainer set over a medium-size bowl to catch the juice. Press with the back of a spoon to drain liquid. There should be $^1/_2$ cup. Finely grate lemon peel from half the lemon and add to pineapple juice. Squeeze 1 tablespoon lemon juice from lemon and add to the pineapple juice. Sprinkle with gelatin.

While gelatin softens, bring the water to a boil. Pour boiling water over gelatin, add sugar and stir until gelatin is dissolved. Place bowl in refrigerator until gelatin is partially set, about 1 hour. Stir in drained pineapple and grated carrots. Refrigerate until salad is firm.

Makes 6 servings.

PER SERVING: Cal 38 • Carbo 10 gm • Prot 1 gm • Total fat 0.1 gm • Sat fat 0 gm • Cal from fat 2% • Chol 0 mg

EDUCATION: While fresh pineapple isn't friendly to gelatin salads, its unique traits can shine in a marinade, tenderizing economical cuts of meat before they head for the grill or broiler. Save the juice from cutting up raw pineapple, and use in marinades for anything from chicken wings to flank steak.

January 19

INSPIRATION: *I won't hold all my thoughts, fears or other feelings inside. Opening up to friends allows me to be real to myself and others.*

Scallop, Shrimp & Clam Seafood Stew

❧ Though clams are favored all over the world, and have been since prehistoric times, they did not "catch on" with the new settlers in North America. Pilgrims in the early 1600s fed New England clams to their pigs, unwilling to dine on what one called "the meanest of God's blessings."

1 1/2 cups chopped onion
1 cup chopped green bell pepper
4 garlic cloves, minced
2 tablespoons olive oil
2 (28-ounce) cans Italian tomatoes with juice
2 tablespoons tomato paste
2 cups bottled clam broth
2 teaspoons dried red hot pepper flakes
1 1/2 teaspoons dried basil
1 1/2 teaspoons dried thyme
1 1/2 teaspoons dried oregano
1 bay leaf
24 hard-shelled cherrystone clams, cleaned (see glossary)
1 1/2 pounds haddock, halibut or cod fillet, cut into 2-inch pieces
3/4 pound shrimp, shelled and deveined (see glossary)
3/4 pound scallops
1/4 cup minced fresh parsley
2 tablespoons freshly grated Parmesan cheese
1 pound linguini, cooked (optional)

Cook onions, bell pepper and garlic in the olive oil in a nonstick Dutch oven over medium-low heat, stirring occasionally until onion is translucent, about 5 minutes. Core and coarsely chop the tomatoes and add with the juice, tomato paste, clam broth, pepper flakes, basil, thyme, oregano and bay leaf. Bring to a boil over medium heat, reduce heat and simmer, uncovered, 1 hour, stirring occasionally.

Bring stew to a boil and add clams. As clams open, transfer to a serving dish with tongs. After 20 minutes, discard any unopened clams. Add fish fillets, shrimp and scallops and bring to a simmer. Cook, covered, 5 to 7 minutes, or until fish is opaque and firm. Remove bay leaf. Stir in clams, parsley and Parmesan cheese. Serve over linguini, if desired. *Makes 6 servings.*

PER SERVING WITHOUT LINGUINI: Cal 423 • Carbo 40 gm • Prot 49 gm • Total fat 7 gm • Sat fat 1 gm • Cal from fat 15% • Chol 182 mg

EDUCATION: Take the day off from work on your birthday. It's a special day, so fill it with special things. Or, donate some time that day to a charity or to someone who can use your help. Celebrate the delightful fact that you're in the world, and notice the ways you make others glad you are, too.

INSPIRATION: *Being open to change and willing to be present in the moment help me to keep growing.*

Apple Cider Dessert Soup

❦ The aroma of this dessert, simmering on the stove on a cold winter day, is as welcome as its hearty flavor.

> *¹/₄ cup chopped pecans*
> *1 teaspoon unsalted butter*
> *¹/₄ cup basmati or other white rice*
> *¹/₄ teaspoon ground cinnamon*
> *Dash of freshly grated nutmeg*
> *3 cups apple cider*
> *¹/₃ cup zante currants or raisins*
> *2 small tart apples*
> *1 teaspoon brown sugar*

Toast pecans over low heat in a heavy-bottomed medium-size saucepan until fragrant, about 3 minutes, stirring frequently. Set pecans aside to cool. In same saucepan, melt butter, then stir in rice, cinnamon and nutmeg. Stir over low heat 2 to 3 minutes.

Add cider and currants or raisins and bring to a boil over medium heat. Cover, reduce heat and simmer until rice is tender, about 20 minutes, stirring once or twice.

Core, peel and cut apples into thin slices. Add to cider mixture with brown sugar. Return to a boil, then simmer just until apples are tender, about 3 minutes. Serve hot, sprinkling each serving with some of the toasted pecans.

Makes 4 servings.

PER SERVING: Cal 246 • Carbo 33 gm • Prot 2 gm • Total fat 6 gm • Sat fat 1 gm • Cal from fat 22% • Chol 3 mg

EDUCATION: To make changes in our lives, we must be willing to see things differently. Soup for dessert? It's a change of pace that allows us to enjoy a low-fat ending to a meal without sacrificing a bit of flavor!

INSPIRATION: *I can renew the world within me each day, turning my view but slightly—just enough to see things in a different light.*

Kaleidoscope Chicken with Couscous

❦ Use all green bell peppers if a variety is not available in your supermarket. For added color, in this case, you could substitute a peeled, seeded tomato for one of the peppers.

> *4 chicken legs, separated into drumsticks*
>   *and thighs*
> *¹/₂ tablespoon olive oil*
> *1 large onion, chopped*
> *2 cups chicken broth*
> *¹/₄ teaspoon salt*
> *¹/₄ teaspoon freshly ground black pepper*
> *¹/₄ teaspoon dried thyme*
> *1 green bell pepper, cut in thin ¹/₂-inch strips*
> *1 red bell pepper, cut in thin ¹/₂-inch strips*
> *1 yellow bell pepper, cut in thin ¹/₂-inch strips*
> *1 cup couscous*
> *¹/₄ cup minced fresh parsley*

Remove skin and fat from chicken. Cook chicken in oil in a nonstick Dutch oven over medium heat, turning occasionally, until browned on all sides. Add onion and cook, stirring frequently, until onion is translucent, about 5 minutes.

Add chicken broth, salt, black pepper and thyme and bring to a boil. Reduce heat to low, cover and simmer until chicken is nearly tender, about 20 minutes. Add bell peppers and cook 10 minutes, until crisp-tender. Stir in couscous and cover pan. Remove from heat and let stand 5 minutes. Stir in parsley and serve.

Makes 6 servings.

PER SERVING: Cal 286 • Carbo 18 gm • Prot 24 gm • Total fat 12 gm • Sat fat 3 gm • Cal from fat 38% • Chol 70 mg

EDUCATION: Think chicken dark meat for economy and variety. Full flavor and ease of preparation make this nutritious dish a change of pace from the "boneless chicken breast syndrome."

INSPIRATION: *When I make a meal for myself, there is just one honored guest.*

Vegetarian Pita Pizza

❧ Crumble dried herbs between your fingers as you add them, to release their flavorful oils.

2 tablespoons chopped onion
$^1/_2$ teaspoon olive oil
$^1/_4$ cup diced green or red bell pepper
1 garlic clove, minced
1 ripe olive, minced
1 whole-wheat pita bread
1 tablespoon tomato paste
$^1/_8$ teaspoon dried basil
$^1/_8$ teaspoon dried oregano
$^1/_4$ cup shredded skim-milk mozzarella cheese

Cook chopped onion with the oil in a small saucepan over medium heat until onion is soft, but not browned, about 5 minutes. Add bell pepper and garlic and continue cooking until the peppers are crisp-tender, about 5 minutes. Stir in minced olive.

Preheat broiler. Broil pita bread briefly on one side until it gets slightly crispy. Remove from broiler, spread unbroiled side with tomato paste and dust with herbs. Arrange vegetable mixture over top and sprinkle with cheese. Broil until cheese is melted and bubbly.

Makes 1 serving.

PER SERVING: Cal 239 • Carbo 30 gm • Prot 12 gm • Total fat 8 gm • Sat fat 3 gm • Cal from fat 30% • Chol 16 mg

EDUCATION: Use herbs to cut down on salt and fats, less healthful flavoring ingredients. When fresh herbs are not available, dried herbs fit the bill. But even dried herbs must be "fresh" to properly flavor dishes. Dried herbs begin to lose flavor after several months. To maintain their flavor as long as possible, store dried herbs in a cool, dry and dark space. Directly above the stove, where herbs will be subjected to heat, is a display spot best avoided.

INSPIRATION: *The process of self-discovery demands my active involvement.*

INSPIRATION: *I am creating the sustaining environment I need to reach my full potential.*

Glazed Carrots

❧ Suitable for a special meal, naturally sweet carrots take on a sophisticated air.

> 8 *medium-size carrots*
> 2 *tablespoons butter*
> 2 *tablespoons brown sugar*
> 2 *teaspoons fresh lemon juice*
> *Dash of freshly grated nutmeg*

Peel and trim carrots. Cut in half crosswise, cutting thicker portions in half lengthwise. Cook carrots with water to cover in a large skillet until tender, about 10 minutes. Drain. Set carrots aside.

In same skillet, melt butter, add brown sugar, lemon juice and nutmeg and stir over medium-low heat until boiling. Return carrots to pan and stir until glazed and heated through. *Makes 6 servings.*

> PER SERVING: Cal 93 • Carbo 14 gm • Prot 1 gm • Total fat 4 gm • Sat fat 2 gm • Cal from fat 38% • Chol 10 mg

EDUCATION: Depressed? It may not be your job or spouse but a simple lack of the vitamin B₆. Start with the recipe above, then continue to add the following foods to your diet: halibut, flounder, cod, raw carrot sticks and bananas. Easy? Sure, and so much more enjoyable than job-hunting or divorce.

Mountain Bread with Sesame Seeds

❧ Ali Baba aside, sesame is familiar as the seeded topping of rolls and bread. Open the versatile sesame seed, however, and find oil, widely used in Oriental cooking; tahini, known as "the butter of the Middle East"; and halvah, a Turkish sweet.

> ¹/₄ *cup lukewarm water*
> 1 *tablespoon honey*
> 1 *tablespoon active dry yeast*
> 1¹/₄ *cups buttermilk*
> 2 *tablespoons canola oil*
> ¹/₂ *teaspoon salt*
> 2 *cups whole-wheat flour*
> ¹/₂ to ³/₄ *cup unbleached*
>   *all-purpose flour*
> 1 *tablespoon butter, melted*
> 2 *teaspoons sesame seeds*

In a large bowl, stir warm water into honey and sprinkle with yeast. When yeast is bubbly, add buttermilk, oil, salt and 1 cup whole-wheat flour. Beat with a hand-held mixer 5 minutes.

Stir in remaining whole-wheat flour. Add unbleached flour ¹/₄ cup at a time, stirring until the dough is firm enough to knead. Turn dough out on a floured surface and knead until smooth, adding enough flour to keep dough from sticking. Form dough into a ball. Lightly oil a large bowl and turn the ball in the bowl until it is coated with oil. Cover with plastic wrap and set in a warm place until dough doubles in bulk. Punch dough down and turn out on a floured surface and knead briefly.

Lightly oil an 8-inch-round cake pan. Form 12 balls of dough, about 2 inches in diameter, and coat lightly with melted butter. Place the balls in pan. Sprinkle with sesame seeds, cover with plastic wrap and set aside to rise. Preheat oven to 400°F (200°C).

When dough has again nearly doubled in bulk, place in oven. Immediately turn heat to 350°F (175°C) and bake about 40 minutes, until loaf is browned and hollow-sounding when tapped. Turn out on a cooling rack. Bread will break apart. *Makes 12 servings.*

PER SERVING: Cal 77 • Carbo 9 gm • Prot 2 gm • Total fat 3 gm • Sat fat 1 gm • Cal from fat 35% • Chol 3 mg

EDUCATION: Take good heart with sesame seeds. Sesame seeds are a good source of protein, figuring prominently in certain ethnic dishes where they are combined with legumes. The seeds can be purchased unhulled or hulled (the bran layer removed) and contain potassium, calcium, and vitamin E, all of which are good for your heart. Sprinkle sesame seeds over cereals, rice, casseroles, salads or desserts.

INSPIRATION: *Being in tune with my body's response to what I eat will help me make health-enhancing decisions.*

Susan's Salmon Salad

❧ Serve as a sandwich spread on whole-grain bread or as an appetizer spread with melba toast, Romaine lettuce leaves or other raw vegetables.

1 (14³/₄-ounce) can red salmon
1 carrot, coarsely chopped
1 celery stalk, coarsely chopped
1 green onion, coarsely chopped
3 tablespoons nonfat yogurt
1 tablespoon reduced-fat mayonnaise
1 tablespoon fresh lemon juice
2 tablespoons minced fresh parsley

Drain salmon and remove skin. In a medium-size bowl, crush salmon bones and flake salmon with a fork. Place carrot, celery and green onion in a food processor and process until finely chopped, or finely mince vegetables with a knife.

Combine yogurt, mayonnaise and lemon juice. Add with vegetables and parsley to salmon and stir to combine. *Makes 6 servings.*

PER SERVING: Cal 112 • Carbo 3 gm • Prot 14 gm • Total fat 5 gm • Sat fat 1 gm • Cal from fat 40% • Chol 39 mg

EDUCATION: Get more calcium in your diet with canned salmon. Mention "calcium" and most of us think "dairy products." But here's a fish story: Canned salmon with bones contains more calcium per serving than certain cheeses, and it's far lower in saturated fat than most cheese. So don't discard the bones in canned salmon. Crushed and folded back into the flaked salmon meat, the bones are virtually undetectable. Canned sardines can also be eaten with the bones for a calcium bonus.

INSPIRATION: *I have a right to feel satisfied after eating. I no longer want to be hurt by guilt or punished with abstinence. I can, and am learning to, find a comfortable way to live in balance with food.*

Three-Bean Chili with Sun-Dried Tomatoes

❧ Despite the long list of ingredients, this recipe is easy, and when done in a slow cooker, there's no presoaking the beans! Rather than purchase sun-dried tomatoes in oil, find plain dehydrated tomatoes. By reconstituting the tomatoes with water, you will be eliminating unnecessary fat.

    1 cup dried red kidney beans
    1/2 cup small dried red chili beans
    1/2 cup dried pinto beans
    6 cups water
    1/4 cup dried green lentils
    1/4 cup chopped sun-dried tomatoes
    1 cup chopped fresh mushrooms
    1 medium-size onion, chopped
    2 jalapeño chiles, seeded
        and minced
    4 garlic cloves, minced
    2 tablespoons paprika
    1 tablespoon chili powder
    1 teaspoon ground cumin
    1 teaspoon ground coriander
    1 teaspoon dried marjoram
    1/4 teaspoon dried oregano
    1/4 teaspoon ground black pepper
    2 large carrots, peeled and sliced
    2 celery stalks, sliced
    8 green onions, sliced
    1 red bell pepper, seeded and cubed
    1 (15-oz.) can stewed tomatoes
    1/4 cup minced fresh parsley
    Cooked brown rice (optional)

GARNISHES

    1/2 cup (2 ounces) shredded extra-sharp
        Cheddar cheese
    1 cup shredded lettuce
    1/2 cup nonfat sour cream
    1/4 cup minced fresh cilantro

Soak beans in water overnight or use the quick-soak method (see January 9).

Combine the water, beans, lentils, sun-dried tomatoes, mushrooms, onion, jalapeños, garlic, spices and herbs in a 3½-quart slow cooker. Cook on HIGH 4 to 5 hours, or on LOW 6 to 8 hours or until beans are tender. Steam carrots, celery, green onions and bell pepper in a small amount of water until tender, about 10 minutes. Add stewed tomatoes and parsley and heat through. Combine with chili in a large serving bowl. Serve over brown rice, if desired, with selection of garnishes.

Makes 6 servings.

PER SERVING: Cal 368 • Carbo 52 gm • Prot 20 gm • Total fat 11 gm • Sat fat 7 gm • Cal from fat 27% • Chol 20 mg

VARIATION

For stovetop cooking, soak beans overnight or use quick-soak method. Cook chili 1½ to 2 hours, then proceed with steaming vegetables.

EDUCATION: Avoid cooking with alcohol if you or those dining with you (including children) could suffer ill effects. Many chili recipes call for beer, while low-fat chicken, meat and seafood recipes often rely on wines and sherry for flavoring in the absence of fats. Substitute stocks, or, for chicken or fish, use fruit juices in place of alcoholic beverages.

INSPIRATION: *Hope is my enemy when it helps me fly from things as they really are.*

Hot Wings √

This delicious appetizer will fly off the buffet table!

4 pounds chicken wings
¹/₂ cup pineapple juice
¹/₄ cup teriyaki sauce
¹/₄ cup water
¹/₄ cup honey
2 tablespoons chili sauce
2 teaspoons minced gingerroot or 1 teaspoon
    ground ginger
2 garlic cloves, pushed through a press
¹/₄ teaspoon ground red (cayenne) pepper,
    or to taste

Preheat oven to 325°F (165°C). Cut wings into 3 pieces, discarding wing tips. Remove skin from wing pieces. Combine remaining ingredients in a large bowl and add wings. Cover and refrigerate 8 hours or overnight.

Arrange wings in a large shallow pan and add marinade. Bake 30 minutes, basting frequently with marinade. Drain before serving. Serve with wooden picks.   *Makes 8 servings.*

PER SERVING: Cal 223 • Carbo 15 gm • Prot 24 gm • Total fat 7 gm • Sat fat 2 gm • Cal from fat 28% • Chol 80 mg

EDUCATION: Help the food budget and your waistline by serving wholesome, satisfying meals. Go hungry after dinner and you are more likely to seek out sugary, high-fat desserts. And no matter how much the cost, if these desserts have little or no nutritious value, they're too expensive. Foods high in protein and fiber provide lasting satisfaction, minimizing the chances that you'll be tempted to splurge later, on less healthy foods.

INSPIRATION: *I will remember to have joy with the gift of food in my life—reverence that I am blessed with abundance.*

Whole-Wheat Breakfast Waffles

❧ Waffles can also be used for lunch or dinner. Top with low-fat creamed chicken or turkey with vegetables. Store leftover waffles in an air-tight plastic bag in the refrigerator or freezer. Thaw, then lightly broil or toast to crisp.

> $^3/_4$ cup whole-wheat flour
> $^1/_2$ cup unbleached all-purpose flour
> 1 teaspoon baking powder
> $^1/_8$ teaspoon salt
> $^1/_8$ teaspoon ground cinnamon
> 2 eggs, beaten
> 1 cup buttermilk
> 1 tablespoon canola oil

Preheat nonstick waffle iron. Combine dry ingredients in a medium-size bowl. In another bowl combine beaten eggs, buttermilk and oil. Stir egg mixture into dry ingredients just until combined. Do not overmix.

Pour $^1/_2$ cup batter on preheated waffle iron. Close iron and bake until golden and crisp, about 3 minutes. Remove and keep warm. Repeat with remaining batter. Serve waffles hot, with topping. *Makes 4 servings.*

PER SERVING: Cal 236 • Carbo 33 gm • Prot 9 gm • Total fat 7 gm • Sat fat 1 gm • Cal from fat 27% • Chol 109 mg

EDUCATION: Make your own quick, nutritious fruit toppings for pancakes and waffles to cut down on sugary syrups. For Strawberry Syrup, hull 1 pint strawberries and process half the berries with $^1/_4$ cup pure maple syrup until pureed. Slice remaining berries and stir in. For Blueberry Syrup, process 1 cup blueberries with $^1/_4$ cup syrup until pureed and stir in 1 cup whole berries. Heat, if desired, before serving.

INSPIRATION: *I remind myself when I'm eating that happiness comes from inside—not outside—of me.*

Victor's Vegetables with Pasta

❧ Victor, the best doctor I've ever met, might enjoy this best in summer with something from the grill. An all-in-one side dish for fish, poultry or broiled chops. The vegetable combination is rich in complimentary flavors, not fat.

> 1 cup fusili or penne pasta
> 1 onion, chopped
> $^1/_2$ tablespoon unsalted butter
> 1 carrot, cut into thin sticks
> 1 small turnip or $^1/_2$ medium-size turnip, diced
> 1 cup sliced portobello, shiitake or regular mushrooms
> 1 garlic clove, minced
> 1 celery stalk, thinly sliced on diagonal
> 2 tablespoons minced fresh parsley
> $^1/_4$ cup tomato juice
> $^1/_2$ teaspoon salt
> Parsley sprigs for garnish

Bring a large saucepan of water to a boil. Add pasta, return to boiling and cook until firm-tender, 5 to 7 minutes.

Meanwhile, add onion and butter to a microwave-safe bowl and microwave on HIGH 1 minute. Stir in carrot and turnip; microwave on HIGH 2 minutes. Add mushrooms and garlic, stir, and microwave on HIGH 3 to 4 minutes, until mushrooms are tender. Stir in celery and parsley and microwave on HIGH 2 to 3 minutes, until celery is crisp-tender. Add tomato juice, salt and pasta and heat through 1 minute on HIGH. Serve hot, garnished with parsley sprigs. *Makes 4 servings.*

PER SERVING: Cal 142 • Carbo 29 gm • Prot 5 gm • Total fat 1 gm • Sat fat 0.4 gm • Cal from fat 6% • Chol 1 mg

VARIATION
The vegetables can be prepared in a large skillet on the stove, beginning with the onion and adding the vegetables, in the order above, until all are firm-tender.

EDUCATION: "Eat your vegetables" is an admonition worth heeding. Most of us had to be coaxed in our early years to eat our vegetables. Now nutrition experts are taking up the chant where our parents left off. To stay healthy, they warn, we have to eat—that's right—more vegetables. Oh, and skip the creamy, cheesy sauces—too much fat.

INSPIRATION: *I will gratefully accept the gentle and quiet small gifts of the day.*

Poached Flounder with Sesame Rice

Toasting sesame seeds brings out their nutty flavor. You can substitute any thin fish fillet for the flounder.

1 tablespoon minced shallots
1 teaspoon canola oil
1 teaspoon sesame seeds
³/₄ cup brown rice
2 cups water

2 green onions, thinly sliced
1 teaspoon unsalted butter
4 small flounder fillets (about ³/₄ pound)
¹/₂ cup low-fat (1%) milk
Pinch of salt
Freshly ground white pepper
2 tablespoons minced fresh parsley
Parsley sprigs for garnish
Lemon slices for garnish

Cook shallots in oil in a medium-size saucepan over medium heat, stirring frequently, until translucent. Add sesame seeds and stir until lightly toasted. Add brown rice and the water and bring to a boil. Cover, reduce heat and steam 40 minutes. Keep warm.

Cook green onions in the butter in a medium-size skillet, stirring frequently, until the green onions are wilted. Lay flounder fillets over green onions and add milk, salt, white pepper and parsley. Bring to a simmer, cover and poach 3 to 4 minutes, until fish fillets are just opaque throughout. Serve over sesame rice garnished with parsley and lemon slices.

Makes 2 servings.

PER SERVING: Cal 490 • Carbo 58 gm • Prot 40 gm • Total fat 9 gm • Sat fat 3 gm • Cal from fat 17% • Chol 90 mg

EDUCATION: Increase your intake of beta-carotene–rich vegetables. Ounce for ounce, parsley ranks among the vegetables highest in beta-carotene content. Your body converts beta-carotene into vitamin A (that's the vitamin that helps keep your skin healthy, your eyes sharp and your immune system in tip-top shape). Luckily, parsley is available and affordable year-round. Instead of just using a sprig or two of parsley as a garnish, get in the habit of mincing several tablespoons of parsley and adding it to soups, salads, vegetables and main dishes, hamburgers, eggs, pasta dishes and stir-frys.

INSPIRATION: *My talents are a gift. They come through me as much as they are "of" me, and it is right to share them.*

Dimm Punch

❧ This nonalcoholic punch is a favorite with children and adults.

White grape or cranberry juice for ice cubes (optional)
3 cups chilled white grape juice
3 cups chilled cranberry juice
1 quart chilled club soda
¹/₂ lemon, seeded and sliced

Make ice cubes from juice, if desired. Combine juices and club soda in a large punch bowl. Float lemon slices in the punch and serve with ice cubes or frozen fruit juice cubes.

Makes 12 servings.

PER SERVING: Cal 75 • Carbo 19 gm • Prot 0.4 gm • Total fat 0.1 gm • Sat fat 0 gm • Cal from fat 1% • Chol 0 mg

EDUCATION: Create your own holiday for family and friends—a noncommercial, joyous celebration. For example, deep in the cold of January, long after the joys of December holidays have passed, our household enjoys a tradition of our own invention: "Dimm, the Festival of Do-Dahs." Instead of experiencing postholiday letdown, we look forward each year to being surrounded by friends and laughter, warmth and hilarity.

Friends gather at our house on the Saturday closest to the official Dimm date, January 31. We share a potluck, then share of ourselves. Some display a talent: magic, music, storytelling or jokes. Others teach: papermaking, foot reflexology, Moravian star-folding, veg-

etable carving, etc. The silly talents are always the favorites!

New friends join us each year, but by the end of the evening they have begun a rare acquaintance with a range of people. Our greatest satisfaction came last year when one newcomer said, "I've never seen so many people having such a great time sober!" We invite you to enjoy Dimm, too, or make up your own holiday to create more fun in your life!

INSPIRATION: *Sometimes I must remember that, just as heat transforms the properties of foo͏ · the better, my trials and diffic.   .y soul.*

Bird's

❧ A change of pac͏   ͏.͏ot side dish—delicate strips   .ıth aromatic spices! For whimsy, place a few cooked peas in each nest. If you really want to go all out, trim and steam pearl onions, then dust with nutmeg for a speckled-egg effect.

4 large carrots
2 teaspoons unsalted butter
¹/₈ teaspoon salt
Dash of ground cinnamon
Dash of ground coriander
Dash of freshly grated nutmeg
2 to 4 tablespoons chicken broth or apple juice

Peel and trim carrots. Using a vegetable peeler, cut long, thin strips from the carrots, ¹/₄ to ¹/₂ inch wide. Melt butter in a medium-size nonstick skillet over medium heat and add salt, cinnamon, coriander and nutmeg. Stir 30 seconds. Add carrots and 2 tablespoons broth or juice and stir to combine with seasonings.

Cook, stirring constantly, until the carrots are firm-tender, about 5 minutes, adding more liquid, if needed, to prevent sticking. Do not brown the carrots. *Makes 4 servings.*

PER SERVING: Cal 53 • Carbo 8 gm • Prot 1 gm • Total fat 2 gm • Sat fat 1 gm • Cal from fat 33% • Chol 5 mg

EDUCATION: Serve carrots more often. The universally accepted orange carrot is a relative newcomer. In earlier times, carrots ranged from yellow to red to purple. Purple carrots are still seen in Central Asian countries, such as Afghanistan. The orange color of our familiar table carrot heralds the abundant presence of beta-carotene. In fact, given their popularity, carrots are the leading source of this nutrient—which the body converts to vitamin A. Light cooking helps break down the sturdy cells of the carrot, making its nutrients more accessible than they are when the carrot is eaten raw.

INSPIRATION: *Peace and quiet is mine for the creating, no matter how busy I have managed to make my life.*

Vermont Apple Bake

In choosing an apple for baking, select a variety that keeps its shape. Rome Beauty, Stayman, York or Jonathan apples are all good choices. McIntosh apples become mushy when cooked.

6 large, tart baking apples
1 tablespoon butter, at room temperature
6 tablespoons apple juice or cider
1/4 cup pure maple syrup
1 teaspoon fresh lemon juice
2 tablespoons finely chopped walnuts

Preheat oven to 350°F (175°C). Wash and core apples. Peel about one-third of the way down the apple from the stem end. Arrange the apples in a 13 × 9-inch shallow casserole dish, stem ends up.

Dot butter over peeled portion of apples. Combine juice or cider, maple syrup and lemon juice and spoon over apples. Bake apples 45 minutes, basting occasionally with cooking juices. Sprinkle with chopped walnuts and bake an additional 15 to 20 minutes, until apples are very tender. Serve hot. *Makes 6 servings.*

PER SERVING: Cal 152 • Carbo 33 gm • Prot 0.7 gm • Total fat 3 gm • Sat fat 1 gm • Cal from fat 18% • Chol 5 mg

EDUCATION: Make it easy to get more apples into your diet. It's easiest to core whole apples with an inexpensive tool made for this purpose: a pointed metal tube attached to a handle. Push the tube into the center of the stem end of an apple through to the blossom end. The core will be removed as you withdraw the corer. If you are filling apples with raisins or nuts, use a knife to core apples and leave about 1/2 inch of apple at the stem end to hold the filling. Cut a funnel-shaped opening at the stem end of the apple to make a spacious cavity for filling.

INSPIRATION: *Drawing happy and enthusiastic people into my life is part of my healing.*

Melt-in-Your-Mouth Buttermilk Rolls

If you have one good recipe for dinner rolls, let it be this one. Prepare to pass the recipe on to guests, who'll be sure to request it!

1 tablespoon dry yeast
1 tablespoon sugar
$1/4$ cup lukewarm water
1 cup buttermilk
3 tablespoons unsalted butter
3 cups unbleached all-purpose flour
$1/2$ teaspoon baking soda
3 tablespoons brown sugar
$1/2$ teaspoon salt
2 tablespoons melted butter
$1/2$ cup yellow cornmeal

Dissolve the yeast and sugar in the water in a large bowl. Let stand until yeast is frothy. Place buttermilk and butter in a small saucepan over low heat just until butter is melted. Cool to lukewarm.

Combine flour, baking soda, brown sugar and salt in a medium-size bowl. Add cooled buttermilk and flour mixtures to yeast in large bowl and beat with a wooden spoon until combined. The dough should be soft and spongy. Set the bowl in a sink partially filled with quite warm water, cover with plastic wrap and let dough rise about 1 hour, until light.

Lightly butter a baking sheet. Beat down dough. Roll pieces of dough about the size and shape of an egg. Lightly coat with melted butter, then roll in cornmeal. Put rolls on baking sheet to rise. Cover and let rise until almost double in size, about 30 minutes. Preheat oven to 400°F (200°C). Bake rolls 20 minutes, or until lightly browned. *Makes 12 rolls.*

PER ROLL: Cal 203 • Carbo 34 gm • Prot 5 gm • Total fat 5 gm • Sat fat 3 gm • Cal from fat 22% • Chol 14 mg

EDUCATION: Turn to buttermilk for a tasty low-fat addition to breads and muffins. It sounds caloric and rich, but buttermilk is actually a tart and tasty low-fat product. Traditionally, buttermilk remained when creamy milk was churned to make butter. These days, however, cultured buttermilk is more readily available. Using low-fat or skim milk, dairies add a culture that converts some of the milk sugar, lactose, to lactic acid. It is this acid that interacts with baking soda to create light and tender quick breads, pancakes, muffins and rolls.

INSPIRATION: *Each day I make better decisions about what goes into my body.*

Hot Dutch Potato Salad

Tangy, no-fat dressing is a hit! Serve with low-fat turkey sausage.

4 to 5 red potatoes
(about 1 1/2 pounds)
1 onion, chopped
1/3 cup cider vinegar
1/4 cup plus 2 tablespoons water
1 teaspoon brown sugar
1/4 teaspoon salt
1/4 teaspoon freshly ground black pepper
1 1/2 teaspoons unbleached all-purpose flour
1/4 teaspoon dry yellow mustard
1/4 cup minced green bell pepper
1/4 cup shredded carrot
2 tablespoons minced fresh parsley

Scrub and cube potatoes with skins on. Place potatoes in a large saucepan, cover with water and bring to a boil over medium heat. Reduce heat to low, cover and simmer potatoes just until tender, 12 to 15 minutes. Drain and return potatoes to pan.

While potatoes are cooking, place chopped onion, vinegar, 1/4 cup water, brown sugar, salt and pepper in a small saucepan. Bring to a boil, reduce heat to low, and simmer 5 minutes. In a small cup, stir flour and mustard into remaining 2 tablespoons water. Add to vinegar mixture and continue cooking, stirring constantly, until mixture thickens.

Stir bell pepper, carrot and parsley into hot potatoes. Pour hot dressing over potato mixture and toss gently to combine. Serve hot.

Makes 4 servings.

PER SERVING: Cal 148 • Carbo 34 gm • Prot 3 gm • Total fat 0.3 gm • Sat fat 0 gm • Cal from fat 2% • Chol 0 mg

EDUCATION: Adapt favorite family recipes to make them lower in fat and calories. When my farming ancestors sat down to hot potato salad, it featured ham, hard-boiled eggs and bacon dressing. But when they got up from the table, the day was spent plowing, planting, harvesting or threshing. Their high-calorie meal provided fuel for a full day's activities.

These days, when plowing is more likely to be through backlogged paperwork than the "south forty," excess fats and calories aren't consumed with physical labor. If we don't find ways to trim our meals, we wind up sitting on hefty assets. But the trick is always to trim calories without losing interest or flavor. Here, colorful pepper and carrots offer an alternative to high-fat meats, and a tasty mustard-vinegar dressing succeeds without bacon.

INSPIRATION: *I am worthy of giving myself the best, treating myself with care and respect.*

Orange, Red Onion & Spinach Salad

A colorful winter salad, rich in vitamins A and C. Sprouting your own alfalfa seeds at home ensures a fresh supply (see glossary).

¹/₄ pound fresh spinach leaves
3 navel oranges
2 red onion slices
¹/₂ cup alfalfa sprouts (see glossary)
2 teaspoons canola oil
1 tablespoon orange juice
2 teaspoons fresh lime juice
¹/₂ teaspoon honey
¹/₄ teaspoon coarsely ground prepared mustard
Dash of salt
Dash of freshly ground white pepper

Wash spinach leaves in a large pot filled with tepid water. Pull off thick stems. Lift spinach out of water, and repeat with fresh water until rinse water is clear. Drain and pat leaves dry with a paper towel.

Peel oranges. Cut them crosswise into thin slices, catching any juices in a bowl. Remove any seeds. Separate onion slices into rings.

On individual plates, arrange spinach leaves. Top with orange slices and onion rings. Garnish with alfalfa sprouts. Combine oil, orange and lime juice, honey, mustard, salt and pepper. Spoon some of the dressing over each salad. Serve chilled.   *Makes 4 servings.*

PER SERVING: Cal 101 • Carbo 18 gm • Prot 2 gm • Total fat 3 gm • Sat fat 0.2 gm • Cal from fat 27% • Chol 0 mg

EDUCATION: Even in the dead of winter, you can experience the pleasure of growing fresh food. One of the easiest crops is sprouts—little powerhouses that burst with nutrition as they germinate. Consider this: by just adding water to alfalfa seeds, for example, you can increase their protein content, boost their B vitamins three to ten times higher and create vitamin C, even when it wasn't present in the original seed! When sprouting any seeds, be sure they are meant for the table and haven't been treated for planting.

INSPIRATION: *Meeting my physical needs for properly nutritious food undergirds my emotional and spiritual recovery.*

Judy's Hearty Baked Penne Pasta

Serve this hearty and colorful vegetarian main dish with a green, leafy vegetable.

8 ounces penne pasta
1 large onion, chopped
¹/₂ cup diced green bell pepper
2 teaspoons olive oil
1 (15-ounce) can tomato sauce
1 tablespoon minced fresh parsley
1 teaspoon dried oregano
1 teaspoon dried basil
¹/₄ teaspoon freshly ground black pepper
1 cup part-skim ricotta cheese
2 cups shredded part-skim mozzarella cheese
    (about 6 ounces)

Preheat oven to 375°F (190°C). Bring a kettle of salted water to a boil. Add pasta and cook just until firm-tender, 6 to 8 minutes. Drain and rinse. Return to pan.

Meanwhile, cook onion and bell pepper in the oil in a medium-size saucepan over medium heat until tender, about 5 minutes. Stir in tomato sauce, parsley, oregano, basil and pepper. Simmer 5 minutes.

Stir ricotta and half the mozzarella together in a medium-size bowl. Combine ricotta mixture with pasta and half the tomato sauce, stirring gently. Turn into a 13 × 9-inch shallow casserole dish. Spoon remaining tomato sauce over pasta and sprinkle with remaining shredded mozzarella. Bake 25 to 30 minutes until cheese is melted and lightly browned.

Makes 6 servings.

PER SERVING: Cal 326 • Carbo 41 gm • Prot 18 gm • Total fat 10 gm • Sat fat 5 gm • Cal from fat 28% • Chol 29 mg

VARIATION

Baked Penne Pasta with Beef Brown ¹/₂ pound lean ground beef with ¹/₂ minced garlic clove over medium heat. Drain off any fat. Toss with penne pasta and cheeses when adding tomato sauce.

EDUCATION: Eat more pasta dishes with low-fat sauces but avoid the rich cream and cheese types that can derive nearly 90 percent of their calories from fat! Pasta, once spurned by dieters, has found new favor among the health-conscious. And for good reason: pasta is high in protein, rich in complex carbohydrates—useful "fuel" for our daily activities—and, most important, low in fat.

INSPIRATION: *If I care for myself first, I will have the strength and serenity to care appropriately for others.*

Apricot Rice Cereal

Make up a large pot of porridge, then refrigerate or freeze in individual portions for future in-a-hurry breakfasts.

1 cup uncooked brown rice
4 cups water
¹/₄ cup chopped apricots
1 tablespoon honey
¹/₄ teaspoon salt
Skim milk

Place the rice, water, apricots, honey and salt in a medium-size saucepan. Bring to a boil over medium heat. Cover, reduce heat to lowest setting, and cook slowly 1 to 1¹/₂ hours or until rice is very soft and the mixture looks like porridge when stirred. Serve with skim milk.

Makes 6 servings.

PER SERVING WITHOUT MILK: Cal 131 • Carbo 28 gm • Prot 3 gm • Total fat 1 gm • Sat fat trace gm • Cal from fat 7% • Chol 0 mg

EDUCATION: Be more aware of foods containing sulfites. Because sulfites can cause severe allergic reactions in some people who are sensitive, their use must be listed on the package label.

Most dried apricots available commercially are treated with sulfur dioxide ("sulfites") to maintain their orange color. You can obtain unsulfured apricots at a natural-food store. These are brown in color, not the bright orange you may associate with dried apricots, but they taste delicious.

INSPIRATION: *I can choose to seek happiness, setting my course for wholeness and wellness.*

Maple Tapioca Pudding

❧ Simple desserts are often best, as this quick tapioca pudding demonstrates.

> *¹/₄ cup quick-cooking tapioca*
> *¹/₄ cup pure maple syrup*
> *2 eggs, lightly beaten*
> *2 cups low-fat (1%) milk*
> *Dash of salt*

Combine tapioca, syrup, eggs, milk and salt in a heavy saucepan. Place over very low heat and let stand 7 minutes without stirring. (If you don't have a heavy saucepan, place ingredients in the top of a double boiler with boiling water beneath.) Increase heat to medium-low and stir until slightly thickened, about 5 minutes. Pudding will thicken more as it cools. Chill, if desired, before serving.   *Makes 4 servings.*

> PER SERVING: Cal 200 • Carbo 29 gm • Prot 7 gm • Total fat 6 gm • Sat fat 3 gm • Cal from fat 27% • Chol 123 mg

VARIATIONS

Macaroon Tapioca Pudding Substitute 3 tablespoons sugar for maple syrup and add 2 teaspoons shredded coconut.

To cook in the microwave, combine ingredients in a large microwave-safe bowl. Microwave on HIGH 3 minutes. Stir and microwave a total of 4 to 5 minutes more, stirring every 2 minutes, until thickened slightly.

EDUCATION: Sometimes a light meal, such as soup and salad, calls for a substantial dessert. In winter, we favor this recipe for tapioca pudding. It is hearty, but low in fat and not too sweet.

Tapioca is processed from the starch extracted from cassava or manioc roots. It is very easily digested. In addition to its use in puddings, tapioca can also be used to thicken soups, fruit juice sauces and other liquids. As a thickener, substitute 1 tablespoon quick-cooking tapioca for 1 tablespoon flour. Always sprinkle on boiling liquids and stir until mixture thickens.

INSPIRATION: *A fresh and joyous spirit waits within me. Today I will begin opening up to set it free.*

Tuna Salad with Raisins

❧ Here is not the oily mayonnaise-based tuna salad you might be used to, but a crunchy, light, sweetly flavored new experience. You can also serve this salad with toasted whole-grain bread, or tuck with the lettuce into pita bread.

> *1 (6¹/₂-ounce) can water-packed*
> *   tuna, drained*
> *2 cups unpeeled diced red apples*
> *¹/₂ cup chopped carrot*
> *¹/₂ cup diced green bell pepper*
> *¹/₂ cup raisins*
> *¹/₄ cup chopped walnuts*
> *¹/₄ cup minced fresh parsley*
> *¹/₃ cup nonfat yogurt*
> *1 tablespoon olive oil*
> *1 tablespoon fresh lemon juice*
> *¹/₂ teaspoon minced shallots*
> *¹/₈ teaspoon ground yellow mustard*
> *Dash of salt*
> *Dash of freshly ground black pepper*
>
> GARNISHES
> *Romaine lettuce leaves*
> *4 small bunches red grapes*
> *4 parsley sprigs*

Flake tuna and toss in a large bowl with apples, carrot, bell pepper, raisins, walnuts and parsley. Combine yogurt, oil, lemon juice, shallots, mustard, salt and pepper in a small bowl. Pour over tuna salad and toss. Serve salad on lettuce leaves, garnished with grapes and parsley sprigs. *Makes 4 servings.*

PER SERVING: Cal 240 • Carbo 30 gm • Prot 17 gm • Total fat 7 gm • Sat fat 1 gm • Cal from fat 26% • Chol 9 mg

EDUCATION: Eat foods that give your jaws a workout! We hear again and again how important exercise is to a healthy body. But exercise is just as important for healthy teeth and gums. Do many of the foods you eat have crunch? Does your diet consist of soft, processed foods—spongy breads, peanut butter, canned vegetables and fruits, puddings, mashed potatoes and applesauce? Or, do you enjoy crusty loaves of bread, raw carrots, apples and pears, nuts and seeds? This salad will give you something to chew on.

February 10

INSPIRATION: *Risking growth means letting go of old ways that haven't worked.*

Jalapeño Beef Stew

❦ Hearty winter beef stew with the punch of a Tex-Mex chili is a welcome dish in cold weather. Serve with whole-grain bread and a crisp salad, then settle down in front of the fire.

1 onion, chopped
3 teaspoons olive oil
6 garlic cloves, minced
1 jalapeño chile, seeded and minced
    (see glossary)
1 1/2 pounds stew beef cubes, trimmed
1 tablespoon ground cumin
1 tablespoon paprika
1/2 teaspoon dried oregano
1/4 teaspoon red (cayenne) pepper

1/4 teaspoon salt
1/4 teaspoon freshly ground black pepper
1 (28-ounce) can whole tomatoes,
    drained and chopped
4 cups beef stock
1 cup frozen whole-kernel corn
6 green onions, thinly sliced
1/4 cup minced fresh parsley

Cook onion in 1 teaspoon of the oil over medium heat in a large nonstick pot, stirring frequently, until onion is soft, about 4 minutes. Add garlic and jalapeño and cook 1 minute more, stirring constantly. Remove onion mixture from the pan and set aside.

Place half the remaining oil in the pan over medium-high heat. Cook half the beef cubes until browned, stirring frequently, about 5 minutes. Remove from pan. Repeat with remaining oil and beef cubes. Return all the beef to the pot and add cumin, paprika, oregano, cayenne, salt and black pepper. Cook, stirring, 30 seconds to develop the flavor of the spices.

Add onion mixture, chopped tomatoes and beef stock to beef. Bring to a boil, reduce heat, cover and slowly simmer until meat is tender, 1 1/2 to 2 hours. Add corn and cook 2 to 3 minutes, until corn is done. Stir in green onions and parsley and serve. *Makes 4 servings.*

PER SERVING: Cal 446 • Carbo 25 gm • Prot 49 gm • Total fat 17 gm • Sat fat 5 gm • Cal from fat 35% • Chol 126 mg

EDUCATION: Try a new flavor tack to revive interest in old favorites. Sometimes all it takes for a jaded appetite is a new twist. This stew, for example, is lifted out of the ordinary with zesty hot chiles and Tex-Mex seasonings. Try the same with your favorite vegetable soup or meat loaf recipe. Hot peppers are rich in vitamin C and add robust flavor with next to no fat or sodium, making them a healthy seasoning choice.

INSPIRATION: *I am willing to begin laying the foundation for a healthier life, and to wait for the results.*

Tossed Green Salad with Blue Cheese Dressing

❧ Made with buttermilk and part-skim ricotta, the creamy dressing is high in taste, low in fat.

> $1/2$ small head romaine lettuce
> 1 cup packed fresh spinach leaves, large stems removed
> $1/2$ cup coarsely shredded cabbage
> 3 green onions, thinly sliced
> 1 carrot, thinly sliced
> $1/4$ cup diced red or green bell pepper
> $1/4$ cup minced fresh parsley
>
> DRESSING:
> $1/4$ cup buttermilk
> $1/4$ cup part-skim ricotta cheese
> 1 teaspoon olive oil
> 1 garlic clove, crushed
> 2 tablespoons crumbled blue cheese
> $1/8$ teaspoon salt
> Dash of freshly ground black pepper

Wash and dry romaine lettuce and spinach. Tear both into large bite-size pieces. Toss greens in a salad bowl with shredded cabbage, green onions, carrot, bell pepper and parsley.

For dressing, combine buttermilk, ricotta, oil and garlic in a blender container. Process on low speed until smooth. Place blended mixture in a serving cup or bowl and stir in crumbled blue cheese, salt and pepper. Serve salad with dressing on the side. *Makes 4 servings.*

PER SERVING: Cal 76 • Carbo 6 gm • Prot 5 gm • Total fat 4 gm • Sat fat 2 gm • Cal from fat 47% • Chol 8 mg

EDUCATION: Add mineral-rich foods to your diet to ease stress. It may seem surprising, but minerals in our diets can be an important part of recovery. Already stressed nerves need adequate supplies of calcium and magnesium to heal. For sources of calcium, look to buttermilk, skim milk, yogurt, tofu, canned salmon with bones crushed and mixed in, broccoli and soybeans. The green, leafy vegetables above are rich in magnesium, as are nuts, peas, brown rice and other whole grains.

INSPIRATION: *I have everything I need for recovery.*

Brenda's Colorful Vegetable Omelet

❧ Serve with herbed potatoes and whole-grain rolls.

> $1/2$ cup chopped onion
> $1/2$ tablespoon unsalted butter, softened
> $1/3$ cup diced red bell pepper
> $1/3$ cup shredded carrots
> $1/3$ cup chopped broccoli flowerets
> $1/8$ teaspoon dried marjoram
> $1/8$ teaspoon salt
> 2 eggs
> 1 egg white
> 1 tablespoon skim milk
> 1 tablespoon minced fresh parsley
> $1/4$ cup alfalfa sprouts
> Parsley sprigs for garnish

In a medium-size bowl, combine onion and 1 teaspoon of the butter. Microwave on HIGH 2 minutes. Stir in bell pepper and carrots and microwave on HIGH 2 minutes. Add broccoli and microwave on HIGH 1 to 2 minutes until vegetables are crisp-tender. Stir in marjoram and salt. (You can also cook in a skillet over medium heat in the order given on top of the stove until vegetables are crisp-tender.) Cover and keep warm.

Beat eggs and extra egg white with skim milk and parsley. Heat a nonstick 8-inch skillet over medium heat until a drop of water dances when sprinkled in the pan. Swirl the remaining $1/2$ teaspoon butter around bottom of pan. When melted, pour in egg mixture. As eggs cook, pull edges of the omelet toward the center of the pan with a table knife, allowing uncooked egg to reach pan. Repeat until eggs are set. Eggs can be slightly soft on top, as they will continue to cook.

Spoon vegetables over half the omelet. Gently fold omelet over vegetables and remove to a serving plate. Top with sprouts and garnish with parsley. *Makes 2 servings.*

PER SERVING: Cal 141 • Carbo 9 gm • Prot 10 gm • Total fat 7 gm • Sat fat 3 gm • Cal from fat 44% • Chol 219 mg

EDUCATION: Make informed choices about the use of butter or margarine. When polyunsaturated oils are processed into margarine, the hydrogenating process creates a type of fat never found in nature. These trans fatty acids have been implicated in a variety of health problems.

To avoid margarines, you may want to cook with small amounts of butter, or, to reduce cholesterol intake, use half butter, half oil. If you do choose to use margarine, get the softest available. The more solid these fats are at room temperature, the more saturated. And the more solid means more hydrogenation—more trans fatty acids.

INSPIRATION: *I am learning that good food can be pleasurable as well as life-sustaining.*

Apple & Banana Winter Muesli

Take advantage of winter fruits in a wholesome combination of nuts and oats. In the summer, add or substitute fresh berries or peaches.

1 apple, cored and diced
$1/2$ banana, diced
$1/2$ cup rolled oats
2 tablespoons raisins
$1/2$ cup nonfat yogurt
1 tablespoon chopped
    walnuts
1 tablespoon chopped
    almonds or pecans
1 teaspoon brown sugar
    (optional)

Combine the apple, banana, oats and raisins in a large cereal bowl. Spoon yogurt over top and garnish with nuts and brown sugar, if desired. *Makes 1 serving.*

PER SERVING: Cal 520 • Carbo 91 gm • Prot 17 gm • Total fat 11 gm • Sat fat 1 gm • Cal from fat 19% • Chol 2 mg

EDUCATION: Eat simple cereals for more complete breakfast nutrition. Many commercial cereals are stripped of fiber and nutrients— then puffed up with sugar, salt and even fats. Rolled oats offer whole-grain fiber and other nutrients and are easy on the food budget, too.

INSPIRATION: *Love starts with me. If I do not love myself, I cannot truly love others. I will honor and love myself today.*

Rock Cornish Game Hen with Couscous Stuffing

❧ The recipe here serves one. If you want to share this holiday, double the stuffing and make two hens. Enjoy with baked potato, carrots and a green salad.

$^1/_2$ *small onion, minced*
1 *shallot, minced*
1 *teaspoon unsalted butter*
$^1/_8$ *teaspoon ground coriander*
1 *tablespoon raisins*
$^1/_3$ *cup chicken broth*
$^1/_4$ *cup couscous*
1 *(1-pound) Rock Cornish*
  game hen

Cook onion and shallot in butter in a medium-size saucepan over medium heat, stirring frequently, until the onion is translucent, about 3 minutes. Stir in coriander and cook 1 minute more. Add raisins and broth and cook, stirring, until the mixture comes to a boil. Add couscous and stir until combined. Cover pan, remove from heat and let stand 5 minutes. Remove cover and let stuffing cool.

Preheat oven to 400°F (200°C). To prepare game hen, rinse and pat dry. Remove any fat from body cavity. Twist wing tips flat against the back of the bird. Stuff cavity with cooled couscous mixture and tie legs together with string.

Place hen breast side up in a shallow baking dish. Roast 45 minutes or until juices run clear, basting twice with pan juices. Untie legs and serve. Remove skin before eating to reduce fat.

Makes 1 serving.

PER SERVING: Cal 481 • Carbo 32 gm • Prot 56 gm • Total fat 14 gm • Sat fat 4 gm • Cal from fat 26% • Chol 235 mg

EDUCATION: Eating alone doesn't have to mean opening a can or taking out a frozen prepackaged dinner. For example, the Rock Cornish game hen is a small, tender and delicious bird just the right size for one! Now, you can treat yourself to an elegant meal without worrying about waste or facing days of leftovers.

INSPIRATION: *I may not have control over many of the things that happen in my life, but I do have choices about how I cope.*

Carrot-Lentil Loaf

The bay leaf, or sweet laurel, used to flavor the lentils has a noble history. This was the crown of laurel sported by victorious Greek athletes and Roman generals in ancient times. Because bay leaf does not soften in cooking, it should never be crushed and added to dishes. Bay leaf must be removed and discarded before serving dishes it has flavored.

> *1 cup lentils*
> *1 small bay leaf*
> *3 cups water*
> *2 carrots*
> *1 onion, quartered*
> *¹/₂ celery stalk, coarsely chopped*
> *1 garlic clove*
> *¹/₂ cup soft whole-wheat bread crumbs*
> *¹/₂ cup skim milk*
> *1 egg, beaten*
> *1 teaspoon ground cumin*
> *¹/₄ teaspoon dried thyme*
> *¹/₄ teaspoon salt*
> *¹/₄ teaspoon freshly ground black pepper*
> *¹/₄ cup ketchup*

Bring the lentils and bay leaf to a boil in the water in a large saucepan over medium heat. Reduce heat, cover and simmer until lentils are firm-tender, 25 minutes. Remove bay leaf.

Preheat oven to 350°F (175°C). Shred one carrot with the large holes of a grater. Set aside. Cut remaining carrot into large pieces and add with onion, celery and garlic to a food processor. Process until finely chopped, or mince ingredients by hand. When lentils are cooked, drain and add shredded carrot, finely chopped vegetables, bread crumbs, milk, egg, cumin, thyme, salt and pepper. Mix until combined.

Place lentil mixture in a lightly oiled or nonstick 8-inch-square shallow casserole dish. Spread ketchup over lentil mixture. Bake 30 minutes.   *Makes 6 servings.*

PER SERVING: Cal 102 • Carbo 18 gm • Prot 6 gm • Total fat 1 gm • Sat fat 0.3 gm • Cal from fat 9% • Chol 36 mg

EDUCATION: Eat well to cope better . We may not be able to control some of the stresses in our lives: pollution, our heredity or exposure to viruses. But choices about our food can help us deal with all of these and move us in the direction of health. Eating a variety of fresh and lightly cooked vegetables, fruits, beans, grains and small amounts of low-fat fish and poultry is an easy way to keep us healthy and emotionally stable.

INSPIRATION: *I will learn to say "yes" more often to foods that enhance my health, and gently "no" to foods that hurt me.*

Sombrero Salsa

Don't counteract the benefits of this low-fat dip with greasy tortilla chips. Choose low-fat or nonfat chips to accompany the salsa.

1 large onion, chopped
1 teaspoon canola oil
2 garlic cloves, minced
2 jalapeño chiles, minced
*   (see glossary)*
3 1/2 cups canned whole tomatoes,
*   drained*
1 cup tomato sauce
1/4 cup canned mild green chiles,
*   chopped*
2 teaspoons ground cumin
2 teaspoons ground coriander
1/2 teaspoon salt
1/4 teaspoon dried oregano
1/4 teaspoon ground black pepper
Low-fat or nonfat corn chips

Place the onion in a large microwave-safe bowl with the oil and microwave on HIGH 2 minutes. Stir in garlic and jalapeños and microwave on HIGH 1 more minute. If you are not using a microwave, cook onion in oil in a skillet over medium heat until translucent. Add garlic and jalapeños and cook, stirring, 1 to 2 minutes. Chop tomatoes, removing tough stem ends.

Stir tomatoes, tomato sauce, mild chiles, cumin, coriander, salt, oregano and black pepper into onion mixture. Serve at once with chips or refrigerate until chilled.

Makes 4 cups, 8 servings.

PER SERVING WITHOUT CHIPS: Cal 52 • Carbo 9 gm • Prot 2 gm • Total fat 2 gm • Sat fat 1 gm • Cal from fat 35% • Chol 0 mg

EDUCATION: Having nutritious, low-fat snacks around the house can help lead us in the direction of healing. "Impulse" eating can be directed by what's available. If what we've stockpiled is a selection of high-fat cookies, desserts and cheeses, that is what we'll turn to. On the other hand, having raw vegetables, fresh fruits, low-fat crackers and tortilla chips and low-fat dips and spreads handy is an automatic plus. Many of the low-fat appetizers in this book can be made up and kept on hand, just for your personal snacking!

INSPIRATION: *I can accept myself today, as I am, becoming more fully individual and alive to my own possibilities.*

Seven-Layer Dip with Guacamole

Avocado turns brown when exposed to air. To keep a fresh, green color, make guacamole just before serving. If storing is necessary, place guacamole in a tall, narrow jar or other container to minimize the surface exposed to air. Stir guacamole before serving.

4 ounces nonfat cream cheese, at
*   room temperature*
1/4 cup nonfat yogurt
1 small garlic clove, pushed
*   through a press*
1/8 teaspoon ground cumin
1 cup Super-Easy Guacamole
*   (see below)*

1 cup Sombrero Salsa (see February 16)
  or bottled salsa thinned
  with tomato juice
1 cup shredded iceberg lettuce
$^1/_2$ cup thinly sliced green onions
$^1/_4$ cup finely chopped ripe olives
$^1/_2$ cup shredded sharp Cheddar cheese
Nonfat tortilla chips

SUPER-EASY GUACAMOLE

1 avocado
2 tablespoons Sombrero Salsa (see February 16)
  or bottled salsa
2 tablespoons nonfat yogurt
$^1/_2$ garlic clove, pushed through a press

Combine cream cheese, yogurt, garlic and cumin. Spread evenly over the bottom of a 10-inch quiche or pie dish. Top with a layer of guacamole, then salsa, and spread evenly over top. Sprinkle with shredded lettuce, then green onions, olives and cheddar cheese. Serve with plenty of nonfat tortilla chips. *Makes 8 servings.*

PER SERVING WITHOUT CHIPS: Cal 134 • Carbo 5 gm • Prot 4 gm • Total fat 5 gm • Sat fat 2 gm • Cal from fat 30% • Chol 10 mg

EDUCATION: Learning to do things the easy way doesn't make us lazy, just smart! For example, guacamole is a tasty dip but can be far simpler to make than many recipes suggest. For a higher-protein snack, add 2 tablespoons part-skim ricotta cheese to Super-Easy Guacamole. Avocado has a higher fat content than most fruits and vegetables, but is rich in minerals and vitamin C.

INSPIRATION: *As I respect myself, I will respect others. As I show care for myself, I can show care for those around me.*

Banana-Cinnamon Whole-Wheat Pancakes

Delicious, with no oil in the batter! Serve with fresh fruit sauce or cinnamon applesauce.

$^1/_2$ cup whole-wheat pastry flour
$^1/_2$ teaspoon ground cinnamon
$^1/_4$ teaspoon baking powder
$^1/_8$ teaspoon salt
$^1/_2$ very ripe banana
1 egg
2 tablespoons skim milk

Place flour, cinnamon, baking powder and salt in a food processor and process until combined. Add banana, egg and milk and process just until smooth.

Heat a small nonstick skillet over medium heat until a drop of water dances when sprinkled on the surface. Lightly butter the bottom of the pan. Spoon batter into the pan. Cook over medium-low heat until bubbles appear on the surface of the pancake and bottom is lightly browned. Turn and brown remaining side. Remove to a plate and serve with desired toppings. *Makes 1 serving.*

PER SERVING: Cal 367 • Carbo 63 gm • Prot 14 gm • Total fat 6 gm • Sat fat 2 gm • Cal from fat 15% • Chol 213 mg

EDUCATION: One way to take care of ourselves is to be frugal. "Waste not, want not" was the mantra while we were growing up in our Pennsylvania Dutch household. The beauty of this recipe is that it makes use of overripe bananas we might not otherwise enjoy. The banana's very ripeness is what creates a tasty, low-fat batter.

INSPIRATION: *By making choices, I reveal my creativity—or, possibly, reveal just what happens to be in my refrigerator on any given day.*

Around-the-World Beef Stir-Fry

❧ By switching a few ingredients, this basic recipe reflects a variety of international cuisines.

MEXICAN:

1 tablespoon canola oil
1 teaspoon dried oregano
1 teaspoon ground cumin
1 garlic clove, minced
1 green bell pepper, cut into strips
1 medium-size onion, sliced
1 jalapeño chile, thinly sliced
    (see glossary)
1 pound lean beef round steak, cut
    into thin strips
3 cups cooked white rice
2 cups thinly sliced lettuce for garnish

In a small bowl, combine oil, oregano, cumin and garlic. In a large nonstick skillet, warm half the seasoned oil over medium heat. Add bell pepper, onion and jalapeño. Stir-fry 2 to 3 minutes, or until crisp-tender. Remove vegetables and set aside. In same skillet, stir-fry beef strips, half at a time, over medium heat in remaining oil, 1 to 2 minutes. Return vegetables and first batch of browned beef to skillet and heat through. Serve over rice and garnish with lettuce.   *Makes 4 servings.*

PER SERVING: Cal 423 • Carbo 48 gm • Prot 31 gm • Total fat 10 gm • Sat fat 2 gm • Cal from fat 21% • Chol 70 mg

VARIATIONS
Middle Eastern Beef Stir-fry Omit oregano; add ¼ teaspoon turmeric. Omit jalapeño and lettuce. Serve over 3 cups cooked rice with yogurt on the side.

Curried Beef Stir-fry Omit oregano; add ½ teaspoon ground coriander, ¼ teaspoon turmeric, ¼ teaspoon paprika and a dash of ground cayenne. Add ½ teaspoon minced gingerroot with bell pepper and onion. Serve over 3 cups cooked basmati rice with yogurt on the side. Garnish with mint sprigs in place of lettuce.

Chinese Beef Stir-fry Omit oregano and cumin; add ¼ cup sliced green onions, 1 tablespoon minced gingerroot and a dash of ground cayenne to the bell pepper and onion. Flavor with a sprinkle of rice vinegar. Omit lettuce and serve over 3 cups cooked rice.

Hungarian Beef Stir-fry Omit oregano and cumin; substitute 1 teaspoon paprika. Omit jalapeño chile and lettuce. Stir 1 teaspoon flour into ½ cup nonfat sour cream. Stir into beef mixture and serve over cooked noodles in place of rice.

Italian Beef Stir-fry Use olive oil. Omit cumin; substitute ¼ teaspoon marjoram and ¼ teaspoon basil. Omit jalapeño pepper and lettuce. Combine ingredients with 1 cup tomato sauce, heat through, and serve over pasta.

EDUCATION: Add variety to your meals to increase your enjoyment of low-fat dishes; sometimes all it takes is a change of seasonings. For example, think of your favorite soup, stew, casserole or meat loaf. Do you always make it the same way? If so, try varying some of the ingredients. Use leeks instead of onions; shallots in place of garlic; parsnips, not carrots; and fennel where you've used celery. Vary the herbs and spices, as above, to give more international flavor to old favorites. Jot down what you've done, so you can repeat your successes.

INSPIRATION: *Positive thoughts can help me build a healthy and strong body. I choose to put my energy into images of health and wholeness.*

Whipped Potatoes with Turnip & Leeks

❧ Potatoes are so good for us, it's fun to find more ways to include them in our diet. Mashing potatoes with other vegetables adds flavor and provides a change of pace.

> *3 large potatoes*
> *1 small turnip*
> *1 cup chopped leeks (see glossary)*
> *2 teaspoons unsalted butter*
> *¼ cup skim milk*
> *2 tablespoons nonfat yogurt*
> *1 tablespoon nonfat sour cream*
> *Dash of salt*
> *Dash of freshly ground white pepper*
> *2 tablespoons minced fresh parsley for garnish*

Peel and cube potatoes and turnip. Place in a large saucepan with enough water to cover and bring to a boil over medium heat. Reduce heat, cover and simmer 20 to 30 minutes, until vegetables are very tender. Meanwhile, cook leeks in the butter in a medium-size skillet over medium-low heat, stirring occasionally, about 10 minutes or until tender. Remove from heat and stir in skim milk, yogurt and sour cream. Drain potatoes and turnip and mash in the pan with the leek mixture. Season with salt and pepper and place in a warmed serving dish. Garnish with parsley.   *Makes 4 servings.*

PER SERVING: Cal 152 • Carbo 30 gm • Prot 4 gm • Total fat 2 gm • Sat fat 1 gm • Cal from fat 12% • Chol 5 mg

EDUCATION: Eat more complex carbohydrates. Who wouldn't like the endurance of an athlete, even if our only weekly run is the half block to the bus stop? Endurance can mean the energy to do our work, take care of the house, see to the children, exercise the pets and still have something left over to enjoy our leisure time, rather than snoozing on the recliner. What athletes know, and many others of us may not, is that complex carbohydrates provide the most efficient energy fuel. Not sugars, but whole grains, potatoes and other vegetables, green salads, and raw fruits are most readily turned into glycogen, the fuel used by working muscles. The body can convert fat or protein to fuel, but the process itself takes energy. Complex carbohydrates are the "high-test" on the highway of life.

INSPIRATION: *Each day I can turn to a power greater than myself to bring the fullness of healing into my life.*

Haddock Fillets with Red Onion Rice

Substitute any white-fleshed fish for the haddock. When you select fish, look for firm flesh and a fresh smell. Allow one-third pound per person when serving fish fillets.

> 1 1/2 cups chicken broth
> 1 1/4 cups quick-cooking brown rice
> 1/8 teaspoon salt
> 2 teaspoons unsalted butter
> 1/3 cup chopped red onion
> 2/3 cup coarsely shredded cabbage
> 1 1/3 pounds haddock fillets
> 1/4 cup water
> 1/4 cup skim milk
> 8 lemon slices for garnish
> 4 parsley sprigs for garnish

Bring broth to a boil in a medium-size saucepan over medium heat. Stir in rice and salt, reduce heat, cover and simmer 10 minutes, until the rice is tender. Keep warm.

Melt butter in a medium-size skillet over medium heat. Stir in onion and cabbage and cook, stirring occasionally, until tender, 8 to 10 minutes. Stir into cooked brown rice.

Place haddock, water and milk in a large skillet. Bring to a boil, reduce heat to low, cover and simmer just until the fish is opaque and firm throughout, about 10 minutes. Serve haddock with rice mixture, garnished with lemon slices and parsley sprigs.

Makes 4 servings.

PER SERVING: Cal 242 • Carbo 17 gm • Prot 33 gm • Total fat 4 gm • Sat fat 1 gm • Cal from fat 15% • Chol 91 mg

EDUCATION: Choose low-fat protein sources. Say "protein" and most people think of meat. But meats offer higher fat content along with protein. Leaning toward the following sources of protein will keep you under the recommended 30 percent total calories from fat: fish, nonfat yogurt, white meat chicken or turkey without skin, split peas, lentils, dried beans, shrimp, scallops and dry-curd cottage cheese.

INSPIRATION: *My life force is a gift to be managed with clarity and love.*

Lentil Soup with Sweet Potato

Sweet potato gives this soup added flavor. We hope it's the best lentil soup you've ever tried!

> 1 large onion, chopped
> 1 tablespoon olive oil
> 3 garlic cloves, thinly sliced
> 1 cup lentils
> 4 cups chicken broth
> 2 carrots
> 2 celery stalks
> 3 or 4 small red potatoes
> 1 large sweet potato
> 1 small head escarole
> 1 1/2 cups tomato juice

Cook onion in oil in a Dutch oven over medium heat, stirring frequently, until onion is translucent, about 5 minutes. Add garlic and cook an additional minute or two, but do not let garlic brown. Add lentils and broth. Bring to a boil, reduce heat to low, cover and simmer 20 minutes. Meanwhile, dice carrots, celery and washed, unpeeled potatoes. After 20 minutes, add vegetables to lentils in Dutch oven. Cook 15 minutes more.

Thinly slice escarole. Add to lentil mixture with canned tomatoes. Cook 10 minutes, until escarole is tender. *Makes 6 servings.*

PER SERVING: Cal 198 • Carbo 34 gm • Prot 9 gm • Total fat 3 gm • Sat fat 0.6 gm • Cal from fat 14% • Chol 0 mg

EDUCATION: Increase resistance to disease by eating foods that contain vitamin A. Vitamin A is like the director of a good play. The director does none of the acting, but helps others do the job well. In a similar way, vitamin A helps the body coordinate immune-system forces to fight off disease, increasing our resistance to illness. Even a few spoonfuls of sweet potato provide a day's worth of recommended dietary allowance, providing an excellent reason to enjoy this vegetable in a variety of dishes. Sweet potatoes are too important to be restricted to Thanksgiving Day!

February 23

INSPIRATION: *I have a new sense of well-being as I make healing choices for myself.*

Delicate Sour Cream Corn Bread

Light and tasty, this corn bread wins converts. Serve it with lentil soup and enjoy a filling, but really low-fat meal.

1 cup unbleached all-purpose flour
3/4 cup yellow stone-ground cornmeal
1 1/2 teaspoons baking powder
1/2 teaspoon baking soda
1/4 teaspoon salt
2 eggs
2/3 cup nonfat yogurt
1/3 cup nonfat sour cream
2 tablespoons melted butter

Preheat oven to 425°F (220°C). Lightly butter a nonstick 8-inch-round baking pan. Combine flour, cornmeal, baking powder, baking soda and salt in a large bowl. In a medium-size bowl, beat eggs, then beat in yogurt, sour cream and butter. Combine with dry ingredients. Pour batter into pan. Bake 25 to 30 minutes or until cake-tester or wooden pick inserted in center comes out clean. Serve warm.

Makes 8 servings.

PER SERVING: Cal 168 • Carbo 24 gm • Prot 6 gm • Total fat 5 gm • Sat fat 4 gm • Cal from fat 28% • Chol 62 mg

VARIATIONS

Cheddar Corn Bread Fold 1/2 cup shredded Cheddar cheese into batter before baking.

Jalapeño Corn Bread Fold 1/2 minced jalapeño chile into batter.

Jalapeño-Cheddar Corn Bread You guessed it; fold in both!

EDUCATION: Plan meals using less processed foods. Highly processed foods most often have had their nutritious and beneficial elements removed and potentially detrimental substances added. Most often removed are fiber, vitamins, minerals and the oil-rich germ of whole grains. Items commonly added are sugar, salt and fat, which must provide flavor to the nutrient-depleted foods. You can see why eating simpler, unprocessed foods is a health-supporting step.

INSPIRATION: *With recovery, I am becoming more whole, no longer hiding parts of myself just to win approval.*

Nancy's Carrot Cake with Creamy ✓ Orange Icing

Many carrot cakes call for as much as a cup of oil. But all that oil isn't necessary for a moist, delicious cake. The orange adds moistness— and terrific flavor! Thanks to Nancy, who brought this cake to our Dimm Celebration (see January 31).

2 or 3 large carrots
1 large navel orange
1 tablespoon raisins
1 cup whole-wheat pastry flour
1 cup unbleached all-purpose flour
2 teaspoons ground cinnamon
2 teaspoons baking powder
2 teaspoons baking soda
1 teaspoon freshly grated nutmeg
¹/₂ teaspoon salt
2 eggs, lightly beaten
¹/₃ cup buttermilk
¹/₂ cup maple syrup
¹/₂ cup packed brown sugar
¹/₃ cup canola oil
4 tablespoons nonfat cream
   cheese, softened
1 teaspoon orange juice
¹/₂ to ²/₃ cup powdered sugar

Preheat oven to 350°F (175°C). Lightly butter a 13 × 9-inch baking pan. Wash and trim carrots and cut into large pieces. Place in a food processor and process until finely chopped, or grate carrots finely, to make 2 cups. Set aside.

Cut orange into 8 wedges. Do not peel. Remove white center and seeds. Cut wedges into 3 or 4 pieces each and puree in a food processor or blender along with the raisins.

Combine flours, cinnamon, baking powder, baking soda, nutmeg and salt in a large bowl. In another bowl, combine eggs, buttermilk, maple syrup, brown sugar, oil, carrots and orange. Stir carrot mixture into dry ingredients until combined.

Spread batter evenly in pan and bake 25 to 30 minutes, until a cake tester or wooden pick inserted in the center comes out clean. Cool cake in pan.

Prepare icing by working cream cheese and orange juice together with the back of a spoon until combined. Stir in enough powdered sugar to obtain a spreadable consistency. When cake is cool, spread top with icing. *Makes 16 servings.*

PER SERVING: Cal 159 • Carbo 26 gm • Prot 2 gm • Total fat 5 gm • Sat fat 1 gm • Cal from fat 28% • Chol 27 mg

EDUCATION: Use spices and herbs to replace flavor provided by fat and sugar. Ground spices, like nutmeg, cinnamon and allspice, quickly lose flavor. Purchase whole spices and grate them as needed for fuller fragrance and flavor. An inexpensive kitchen gadget, sold as a nutmeg grater, can be used for any hard spice. Grate spices into a small cup, then measure before adding.

INSPIRATION: *Creating something allows me to experience a union of my spiritual, emotional and physical energies.*

Dawn's Crusty Whole-Wheat Bread

Crusty whole-wheat bread from the oven is one of the real pleasures of baking. A great weekend activity, too!

> 1 cup buttermilk
> 1 tablespoon active dry yeast
> 2 tablespoons brown sugar
> 1 1/2 cups whole-wheat flour
> 1 1/2 cups unbleached all-purpose flour
> 1/4 cup rolled oats or oat bran
> 1/2 teaspoon salt
> 2 tablespoons safflower oil
> 1 tablespoon skim milk

Heat buttermilk to lukewarm. Pour yeast into a small bowl and stir in buttermilk and brown sugar. Let stand until foamy, 10 minutes.

Meanwhile, in a large bowl, combine flours, oats and salt. Pour yeast mixture and oil into flour mixture and stir to combine. Use your hands to combine and gradually work the dough into a ball as it becomes firmer. Turn out dough on a lightly floured surface and knead 10 minutes.

Set dough in an oiled bowl and turn so its surface is lightly coated with oil. Cover the bowl with plastic wrap and allow dough to rise in a warm place until doubled in size, 30 to 45 minutes.

Oil a 9 × 5-inch loaf pan. Punch dough down with your fist, then form it into a loaf and set it in the loaf pan. Cover and let rise again until almost doubled in size, about 30 minutes.

Preheat oven to 350°F (175°C). Brush the top of the dough with milk, then bake 35 minutes. Remove bread from the pan and set it directly on the oven rack. Turn off oven; remove bread after 5 minutes for a crisp crust.

Makes 1 loaf, 12 slices.

PER SLICE: Cal 159 • Carbo 28 gm • Prot 4 gm • Total fat 3 gm • Sat fat 0.3 gm • Cal from fat 17% • Chol trace

EDUCATION: For a wide range of tactile and sensual experiences, bake your own bread. There are few cooking techniques to rival it. The first experience comes from watching the bread come alive, expanding from a cold lump of dough to a sensuous, billowing mass. Punching down the dough, then shaping it, provides a creative experience. The swelling and browning of the baking bread accompanies one of the kitchen's most satisfying aromas. Slicing through the crisp crust into the still warm, soft interior precedes the incomparable taste of fresh bread straight from the oven. Then, sharing your creation! An insight into why "breaking bread" together is a universal symbol of peace.

INSPIRATION: *I will relax into changes that are in my best interest, gently letting go of bad food habits.*

Bonnie's Slow-Cooker Creamy Potato Soup

✗ If you don't have a slow cooker, follow the easy directions for stove cooking. Bonnie enjoys having enough soup in the freezer to get her through long North Dakota winters.

> 1 onion, finely chopped
> 2 teaspoons unsalted butter
> 2$^1/_2$ cups chicken broth
> 4 cups low-fat milk
> 5 large potatoes, peeled
>   and diced
> $^1/_2$ teaspoon salt
> $^1/_2$ teaspoon freshly ground
>   white pepper
> 1 (12-ounce) can skim evaporated milk
> $^1/_4$ cup unbleached all-purpose flour

In a medium-size skillet, cook onion in butter over medium heat until lightly browned. Add broth and heat to boiling. Place low-fat milk, potatoes, salt, pepper, onion and broth in a 3$^1/_2$-quart slow cooker. Cook on LOW 6 hours, or HIGH 4 hours, until potatoes are tender.

Place evaporated milk in a blender and add flour a little at a time until blended. Add 1 cup of potatoes and soup from cooker and process until smooth. Pour back in cooker and heat through for 30 minutes.

If you don't have a slow cooker, brown onion in butter in a Dutch oven, add broth, low-fat milk and potatoes and cook over medium-low heat 1 hour. Season with salt and pepper. Blend evaporated milk and flour with some of the soup, as above, and cook until heated through and slightly thickened.

Makes 10 servings.

PER SERVING: Cal 160 • Carbo 26 gm • Prot 9 gm • Total fat 2 gm • Sat fat 1 gm • Cal from fat 11% • Chol 7 mg

EDUCATION: Prevent illnesses by following safe food-handling practices in your kitchen. Refrigerate leftovers immediately; don't wait for soup to cool to room temperature.

When freezing leftover soups, choose a container close in size to the amount of soup you are storing. This minimizes the amount of food surface exposed to air and helps prevent freezer burn. Jars with airtight lids can be used, but allow enough space for the liquid to expand as it freezes. Soups can also be frozen in heavy-duty self-sealing plastic freezer bags. Eliminate as much air as possible from the bag before sealing. Store bags flat in freezer. Next time you need a quick, healthy meal, just defrost and heat!

INSPIRATION: *I am open to new ideas today—new sights, new sounds, new tastes and new feelings.*

Maura's Winter Vegetable Salad

✗ Try vegetables in a different form: uncooked and shredded, as a salad—a refreshing change for winter! Vary the vegetables according to what you find at the supermarket. Turnips, jicama, celery or cabbage can be used.

3 carrots
1 parsnip
1 kohlrabi
1/3 cup nonfat yogurt
2 tablespoons olive oil
2 tablespoons minced fresh parsley
2 teaspoons fresh lemon juice
1/2 garlic clove, pushed through a press
1/8 teaspoon dry yellow mustard
Dash of salt
Dash of freshly ground white pepper

Peel and coarsely shred root vegetables. Mince leaves of the kohlrabi and add to the shredded vegetables, tossing to combine. Combine yogurt, olive oil, parsley, lemon juice, garlic, mustard, salt and pepper. Spoon dressing over shredded vegetables. Toss before serving. *Makes 4 servings.*

PER SERVING: Cal 170 • Carbo 26 gm • Prot 4 gm • Total fat 6 gm • Sat fat 1 gm • Cal from fat 31% • Chol 1 mg

EDUCATION: Eat about 20 grams of soluble and insoluble fiber each day. Many of us have heard of how eating a diet with adequate "roughage" can benefit our digestive system. Roughage translates to "fiber," and a high-fiber diet has been shown to alleviate a host of digestive ills, from simple irregularity to heartburn and diverticulitis. Insoluble fiber, the kind that absorbs water and adds bulk to the residue of foods we eat, is important to digestive health. Increasing our intake of vegetables and grains helps provide adequate roughage to meet our body's needs.

INSPIRATION: *Finding foods that help me stay in balance is no longer difficult when I tune in to my body.*

Elsie's Apple Muffins

❦ Serve with applesauce, apple butter or nonfat cream cheese.

2 1/2 cups whole-wheat pastry flour
2 1/2 teaspoons baking powder
1 teaspoon ground cinnamon
1 cup diced apples
1/2 cup sunflower seeds
3/4 cup buttermilk
2 eggs, beaten
1/4 cup honey

Preheat oven to 375°F (190°C). Lightly butter 12 (2¾-inch) muffin cups. Combine flour, baking powder and cinnamon in a large bowl. In a medium-size bowl, combine apples, sunflower seeds, buttermilk, eggs and honey. Stir apple mixture into the dry ingredients just until combined.

Divide batter among muffin cups. Bake 25 to 30 minutes or until golden brown.

Makes 1 dozen.

PER MUFFIN: Cal 167 • Carbo 28 gm • Prot 5 gm • Total fat 4 gm • Sat fat 1 gm • Cal from fat 21% • Chol 35 mg

EDUCATION: If you crave something sweet, think "whole wheat." Fiber can help balance sweetness by allowing your body to process the sugars more slowly, delaying their entry into your bloodstream. As you learn to cook new recipes, use fruit to provide some of the sweetness for baked goods and desserts. By reducing sugar and increasing fiber, you'll help your body achieve and maintain balance.

INSPIRATION: *I will focus on enjoying this day exactly as it is, knowing I will never experience another just like it.*

Mom's Beef Pot Roast
with Vegetables

Slow oven-simmering yields a tender roast and flavorful vegetables. Serve crusty bread and a crisp green salad to add contrast to the tender vegetables.

1 (2¹/₂- to 3-pound) rump roast
6 carrots
4 potatoes
1 small fennel bulb
1 large onion
1 tomato
1 celery stalk
3 cups beef stock
1 tablespoon minced fresh parsley
1 bay leaf
1 garlic clove, peeled
¹/₄ teaspoon dried marjoram
¹/₄ teaspoon freshly ground
    black pepper

Preheat oven to 325°F (165°C). Trim any excess fat from pot roast, rinse and pat dry. Peel carrots and halve them crosswise. Peel and halve or quarter potatoes, depending on size. Trim stems and root end from fennel. Quarter lengthwise. Peel and quarter onion lengthwise. Peel, seed and chop tomato. Trim celery and cut into 4 pieces.

Place vegetables in the bottom of a small roasting pan. Add stock, parsley, bay leaf, garlic clove, marjoram and pepper. Place roast on top of the vegetables. Roast 2 hours, until meat and vegetables are fork-tender. Remove bay leaf. Thinly slice roast and serve with vegetables on the side. *Makes 6 servings.*

PER SERVING: Cal 480 • Carbo 29 gm • Prot 58 gm • Total fat 13 gm • Sat fat 4 gm • Cal from fat 24% • Chol 146 mg

EDUCATION: Enjoy small amounts of meat occasionally. While it is true that vegetarians suffer less major disease than meat-eaters, you may not be ready or willing to eliminate meat altogether from your diet. But there is good news for meat-eaters. Minerals essential to good health, such as iron and zinc, are absorbed by the body much more readily from animal, rather than vegetable, sources.

Sliced leftover beef from this meal can be enjoyed in sandwiches made with whole-grain bread, topped with lettuce, tomato, onion, chopped green onions and alfalfa sprouts.

INSPIRATION: *The door to personal freedom and serenity waits inside of me—and only I hold the key.*

Uncle Jay's Hamburger Pie

No crust, just a simple topping of mashed potatoes with cheese. Serve with a green salad.

> 2 large potatoes, peeled and cubed
> 1 small turnip, peeled and cubed
> 1 cup chopped onion
> 1 cup diced carrots
> 1 cup chopped celery
> 1/3 cup chopped green bell pepper
> 1 teaspoon olive oil
> 3/4 pound extra-lean ground beef
> 2 garlic cloves, minced
> 1 tablespoon whole-wheat pastry flour
> 2 teaspoons chili powder
> 1/2 teaspoon salt
> 1/4 teaspoon dried oregano
> 1/4 teaspoon freshly ground black pepper
> 3/4 cup tomato juice
> 1/2 cup frozen whole-kernel corn
> 1/4 cup skim milk
> 1/3 cup shredded Cheddar cheese

Cook potatoes and turnips in water to cover in a medium-size saucepan over medium heat until tender, 10 to 15 minutes.

Cook onion, carrots, celery and bell pepper in oil in a large, nonstick pot, stirring frequently, until onion is translucent, 4 or 5 minutes. Add beef and garlic to pan and brown meat, breaking it up into small pieces as it cooks. Sprinkle flour, chili powder, salt, oregano and pepper over meat and stir to combine. Add tomato juice and corn and stir. Bring to a boil, reduce heat, cover and simmer 2 or 3 minutes, until corn is tender.

Preheat oven to 425°F (220°C). When potatoes are tender, mash with skim milk. Stir in cheese. Spread hamburger mixture into an 8-inch pie pan for a crust. Spoon mashed potato mixture over top and spread to cover filling. Bake 15 minutes or until top is lightly browned.

Makes 4 servings.

PER SERVING: Cal 350 • Carbo 35 gm • Prot 23 gm • Total fat 14 gm • Sat fat 8 gm • Cal from fat 36% • Chol 67 mg

EDUCATION: Choose comfort foods that have some redeeming nutritional value: milk toast, mashed bananas sprinkled with a bit of sugar, peanut butter on crackers, or vanilla custard. Hamburger Pie is one of those comforting foods that cozies up to your mouth like it belongs there, and reminds us of simpler times. Its variety of vegetables, fiber and nutrients, however, provides not just comfort, but sustenance as well. When we're looking for comfort, it's best to think in the long term, too!

INSPIRATION: *Instead of being confused by my persistent and myriad "wants," let me focus on my far fewer "needs."*

Tortillas Stuffed with Broccoli & Mushrooms

1 onion, chopped
$^1/_2$ green bell pepper, diced
1 teaspoon canola oil
$^1/_2$ cup sliced mushrooms
1 garlic clove, minced
$^1/_2$ cup chopped broccoli flowerets
$^1/_2$ cup shredded carrots
1 cup thinly sliced fresh spinach or romaine lettuce leaves
$^1/_3$ cup nonfat yogurt
$^1/_3$ cup shredded sharp Cheddar cheese
4 flour tortillas
1 cup Sombrero Salsa (February 16) or $^1/_2$ cup bottled salsa thinned with $^1/_2$ cup tomato juice
$^1/_2$ cup thinly sliced green onions for garnish
$^1/_4$ cup minced fresh parsley for garnish

Combine onion and bell pepper with oil in a large microwave-safe bowl. Microwave 3 minutes on HIGH or cook in a skillet over medium heat until translucent. Add mushrooms and garlic. Microwave on HIGH 3 or 4 minutes or cook over medium heat until mushrooms are slightly tender.

Stir in broccoli, carrots and spinach or lettuce. Microwave on HIGH 3 or 4 minutes or cook until broccoli is crisp-tender. Combine yogurt and Cheddar cheese. Stir into vegetables. Warm tortillas on HIGH 10 seconds each in microwave, or in a hot cast-iron pan set over medium heat.

When each tortilla is pliable, fill with $^1/_4$ of the vegetable mix and roll up. Place seam side down in an 8 × 8-inch shallow casserole dish. Spoon salsa over tortillas and microwave on MEDIUM until heated through, 4 to 5 minutes. Or bake in a preheated 350°F (175°C) oven 20 to 25 minutes, until tortillas are heated through. *Makes 4 servings.*

PER SERVING: Cal 194 • Carbo 29 gm • Prot 7 gm • Total fat 7 gm • Sat fat 2 gm • Cal from fat 32% • Chol 10 mg

EDUCATION: Eat fresh vegetables in season for maximum taste and nutrition. When it comes to healthful vegetables, broccoli is at the head of its class. In fact, broccoli and other cruciferous vegetables (such as cabbage, cauliflower and Brussels sprouts) are considered potent enough to help prevent cancer. Broccoli is also high in calcium and vitamin C—rivaling milk and oranges in providing these two nutrients.

For best flavor, choose broccoli with tight green or purplish-green flowerets. Yellowing flowerets signal the broccoli is past its prime. Store broccoli in the crisper section of your refrigerator in a perforated plastic bag. Finely chop or puree leftover cooked broccoli and add to casseroles or soups.

INSPIRATION: *Taking some quiet time each day helps me feel in harmony with my life as it unfolds.*

Molasses-Spice Breakfast Cake

Serve spread with ricotta cheese and applesauce. This whole-grain coffee cake is a fiber-rich start to your day.

2¹/₂ cups whole-wheat pastry flour
2 teaspoons baking soda
1 teaspoon ground cinnamon
1 teaspoon freshly grated nutmeg
¹/₄ teaspoon ground cloves
¹/₄ teaspoon ground allspice
¹/₄ teaspoon ground cardamom
1¹/₃ cups buttermilk
¹/₂ cup medium unsulfured molasses
1 egg, beaten
1 tablespoon canola oil

TOPPING:
¹/₃ cup rolled oats
1 tablespoon brown sugar
1 tablespoon melted butter
1 tablespoon finely chopped walnuts
¹/₂ teaspoon ground cinnamon

Preheat oven to 350°F (175°C). Lightly butter an 8-inch-square baking pan. Combine the flour, baking soda, cinnamon, nutmeg, cloves, allspice and cardamom in a large bowl. In a medium-size bowl, combine buttermilk with the molasses, egg and oil. Add buttermilk mixture to dry ingredients and stir just until combined. Spread batter in baking pan.

For topping, combine oats, brown sugar, butter, nuts and cinnamon. Sprinkle over batter and bake 30 to 35 minutes, until a wooden pick inserted in the center comes out clean.

Makes 9 servings.

PER SERVING: Cal 208 • Carbo 38 gm • Prot 5 gm • Total fat 4 gm • Sat fat 1 gm • Cal from fat 17% • Chol 5 mg

EDUCATION: Put balance in your life by offsetting high-fat indulgences with low-fat enjoyments. Making a festive low-fat breakfast or brunch does not have to mean major sacrificing. The creative use of spices, above, results in a delicious breakfast cake with admirably little fat.

INSPIRATION: *Taking responsibility for my life brings me more confidence and adds to my maturity.*

Cabbage, Carrot & Fruit Salad with Citrus Dressing

Cabbage tastes zesty when combined with fruit and topped with a tangy dressing.

3 cups coarsely shredded cabbage
1 (8-ounce) can crushed pineapple, drained
1 cup seedless grapes, halved
¹/₂ cup shredded carrots
1 tablespoon minced fresh parsley
3 tablespoons orange juice
1 tablespoon olive oil
1 tablespoon fresh lemon juice
1 garlic clove, pushed through a press
1 teaspoon paprika
¹/₄ teaspoon freshly grated orange peel
¹/₈ teaspoon salt

Combine cabbage, pineapple, grapes, carrots and parsley in a large serving bowl. Stir the orange juice, olive oil, lemon juice, garlic, paprika, orange peel and salt together in a small bowl. Pour dressing over cabbage mixture, toss and serve. *Makes 6 servings.*

PER SERVING: Cal 87 • Carbo 17 gm • Prot 1 gm • Total fat 3 gm • Sat fat 0.4 gm • Cal from fat 31% • Chol 0 mg

EDUCATION: Eat more cabbage—and members of the cabbage family, including broccoli, cauliflower and Brussels sprouts—to prevent cancer. Researchers have found evidence that compounds, called "indoles," in these cruciferous vegetables play the protective role. In addition, cabbage is high in vitamin C and fiber, two more potent cancer fighters. To make cabbage more appealing, serve it raw, as in the salad above, or lightly cooked.

INSPIRATION: *There is no single recipe for everyone to find joy; I must cook up my own kind of happiness.*

Brunswick Stew

❧ Colorful, vegetable-studded chicken stew is a southern favorite, low in fat, long on nutrition.

> 1 1/2 cups thinly sliced onions
> 1/2 tablespoon unsalted butter
> 1 (3- to 3 1/2-pound) frying chicken,
>   quartered
> 2 cups water
> 1 (28-ounce) can whole tomatoes, chopped,
>   with juice
> 2 large potatoes, peeled and diced
> 1 1/2 cups frozen baby lima beans
> 1 1/2 cups frozen whole-kernel corn
> 1/2 teaspoon salt
> 1/4 teaspoon freshly ground black pepper
> Dash of red (cayenne) pepper

Cook onions in butter in a large, nonstick pot over medium heat, stirring frequently, until onions are translucent, about 5 to 6 minutes. Remove onions and set aside.

Remove skin from chicken. Place chicken in pot and add water and tomatoes with juice. Bring to a boil, reduce heat, cover and simmer 1 hour or until chicken is tender.

Remove chicken and set aside. Add potatoes to cooking liquid in the pot and cook 10 minutes or until potatoes are firm-tender. Stir in onions, lima beans, corn, salt, pepper and cayenne and cook 3 to 4 minutes, until vegetables are tender. Cut chicken into serving pieces and return to the pot, heat through and serve.

Makes 4 servings.

PER SERVING: Cal 571 • Carbo 52 gm • Prot 49 gm • Total fat 19 gm • Sat fat 6 gm • Cal from fat 30% • Chol 128 mg

EDUCATION: Make meals more appealing by choosing foods in a variety of colors and shapes. When cutting up vegetables for soups or salads, dice some, cut others into long, thin sticks and thinly slice yet others. This adds texture and eye appeal which can stimulate the appetite and make your meals more fun, too!

INSPIRATION: *I am ready and able to bring healing into my life.*

Baked Butternut Squash with Fruit

❧ A good side dish when the oven is already in use for roasting chicken or baking bread. Add a crisp, green salad to the meal.

> 4 cups peeled, cubed butternut squash
> 2 apples, peeled, cored and cubed
> 1 orange, peeled, seeded and cubed
> 1/4 cup chopped pitted prunes
> 1 tablespoon minced dried apricots
> 1/2 cup orange juice
> 1/4 cup apple juice
> Dash of ground cinnamon
> Dash of freshly grated nutmeg

Preheat oven to 350°F (175°C). Combine squash, apples, orange, prunes, apricots, juices, cinnamon and nutmeg in a medium-size casserole dish. Cover and bake 1 hour, or until squash is tender, stirring once. Remove lid for final 15 minutes or so of baking.

Makes 6 servings.

PER SERVING: Cal 122 • Carbo 32 gm • Prot 2 gm • Total fat 0.4 gm • Sat fat trace • Cal from fat 3% • Chol 0 mg

EDUCATION: Fight cancer by eating more beta-carotene. Butternut squash is a golden-rich source of carotene. There are many ways to get more butternut squash in your diet, including using cubed squash as a substitute for potatoes in soups and stews or as a side dish. Butternut squash can also be substituted for pumpkin in pies or baked puddings.

March 7

INSPIRATION: *I am beginning to reclaim parts of myself I buried or ignored in my need to be accepted by others.*

Mediterranean Sole

❦ Sole, or flounder, flavored with tomatoes, garlic, olive oil and herbs, can be complemented with rice, French-cut green beans, and a crisp salad.

> *1 small onion, chopped*
> *1 teaspoon olive oil*
> *2 green onions, thinly sliced*
> *2 garlic cloves, minced*
> *4 tomatoes, peeled, seeded and finely chopped*
> *8 fresh basil leaves or ¹/₂ teaspoon dried basil*
> *2 tablespoons minced fresh parsley*
> *1¹/₂ pounds sole fillets*
> *4 lemon wedges for garnish*
> *4 parsley sprigs for garnish*

Cook chopped onion in oil in a large non-stick skillet over medium heat, stirring frequently, until the onion is translucent, about 5 minutes. Add the green onions and garlic and cook until the green onions are wilted.

Stir in tomatoes and herbs. Bring to a boil and stir. Place fish fillets in a single layer over the tomato mixture. Reduce heat, cover and simmer 7 to 10 minutes, until the fish is opaque throughout. Remove fish to a serving plate and top with the tomato mixture. Garnish with lemon and parsley.   *Makes 4 servings.*

PER SERVING: Cal 203 • Carbo 8 gm • Prot 33 gm • Total fat 4 gm • Sat fat 1 gm • Cal from fat 17% • Chol 82 mg

EDUCATION: Decrease the amount of salt in your diet. Excess sodium (salt) intake is linked to hypertension or high blood pressure in many individuals. Cutting back on salt can be accomplished in many ways. One is to reduce salt in cooking. Choose herbs and other flavoring agents to perk up the taste buds without sodium.

In the recipe above, onions, garlic, green onions and tomato all add flavor to the fish, which is further accented with basil and parsley. Use similar techniques with other fish or with meat and poultry.

Also, don't encourage salt use at the table. You might set out some fresh or dried herb mixes or sesame seeds for sprinkling on food, instead, or garnish dishes with lemon wedges, which can be squeezed onto foods for a tangy lift.

INSPIRATION: *My Higher Power is gently guiding me to be the best that I can be.*

Chinese Cabbage with Noodles

Chinese cabbage (bok choy or celery cabbage, as it is sometimes called) becomes a main course in a colorful dish. You can substitute any cabbage in this recipe, however.

1 pound Chinese or celery cabbage
1 cup chopped onions
1/2 tablespoon unsalted butter
1 garlic clove, minced
2 carrots, coarsely shredded
1/2 cup water
1 teaspoon finely grated lemon zest
1/4 teaspoon dried sage
1/4 teaspoon salt
3/4 pound wide egg noodles
1 cup low-fat cottage cheese
2 tablespoons nonfat sour cream
2 tablespoons skim milk
1/4 cup minced fresh parsley for garnish
8 thinly sliced rings of red bell pepper for garnish

Separate cabbage leaves and rinse well. Cut across the ribs into thin slices. Set aside.

Cook onions in the butter over medium heat in a large skillet, stirring frequently, until the onions are translucent, about 5 minutes. Add garlic and cook, stirring, 1 minute. Add the cabbage, carrots, water, lemon zest, sage and salt. Bring to a boil, reduce heat, cover and simmer 20 to 25 minutes, until cabbage is tender.

Meanwhile, in a large pot of boiling water, cook noodles until firm-tender. Drain noodles. Stir the cottage cheese into the cabbage mixture and heat through.

Serve noodles on individual plates, topped with cabbage mixture. Thin sour cream with milk and spoon a tablespoon of the mixture over each serving. Sprinkle with parsley and top with bell pepper. *Makes 4 servings.*

PER SERVING: Cal 455 • Carbo 74 gm • Prot 22 gm • Total fat 8 gm • Sat fat 3 gm • Cal from fat 16% • Chol 90 mg

EDUCATION: Eat more green leafy vegetables for better health. Chinese cabbage is more nutritious than other types of cabbage; it provides a substantial amount of beta-carotene (60 percent of the Recommended Daily Allowance in 1 1/2 cups, shredded) and significant calcium content. Like other cabbages, Chinese cabbage is rich in vitamin C, folacin, potassium and fiber.

INSPIRATION: *Today I will put time and energy into pursuits that nurture my body and my spirit.*

Nan's Chicken Milanaise with Vegetable Rice

A quick meal with nutrition in mind, perfect for Nan's and George's busy life in Rochester, complete with active kids. Just add salad!

1 egg, beaten
1 tablespoon water
⅓ cup dried whole-wheat bread crumbs
2 tablespoons freshly grated Parmesan cheese
4 boneless, skinless chicken breast halves
¼ cup unbleached flour
1½ cups chicken broth
1¼ cups quick-cooking brown rice
2 teaspoons olive oil
½ cup chopped onion
1 teaspoon butter
½ cup diced red bell pepper
¼ cup minced green onions
¼ cup minced fresh parsley
8 lemon wedges for garnish
Parsley sprigs for garnish

Combine beaten egg and water in a shallow bowl. Combine bread crumbs and Parmesan cheese. Dredge chicken breast halves in the flour, shaking off excess. Dip floured chicken breasts in the egg, then in the bread crumb mixture. Set aside.

Bring chicken broth to a boil in a medium-size saucepan. Stir in rice, reduce heat, cover and simmer 10 minutes.

Heat olive oil in a large nonstick skillet over medium heat and add the chicken. Cook, turning once, until golden brown, about 10 minutes.

Meanwhile, cook chopped onion in butter over medium heat in a small saucepan, stirring frequently, until onion is translucent. Stir in bell pepper and cook, stirring frequently, until firm-tender, 3 to 4 minutes. Stir in green onions and cook 1 or 2 minutes, stirring frequently, until wilted. Stir in minced parsley and remove from heat.

When rice is done, remove from heat and add vegetable mixture, stirring to combine. Serve chicken accompanied by rice.

Makes 4 servings.

PER SERVING: Cal 542 • Carbo 31 gm • Prot 66 gm • Total fat 15 gm • Sat fat 5 gm • Cal from fat 25% • Chol 214 mg

EDUCATION: Start your own garden for maximum nutrition and relaxation. Start small, share space with a friend or look into a community plot if you don't have land. Even cities are beginning to make land available for people to grow their own food. Not only will you enjoy fresh, nutritious produce, but you will get exercise and develop patience, diligence and optimism! Another benefit is feeling connected to the cycle of living things, from germination to fruiting, to harvest and completion.

INSPIRATION: *Forgiving myself for past mistakes and making amends where I can frees me to enjoy my humanness today.*

Rice Pudding with Currants

❧ Cooking up extra brown rice is easy. It's convenient to have it on hand, because all it takes is a little reheating and you've got a fiber-filled nutritious side dish. But don't overlook the possibility of a hearty old-fashioned rice pudding. Winter is just the time to enjoy this comforting dessert.

> 2 cups cooked short-grain brown rice
> $^1/_4$ cup dried currants
> $^1/_4$ cup packed brown sugar
> 1 tablespoon butter, softened
> 2 eggs
> 1 cup skim milk
> $^1/_4$ teaspoon freshly grated
>   lemon peel
> $^1/_8$ teaspoon salt
> $^1/_2$ teaspoon granulated sugar
> $^1/_4$ teaspoon ground cinnamon

Preheat oven to 325°F (165°C). Combine rice, currants, brown sugar and butter in a large bowl. Beat the eggs in a medium-size bowl, then add milk, lemon peel and salt and stir until combined.

Lightly butter a deep casserole dish. Stir egg mixture into the rice, then pour into prepared casserole. Combine granulated sugar and cinnamon and sprinkle over top. Bake about 50 minutes, or until pudding is set, though there may be a small amount of liquid on the top. Serve hot or chilled.   *Makes 8 servings.*

PER SERVING: Cal 66 • Carbo 16 gm • Prot 1 gm • Total fat trace • Sat fat trace • Cal from fat 10% • Chol 9 mg

EDUCATION: Eat more whole grains such as brown rice for their nutritional advantage. Brown rice has lots going for it. One, it has a satisfying nutty flavor that complements almost any main dish. Two, brown rice is high in lysine, an amino acid, making it a natural for vegetarian combinations with lentils, beans or tofu. Three, when considering nutrition, brown rice shines. Only the husk of brown rice is removed during milling. That leaves the bran layer, with all its fiber and germ, intact. Brown rice, therefore, has more folacin, iron, riboflavin, potassium, phosphorus, zinc, trace minerals copper and manganese than any other rice. Brown rice also contains the antioxidant vitamin E, missing from refined white rices.

INSPIRATION: *I trust my Higher Power to provide me with equilibrium and guidance.*

Pecan Porridge with Dates

❧ Dress up breakfast and enjoy the natural sweetness of dates. The pecans add extra protein for a filling start to the day.

> $^3/_4$ cup water
> 1 tablespoon chopped pitted dates
> 1 tablespoon chopped pecans
> $^1/_3$ cup rolled oats
> $^1/_8$ teaspoon ground cinnamon
> Dash of salt
> Skim milk

Combine water, dates and pecans in a small saucepan. Bring to a boil. Stir in oats and simmer 5 to 7 minutes or until thickened, stirring occasionally. Serve hot with milk.

Makes 1 serving.

PER SERVING WITHOUT MILK: Cal 179
• Carbo 28 gm • Prot 5 gm • Total fat 6 gm • Sat
fat 1 gm • Cal from fat 32% • Chol 0 mg

EDUCATION: Strive for balance in your day.
Eating a breakfast laced with lots of sugar and
caffeine puts your energy cycle on a yo-yo
course—lifting you up at first, but leaving you
flat in the dumps by mid-morning. That leads
to the temptation of more sweets and caffeine,
and the cycle continues. A breakfast with plenty of fiber and protein will stay with you all
morning, giving you a balanced supply of energy to get things done.

March 12

INSPIRATION: *I will take time today to reward
myself: eat well, take a walk, plan a garden or talk to
a friend.*

Eggplant Soup with Shell Pasta

Choose any pasta to vary this dish. If using
larger pastas, like wagon wheels, increase
amount to 1 cup.

1 cup chopped onion
1/2 cup thinly sliced celery
1 tablespoon olive oil
3 garlic cloves, minced
2 cups diced eggplant
1 (28-ounce) can whole tomatoes
2 cups chicken broth
1/4 teaspoon dried marjoram
1/4 teaspoon dried oregano
1/8 teaspoon dried thyme
1/8 teaspoon salt
1/8 teaspoon freshly ground black pepper
1/2 cup cooked tiny shell pasta
1/4 cup minced fresh parsley

Cook onion and celery in oil in a Dutch
oven over medium heat, stirring frequently,
until onion is tender, about 3 minutes. Stir in
garlic and cook 1 minute more, stirring constantly.

Add eggplant, reduce heat to low, cover pan
and cook 10 minutes, stirring occasionally,
until eggplant is firm-tender.

Chop tomatoes and add with their juice,
the broth, marjoram, oregano, thyme, salt and
pepper to eggplant. Bring to a boil, reduce
heat, cover and simmer 20 minutes or until
eggplant is quite tender. Stir in cooked pasta
and parsley and heat through.

Makes 4 servings.

PER SERVING: Cal 175 • Carbo 27 gm • Prot 7
gm • Total fat 5 gm • Sat fat 1 gm • Cal from fat
26% • Chol 0 mg

EDUCATION: Reduce fat in your diet by using
cooking techniques other than frying when
you prepare eggplant and other foods that have
an affinity for oil. In fact, eggplant can absorb
more oil than any other vegetable. Steaming,
stewing and stuffing are three ways to enjoy
eggplant without having a finished dish swim-
ming in oil.

INSPIRATION: *I deserve all the time I need for myself.*

INSPIRATION: *I trust my inner spirit and my body wisdom to know what is right for me.*

Artichokes with Lemon-Yogurt Vinaigrette

❧ Artichokes are often served with mayonnaise-based dipping sauces. This lighter sauce won't overshadow their delicate flavor.

> 4 large artichokes
> 1 tablespoon olive oil
> $^1/_2$ cup nonfat yogurt
> 1 small garlic clove, pushed through a press
> $^1/_4$ teaspoon freshly grated lemon peel
> $^1/_8$ teaspoon dry mustard
> $^1/_8$ teaspoon salt
> Dash of freshly ground white pepper

Trim artichoke stems even with artichoke bottoms and remove any damaged leaves. If you like, trim each leaf with kitchen shears or a sharp knife to remove the thorny tip. Steam artichokes in a large kettle over boiling water 45 to 50 minutes or until bottoms are quite tender.

Combine oil, yogurt, garlic, lemon peel, mustard, salt and pepper. Divide sauce among 4 small dipping bowls and serve with hot artichokes. *Makes 4 servings.*

PER SERVING: Cal 109 • Carbo 16 gm • Prot 6 gm • Total fat 4 gm • Sat fat 1 gm • Cal from fat 33% • Chol 2 mg

EDUCATION: Add fun to your life by eating finger foods such as artichokes. Artichokes do not contain large amounts of any one nutrient, but they do offer magnesium, potassium, calcium, iron, phosphorus and fiber. If they are served with low-fat dipping sauces, artichokes can be a healthful addition to your diet.

Nancy's Creamy Broccoli Soup

❧ A quick, nutritious soup that chases away the chill. Serve with whole-grain bread and a salad for a light dinner.

> $^3/_4$ pound broccoli
> 1 cup chopped onion
> 1 teaspoon olive oil
> 1 teaspoon unsalted butter
> 1 large potato, peeled and chopped
> 2 cups chicken broth
> $^1/_2$ teaspoon dried basil
> $^1/_4$ teaspoon dried thyme
> $^1/_4$ teaspoon dried oregano
> $^1/_4$ teaspoon paprika
> $^1/_4$ teaspoon dry yellow mustard
> $^1/_4$ teaspoon salt
> $^1/_8$ teaspoon freshly ground black pepper
> 1 cup skim milk
> $^1/_2$ cup shredded Cheddar cheese
> $^1/_4$ cup minced fresh parsley

Peel stems and chop the broccoli. Cook onion in the oil and butter over medium heat in a large nonstick pot, stirring frequently, until the onion is translucent. Add broccoli and potato and stir to combine with the onion.

Add broth, basil, thyme, oregano, paprika, mustard, salt and pepper. Bring to a boil, reduce heat, cover and simmer 20 to 25 minutes or until vegetables are tender.

Let soup cool slightly, then puree in a food processor or blender, just until smooth. Pour pureed broccoli mixture back into pot and add milk. Heat through slowly, stirring constantly, until soup is hot. Remove from heat, add cheese and parsley and stir until cheese is melted.

Makes 4 servings.

PER SERVING: Cal 189 • Carbo 19 gm • Prot 12 gm • Total fat 8 gm • Sat fat 4 gm • Cal from fat 39% • Chol 19 mg

EDUCATION: Be adventurous to feed your soul. Travel to a foreign country to see and be among the people, instead of isolating yourself on a sandy beach. Stretch yourself physically on a hike or climb. Unpack some of your emotional baggage by having an honest talk with someone you may have been avoiding.

INSPIRATION: *My attitude is what determines how fully I will live life today.*

Orange-Date-Walnut Fruit Cup Dessert

🌿 Winter fruit desserts don't have to be boring. Combine a variety of textures and flavors to maximize their appeal.

> 2 navel oranges
> 2 tart red apples
> $^1/_4$ cup nonfat yogurt
> 1 tablespoon chopped
>   pitted dates
> $^1/_2$ teaspoon brown sugar
> Dash of ground cinnamon
> 2 teaspoons chopped walnuts

Peel and cube oranges, removing any seeds. Core and dice apples. Combine fruit in a medium-size bowl with yogurt, dates, sugar and cinnamon. Cover and refrigerate until chilled. Stir in nuts before serving. *Makes 4 servings.*

PER SERVING: Cal 95 • Carbo 22 gm • Prot 2 gm • Total fat 1 gm • Sat fat trace • Cal from fat 9% • Chol 1 mg

EDUCATION: Cut down on sugar for a positive effect on your mental state. Start by reducing the granulated sugar called for in your favorite dessert recipes by as much as a third. In most cases, you'll barely notice the difference— except in your ability to cope. Then, begin exploring fresh fruit desserts. Fruits contain natural sweetness, reducing the need for sugar. By buying ripe fruits in season, you'll enjoy peak flavor and save money with lower seasonal costs.

INSPIRATION: *Today I will share of myself because I want to, not because I have to. I can experience real joy in being giving.*

Irish Soda Bread with Oats & Currants

❧ Made with whole-wheat pastry flour and old-fashioned rolled oats, Irish Soda Bread is easy to bake and substantial. Sure 'n' begorra, won't you just have enough to keep a loaf and give a loaf away for St. Patrick's Day.

> 2¼ to 2½ cups whole-wheat
>   pastry flour
> 2 cups unbleached all-purpose flour
> 1 cup old-fashioned rolled oats
> 2 teaspoons baking soda
> 1 teaspoon baking powder
> 1 teaspoon salt
> ½ cup dried currants
> 2 cups buttermilk
> 1 egg, beaten

Preheat oven to 350°F (175°C). Lightly oil a large baking sheet. Combine 2¼ cups whole-wheat pastry flour, unbleached flour, oats, baking soda, baking powder and salt in a large bowl. Stir currants into flour mixture. Add buttermilk and egg and stir until the mixture forms a dough.

By hand, knead in enough additional whole-wheat pastry flour to make a manageable, but sticky dough. Halve the dough and form each half into a round loaf. Dust loaves with whole-wheat pastry flour and cut an "X" in the top, about an inch deep, with a serrated knife. Put the loaves on prepared baking sheet. Bake 40 to 45 minutes, or until they are nicely browned and sound hollow when tapped.

Makes 2 loaves (24 slices).

PER SLICE: Cal 113 • Carbo 22 gm • Prot 4 gm • Total fat 1 gm • Sat fat trace • Cal from fat 8% • Chol 10 mg

EDUCATION: Show someone you love how you feel. Words help, but by our actions we can more deeply express what is in our hearts. Think about what would make this loved one happy, and respond.

INSPIRATION: *I will rejoice in the connection I feel with other people today—celebrating our sameness rather than dwelling on our differences.*

St. Patty's Sautéed Swiss Chard

❧ St. Patrick's Day is traditional for "putting on the green," so don't forget your dinner table! And don't be shy about trying these greens—you'll find they are delicious! The high percentage of calories from fat is only because the greens themselves are so low in calories.

> 1 bunch red Swiss chard or
>   beet greens
> 1 teaspoon unsalted butter
> 1 small garlic clove, pushed
>   through a press

Thoroughly rinse greens under lukewarm running water. Tear off stems. Coarsely tear up leaves. Melt butter in a medium-size nonstick skillet over medium heat. Add garlic and greens, with just the water that clings to the rinsed leaves. Stir until greens are wilted, about 5 minutes. Reduce heat to low, cover and steam 2 or 3 minutes, just until greens are tender.

Makes 2 servings.

PER SERVING: Cal 31 • Carbo 3 gm • Prot 1 gm • Total fat 2 gm • Sat fat 1 gm • Cal from fat 61% • Chol 5 mg

EDUCATION: Eat a variety of vegetables, not just a familiar few. If you mosey from the carrots to celery, from the green onions to the iceberg lettuce and avoid the section of the store with dark green, leafy vegetables, you're passing up some of the best nutrition in your supermarket. Next time when you get to the greens, pull over. You may be surprised at the variety: mustard greens, chicory, collard greens, kale, spinach, turnip greens, beet greens and Swiss chard. Try thinly sliced greens in soups and stews.

March 18

INSPIRATION: *Let me do today what it is possible to do—and let me trust my Higher Power to handle the rest.*

Chicken Enchiladas
with Mozzarella

Serve with corn and a big tossed salad with carrots, green onions, celery and sprouts.

2 boneless, skinless chicken
    breast halves
1/2 cup chicken broth
1 onion, chopped
1 (28-ounce) can whole
    tomatoes, drained
2 teaspoons chili powder
1 teaspoon ground cumin
1/2 cup shredded part-skim
    mozzarella cheese
4 (8-inch) flour tortillas

Bring chicken breast halves and broth to a boil in a medium-size saucepan over medium heat. Reduce heat, cover and simmer 8 minutes, or until chicken is cooked through. Set chicken aside, saving broth.

Return broth to a boil in the saucepan, add the onion, cover and simmer 2 or 3 minutes, until the onion is firm-tender. Chop tomatoes and add to onion with chili powder and cumin. Bring to a boil, reduce heat, cover and simmer 2 or 3 minutes, to blend flavors. Set aside half of the tomato mixture.

Preheat oven to 350°F (175°C). Lightly oil a 9-inch-square baking dish. Coarsely chop chicken and add with half the mozzarella to the remaining tomato sauce. Place 2/3 cup of the chicken mixture down the center of each tortilla, and fold the tortilla around the filling. Place folded tortillas seam side down in baking dish.

Spoon remaining tomato mixture over the stuffed enchiladas. Sprinkle with remaining mozzarella. Bake 15 minutes or until enchiladas are heated through. *Makes 4 servings.*

PER SERVING: Cal 341 • Carbo 31 gm • Prot 37 gm • Total fat 8 gm • Sat fat 2 gm • Cal from fat 21% • Chol 81 mg

EDUCATION: Get your priorities straight and stick to them to conserve your energies. What is most important to you? Family? Relationships? Emotional growth? Spiritual healing? Does your life-style reflect your priorities, or do you need to make changes? To be meaningful, values need to be lived.

INSPIRATION: *I will take several moments today to stop what I "have" to do, and just notice what is going on around me.*

Chile Corn Bread & Lentil Casserole

❧ A main dish with robust flavor, with a spicy jalapeño corn bread topping.

1 cup chopped onion
1 cup chopped green bell pepper
1 tablespoon olive oil
4 garlic cloves, minced
1 cup dried lentils
2 cups chicken broth
2 cups tomato sauce
1 tablespoon chili powder
1 teaspoon ground cumin
$^1/_2$ teaspoon dried oregano
$^1/_4$ teaspoon dried thyme
$^1/_4$ teaspoon salt
$^1/_4$ teaspoon freshly ground black pepper
$^3/_4$ cup ground yellow cornmeal
$^1/_4$ cup unbleached flour
1 teaspoon baking soda
1 egg, beaten
2 cups buttermilk
1 teaspoon minced jalapeño chile
$^1/_4$ cup shredded Cheddar cheese

Cook onion and bell pepper in oil in a Dutch oven over medium heat, stirring frequently, until the onion is translucent. Add garlic and cook, stirring, 1 minute. Add lentils, broth, tomato sauce, chili powder, cumin, oregano, thyme, salt and pepper. Bring to a boil, reduce heat, cover and simmer 30 minutes or until lentils are firm-tender.

Preheat oven to 400°F (200°C). Meanwhile, combine the cornmeal, flour and baking soda in a large bowl. Combine beaten egg, buttermilk and jalapeño in a medium-size bowl.

When the lentils are done, place the lentil mixture in the bottom of an 8-inch-square casserole dish. Combine egg mixture with dry ingredients in the large bowl. Carefully spoon the cornmeal batter over the lentils. Sprinkle with cheese. Bake casserole 35 to 40 minutes, until the corn bread topping begins to brown and shrink from the sides of the dish. *Makes 6 servings.*

PER SERVING: Cal 268 • Carbo 40 gm • Prot 13 gm • Total fat 7 gm • Sat fat 2 gm • Cal from fat 23% • Chol 43 mg

EDUCATION: Eat more vegetarian meals for better health. Vegetarians tend to have blood pressure lower than those who regularly eat meat. In fact, some studies show vegetarians enjoy better health in general. By increasing your repertoire of delicious vegetarian recipes, you can cut down on meat and animal products. That means less saturated fat and cholesterol, and more fiber in your diet, all beneficial to your body.

INSPIRATION: *The beginning of spring may not be obvious from the weather, but I know it's arriving. My recovery may not be obvious to those around me, but I feel its budding.*

Kashmiri-style Curried Cauliflower

❧ In tiny houseboat kitchens, cooks in Kashmir in Northern India create an astonishing array of foods for their guests. The curried dishes are varied, and flavorful.

1 (1-pound) head cauliflower
1 teaspoon mustard seeds
1 tablespoon canola oil
1 teaspoon peeled grated gingerroot
$^1/_2$ teaspoon ground coriander
$^1/_8$ teaspoon turmeric

¹/₈ teaspoon paprika
¹/₂ cup water
¹/₂ cup frozen green peas
1 teaspoon fresh lemon juice

Cut the cauliflower into small flowerets, about 1 inch across. Cook the mustard seeds in the oil in a large saucepan over medium heat, stirring frequently, until the seeds stop "popping." Add gingerroot, coriander, turmeric and paprika and cook, stirring, 30 seconds. Add the cauliflower, stirring to coat it with seasonings, and the water. Reduce heat to low, cover and steam cauliflower until crisp-tender, 5 to 8 minutes, adding a few drops of water, if necessary, to prevent sticking. Stir in peas, cover and steam 1 to 2 minutes, just until peas are cooked and cauliflower is firm-tender. Sprinkle lemon juice over the cauliflower mixture, toss and serve. *Makes 4 servings.*

PER SERVING: Cal 57 • Carbo 9 gm • Prot 3 gm • Total fat 2 gm • Sat fat trace • Cal from fat 27% • Chol 0 mg

EDUCATION: Celebrate spring! Just as bodies are enriched with a nutritious, balanced diet, spirits can be enriched with small celebrations of beauty. Splurge on some flowers in the house, at the windows and on the table. Make a small celebration of seeing spring come back in your life again!

M a r c h   2 1

INSPIRATION: *Though my journey toward health and wholeness is not without difficulties, I can stay with the process.*

Lemon Meringue Pie with Graham Cracker Crust

🌿 Buying a prepared crust makes this easy to prepare. The meringue is truly impressive!

1¹/₂ cups sugar
6 tablespoons cornstarch
Dash of salt
²/₃ cup fresh lemon juice
¹/₃ cup cold water
3 egg yolks, well-beaten
1¹/₂ cups boiling water
1 tablespoon butter
1¹/₂ teaspoons freshly grated lemon peel
6 egg whites
¹/₄ teaspoon cream of tartar
3 tablespoons vanilla sugar (see glossary)
1 (9-inch) ready-to-use graham cracker crust

Combine sugar, cornstarch and salt in a sifter and sift into a medium-size saucepan. Gradually stir in lemon juice and cold water until smooth. Stir in egg yolks. Stirring constantly, gradually add boiling water. Add butter.

Bring mixture to a boil over medium-low heat, stirring constantly. When mixture thickens, reduce heat and simmer 1 minute. Remove from heat and stir in lemon peel. Set aside to cool slightly.

Preheat oven to 350°F (175°C). Beat egg whites in a large bowl until frothy. Add cream of tartar. Beat until stiff but not dry. Beat in vanilla sugar 1 tablespoon at a time; do not overbeat.

Spread lemon filling in crust. Top with meringue, spreading to edge of pan. Bake 15 to 20 minutes or until top of meringue is lightly browned. *Makes 8 servings*

PER SERVING: Cal 390 • Carbo 260 gm • Prot 4 gm • Total fat 11 gm • Sat fat 3 gm • Cal from fat 25% • Chol 84 mg

EDUCATION: Eat low-fat desserts. One of the highest-fat portions of pies is the crust. In fact, the general rule of thumb is, to cut dessert calories in half, eat the pie filling and leave the crust behind.

INSPIRATION: *By getting out of my own way, I may suddenly find the path ahead an easier one.*

Garlic Shrimp with Spinach

❧ Serve with a bulgur or rice pilaf, steamed carrots and bread.

1 1/4 *pounds medium-size shrimp*
1/4 *cup minced fresh parsley*
1 *tablespoon minced shallots*
1 *tablespoon minced garlic*
2 *teaspoons olive oil*
1/4 *teaspoon freshly grated*
    lemon peel
1/4 *teaspoon salt*
1/8 *teaspoon freshly ground*
    black pepper
1 *pound fresh spinach*
Lemon wedges for garnish

Peel and devein shrimp (see glossary). Combine parsley, shallots, garlic, oil, lemon peel, salt and pepper in a medium-size bowl. Add shrimp and toss to coat with marinade. Refrigerate while preparing spinach.

Wash spinach well in lukewarm water to remove any sand. Drain, pull off stems and tear leaves into large pieces. Cook spinach in a covered large saucepan over low heat, stirring frequently, until tender, about 5 minutes. Keep warm.

Cook shrimp in the marinade in a medium-size nonstick skillet over medium heat, stirring constantly, just until shrimp turn pink, 3 or 4 minutes.

Drain spinach well. Place on a serving plate and top with shrimp. Garnish with lemon wedges. *Makes 4 servings.*

PER SERVING: Cal 203 • Carbo 7 gm • Prot 32 gm • Total fat 5 gm • Sat fat 1 gm • Cal from fat 23% • Chol 218 mg

EDUCATION: Choose dark green leafy vegetables for salads and side dishes. Deep green vegetables are rich in chlorophyll, which some researchers regard as a cancer preventative. Add parsley, broccoli and spinach to salads, soups or stews. Serve meats, poultry or fish on a bed of spinach, like the recipe above, where it adds not only nutrition, but eye appeal.

INSPIRATION: *Hospitality allows me to feel good about myself and to share my good feelings with others.*

Pamela's Fiery Artichoke Spread

❧ Add your favorite hot pepper sauce to taste, as hot as you like it! This is a popular item at Pamela's parties.

> 1 (14-ounce) can artichoke hearts
> 1 tablespoon diced red bell pepper
> 1 tablespoon reduced-fat mayonnaise
> 1 1/2 teaspoons hot pepper sauce,
>   or to taste
> 1 teaspoon minced garlic
> 1 teaspoon fresh lemon juice
> 1 teaspoon minced fresh dill
> 2 (5-ounce) boxes melba toast rounds
> 1 ring red bell pepper for garnish
> Dill sprigs for garnish

Drain and finely chop artichoke hearts. Combine with the next 6 ingredients in a medium-size bowl. Place in a small serving bowl and refrigerate until chilled.

Place dip on a platter surrounded by melba toast. Garnish top of dip with a thin ring trimmed from the bell pepper and some sprigs of dill. *Makes 8 servings.*

PER SERVING: Cal 153 • Carbo 29 gm • Prot 9 gm • Total fat 1 gm • Sat fat trace • Cal from fat 4% • Chol 1 mg

EDUCATION: When entertaining, stretch yourself beyond your work setting or usual social strata. Think of the people you "connect" with from all walks of life and invite them to your home. You may find it far more interesting and fun than limiting your socializing to a homogenized group.

INSPIRATION: *Accepting myself exactly, precisely as I am, with no conditions, is a goal I will relax into.*

Tomato-Herb Brown Rice

❧ Served with fish or chicken, the rosy hue of the rice adds color appeal to the meal.

> 1 small onion, chopped
> 2 teaspoons olive oil
> 1 cup brown rice
> 2 garlic cloves, minced
> 3/4 cup chicken broth
> 1 (14 1/2-ounce) can stewed
>   tomatoes
> 1/4 cup minced fresh parsley

Cook onion in oil in a large saucepan over medium heat, stirring frequently, until translucent. Add the rice and garlic and stir until combined. Add broth and tomatoes.

Bring to a boil over medium-high heat, then cover and reduce heat to low. Cook 30 to 35 minutes, until the rice is tender and the liquid is absorbed. Stir in minced parsley and serve.

Makes 4 servings.

PER SERVING: Cal 236 • Carbo 45 gm • Prot 6 gm • Total fat 4 gm • Sat fat 1 gm • Cal from fat 16% • Chol 0 mg

EDUCATION: Use some minimally processed foods to save time in the kitchen. Look for foods, such as stewed tomatoes, where not much has been added or taken away from the original ingredients. Like most canned foods, stewed tomatoes are higher in sodium than their fresh counterparts. When using stewed tomatoes to flavor dishes, don't add additional salt to the dish.

INSPIRATION: *I support myself in attaining peace and fullness on the physical and spiritual levels.*

Ril's Red Lentil Soup

❧ Makes a light supper accompanied by whole-grain rolls and a green salad. For a heartier soup, stir in ½ cup cooked bulgur.

1 cup red lentils
1 cup chopped onion
2 teaspoons canola oil
5 garlic cloves, minced
1 tablespoon peeled, grated gingerroot
1 teaspoon ground coriander
1 teaspoon ground cumin
4 cups chicken broth
1 (14¹/₂-ounce) can whole tomatoes, drained
  and chopped
1 tablespoon minced fresh parsley
¹/₄ cup nonfat sour cream for garnish
Parsley sprigs for garnish

Rinse lentils in a sieve and set aside to drain. Cook onion in oil in a large saucepan over medium heat, stirring frequently, until onion is translucent. Add garlic and gingerroot and cook, stirring, 1 minute. Add coriander and cumin and cook, stirring, 30 seconds more.

Add lentils and broth and bring to a boil. Reduce heat to low, cover and simmer 15 minutes, until lentils are nearly tender. Stir in chopped tomatoes and cook 5 minutes more. Stir in minced parsley before serving. Garnish with sour cream and parsley sprigs. *Makes 6 servings.*

PER SERVING: Cal 126 • Carbo 14 gm • Prot 8 gm • Total fat 4 gm • Sat fat 2 gm • Cal from fat 33% • Chol 0 mg

EDUCATION: Appreciate the person you are becoming. No one is finished growing, changing or becoming whole. We are always integrating new thoughts, expressions, experiences, joys and sorrows. Pay attention to yourself as you grow and heal. Notice the contributions you are now able to make, even though they may seem modest, to making the world a better place.

INSPIRATION: *I will not use food to build barriers to my feelings today.*

Pam's Pumpkin Muffins with Sunflower Seeds

❧ For breakfast or lunch, pumpkin muffins are filling. High in fiber, they "stick to the ribs," so you don't overeat later in the day.

1 cup whole-wheat pastry flour
1 cup unbleached all-purpose flour
1¹/₂ teaspoons baking powder
1¹/₂ teaspoons baking soda
1 teaspoon ground cinnamon
¹/₄ teaspoon ground cloves
¹/₄ teaspoon freshly grated nutmeg
¹/₄ teaspoon salt
2 eggs
1 cup canned pumpkin (see glossary)
²/₃ cup buttermilk
¹/₃ cup brown sugar
¹/₄ cup canola oil
¹/₂ cup raisins
¹/₄ cup sunflower seeds

Preheat oven to 400°F (200°C). Lightly butter 24 (2³/₄-inch) muffin cups. Combine flours, baking powder, baking soda, cinnamon, cloves, nutmeg and salt in a large bowl.

Beat eggs in a medium-size bowl and stir in pumpkin, buttermilk, sugar and oil. Stir egg mixture, raisins and sunflower seeds into dry ingredients just until combined. Spoon batter into prepared muffin cups. Bake 25 minutes or until a wooden pick inserted in the centers comes out clean. Cool muffins in pans on a wire rack 5 minutes. Remove from pans and cool completely. *Makes 24 muffins.*

PER MUFFIN: Cal 100 • Carbo 15 gm • Prot 3 gm • Total fat 4 gm • Sat fat trace • Cal from fat 36% • Chol 18 mg

EDUCATION: Learn something new to expand your mind. You may want to enroll in a course at your local high school or community college, take up a hobby or see an opera. Push back the unknown corners of your life to discover yourself enjoying a new experience.

March 27

INSPIRATION: *It is not just a change in what I keep in my refrigerator, but a change inside myself, that will make the difference in my relationship to food.*

Sandy's Tofu Satay with Green-Onion Rice

Indonesian-style satay sauce defines this exotic, flavorful dish. Serve with cooked carrots and celery sticks.

1 small onion, minced
1 teaspoon canola oil
1 tablespoon minced garlic
1 tablespoon peeled, grated gingerroot
1 teaspoon minced jalapeño chile
    (see glossary)
1/2 cup low-fat coconut milk or fresh coconut milk (see glossary)
1/3 cup natural peanut butter
2 tablespoons fresh lime juice
1 teaspoon ground coriander
1/2 teaspoon ground cumin
1/4 teaspoon freshly ground black pepper
1/4 teaspoon ground red (cayenne) pepper
5 cups chicken broth

2 1/2 cups quick-cooking brown rice
1/4 teaspoon salt
1 pound light firm tofu
1/3 cup thinly sliced green onions
1 tablespoon minced fresh parsley

Cook minced onion in oil in a medium-size skillet over medium heat, stirring frequently, until onion is translucent. Stir in garlic, gingerroot and jalapeño and cook, stirring, 1 minute.

Place onion mixture in a blender or food processor with the coconut milk, peanut butter, lime juice, coriander, cumin, pepper and cayenne. Process until smooth to make a sauce.

Bring broth to a boil in a medium-size saucepan. Stir in rice and salt. Reduce heat, cover and simmer 10 minutes, until rice is tender and liquid is absorbed.

Cut tofu into cubes and place in the medium-size skillet in which the onion was cooked. Spoon sauce over tofu. Cover and cook over low heat until mixture is bubbling and flavors have blended, 8 to 10 minutes.

Stir green onions and minced parsley into brown rice. Serve rice topped with tofu and sauce. *Makes 6 servings.*

PER SERVING: Cal 463 • Carbo 70 gm • Prot 20 gm • Total fat 21 gm • Sat fat 3 gm • Cal from fat 40% • Chol 0 mg

VARIATIONS
Substitute 1 pound cooked, cubed lean pork or 2 cooked chicken breast halves for tofu. Substitute 3/4 cup chicken broth for coconut milk in satay sauce.

EDUCATION: Breathe deeply to relax. When we are worried or anxious, our breathing becomes shallow and fast. A deep, cleansing breath slows down our body's systems and provides a calming influence. Luxuriate in the ability to fill your lungs with air. It can help you to calm down as well as benefit your body with oxygen.

INSPIRATION: *The choice is mine on how to spend or how to conserve my time and efforts.*

Julie's Baked Sweet Onions

❧ Large, mild onions—such as Vidalia, Texas or Maui sweet onions—are delicious when roasted. Serve with meat, a green or yellow vegetable and salad.

2 large sweet onions
1 teaspoon unsalted butter, softened
¹/₄ cup chicken broth
Dash of salt
Dash of freshly grated nutmeg

Preheat oven to 350°F (175°C). Peel onions and trim stem and root ends so onions will stand upright in the baking dish. Cut in half, crosswise, and arrange cut sides up in a shallow baking dish. Spread a small amount of butter on top of onions. Spoon broth over onions and season with salt and nutmeg. Bake, uncovered, 35 to 45 minutes, until onions are tender.

Makes 4 servings

PER SERVING: Cal 42 • Carbo 7 gm • Prot 1 gm • Total fat 1 gm • Sat fat 1 gm • Cal from fat 26% • Chol 3 mg

EDUCATION: Choose easy side dishes when creating involved main courses. This allows you to focus your energy on the more complicated task. This onion dish looks elegant but is easy to prepare. Let the oven do double duty by selecting another dish that cooks at the same temperature.

INSPIRATION: *I will not waste energy fighting the old, but spend my energy building the new.*

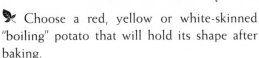

Scrumptious Low-Fat Scalloped Potatoes

❧ Choose a red, yellow or white-skinned "boiling" potato that will hold its shape after baking.

3 or 4 large potatoes
1 cup low-fat (1%) milk
1 garlic clove, pushed through a press
Dash of salt
Dash of freshly ground white pepper
2 teaspoons unsalted butter, softened

Preheat oven to 425°F (220°C). Peel and slice potatoes about ¹/₈ inch thick. You should have 4 to 5 cups. Scald milk in the microwave 2 to 2¹/₂ minutes on HIGH, or in a saucepan over medium heat. Stir garlic into the milk and pour into a shallow 8-inch-square casserole dish. Spread the potato slices in the casserole, dot with butter and season with salt and pepper.

Bake 25 to 35 minutes, or until the potatoes are browned and the liquid is nearly absorbed.

Makes 4 servings.

PER SERVING: Cal 132 • Carbo 23 gm • Prot 4 gm • Total fat 3 gm • Sat fat 1 gm • Cal from fat 19% • Chol 8 mg

EDUCATION: When you include potatoes in your diet, keep them low in fat. No matter how humble they seem, plain old potatoes are a worthy staple in a healthy diet. They are the world's most popular vegetable. Low in fat and sodium—as long as we keep it that way—potatoes offer prodigious amounts of fiber and potassium, as well as protein and vitamin C.

INSPIRATION: *I can allow myself to feel and show enthusiasm.*

Chile Olé Bean Dip

People keep coming back for more! Tasty, low-fat bean dip can be served with vegetable sticks or low-fat corn chips. Either way, they'll be scraping the bowl!

> *1 (16-ounce) can vegetarian refried beans*
> *1 cup nonfat sour cream*
> *1 (8-ounce) package nonfat cream cheese, softened*
> *²/₃ cup thinly sliced green onions*
> *2 tablespoons minced canned mild green chiles*
> *1 tablespoon chili powder*
> *2 teaspoons ground cumin*
> *1 teaspoon ground coriander*
> *¹/₂ teaspoon dried oregano*
> *¹/₂ teaspoon salt*
> *¹/₄ teaspoon freshly ground black pepper*
> *¹/₈ teaspoon ground red (cayenne) pepper*
> *20 drops hot pepper sauce or to taste*
> *¹/₃ cup shredded Cheddar cheese*
> *¹/₃ cup shredded Monterey Jack cheese*
> *1 tablespoon minced fresh parsley for garnish*

Preheat oven to 350°F (175°C). Combine refried beans, sour cream, cream cheese, green onions, chiles, chili powder, cumin, coriander, oregano, salt, pepper, cayenne, hot pepper sauce in a large bowl. Combine the shredded cheeses in a small bowl.

Place half the bean mixture in a 1¹/₂-quart casserole dish; sprinkle with half the cheese. Add remaining bean mixture and sprinkle with remaining cheese. Bake 20 minutes or until bubbly. *Makes about 4 cups.*

PER ¹/₄ CUP: Cal 138 • Carbo 8 gm • Prot 5 gm • Total fat 4 gm • Sat fat 3 gm • Cal from fat 26% • Chol 13 mg

EDUCATION: Enjoy eating with friends in your home without a lot of hassle. Many of us don't have time to plan, cook and serve elaborate dinner parties. That doesn't have to stop us from entertaining. Invite a few friends over for appetizers before stepping out for dinner. As with the bean dip here, you can find recipes that require little or no cooking. And cleanup is kept to a minimum, too. You'll be able to share the intimacy of your home and your hospitality with a minimum of effort.

INSPIRATION: *Healing is a natural process that my body knows how to do.*

Banana Bread ✓

🌿 A slice of banana bread spread with peanut butter or nonfat cream cheese is a quick breakfast.

> 1 1/2 cups whole-wheat pastry flour
> 1/4 cup unprocessed wheat bran
> 1 teaspoon baking powder
> 1 teaspoon baking soda
> 1/4 teaspoon salt
> 1/3 cup packed brown sugar
> 3 tablespoons unsalted butter,
>   softened
> 1 egg, beaten
> 1 egg white
> 1 cup mashed ripe bananas
> 1/4 teaspoon freshly grated
>   lemon peel

Preheat oven to 350°F (175°C). Lightly butter a 9 × 5-inch loaf pan. Combine flour, bran, baking powder, baking soda and salt in a large bowl. In a medium-size bowl, beat sugar and butter until combined. Beat in egg, egg white, bananas and lemon peel.

Stir egg mixture into dry ingredients just until combined. Spoon batter into prepared pan. Bake 1 hour or until a wooden pick inserted in the center comes out clean. Remove from pan and let cool on a wire rack.

Makes 1 loaf (10 slices).

PER SLICE: Cal 211 • Carbo 28 gm • Prot 4 gm • Total fat 10 gm • Sat fat 6 gm • Cal from fat 42% • Chol 46 mg

EDUCATION: Add fiber to your diet. If you haven't yet made a habit of choosing whole-grain breads and cereals, you may want to add a little unprocessed wheat bran into your life. Just 1 to 2 tablespoons a day will help regulate your entire digestive system, if you're not already eating a diet high in insoluble fiber. Because bran can absorb and hold water, it provides the bulk necessary for proper functioning of the digestive system. Try adding small amounts of bran to hot cereals, pancake and muffin batters, meat loaf, meatballs, casseroles, stuffing and cooked fruit desserts. As your intake of whole foods rich in fiber increases, your need for a bran "supplement" will diminish.

INSPIRATION: *I can allow the healing presence of humor and laughter in my life.*

Funny Cake ✓

🌿 One of the funny things about this traditional Pennsylvania Dutch cake is that it is usually baked in a pie shell. We've used a non-traditional crust here to cut back on fat. Then, the chocolate topping—well, I'll let you see for yourself.... April Fools!

> 2 sheets filo pastry
> 1 tablespoon unsalted butter very soft, but not
>   melted
> 3/4 cup vanilla sugar (see glossary)
> 2 tablespoons unsalted butter, softened
> 1 egg, beaten
> 1 cup unbleached all-purpose flour
> 1 teaspoon baking powder
> 1/2 cup milk

CHOCOLATE TOPPING

¹/₂ cup sugar

¹/₄ cup cocoa powder

¹/₂ teaspoon instant vanilla or hazelnut coffee granules

¹/₃ cup boiling water

Preheat oven to 350°F (175°C). Lightly butter a 9-inch pie plate and line with 1 sheet of filo dough. Brush with a thin layer of very soft butter. Place half of the remaining sheet of filo on top of pie plate and brush lightly with butter. Add remaining layer of filo and brush lightly with remaining very soft butter. Fold edges into edge of pie plate.

Beat together vanilla sugar and softened butter until combined. Stir in egg. Combine flour and baking powder in a small bowl. Add flour mixture and milk to egg mixture, stirring just until combined.

For topping, combine sugar with cocoa powder and coffee and stir into boiling water until mixture is smooth.

Spoon batter into filo pastry shell. Pour chocolate topping over batter. Bake 30 to 35 minutes or until a wooden pick inserted in the center comes out clean. Allow to cool before cutting. *Makes 8 servings.*

PER SERVING: Cal 198 • Carbo 42 gm • Prot 3 gm • Total fat 3 gm • Sat fat 1 gm • Cal from fat 18% • Chol 32 mg

EDUCATION: Spend time reading good books to develop your mind. Like any other part of our bodies, our minds can become flabby with disuse. Occasionally read something with a viewpoint quite different from your own. Observe yourself as you confront new ideas, and learn from your reactions.

INSPIRATION: *Dealing with the reality of my physical situation may help me be open to the possibilities of healing change.*

Steamed Cabbage with Apples & Peanuts

❧ Cabbage—high in vitamin C and seen as a cancer-fighter—is a good food buy!

1 medium-size head green cabbage

2 tart apples, peeled, cored and sliced

2 teaspoons unsalted butter

2 or 3 tablespoons apple juice

¹/₂ cup chopped peanuts

Chop cabbage coarsely. Cook sliced apples in butter in a nonstick Dutch oven over medium heat, stirring frequently, until apples are firm-tender, 5 to 6 minutes. Add cabbage, cover and steam, stirring occasionally, just until cabbage is firm-tender, 7 to 10 minutes, adding apple juice as needed to prevent scorching. Do not overcook. Stir in peanuts. *Makes 6 servings.*

PER SERVING: Cal 127 • Carbo 12 gm • Prot 4 gm • Total fat 7 gm • Sat fat 2 gm • Cal from fat 49% • Chol 4 mg

EDUCATION: Increase your intake of fresh fruits. Apples are terrific winter fruit! When you're looking to add an apple each day, an easier-than-pie way to enjoy them is to slice thin, then sprinkle with lemon juice and cinnamon. The pectin in the apple is a valuable source of soluble fiber that has been shown to help lower cholesterol.

INSPIRATION: *One action leads to another—my positive actions to heal myself will build on one another.*

Kansas City Oatmeal Bread

🌿 Oats offer a moist, sweet element to bread, in addition to high fiber.

1 tablespoon active dry yeast
¹/₄ cup lukewarm water
¹/₃ cup packed brown sugar
2 cups skim milk
2 cups rolled oats
2 tablespoons unsalted butter
3³/₄ to 4 cups unbleached all-purpose flour
1 teaspoon salt

Place yeast, water and sugar in a small bowl and let stand until frothy. Heat milk in a small pan until scalding hot. Place oats and butter in a large bowl, stir in scalded milk and let stand until mixture is lukewarm.

Add yeast mixture and 1 cup of flour to the oats and beat until well combined. Cover with a towel and let the dough rise in a warm place until light. Beat down dough and stir in enough of the remaining flour to make a moderately firm dough. Knead dough on a floured surface until light. Let rise in a large, oiled bowl until doubled in size.

Preheat oven to 400°F (200°C). Lightly oil 2 nonstick 9 × 5-inch loaf pans. Punch down dough and shape into two loaves. Place loaves in pans. Cover with plastic wrap and let rise until dough is level with top of the pans. Bake 20 minutes, reduce oven temperature to 350°F (175°C) and bake 25 minutes more, or until bread sounds hollow when tapped.

Makes 2 loaves (24 slices).

PER SLICE: Cal 125 • Carbo 23 gm • Prot 4 gm • Total fat 2 gm • Sat fat 1 gm • Cal from fat 14% • Chol 3 mg

EDUCATION: Find healthy ways to reduce stress and experience tranquility. During the course of teaching stress management, I often related the story of a "friend" who found that kneading dough was a perfect vent for frustrations. I'd describe how she punched the dough and slapped it on the counter, twisted, pinched and pounded it. Until one day, I heard a voice from the back of the room: "But who'd want to eat the bread with all that negative energy in it?" Since then I've chosen to kick empty boxes in the basement when I'm upset, and to appreciate a more gentle spirit of bread-making.

INSPIRATION: *Every end brings a new beginning, a balance in the process of life.*

Terry's Turkey Meatball Sandwiches

🌿 Terry's three children enjoy mom's meatball sandwiches. Doug, Emily and Jeff occasionally make a meal for mom, too.

1 pound ground skinless
    turkey breasts
¹/₄ cup minced onion
1 tablespoon minced fresh parsley
2 teaspoons fresh lemon juice
¹/₂ teaspoon dried oregano
¹/₄ teaspoon dried mint

¹/₄ teaspoon freshly ground black pepper

1 garlic clove, minced

¹/₃ cup nonfat sour cream

¹/₂ small cucumber, peeled and
    finely chopped

2 large whole-wheat pita breads, cut in half

1 cup shredded lettuce leaves

1 cup peeled, seeded and chopped tomato

Combine ground turkey, onion, parsley, half the lemon juice, oregano, mint, pepper and garlic. Shape into 12 balls. Cook in a lightly oiled nonstick skillet over medium heat, stirring occasionally, 8 to 10 minutes, until browned and cooked throughout. Meanwhile, combine sour cream, cucumber and the remaining lemon juice. Place in a small serving dish.

When meatballs are done, place 3 in each pita half. Top with lettuce and tomato. Serve accompanied by sour cream sauce.

Makes 4 servings.

PER SERVING: Cal 161 • Carbo 4 gm • Prot 26 gm • Total fat 4 gm • Sat fat 1 gm • Cal from fat 22% • Chol 59 mg

EDUCATION: To cut back on calories, pay attention to fats. Ounce for ounce, fats have more than twice as many calories as carbohydrates. Many processed foods are loaded with fat, often listed simply as "vegetable" oil. Often this is coconut oil, the worst kind for your health because it is so highly saturated. Begin with low-fat ingredients, like those above, cooked in a low-fat way, and you'll be on the right road to proper calorie balance.

INSPIRATION: *I will take the possibilities of today and make of them what I can.*

Mashed Sweet Potatoes with Carrots & Spices

🌿 Cinnamon and spices add a fragrant note to this healthful dish. Choose the dark orange sweet potatoes, often referred to as "yams."

2 large sweet potatoes

2 carrots

¹/₄ cup nonfat yogurt

1 teaspoon brown sugar

¹/₄ teaspoon ground
    cinnamon

¹/₈ teaspoon ground
    coriander

¹/₈ teaspoon ground ginger

¹/₈ teaspoon salt

Peel and cube sweet potatoes. Peel and slice carrots. Place vegetables in a steaming basket over boiling water and steam 20 to 25 minutes, until tender. Mash in a large bowl and stir in yogurt, brown sugar, cinnamon, coriander, ginger and salt. Serve hot. *Makes 4 servings.*

PER SERVING: Cal 87 • Carbo 20 gm • Prot 2 gm • Total fat trace • Sat fat trace • Cal from fat 4% • Chol 1 mg

EDUCATION: Eat foods high in vitamin A. Vitamin A is the maintenance-worker-in-chief that maintains and repairs the epithelium, the thin tissue that lines all of our major organs, covers our body and lines its various passageways. A healthy epithelium is an important line of defense. With vitamin A so necessary to healthy tissues, it's nice to know how easy it is to come by. Just ¹/₂ cup of cooked sweet potatoes offers twice the minimum daily allowance recommended by nutritionists.

INSPIRATION: *I don't need to be perfect, I just need to be myself!*

Anne's Pasta with Cauliflower

Delicious vegetarian ingredients prove pasta's versatility. Serve with Italian bread and a tossed green salad.

$3/4$ pound linguini
1 onion, halved and thinly sliced
1 carrot, diced
$1/2$ red bell pepper, diced
$1/2$ tablespoon olive oil
2 garlic cloves, minced
1 small head cauliflower
$1/2$ cup water
1 bay leaf
$1/4$ teaspoon dried marjoram
$1/4$ teaspoon dried basil
$1/4$ teaspoon salt
$1/8$ teaspoon freshly ground black pepper
2 cups tomato sauce
$1/4$ cup minced fresh parsley
$3/4$ cup (3 ounces) shredded Cheddar cheese

Bring a large pot of water to a boil. Add pasta, return to a boil, then reduce heat and cook about 8 minutes, until quite firm, but beginning to become tender. Turn off heat but do not drain.

Meanwhile, cook onion, carrot and bell pepper in the oil in a large skillet over medium heat, stirring frequently, until the onion is translucent, about 10 minutes. Stir in garlic and cook 1 or 2 minutes more. Break cauliflower into bite-size flowerets. Add to pan with water, bay leaf, marjoram, basil, salt and pepper. Bring to a boil, reduce heat, cover and simmer 6 to 8 minutes, until the cauliflower is crisp-tender. Add tomato sauce and parsley, bring to a boil, reduce heat and simmer 2 or 3 minutes, stirring frequently. Remove from heat, remove bay leaf, and stir in cheese until cheese is melted. Drain linguini. Serve cauliflower sauce over pasta.

Makes 4 servings.

PER SERVING: Cal 291 • Carbo 40 gm • Prot 13 gm • Total fat 10 gm • Sat fat 5 gm • Cal from fat 30% • Chol 51 mg

EDUCATION: Refrain from draining your diet of nutrients. Cauliflower is an excellent source of folacin, also known as folic acid. When cooked, however, over three-fourths of the folacin can be lost. Since most of this vitamin winds up in the cooking water, choose recipes that conserve this water, as above, or save drained water for use in other dishes. Cook cauliflower only until crisp-tender or serve it raw in salads or with low-fat dips to maximize your intake of this vitamin. Folacin is important to the growth and function of your body's new cells.

INSPIRATION: *I can see myself as an adventure; discovering me is more exciting than giving in to the compulsions that smother my creative self.*

Italian Potatoes with Ripe Olives

Stewed tomatoes flavored with garlic, olives and capers change the pace with this potato side dish.

4 large potatoes
1 teaspoon olive oil
2 garlic cloves, minced

$^1/_8$ teaspoon red pepper flakes
1 (14$^1/_2$-ounce) can stewed tomatoes
$^1/_4$ cup pitted ripe olives, minced
1 tablespoon capers, minced
$^1/_4$ teaspoon dried rosemary
$^1/_8$ teaspoon freshly ground
    black pepper
$^1/_4$ cup minced fresh parsley
2 tablespoons freshly grated
    Parmesan cheese
Whole pitted ripe olives for garnish
Parsley sprigs for garnish

Peel potatoes and cut into bite-size pieces. Place in a large saucepan, cover with water and bring to a boil. Reduce heat, cover and simmer 10 or 12 minutes or until potatoes are tender. Drain, cover pan with a kitchen towel and replace lid.

Meanwhile, heat oil in a large nonstick skillet over medium heat. Add garlic and pepper flakes and stir 1 minute. Add stewed tomatoes, olives, capers, rosemary and pepper. Bring to a boil, reduce heat and simmer, uncovered, 5 minutes or until sauce thickens slightly. Stir in parsley and Parmesan cheese and remove from heat. Place potatoes on a serving plate and top with tomato mixture. Garnish with olives and parsley. *Makes 4 servings.*

PER SERVING: Cal 181 • Carbo 35 gm • Prot 5 gm • Total fat 3 gm • Sat fat 1 gm • Cal from fat 15% • Chol 3 mg

EDUCATION: Take time to enjoy eating, especially with loved ones. Try to set aside one meal a day when everyone in the house can sit down to a leisurely meal. Turn off the television to allow conversation to develop. Keep topics light. No one can digest well if he or she is arguing or being criticized.

April 8

INSPIRATION: *My Higher Power offers reliable direction to achieving my goals of self-care.*

Whole-Wheat Honey Muffins

Simple and easy to make, whole-wheat muffins are delicious with any meal of the day.

1$^3/_4$ cups whole-wheat
    pastry flour
2 teaspoons baking powder
$^1/_4$ teaspoon ground
    cinnamon
$^3/_4$ cup buttermilk
$^1/_4$ cup honey
3 tablespoons canola oil
1 egg, beaten

Preheat oven to 375°F (190°C). Lightly oil 12 (2$^3/_4$-inch) nonstick muffin cups. Combine flour, baking powder and cinnamon in a medium-size bowl. In a small bowl, stir together buttermilk, honey, oil and egg. Add the egg mixture to the dry ingredients and stir just until combined. Spoon batter into muffin cups. Bake 20 to 25 minutes, or until a wooden pick inserted in the center of the muffins comes out clean. *Makes 12 muffins.*

PER MUFFIN: Cal 131 • Carbo 21 gm • Prot 3 gm • Total fat 4 gm • Sat fat trace • Cal from fat 28% • Chol 18 mg

EDUCATION: Be a label reader to make sure you're getting what you expect. If you don't have time to bake your own breads, be sure to read labels when shopping for whole-grain muffins and breads. "Wheat" bread may contain little or no whole grain. Look for "whole-wheat flour" listed first in the order of ingredients to be sure of a substantial whole-grain content.

INSPIRATION: *In choosing healing and nutritious foods, I will focus on how I feel in response to these changes, not on my external appearance.*

Sandra's Chicken Fried Rice

🌿 Served with a soup and salad, this simple dish is a meal. Having cooked brown rice on hand (see glossary) speeds preparation.

> 1 1/2 cups brown rice
> 3 cups chicken broth
> 1 boneless and skinless
>   chicken breast half
> 1/4 cup water
> 3/4 cup chopped onion
> 3/4 cup diced green bell
>   pepper
> 1/4 cup thinly sliced green
>   onions
> 2 teaspoons canola oil
> 1 garlic clove, minced
> 1 egg
> 1 tablespoon skim milk
> 1 tablespoon minced
>   fresh parsley

Place rice and broth in a large saucepan. Bring to a boil, reduce heat, cover and simmer 35 to 40 minutes, until water is absorbed and rice is tender. Place chicken and water in a small skillet. Bring to a boil, reduce heat, cover and simmer 8 to 10 minutes, just until the chicken is cooked through. Drain and set aside to cool.

Combine onion, bell pepper and green onions in a large, nonstick skillet with the oil over medium heat and cook, stirring frequently, 10 to 15 minutes, until the vegetables are tender. Stir in garlic and cook 1 or 2 minutes more. Remove vegetables from the pan and place in a large serving bowl. Beat egg with skim milk. Lightly oil a large skillet and pour in egg mixture. Cook, without stirring, until egg is cooked throughout. Cool egg and cut into thin strips. Finely chop cooled chicken breast.

To assemble dish, combine chicken, cooked vegetables, egg and parsley with rice in a large saucepan. Heat through.   *Makes 4 servings.*

PER SERVING: Cal 383 • Carbo 60 gm • Prot 18 gm • Total fat 7 gm • Sat fat 1 gm • Cal from fat 16% • Chol 72 mg

EDUCATION: Stay within your budget by choosing wisely. Living economically is another way of taking care of ourselves. By avoiding highly processed, expensively advertised prepared foods, we put our money where it does the most good—on wholesome ingredients. Easily prepared dishes made with whole foods are healthier, too. We can see to it that they contain less fat, sugar and sodium than their processed counterparts. Save money, stay healthy—we win two ways!

April 10

INSPIRATION: *Interacting with those around us, sharing our experiences of healing, helps all of us grow, forgive and trust.*

Corn & Red Pepper–Scrambled Egg Tortillas

Tasty and colorful with a cornucopia of herbs and vegetables. Flour tortillas, warmed for 20 seconds in a microwave, can be substituted. Serve with salsa as a variation.

> ¹/₂ small onion, chopped
> ¹/₂ small red bell pepper,
>   chopped
> 1 green onion, thinly sliced
> 1 teaspoon canola oil
> 1 cup frozen whole-kernel corn
> 2 tablespoons minced
>   fresh parsley
> ¹/₈ teaspoon ground coriander
> Dash of freshly ground
>   black pepper
> 2 eggs
> 2 egg whites
> 1 tablespoon skim milk
> 4 corn tortillas
> Red pepper rings for
>   garnish
> Parsley sprigs for garnish

Cook onion, bell pepper and green onion in a nonstick skillet over medium heat, stirring frequently, until vegetables are firm-tender. Stir in corn, parsley, coriander and pepper and cook 2 or 3 minutes, until the corn is tender. Beat eggs, egg whites and milk together while the corn is cooking. Pour over the corn mixture and stir occasionally until cooked through.

Boil a small amount of water in a small skillet. Dip each corn tortilla briefly in the boiling water to soften. (Do not let tortillas cook more than a few seconds or they will fall apart.) Fold tortillas in quarters and fill two "pockets" of each with the scrambled egg mixture. Place 2 filled tortillas on each plate and garnish with pepper rings and parsley.   *Makes 2 servings.*

PER SERVING: Cal 336 • Carbo 48 gm • Prot 17 gm • Total fat 10 gm • Sat fat 2 gm • Cal from fat 26% • Chol 213 mg

EDUCATION: Eat eggs occasionally as part of a healthy diet. Eggs are versatile, a good source of protein, and full of valuable vitamins and minerals. Good news for egg lovers: according to the USDA, the average large egg today contains only 213 milligrams of cholesterol, nearly 25 percent less than in the previous decade. The reason? Hens are receiving lower-fat feed, which translates to lower-fat eggs. Because of this, the American Heart Association has increased its recommended maximum allowance of yolks, which contains the cholesterol, from three to four per week. Be sure to count eggs in puddings and baked goods when calculating your intake.

INSPIRATION: *Gathering information is a daily step in creating a healthier life-style for myself.*

Jo's Fast & Fabulous Fish & Vegetable Stew

🌿 Ready in under half an hour, this main-dish cod and vegetable combination can be served with crusty rolls. For variety, you can also add hot red pepper flakes to taste and serve over linguini.

    1 large onion
    1 teaspoon olive oil
    2 garlic cloves, minced
    5 medium-size red potatoes
    2 cups chicken broth
    1/4 cup minced fresh parsley
    1/4 teaspoon dried thyme
    1/4 teaspoon salt
    1/4 teaspoon freshly ground black pepper
    1 1/2 pounds cod fillet
    1/2 pound fresh spinach,
       thoroughly rinsed
    1 (28-ounce) can whole plum tomatoes
    Lemon slices for garnish
    Parsley sprigs for garnish

Cut onion in half lengthwise, then thinly slice crosswise. Cook onion in the oil in a non-stick Dutch oven over medium heat, stirring frequently, until onion is translucent. Stir in garlic and cook, stirring, 1 or 2 minutes. Remove from heat.

Cut unpeeled potatoes into bite-size pieces. Combine potatoes, broth, parsley, thyme, salt and pepper with onion mixture and bring to a boil. Reduce heat, cover and simmer 10 minutes, until potatoes are almost tender. Meanwhile, cut cod fillet into bite-size pieces. Discard stems from spinach and coarsely slice leaves. Reserving 1 cup of liquid, drain and chop tomatoes.

Add tomatoes, reserved tomato juice, cod and spinach to pan. Bring to a boil, reduce heat, cover and simmer 5 minutes or until cod is cooked through and potatoes are tender. Spoon into large soup bowls and garnish with lemon slices and parsley. *Makes 4 servings.*

PER SERVING: Cal 396 • Carbo 51 gm • Prot 40 gm • Total fat 4 gm • Sat fat 1 gm • Cal from fat 9% • Chol 74 mg

EDUCATION: Spend some time in the natural world to feel your connection with the earth. You don't have to hike into the wilderness. Take off your shoes and feel grass under your feet. Visit a park and take a really close-up look at the flowers. Pay attention to a sunrise or sunset.

INSPIRATION: *Resisting a new path can prevent me from changing the things I can.*

Miriam's Turkey Cutlet Parmesan

🌿 Turkey cutlets offer a delicious alternative to a traditional Italian dish. Serve with a side dish of pasta and vegetables.

    3 tablespoons unbleached all-purpose flour
    1/4 teaspoon salt
    1/4 teaspoon dried marjoram
    1/4 teaspoon dried basil
    1/8 teaspoon freshly ground
       black pepper
    1/2 cup dried whole-wheat bread crumbs
    2 tablespoons freshly grated Parmesan cheese
    1 egg white
    1 tablespoon water
    4 turkey breast cutlets (about 1 pound)
    1/2 tablespoon olive oil

1 cup marinara or spaghetti sauce
1/3 cup shredded part-skim
    mozzarella cheese

Preheat oven to 400°F (200°C). On a large plate, mix flour, salt, marjoram, basil and pepper. On another plate, mix bread crumbs and Parmesan cheese. In a pie pan, beat egg white with water. Coat turkey cutlets with flour mixture, then egg white mixture and finally crumbs.

Brown breaded cutlets in the oil in a large nonstick skillet over medium heat. Place in a 13 × 9-inch shallow casserole dish. Top each with 1/4 cup sauce and bake 10 minutes, until turkey cutlets are cooked through. Top with mozzarella cheese and bake 1 or 2 minutes, just until cheese is melted.   *Makes 4 servings.*

PER SERVING: Cal 337 • Carbo 20 gm • Prot 32 gm • Total fat 14 gm • Sat fat 4 gm • Cal from fat 37% • Chol 72 mg

EDUCATION: Avoid striving toward a totally nonfat diet. Even if we could, we wouldn't want to banish all of the fat in our diet. Dietary fats are vital to our well-being, essential to the absorption and utilization of the fat-soluble vitamins A, D, E and K. Our body's fat cells, though we spend so much effort trying to reduce them, are important, too. They help us to maintain our body temperature, serve as storage areas for the fat-soluble vitamins listed above, and are a source of energy when the body is in need of calories. What we want to avoid are not fats themselves, but their over consumption.

April 13

INSPIRATION: *I am nourished by sharing and giving to others.*

Ellen's Low-Fat Raisin Cake

❧ Raisins give a rich texture to this low-fat cake. Spicy and moist, it needs no frosting.

2 cups raisins
1 cup packed dark brown sugar
1 1/3 cups water
3 tablespoons unsalted butter
2 teaspoons ground cinnamon
1/2 teaspoon freshly grated nutmeg
1/2 teaspoon ground cloves
2 cups whole-wheat pastry flour
1 teaspoon baking powder
1/2 teaspoon baking soda
1/2 teaspoon salt

Combine raisins, sugar, water, butter, cinnamon, nutmeg and cloves in a medium-size saucepan. Bring to a boil over medium heat, stirring frequently, then reduce heat and simmer 3 minutes. Set aside to cool.

Preheat oven to 325°F (165°C). Lightly butter a nonstick 8-inch-square baking pan. Combine flour, baking powder, baking soda and salt in a large bowl. When raisin mixture is cool, stir it into the dry ingredients. Pour batter into prepared pan. Bake 45 to 50 minutes or until a wooden pick inserted in the center of the cake comes out clean.   *Makes 8 servings.*

PER SERVING: Cal 366 • Carbo 80 gm • Prot 4 gm • Total fat 5 gm • Sat fat 3 gm • Cal from fat 12% • Chol 12 mg

EDUCATION: Avoid crash diets. They are hard on emotional stability. Those of us who've tried them (and the people who've had to tolerate us) have ample evidence of that. But insufficient calories can also impair our immune systems, making us more susceptible to infection and illness. By eating low-fat foods that are high in complex carbohydrates and fiber, we allow our bodies to regulate our appetites and weight, without sacrificing any of the nutrients needed for our physical and emotional well-being.

INSPIRATION: *I am: ready for change, open to healing, in tune with recovery.*

Cornmeal Pancakes with Cinnamon Applesauce

🌿 Cornmeal and whole-wheat flour combine to create a hearty and flavorful breakfast pancake. Top with hot cinnamon applesauce.

1 cup stone-ground yellow
    cornmeal
3/4 cup whole-wheat pastry flour
1 1/2 teaspoons baking powder
1/2 teaspoon baking soda
2 eggs, beaten
1 tablespoon canola oil
1 1/4 to 1 3/4 cups buttermilk
2 cups applesauce
2 tablespoons maple syrup
1/2 teaspoon ground cinnamon

Combine cornmeal, flour, baking powder and baking soda in a large bowl. In a small bowl, combine eggs and oil.

Stir egg mixture and 1 1/4 cups buttermilk into the dry ingredients just until combined. Add additional buttermilk if batter is too thick.

For each pancake, pour about 1/3 cup of batter onto a lightly oiled, hot, nonstick griddle. When bubbles have formed on top of the pancake and the bottom is well browned, turn the pancake and cook until remaining side is browned. Keep griddle hot and cook remaining pancakes. For topping, combine applesauce, maple syrup and cinnamon in a small saucepan. Heat and serve with pancakes.

Makes 4 servings.

PER SERVING: Cal 437 • Carbo 82 gm • Prot 11 gm • Total fat 8 gm • Sat fat 2 gm • Cal from fat 16% • Chol 109 mg

EDUCATION: Turn off the television to enjoy some peace. Violence and acrimony, real and produced, fill the screen each day and night. Select what you watch with care, then spend your freed-up time connecting more fully with the real world that surrounds you.

INSPIRATION: *Let me see myself and those around me with fresh eyes, appreciating rather than criticizing what I encounter.*

Bev's Tuna Salad Pita Sandwiches with Sprouts

🌿 Adding bell pepper, carrot, onion, green onions and olives to low-fat tuna salad maximizes taste, nutrition and visual appeal.

1/2 small green bell pepper, finely diced
1/2 carrot, grated
1/2 small onion, grated
1 (6 1/2-ounce) can water-packed tuna,
    drained
2 green onions, thinly sliced
2 ripe olives, minced
2 tablespoons minced fresh parsley
2 tablespoons reduced-fat mayonnaise
1 tablespoon nonfat yogurt
1/4 teaspoon dried basil
1/8 teaspoon salt
1/8 teaspoon freshly ground
    black pepper
2 whole-wheat pita sandwich breads
1/2 cup alfalfa sprouts

Combine bell pepper, carrot, onion, tuna, green onions, olives, parsley, mayonnaise, yogurt, basil, salt and pepper in a medium-size bowl. Cut pita breads in half to form 2 pockets each. Stuff ¼ of the tuna salad in each pita pocket half and top with sprouts.

Makes 2 servings.

PER SERVING: Cal 301 • Carbo 28 gm • Prot 33 gm • Total fat 6 gm • Sat fat trace • Cal from fat 18% • Chol 22 mg

EDUCATION: Drink 8 to 10 glasses of water each day. When you think about your body's needs, don't forget the most important of all— plain, clean water. While human beings can live several weeks without food, without water we perish in a matter of days. Whether in liquid meals like soup, in fruits, vegetables or out of a glass, substantial amounts of water are needed each day to: allow organs to function properly, transport nutrients to and waste products from each cell, keep skin and mucous membranes healthy as a first barrier against injury and disease and maintain adequate blood volume. For all of us, that extra glass of water may be just what our body is calling for instead of more food.

April 16

NSPIRATION: *Gifts of the universe are mine for the taking. I can accept and share love and peace of mind.*

Lou's Garlic-Herb Leg of Lamb

❧ When I worked in Washington, D.C., it was exciting to meet people of various nationalities, especially those who were as fond of food as I am. Many recipes were discovered and exchanged in those days, including this one for a garlic and herb Mediterranean touch to leg of lamb. Serve with cooked greens, mashed squash, salad and rolls.

1 (5-pound) leg of lamb
1 lemon slice

4 garlic cloves, cut into
large slivers
1 tablespoon dried rosemary
1 tablespoon dried thyme
½ teaspoon salt
¼ teaspoon freshly ground
black pepper

Remove papery outer covering, called the "fell," from leg of lamb. Trim away excess fat. Rub meat with the lemon slice. With a sharp knife, cut slits in the meat and in each slit insert a sliver of garlic. Combine rosemary, thyme, salt and pepper. Place lamb, fat side up, on a roasting rack in a shallow pan. Pat herbs on top of the leg of lamb. Let lamb rest at room temperature while preheating oven.

Preheat oven to 450°F (225°C). When oven is hot, place the lamb on a rack in the center of the oven. Immediately reduce heat to 350°F (175°C). Roast the leg of lamb about 2½ hours (30 minutes to the pound), or until the internal temperature registers 160° to 165°F (75°C) for rare or 175° to 180°F (80°C) for well done. Do not cover pan or baste the lamb as it roasts.

Makes 8 servings.

PER SERVING: Cal 326 • Carbo 1 gm • Prot 48 gm • Total fat 13 gm • Sat fat 5 gm • Cal from fat 36% • Chol 151 mg

EDUCATION: Choose lean cuts of meat to reduce fat. The leg of lamb is the leanest, most nutritious lamb cut. Lamb is rich in iron, like most meats. And a little lamb, like other meats, will help you better absorb iron from the non-meat portions of your meal.

INSPIRATION: *I will trust my instincts about the sort of healthful changes my body needs.*

Mixed Vegetable & Cabbage Coleslaw

❧ Colorfully studded with radishes, broccoli and carrot, this coleslaw wins points for flavor, too.

> *4 cups shredded cabbage*
> *2 celery stalks, thinly sliced on diagonal*
> *2 radishes, thinly sliced*
> *1 carrot, shredded*
> *1/2 cup chopped broccoli flowerets*
> *1/4 cup minced fresh parsley*
> *3 tablespoons nonfat yogurt*
> *1 tablespoon canola oil*
> *1/2 teaspoon brown sugar*
> *1/4 teaspoon salt*
> *1/8 teaspoon ground coriander*

Combine cabbage, celery, radishes, carrot, broccoli and parsley in a large bowl. Combine the yogurt, oil, brown sugar, salt and coriander in a small bowl. Pour dressing over the vegetables and toss to coat. *Makes 6 servings.*

PER SERVING: Cal 51 • Carbo 6 gm • Prot 1 gm • Total fat 2 gm • Sat fat trace • Cal from fat 35% • Chol trace

EDUCATION: Eat extra-high vitamin C foods when you're stressed. Stress, injury, fever or infection can rapidly deplete vitamin C reserves in the body. So, step up your intake of vitamin C with dishes like the cabbage coleslaw above to guarantee you have enough to keep you healthy.

INSPIRATION: *Emerging as a whole person means allowing the transformation to occur each moment.*

Quick Brown Rice & Banana Porridge

❧ Leftover cooked brown rice is all you need for an easy, delicious, hot, whole-grain breakfast. It's as comforting as a dessert pudding, but it sticks to the ribs, not your hips!

> *2/3 cup cooked brown rice*
> *1/3 cup skim milk*
> *1 teaspoon brown sugar*
> *Dash of ground cinnamon*
> *1/2 banana, peeled and diced*

Combine rice, milk, sugar and cinnamon in a microwave-safe cereal bowl. Microwave on HIGH 2 minutes. Stir in banana.

Makes 1 serving.

PER SERVING: Cal 243 • Carbo 52 gm • Prot 7 gm • Total fat 2 gm • Sat fat trace • Cal from fat 6% • Chol 1 mg

VARIATIONS
Plan "leftovers" when you cook brown rice. Vary breakfast by adding a selection of ingredients to the recipe above. Omit banana. Cook 1/2 peeled chopped apple with the rice. Add 1 tablespoon chopped walnuts and 1 tablespoon raisins before microwaving. Stir 1/2 cup diced strawberries into bowl.

EDUCATION: Starch up your diet to prevent drooping. There is a vast difference between how the body processes starches and sugars. Starches—such as potatoes, pastas, bread, cereals, cornmeal, vegetables and rice—are "complex" carbohydrates. The body breaks them down slowly: complex starches to complex sugars, complex sugars to simple sugars, and finally the simple sugars enter the bloodstream. This slow process keeps blood-sugar levels on an even keel. Refined carbohydrates—such as table sugar and syrups—enter the bloodstream almost immediately, quickly boosting blood-sugar levels. The body reacts by pumping extra insulin and adrenaline into the bloodstream. Sugar levels plummet, setting the course for fatigue, depression and mood swings.

Try these approaches to balance your sugar intake: Avoid breakfast cereals or other processed foods where the main ingredient is sugar. Read labels: sugar, dextrose, corn syrup, beet sugar, brown sugar, fructose, etc., are all ways of adding sugar. Many foods contain two, three or more. Besides cutting down on sugar at breakfast, take care with desserts. Only have desserts after a large meal that contains lots of protein and fiber. When you are making your own sweet desserts, substitute fiber-rich whole grain flour for all or part of refined flours. Select smaller portions of desserts and enjoy them with some fresh fruit.

April 19

INSPIRATION: *Letting gently go of negative ways of coping with stress and anxiety will make room in my life for more positive responses.*

Stir-fried Asparagus with Cherry Tomatoes

❧ When it's off-season for tomatoes, you'll find cherry tomatoes often have more flavor than the large tomatoes in the supermarket.

1 pound asparagus
1/2 pint cherry tomatoes
1 teaspoon olive oil
1 teaspoon pine nuts
1 tablespoon minced fresh
    parsley
1/4 teaspoon salt

Hold base of each asparagus stalk and bend until end breaks off. This will be the spot beyond which the bottoms are too tough to eat. Discard ends and trim scales from stems. Cut asparagus diagonally into 3-inch pieces. Slice cherry tomatoes in half.

Heat oil in a large nonstick skillet over medium heat. Add pine nuts and cook, stirring, 1 minute. Add asparagus and cook, stirring, about 3 minutes, until asparagus is crisp-tender. Add cherry tomatoes, parsley and salt and cook, stirring, until heated through.

Makes 4 servings.

PER SERVING: Cal 52 • Carbo 7 gm • Prot 3 gm • Total fat 2 gm • Sat fat trace • Cal from fat 34% • Chol 0 mg

EDUCATION: Look for fresh, nutritious, fast-cooking, colorful vegetables to add to meals when you're in a hurry. Cherry tomatoes are one answer. Cherry tomatoes need only to be cooked until hot. Season with a few drops of honey or add minced fresh herbs or garlic. Feta cheese, cooked peas or a sprinkle of freshly grated Parmesan are other possible additions.

INSPIRATION: *Real communication nourishes the soul. Let me listen to others carefully, and seek out those who hear me in turn.*

Olive-Lentil Party Spread

Greek olives impart a distinctly succulent flavor to this spread, developed by Pamela as an alternative to creamy dairy dips. Greek olives can be found at ethnic food stores or often in the supermarket. Ripe olives can be substituted, but the dish isn't as flavorful. Also good as a sandwich spread topped with shredded vegetables.

$3/4$ cup French or green lentils
$2 1/4$ cups chicken broth, fat removed
2 large garlic cloves, peeled
$1/3$ cup pitted chopped Greek olives
3 tablespoons minced fresh parsley
1 teaspoon olive oil
1 teaspoon brown rice vinegar
$1/8$ teaspoon salt
Dash of freshly ground black pepper
2 (5-ounce) boxes melba toast rounds

Rinse and pick over lentils. Place in a medium-size saucepan with the broth and garlic and bring to a boil over medium heat. Reduce heat, cover and simmer 30 to 40 minutes or until tender, but not mushy. Drain lentils and allow them to cool completely.

Place the lentils and garlic, olives, 2 tablespoons parsley, oil, vinegar, salt and pepper in a food processor. Process in short bursts just until ingredients are finely chopped. Turn spread into a small bowl and sprinkle with remaining parsley. Place bowl on a serving dish and surround with melba toast. *Makes 8 servings.*

PER SERVING: Cal 237 • Carbo 38 gm • Prot 16 gm • Total fat 3 gm • Sat fat trace • Cal from fat 11% • Chol 0 mg

EDUCATION: Lower your fat intake with nonfat choices of spreads. Crackers can be higher in fat than the low-fat spreads you'll be choosing to serve with them. For parties or home snacking, accompany spreads and dips with melba toast; vegetables, such as broccoli, carrots, romaine lettuce leaves; or apples and other firm, sliced fruits. These selections will add fiber and nutrients, supporting your attempts at healthful changes rather than undermining them.

INSPIRATION: *Serenity is being content with what I have, not in getting whatever I want.*

Quick Wheat Pilaf with Green Onions & Peas

❧ For a change of pace, add a variety of vegetables to your bulgur pilaf. Add a grated carrot when adding chicken broth, or stir in cooked lima beans or snow peas.

1 onion, finely chopped
2 teaspoons butter
1 garlic clove, minced
¹/₄ teaspoon ground coriander
¹/₄ teaspoon paprika
1 cup bulgur
2 cups chicken broth
¹/₂ cup frozen green peas
¹/₄ cup thinly sliced green onions
2 tablespoons minced fresh parsley

Cook onion in butter in a large saucepan over medium heat, stirring frequently, until onion is translucent. Add garlic, coriander and paprika and cook, stirring, an additional 30 seconds. Add bulgur and stir until combined with onion mixture.

Add broth and bring to a boil. Reduce heat, cover and simmer 5 minutes, until liquid is absorbed. Meanwhile, cook peas in a small amount of boiling water in a small saucepan just until firm-tender, about 2 minutes. Keep warm.

Stir peas, green onions and parsley into cooked bulgur, cover and let stand 2 to 3 minutes before serving.   *Makes 4 servings.*

PER SERVING: Cal 192 • Carbo 34 gm • Prot 8 gm • Total fat 3 gm • Sat fat 1 gm • Cal from fat 16% • Chol 6 mg

EDUCATION: Choose quick-cooking bulgur to make menu planning easier. As far back as ancient Persia, cooks have enjoyed the convenience of bulgur, a parboiled, cracked grain. Whole-wheat berries are boiled, then dried and cracked. Because it is precooked, bulgur is a snap to prepare, making it easy for you to add more whole grain to your diet. Stir cooked bulgur into hot cereals, bread dough, soups or casseroles, or use for stuffings. Bulgur is available in health-food stores.

INSPIRATION: *If I give up my need to control every-thing, every day, my life can fulfill its promise of adventure.*

California-style Veggieburgers

A vegetarian alternative to hamburgers, with a built-in salad on the roll. These burgers are surprisingly tasty!

1/2 cup finely grated carrots
1/2 cup finely chopped celery
1/3 cup pecan halves, finely ground
1/2 cup fresh bread crumbs
1/4 cup grated onion, lightly pressed in
    a sieve to remove excess liquid
2 tablespoons finely diced green bell pepper
2 tablespoons minced fresh parsley
1 egg, beaten
1/4 teaspoon paprika
1/8 teaspoon dried thyme
1/8 teaspoon salt
Dash of freshly ground black pepper
1 tablespoon nonfat yogurt
1 tablespoon nonfat mayonnaise
4 whole-grain hamburger rolls
1/2 cup shredded lettuce
2 thin slices red onion
2 thin slices green bell pepper
2 thin slices tomato
Alfalfa sprouts

Preheat oven to 350°F (175°C). Lightly butter or oil a shallow baking pan. Combine carrots, celery, ground nuts, bread crumbs, grated onion, diced bell pepper, parsley, egg, paprika, thyme, salt and pepper in a medium-size bowl. Shape into 4 patties.

Arrange patties in pan. Bake 15 minutes or until patties begin to brown. Turn and bake until remaining sides are brown, 10 to 15 minutes.

Combine yogurt and mayonnaise. Spread rolls with yogurt mixture. Place a veggieburger on the bottom of each roll and top with some lettuce, a slice of onion, bell pepper and tomato and some alfalfa sprouts. *Makes 4 servings.*

PER SERVING: Cal 182 • Carbo 20 gm • Prot 5 gm • Total fat 8 gm • Sat fat 1 gm • Cal from fat 35% • Chol 55 mg

EDUCATION: To reduce fat consumption, be conservative in your use of nuts. Like eggs, nuts can add flavor and nutritional benefits to your diet when used in moderaton. Nuts, like eggs, come in their own disposable containers. Like eggs, nuts are high in protein, but also high in fat. An advantage to nuts is that they are rich in monounsaturated oils, believed to have potential benefit to the heart and circulation.

Nuts contain some of the tastiest oils available, so small amounts can have flavorful impact. Try hazelnut, walnut or macadamia nut oil for a delicate taste treat in salad dressings. One tip: to increase the nutty flavor, lightly toast nuts in a dry skillet over medium heat before adding to your recipe. It helps make a little go a long way, tastewise.

INSPIRATION: *By not numbing myself with food, I am more open to my emotional joys and sorrows, and to the lessons I can learn from them.*

Jean's Beef Goulash

❧ Serve with steamed cabbage and a big green salad. To have the lowest intake of fat, trim beef cubes as needed.

> 1 pound lean stew beef cubes
> ¹/₂ tablespoon olive oil
> 3 onions, halved and thinly sliced
> 1 green bell pepper, diced
> 2 garlic cloves, minced
> 1 tablespoon paprika
> 1 tablespoon unbleached all-purpose flour
> 1 tablespoon tomato paste
> 3 cups chicken or beef broth
> 1 cup tomato juice
> 2 bay leaves
> ³/₄ pound wide noodles
> 2 tomatoes, peeled, seeded and
>   cut into strips
> ¹/₄ teaspoon salt
> ¹/₄ teaspoon freshly ground black pepper
> ¹/₂ cup nonfat sour cream
> 2 tablespoons minced fresh parsley

Brown meat in oil in a nonstick Dutch oven over medium heat. Remove meat, add onions and bell pepper and cook, stirring frequently, until onions are translucent. Add garlic and paprika and stir 1 minute. Stir in flour, tomato paste, broth, tomato juice and bay leaves.

Return meat to Dutch oven. Return mixture to a boil, reduce heat, cover and simmer 1¹/₂ to 2 hours, stirring occasionally, until the meat is very tender.

Meanwhile, bring a large pot of water to a boil. Add noodles and cook until tender, 7 to 8 minutes. Drain noodles.

Add tomatoes, salt and pepper to goulash and cook 10 minutes more. Remove bay leaves. Spoon goulash over noodles and garnish with sour cream and parsley.   *Makes 4 servings.*

PER SERVING: Cal 674 • Carbo 72 gm • Prot 23 gm • Total fat 24 gm • Sat fat 8 gm • Cal from fat 32% • Chol 147 mg

EDUCATION: Make your life easier by cooking some dishes in the oven. Dishes like the goulash above can also be simmered in a 350°F (175°C) oven in a covered casserole dish 1¹/₂ to 2 hours, instead of simmering on the stove. This leaves you free to walk the dog, enjoy the rain, take a nap or call a friend. Choose long-cooking dishes with liquid for oven simmering, such as soups, stews or bean dishes.

INSPIRATION: *Living creatively means I am willing to take risks, to try something new, to give up old patterns of self-destructive behavior.*

Green Pea Soup with Tarragon

❧ Serve hot or chilled as an appetizer soup for a spring dinner. Make it a party!

1 pound fresh green peas in shells
1 small onion, finely chopped
1/2 tablespoon butter
1 tablespoon unbleached flour
2 cups chicken broth
2 teaspoons minced fresh tarragon
1/4 teaspoon salt
1 1/2 cups skim milk
1/3 cup nonfat sour cream
6 tarragon sprigs for garnish

Shell peas. Cook onion in butter in a large saucepan over medium heat, stirring frequently, until onion is tender, 5 to 7 minutes. Add flour and stir 2 minutes. Gradually stir in broth. Add peas, tarragon and salt. Bring to a boil, reduce heat, cover and simmer, stirring occasionally, until peas are very tender, about 15 minutes.

Puree soup in food processor. Return to saucepan and add milk. Heat through and serve, garnishing each bowl with a dollop of sour cream and a sprig of tarragon.

Makes 4 servings.

PER SERVING: Cal 194 • Carbo 21 gm • Prot 11 gm • Total fat 7 gm • Sat fat 5 gm • Cal from fat 32% • Chol 9 mg

EDUCATION: For low-fat protein, pass the peas, please. You may, by now, be associating dried beans with high protein. But peas, also a member of the legume family, are also protein-rich. And, because they are fresh, they cook up quickly and easily. Surprisingly, a 3/4-cup portion of peas contains more protein than an egg—with a mere half gram of fat! Add fresh peas this spring to soups during the last 10 to 12 minutes of cooking, or add raw to green salads. You may also find, as I do, that freshly shelled green peas are a tasty snack!

INSPIRATION: *I rejoice in the freedom of finding my own way, instead of trying to copy the success of someone else.*

Prune Bread ✓

❧ Deliciously flavored, there's no need for jams or jellies to appreciate this loaf!

3/4 cup Pureed Prunes (see below)
1 3/4 cups whole-wheat pastry flour
1 teaspoon baking powder
1/2 teaspoon baking soda
1 teaspoon ground cinnamon
1/2 teaspoon freshly grated nutmeg
1/2 teaspoon ground cloves
1/2 teaspoon ground allspice
1/4 cup butter, softened
3/4 cup packed brown sugar
1/2 cup nonfat sour cream
1 egg, separated
2 additional egg whites

PUREED PRUNES
1 cup tightly packed pitted prunes
1/2 cup water
1/2 teaspoon freshly grated lemon peel

Preheat oven to 350°F (175°C). Lightly oil a nonstick 9 × 5-inch loaf pan.

To make Prune Puree, bring prunes, water and lemon peel to a boil in a saucepan. Reduce heat, cover and simmer 8 to 10 minutes, until the prunes are soft and the water is nearly absorbed. Remove lid and simmer until all liquid has evaporated. Puree prunes in a blender or food processor. Set aside.

Combine flour, baking powder, baking soda, cinnamon, nutmeg, cloves and allspice in a large bowl. In a medium-size bowl, beat butter and brown sugar until smooth. Add puree, sour cream and egg yolk. Stir prune mixture into dry ingredients just until combined. Stiffly beat egg whites and gently fold into batter. Spoon batter into loaf pan. Bake 30 to 35 minutes, until a wooden pick inserted in the center comes out clean. *Makes 1 loaf, 10 slices.*

PER SLICE: Cal 244 • Carbo 41 gm • Prot 4 gm • Total fat 7 gm • Sat fat 5 gm • Cal from fat 26% • Chol 34 mg

EDUCATION: Prune your diet of fat with the creative use of dried fruit. Prunes are a rich source of iron and fiber. Pureed prunes can be used as a tasty, low-fat, low-sugar spread on toast or muffins, as well as a flavorful ingredient in this quick bread.

INSPIRATION: *Fear of the unknown wears many disguises. Today I will reach past just one fear to enjoy discovery.*

Mike's Fresh Spinach & Couscous Salad

Garden-fresh, tender leaves of spinach thread their way through this delicately flavored couscous mixture. Allow couscous to cool completely before adding spinach and herbs.

1 1/2 cups couscous
2 1/4 cups boiling water
1/4 teaspoon salt
2 tablespoons olive oil
2 tablespoons fresh lemon juice
1/4 teaspoon finely grated lemon peel
2 cups washed, finely sliced
    spinach leaves
1/2 cup thinly sliced green onions
3 tablespoons minced fresh dill
1 tablespoon minced fresh parsley

Place couscous in a large bowl. Stir in boiling water and salt. Cover with plastic wrap and let stand 5 minutes. Fluff couscous with a fork. Stir in oil, lemon juice and lemon peel. Set aside until completely cooled. Toss couscous with spinach, green onions, dill and parsley. Cover and refrigerate salad 2 hours or more before serving. *Makes 6 servings.*

PER SERVING: Cal 164 • Carbo 21 gm • Prot 4 gm • Total fat 5 gm • Sat fat 1 gm • Cal from fat 31% • Chol 0 mg

EDUCATION: Gain muscle with greens and grains. Magnesium is important for muscle tone. When muscles lack sufficient magnesium, they can cramp or even become spastic. Good sources, in addition to the spinach in the recipe here, include other dark green leafy vegetables, brown rice, nuts, peas, soybeans and whole grains.

INSPIRATION: *Nurturing my relationships supports my recovery; sharing fun, good food, ideas and feelings is part of my growing intimacy with myself and others.*

Party Chicken Salad with Raw Vegetables

Colorful vegetables surrounding this spread makes for an eye-catching presentation.

2 boneless skinless chicken breast
    halves
$^1/_2$ cup chicken broth
1 tablespoon grated onion
1 tablespoon bottled steak sauce
2 garlic cloves, pushed through a press
$^1/_2$ teaspoon Madras curry powder
$^1/_4$ cup chopped celery
$^1/_4$ cup minced fresh parsley
1 tablespoon minced red bell pepper
2 (8-ounce) packages nonfat cream
    cheese, softened
$^1/_3$ cup pecans, toasted (see glossary) and
    chopped
6 celery stalks, cut into 2-inch lengths
2 green bell peppers, seeded and cut into
    1-inch-wide strips
2 red bell peppers, seeded and cut
    into 1-inch-wide strips
$^1/_2$ cauliflower, separated into flowerets
1 broccoli stalk, separated into flowerets

Simmer chicken in broth in a small skillet over medium-low heat 15 to 20 minutes, until opaque throughout. Drain and refrigerate to cool. Meanwhile, drain liquid from grated onion by pressing onion in a small strainer with the back of a spoon. Combine onion with steak sauce and garlic. Stir in curry powder, celery, 2 tablespoons of the parsley and the minced bell pepper.

Beat cream cheese with curry mixture. Finely chop cooked breasts and blend with cream cheese mixture. Form chicken spread into a log or ball. Wrap in plastic and chill 4 hours or overnight.

To serve, combine remaining parsley with chopped nuts. Press into surface of log or ball. Place on a platter with vegetables.

Makes 10 servings.

PER SERVING: Cal 181 • Carbo 13 gm • Prot 8 gm • Total fat 4 gm • Sat fat 1 gm • Cal from fat 20% • Chol 25 mg

VARIATIONS
Serve with melba toast or crackers in place of raw vegetables. Omit nuts, stir all of parsley into chicken mixture and serve as a sandwich spread.

EDUCATION: Avoid inviting bacteria to your party. Parties, unfortunately, can be an opportunity for foodborne illness. Food left at room temperature too long is an excellent host to bacteria. Their presence in foods may not be detected by taste or smell. To prevent an uncomfortable ending to your party, remember to keep hot foods hot and chilled foods cold. Serve creamy dips in bowls over ice, hot foods in a chafing dish or on a hot serving tray. If food must stand at room temperature, let it do so no longer than 2 hours.

INSPIRATION: *Whatever my challenges today, I know I can more competently meet them if my body is properly nourished.*

Vegetable Pie with Three Cheeses

Vegetables and a trio of cheeses make a vegetarian main dish delicious and satisfying.

1 large onion, halved and thinly sliced
2 large carrots, cut into julienne strips
1 cup chopped cauliflower flowerets
1 cup coarsely shredded cabbage
1 cup broccoli flowerets
¹/₂ cupnonfat ricotta cheese
2 tablespoons crumbled feta cheese
2 sheets filo pastry
1 tablespoon butter, softened
¹/₃ cup shredded skim-milk mozzarella cheese

Preheat oven to 350°F (175°C). Place onion, carrots, cauliflower, cabbage and broccoli in a large colander. Set colander in a kettle over boiling water and steam vegetables 5 to 7 minutes, until just crisp-tender. In a small bowl, combine ricotta and feta cheeses, then stir ricotta mixture into vegetables.

Lightly butter a 9-inch pie plate and line with 1 sheet of filo dough. Brush with a thin layer of very soft butter. Place half of the remaining sheet of filo on top of pie plate and brush lightly with butter. Add remaining layer of filo and brush lightly with remaining very soft butter. Fold edges into edge of pie plate.

Fill filo pastry shell with vegetable mixture. Sprinkle with mozzarella cheese. Bake 20 to 30 minutes, until cheese is golden and vegetables are tender.   *Makes 8 servings.*

PER SERVING: Cal 121 • Carbo 13 gm • Prot 8 gm • Total fat 4 gm • Sat fat 3 gm • Cal from fat 30% • Chol 15 mg

EDUCATION: Taking a walk outdoors on a beautiful day does wonders for the soul. But it also does something you can feel down to your very bones: Sunshine enables vitamin D to be manufactured by the body. Vitamin D is necessary for the absorbtion of calcium, such as that contained in the low-fat cheeses, above. Sufficient calcium absorption, we know, is essential for healthy teeth and bones.

INSPIRATION: *Today I will be open to spontaneity—I will rejoice in the unexpected.*

Dad's Easy Spaghetti with Meat Sauce

✹ Simple and delicious, made in a cast-iron skillet the way my Dad cooked it. Serve with a salad and crusty whole-grain bread.

> *1 cup chopped onion*
> *¹/₂ cup chopped green bell pepper*
> *1 tablespoon olive oil*
> *³/₄ pound extra-lean ground beef*
> *4 garlic cloves, minced*
> *2 (28-ounce) cans Italian plum tomatoes*
> *   with juice*
> *¹/₂ teaspoon dried marjoram*
> *¹/₄ teaspoon dried oregano*
> *¹/₈ teaspoon freshly ground black pepper*
> *¹/₂ pound thin whole-wheat spaghetti*
> *¹/₄ cup minced fresh parsley*
> *¹/₄ cup freshly grated Parmesan cheese*

Cook onion and bell pepper in oil in a large cast-iron skillet over medium-low heat, stirring frequently, until the onion is translucent. Add beef and garlic to pan and brown meat, breaking it up into small pieces as it cooks.

Chop tomatoes and add with their juice, the marjoram, oregano and pepper. Bring ingredients to a boil, reduce heat, cover and simmer 30 minutes.

Meanwhile, bring a large pot of water to a boil. Add pasta and cook just until firm-tender, 4 to 6 minutes. Serve pasta topped with meat sauce. *Makes 4 servings.*

PER SERVING: Cal 572 • Carbo 66 gm • Prot 30 gm • Total fat 22 gm • Sat fat 8 gm • Cal from fat 34% • Chol 62 mg

EDUCATION: Preserve your health with fewer preservatives. Some food additives have been shown to diminish the body's ability to absorb iron. EDTA, a commonly used preservative, may cut iron absorption in half. The tannic acid in tea also inhibits iron absorption, as do phosphates, which are additives found in sodas, baked goods and ice cream and candy. Sufficient iron helps us perform at peak energy levels. One way to safely increase iron levels is to haul out that old-fashioned cast-iron skillet. Cooking acid-rich foods, such as tomato sauce, in the skillet will result in the migration of small, but important, amounts of iron into your food. Food sources of iron include beef, liver, sunflower seeds, dried apricots and blackstrap molasses.

INSPIRATION: *Living well and taking care of myself today is my best preparation for tomorrow.*

Snow Pea Sauté

✹ Spring vegetables perk up dinnertime in a colorful combination, with the added zip of lemon juice. A light entrée of chicken or fish would go well with this dish.

> *1 pound snow peas*
> *1 celery stalk*
> *3 green onions*
> *3 radishes*
> *¹/₂ tablespoon canola oil*
> *1 garlic clove, minced*
> *1 tablespoon fresh lemon juice*
> *Lemon slices for garnish*
> *Parsley sprigs for garnish*

Remove stem end and strings along both sides of pea pods. Slice celery on the diagonal into thin slices. Cut green onions on the diagonal into 1-inch pieces. Trim stem ends and cut radishes into thin slices.

Cook snow peas, celery, green onions and radishes in oil over medium heat in a large non-stick skillet, stirring frequently, until vegetables are crisp-tender. Add garlic and stir 1 or 2 minutes. Sprinkle with lemon juice. Serve garnished with lemon slices and parsley.

Makes 4 servings.

PER SERVING: Cal 65 • Carbo 10 gm • Prot 3 gm • Total fat 2 gm • Sat fat trace • Cal from fat 26% • Chol 0 mg

EDUCATION: Spring for more vitamin C in your diet. Besides bringing a touch of spring to the dinner table, this dish offers copious amounts of vitamin C. Snow peas alone provide 100 percent of the RDA in one serving, while green onion tops are another source. To increase your intake of these tasty, C-rich vegetables, thinly slice and slip them into salads or soups during the last few minutes of cooking. Left whole, they make an attractive addition to raw vegetable platters, surrounding a low-fat (of course!) dip.

INSPIRATION: *I will look for the best in everyone I encounter today. I will offer my best in return.*

Minted Peas with Lettuce

Fresh peas, a refreshing hint of mint and, if you have a garden, your own lettuce, too! It's spring!

> 2 cups shelled fresh peas
>   (2 pounds unshelled)
> 10 to 15 large garden lettuce leaves
>   or 3 Boston lettuce leaves
> 2 teaspoons butter
> 2 teaspoons minced fresh mint
> Dash of salt
> Dash of freshly ground pepper

Steam peas over boiling water 10 to 15 minutes or until bright green and tender. Wash lettuce and slice into strips. Melt the butter in a large, nonstick skillet over medium heat. Add lettuce and stir 1 minute or until lettuce wilts. Add peas and mint and stir until combined with lettuce. Season with a little salt and pepper.

Makes 4 servings.

PER SERVING: Cal 81 • Carbo 11 gm • Prot 4 gm • Total fat 2 gm • Sat fat 1 gm • Cal from fat 22% • Chol 6 mg

EDUCATION: Add mint to fresh iced fruit juices and serve as an alternative to alcoholic beverages. Fresh mint is a versatile flavoring, complementing as it does both fruits and vegetables. Mint can make a healthy fresh fruit salad more appealing and add zest to fruit soups. Mint also goes well with peas, as above, in fresh pea soup and in tabbouleh, a cracked wheat salad of the Middle East.

INSPIRATION: *Making small steps each day to become healthy and whole is my process.*

Oat Scones with Currants

🌿 Rolled oats can be whizzed up in the blender or food processor to make oat flour. Good for breakfast or with fresh fruit for dessert.

> 1 1/4 cups unbleached
>   all-purpose flour
> 3/4 cup oat flour
> 3 tablespoons brown sugar
> 1 tablespoon baking powder
> 1/2 teaspoon salt
> 4 tablespoons unsalted butter
> 1 egg, beaten
> 1/3 to 1/2 cup buttermilk
> 3 tablespoons dried currants

Preheat oven to 400°F (200°C). Combine the flours, brown sugar, baking powder and salt in a large bowl. Cut in butter with a pastry blender until the mixture resembles coarse meal. In a small bowl, combine egg, 1/3 cup buttermilk and currants. Stir egg mixture into dry ingredients just until combined, adding additional buttermilk, if needed, to make a soft dough that can be rolled out.

Roll out dough to about 5 inches wide and 3/4 inch thick. Cut dough in triangles. Bake on a lightly oiled baking sheet 15 to 18 minutes, until a wooden pick inserted in the center comes out clean.   *Makes 6 scones.*

PER SERVING: Cal 69 • Carbo 11 gm • Prot 2 gm • Total fat 2 gm • Sat fat 1 gm • Cal from fat 26% • Chol 57 mg

EDUCATION: Expand your take on oats beyond hot breakfast cereal. Becoming familiar with oats' versatility will help you include more of this healthful, high-fiber grain in your diet. High in protein, oats also contain impressive levels of iron. Eating vitamin C–rich foods, remember, will help you absorb the iron more easily.

INSPIRATION: *I will not let fear of change prevent me from taking advantage of new ways to care for myself.*

Beef & Lentil Hamburger Patties

🌿 Cut down on meat, but enjoy the hearty flavor of these burgers. Serve on whole-grain rolls for added fiber.

> 1 cup lentils, cooked , mashed
>   (see below)
> 1 pound lean ground beef
> 1 small onion, minced
> 1 egg, beaten
> 2 tablespoons minced fresh parsley
> Dash of freshly ground black pepper
> 6 whole-grain hamburger rolls
> 6 red onion slices
> 6 lettuce leaves
> 1/2 cup alfalfa sprouts
>
> LENTILS
> 1 cup lentils
> 1/2 onion, minced
> 3 cups water

To cook lentils, place lentils, minced onion and 3 cups water in a large saucepan. Bring to a boil, reduce heat, cover and simmer 45 minutes to 1 hour, until the lentils are tender. Drain lentils and set aside.

Combine the beef, lentils, onion, egg, parsley and pepper in a medium-size bowl. Form into 6 patties. Cook in a small amount of oil in a large, nonstick skillet, turning until both sides are browned and the burgers are cooked through.

Serve on rolls, topped with red onion, lettuce and sprouts.   *Makes 6 servings.*

PER SERVING: Cal 379 • Carbo 30 gm • Prot 21 gm • Total fat 19 gm • Sat fat 7 gm • Cal from fat 45% • Chol 91 mg

EDUCATION: Have cooked lentils on hand to make it easier to add these flavorful, fiber-full legumes to meat loaves, soups or the hamburgers, above. Use lentils in tomato sauce for vegetarian spaghetti or season with salsa and tuck them into tortillas. Lentils do not have to be presoaked, so they are relatively quick to prepare.

May 4

INSPIRATION: *In developing positive attitudes about myself, I discover more that is positive in the people around me.*

Chicken Soup with Coconut Milk

❧ Quick and easy, tasty and colorful—make it an authentic Thai dish by adding a tablespoon of *nuoc mam* fish sauce with the broth. It's available in Asian markets and some supermarkets, as is coconut milk.

3 cups chicken broth
4 thin slices gingerroot
1 pound boneless skinless chicken breasts
1/2 cup low-fat coconut milk or fresh coconut
    milk (see glossary)

2 tablespoons fresh lime juice
1/8 teaspoon crushed red pepper flakes
1/2 cup snow peas, sliced in half on diagonal
1/2 cup coarsely shredded carrots
1/4 cup minced fresh cilantro
1 cup cooked brown rice
1 tablespoon minced fresh parsley

Place broth and gingerroot in a large saucepan. Bring to a boil, reduce heat and simmer 5 minutes. Cut chicken into thin 2-inch strips. Add chicken, coconut milk, lime juice and pepper flakes to broth. Return to a boil, cover and simmer 4 to 5 minutes, until chicken is cooked through. Add snow peas, carrots and cilantro and cook 1 to 2 minutes, until vegetables are crisp-tender. Stir in rice and parsley, heat through and serve.   *Makes 6 servings.*

PER SERVING: Cal 227 • Carbo 12 gm • Prot 29 gm • Total fat 6 gm • Sat fat 2 gm • Cal from fat 23% • Chol 68 mg

EDUCATION: Join the world in appreciating the primary role of rice in a sustaining diet. For more than half of the world's population, rice is the very basis of their cuisine. We can take advantage of the bountiful nutrition in rice by enjoying it unpolished. Eating brown rice enables us to benefit from an entire range of vitamins and minerals, as well as fiber, almost all of which is removed from white rice.

INSPIRATION: *As I see myself letting go of my need for control and entering into the rhythm of life, I gradually discover signs of my growth and healing.*

Waldorf Salad with Pears & Raisins

❧ Anjou and Bosc pears are still in season, and give a sweet twist to Waldorf salad. Firm and crisp, these pears are perfect for salads.

³/₄ cup cored diced pears
³/₄ cup diced celery
¹/₄ cup raisins
¹/₄ cup chopped walnuts
¹/₄ cup nonfat yogurt
3 tablespoons reduced-fat mayonnaise
¹/₄ teaspoon freshly grated lemon peel
Lettuce leaves
2 tablespoons minced fresh parsley
*   for garnish*

In a medium-size bowl, combine diced pears, celery, raisins and walnuts. In a small bowl, stir together mayonnaise, yogurt and lemon peel. Stir yogurt mixture into salad. Arrange lettuce leaves on individual plates and garnish with minced parsley.   *Makes 4 servings.*

PER SERVING: Cal 150 • Carbo 23 gm • Prot 3 gm • Total fat 6 gm • Sat fat trace • Cal from fat 39% • Chol 5 mg

EDUCATION: Pear-up for heart health! When eaten with their skins, pears are even higher in fiber than apples. And the fiber has special benefits for your circulation. Nutritionally similar to apples, but often sweeter, pears can be substituted for apples in a variety of dishes. Keeping the skin on also ensures that you get the benefit of vitamin C from fresh pears, since most of it is concentrated in the skin. Don't forget, too, pears are a great snack, with no preparation time!

INSPIRATION: *I will not compare myself, or my accomplishments, with others, today, but will appreciate each of us as the unique individuals we are.*

Eddie's Fresh Spinach & Brown Rice Casserole

❧ If you have cooked brown rice on hand, just substitute 1¹/₂ cups for the quick-cooking rice. Serve with soup and salad for a meatless meal.

1 cup vegetable stock or chicken broth
³/₄ cup quick-cooking brown rice
2 pounds spinach
¹/₂ cup chopped onion
2 teaspoons unsalted butter
1 garlic clove, minced
¹/₄ teaspoon dried thyme
¹/₈ teaspoon crumbled dried rosemary
Dash of freshly grated nutmeg
¹/₂ cup shredded part-skim
*   mozzarella cheese*
2 tablespoons dry whole-wheat
*   bread crumbs*
1 tablespoon freshly grated
*   Parmesan cheese*

Preheat oven to 350°F (175°C). Bring stock to a boil in a medium-size saucepan over medium heat. Stir in rice, reduce heat, cover and simmer 10 minutes. Keep warm.

Meanwhile, wash spinach well and remove stems. Slice into thin strips. Cook the onion in the butter over medium heat in a large, non-stick skillet, stirring frequently, until onion is translucent, 2 to 3 minutes. Stir in the garlic, thyme, rosemary and nutmeg. Add spinach and cook, stirring, 1 to 2 minutes. Remove from heat. Stir rice and shredded mozzarella into spinach. Place mixture in a lightly buttered 2-

quart casserole dish. Combine bread crumbs and Parmesan and sprinkle over top. Bake 30 minutes, until top is lightly browned.

Makes 4 servings.

PER SERVING: Cal 179 • Carbo 22 gm • Prot 14 gm • Total fat 6 gm • Sat fat 3 gm • Cal from fat 30% • Chol 13 mg

EDUCATION: Add citrus fruits or peppers to your meals when you serve spinach. Anyone who's heard of Popeye knows spinach is good for you. High in beta-carotene, iron and folic acid, spinach is also a surprising source of protein. Combined with rice or other grains, spinach makes a great meatless meal. Having vitamin C present in the meal will help take advantage of the iron content in spinach, making it more readily absorbed.

INSPIRATION: *When I am too busy is the very time I should be caring for myself.*

Greek-Salad Pita Sandwiches

Serve with a fish stew for a Mediterranean-style meal.

2 cups coarsely shredded cabbage
1 carrot, shredded
¹/₄ cup feta cheese, crumbled
¹/₄ cup minced fresh parsley
2 tablespoons nonfat yogurt
1 tablespoon olive oil
1 tablespoon lemon juice
¹/₈ teaspoon dried thyme
Dash of freshly ground black pepper
4 large whole-wheat pita breads
Parsley sprigs for garnish

Combine the cabbage, carrot, cheese and parsley in a large bowl. In a cup measure, combine the yogurt, oil, lemon juice, thyme and pepper. Toss with cabbage mixture.

Cut pita breads in half crosswise. Open each half and stuff with some of the cabbage mixture. Arrange on a serving plate and garnish with parsley. *Makes 4 servings.*

PER SERVING: Cal 179 • Carbo 26 gm • Prot 6 gm • Total fat 6 gm • Sat fat 2 gm • Cal from fat 29% • Chol 7 mg

EDUCATION: Keep a healthy smile to improve your physical and emotional well-being. Vitamin C and calcium, found in the recipe above, are important to a healthy smile. The cells lining the gums have one of the highest turnover rates in the body, being completely replaced every three to seven days. Without sufficient vitamin C, this epithelium tissue is less able to resist bacteria, which can lead to dental problems. It's one more way that eating well can keep us smiling.

INSPIRATION: *I won't use food as a crutch today to keep me limping through life at arm's length from my feelings.*

Wheat-Germ Bread with Olive Oil

❧ Use raw wheat germ from the health-food store, not the toasted cereal, for best flavor.

1 tablespoon yeast
¹/₄ cup lukewarm water
3 tablespoons honey
1¹/₃ cups skim milk
1 teaspoon salt
3 cups unbleached all-purpose
  flour
³/₄ cup wheat germ
3 tablespoons olive oil

Preheat oven to 400°F (200°C). Place the yeast, water and honey in a small bowl and let stand until frothy. Heat milk in a small pan until scalding hot. Stir in salt and let stand until lukewarm.

Combine the flour and wheat germ in a large bowl. Add yeast mixture and milk. While mixing ingredients add oil. Knead dough in the bowl for 5 minutes. Cover with a tea towel and let the dough rise in a warm place until light. Punch down and place dough in a lightly oiled, nonstick 9 × 5-inch bread pan. Let rise until dough is even with top of the bread pan. Bake 15 minutes, turn oven down to 350°F (175°C) and bake 25 minutes more or until bread sounds hollow when tapped.

Makes 1 loaf (12 slices).

PER SLICE: Cal 197 • Carbo 33 gm • Prot 6 gm • Total fat 4 gm • Sat fat 1 gm • Cal from fat 18% • Chol trace

EDUCATION: Add the "heart" of the wheat to breads, casseroles, pancakes, baked goods and breakfast cereals just for the health of it. Wheat germ is a storehouse of nutrients, rich in vitamin E, thiamin, riboflavin and iron, as well as protein and fiber. When baking, substitute 1 or 2 tablespoons of wheat germ for flour and proceed according to your recipe. Toasted honey wheat germ can be sprinkled on yogurt or breakfast cereals for added flavor and nutrition. Remember, too, that whole-wheat flour already contains the "germ."

INSPIRATION: *It is possible to be satisfied with the good things I have in my life without always seeking more.*

Pineapple Chicken

❧ Fresh pineapple is at its peak during spring, from March to June, and is worth the extra effort of preparing. It is far more flavorful than the canned variety. Here, pineapple adds a sweet change of pace to easy, skillet-cooked chicken. Serve with noodles and a green salad.

¹/₂ medium-size ripe pineapple
4 skinless and boneless chicken
  breast halves
1 tablespoon unbleached
  all-purpose flour
¹/₄ teaspoon salt
2 teaspoons canola oil
¹/₂ cup pineapple juice
1 tablespoon honey
1 tablespoon teriyaki sauce
1 tablespoon chopped fresh
  chives for garnish

Cut off top and bottom of pineapple and slice into rings. With a sharp knife, peel and remove core from each ring. Refrigerate half of the rings for future use. Cut the remaining rings in quarters. Set aside.

Between two sheets of waxed paper, flatten chicken breast halves to an even thickness using a rubber mallet. On another sheet of waxed paper, mix flour and salt. Coat chicken breast halves with the mixture. Cook the chicken breasts in the oil over medium heat in a large, nonstick skillet 10 minutes, turning once or until the breasts are golden brown and tender. Remove chicken to a warm platter and keep warm.

Add pineapple juice, honey and teriyaki sauce to skillet and stir to combine with drippings in the pan. Add pineapple pieces and cook 2 to 3 minutes, until pineapple is tender. Arrange pineapple with chicken and pour sauce over both. Garnish with fresh chives.

Makes 4 servings.

PER SERVING: Cal 296 • Carbo 18 gm • Prot 31 gm • Total fat 11 gm • Sat fat 3 gm • Cal from fat 33% • Chol 83 mg

EDUCATION: Follow your nose to select a ripe, flavorful pineapple. You won't be disappointed or waste your money. A good pineapple is sweetly fragrant. The fruit should appear firm and plump. Turn the pineapple upside down. If it smells sour or fermented or the bottom is moldy, pass it up.

Pineapples will not become sweeter once picked, so air-shipped pineapples that reach market a day or two after harvest, when they are ripe, are a best bet. Pineapples are rich in vitamin C, which helps your body absorb iron from the chicken or from any accompanying dishes.

May 10

INSPIRATION: *I can go through difficult times without escaping into overeating or other harmful ways of coping.*

Spring Rice Pilaf

The season's fresh spinach weaves its colorful way through this delicious side dish.

1 carrot, cut in small strips
1 small onion, halved and thinly sliced
2 teaspoons unsalted butter
1 cup basmati or regular
*   long-grain rice*
1 3/4 cups chicken broth
1/2 pound fresh spinach
1 tablespoon minced fresh parsley

Cook carrot and onion in butter in a large, nonstick skillet over medium heat, stirring frequently, until vegetables are tender, about 3 to 4 minutes. Add rice and cook 1 minute, stirring constantly. Add broth and bring to a boil. Reduce heat, cover and simmer 15 minutes.

Meanwhile, wash spinach and remove stems. Cut leaves into thin strips. Stir spinach into rice mixture, cover, and continue to simmer 5 minutes or until spinach is tender and liquid is absorbed. Toss pilaf with parsley and serve.

Makes 4 servings.

PER SERVING: Cal 232 • Carbo 43 gm • Prot 7 gm • Total fat 3 gm • Sat fat 1 gm • Cal from fat 12% • Chol 6 mg

EDUCATION: Enjoy a daily supply of water-soluble vitamins in your diet. Vitamins are essential to our metabolism. They enable enzymes in our bodies to carry out the most basic functions of life. Our bodies do not manufacture vitamins, so we depend upon the foods we eat to supply these vital nutrients. Water-soluble vitamins, which include C and the range of B vitamins, are generally flushed out of the body if our intake exceeds our body's demand. But that also means these vitamins are not easily stored, so a constant supply—like the vitamin-rich combination above—is needed in the diet.

INSPIRATION: *I can do no more than my best, realizing that failures are valuable signposts leading to success.*

Fifteen-Minute Beef & Macaroni

🌿 Onion and carrot combine to reduce the amount of ground beef needed for this quick skillet meal. Stir in cooked mushrooms or other cooked vegetables before serving, if you like. Fast and delicious.

> 1 medium-size onion
> 1 carrot
> 1 garlic clove, peeled
> Dash of salt
> 1/2 pound extra-lean ground beef
> 1/2 teaspoon dried basil
> Dash of freshly ground black pepper
> 3/4 pound elbow macaroni
> 1 (14-oz.) jar spaghetti sauce

Peel and quarter onion. Peel and coarsely chop carrot. Add onion, carrot and garlic to a food processor. Process until finely chopped or mince by hand.

Sprinkle a little salt in a large nonstick skillet. Add ground beef and minced vegetables. Cook over low heat, stirring to break up meat, about 10 minutes or until vegetables are tender and beef is cooked. Season with basil and pepper.

Meanwhile, bring a large saucepan of water to a boil. Add macaroni and cook until firm-tender, 7 to 9 minutes.

Drain macaroni and add with spaghetti sauce to skillet, stirring until combined. Heat through and serve.   *Makes 4 servings.*

PER SERVING: Cal 525 • Carbo 79 gm • Prot 25 gm • Total fat 12 gm • Sat fat 4 gm • Cal from fat 21% • Chol 43 mg

EDUCATION: Eat more onions (and that includes leeks, green onions and shallots) to keep you in circulation. Studies indicate onions help lower blood pressure in addition to lowering cholesterol levels in the blood. These are two heart-healthy reasons to include more of them in your diet. Avoid onions cooked in a lot of fat, which will counteract their healthful benefits. Large spring onions, such as Vidalia, are so mild they can be added raw to sandwiches and salads.

INSPIRATION: *I am beginning to take things as they come, trusting that I have the resources I need to cope in a healthy way.*

Strawberry-Rhubarb Cobbler with Crème Fraîche

🌿 If you buy rhubarb with the leaves attached, cut off the leaves and discard them. They are toxic if eaten.

4 cups sliced rhubarb

2 cups stemmed and halved strawberries

³/₄ cup packed brown sugar

2 tablespoons cornstarch

2 tablespoons cold water

1 cup unbleached flour

³/₄ cup whole-wheat pastry flour

3 teaspoons baking powder

2 teaspoons sugar

¹/₂ teaspoon salt

4 tablespoons cold unsalted butter

1 cup skim milk

¹/₄ teaspoon ground cinnamon

LOW-FAT CRÈME FRAÎCHE

3 tablespoons nonfat cream cheese, softened

¹/₃ cup nonfat sour cream

¹/₂ cup buttermilk

Preheat oven to 425°F (220°C). Combine rhubarb, strawberries, brown sugar, cornstarch and water in a large saucepan. Bring to a boil, stirring frequently. Remove from heat.

Combine flours, baking powder, sugar and salt in a large bowl. Cut in butter with a pastry blender until the mixture resembles coarse meal. Stir in milk lightly, just until combined. Pour rhubarb mixture into a 9-inch-square baking dish. Drop spoonfuls of dough over top. Sprinkle with cinnamon. Bake 30 minutes or until bubbly and top is browned.

For crème fraîche, combine cream cheese with ¹/₃ cup nonfat sour cream in a small bowl, stirring until very smooth. Add buttermilk and stir until combined. Serve over cobbler.

Makes 8 servings.

PER SERVING: Cal 395 • Carbo 7 gm • Prot 1 gm • Total fat 1 gm • Sat fat trace • Cal from fat 2% • Chol 2 mg

EDUCATION: Substitute low-fat versions of traditional high-fat ingredients to cut fat while enjoying old favorites. The French enjoy spooning a rich, natural cream, called crème fraîche, over fruit and desserts. And, although it is very high in fat, a very low-fat imitation approximates the creamy texture and slight tang that characterizes crème fraîche. Letting this Low-Fat Crème Fraîche mixture mature in the refrigerator overnight allows its flavor to develop. You can also use this lower-fat topping in place of whipped cream on other fruit desserts.

INSPIRATION: *Sharing, talking, listening, laughing are all healing activities that can take place around the dinner table.*

Fran's Swordfish Steaks with Ginger-Orange Sauce

🌿 Salmon steaks also work in place of swordfish. If you don't have fresh ginger on hand, you can substitute ¼ teaspoon ground ginger, but the flavor is less intense.

> 1½ pounds swordfish steaks,
>   about ¾ inch thick
> 2 teaspoons unsalted butter
> 2 green onions, sliced on diagonal
> ½ cup orange juice
> ½ cup fish or chicken broth
> 1 teaspoon Worcestershire sauce
> 1 teaspoon grated gingerroot
> ⅛ teaspoon freshly ground black pepper
> Orange slices for garnish
> Parsley sprigs for garnish

Cook the swordfish steaks in 1 teaspoon butter in a large nonstick skillet over medium heat, turning once, 8 to 10 minutes or until the fish is cooked through. Remove steaks to a warm platter and keep warm.

Add remaining butter to skillet and cook green onions, stirring frequently, until crisp-tender, 2 to 3 minutes. In a small bowl, mix orange juice, broth, Worcestershire sauce, gingerroot and pepper. Add to skillet, bring to a boil, stirring constantly, and boil 1 minute. Pour some of the sauce over swordfish and serve remaining sauce separately. Garnish swordfish with orange slices and parsley sprigs.

Makes 4 servings.

PER SERVING: Cal 243 • Carbo 4 gm • Prot 34 gm • Total fat 9 gm • Sat fat 4 gm • Cal from fat 33% • Chol 74 mg

EDUCATION: For freshness and safety, use fish promptly after purchase. Fish is a healthful part of a low-fat diet, but highly perishable. If you follow a few simple rules, you'll enjoy fresh-tasting, wholesome fish. Get seafood into the refrigerator as soon as possible after purchase. If you shop at a separate store for your seafood, make it the last stop. In hot weather, or if you will be delayed, bring along a small ice chest with ice to keep fish cold. Cook fish as soon as possible. Even stored in the coldest part of your refrigerator, fish will begin to deteriorate within a day or two.

INSPIRATION: *As my mind becomes quieter, it is easier to see options and answers in my life.*

Buckwheat Molasses-Buttermilk Muffins

🌿 The hearty, nutlike flavor of buckwheat—most familiar, perhaps, in pancakes—is complemented by molasses.

> 1 cup buckwheat flour
> ½ cup stone-ground yellow cornmeal
> 2 teaspoons baking powder
> ½ teaspoon baking soda
> ¼ teaspoon salt
> 1½ cups buttermilk
> 3 tablespoons melted butter
> 2 tablespoons medium
>   unsulfured molasses
> 1 egg yolk
> 2 egg whites, beaten
>   until stiff

Preheat oven to 350°F (175°C). Lightly grease 12 (2¾-inch) muffin cups. Combine buckwheat, cornmeal, baking powder, soda and salt in a large bowl. In a medium-size bowl, combine the buttermilk, butter, molasses and egg yolk. Stir the buttermilk mixture into the dry ingredients just until combined, then gently fold in the stiffly beaten egg whites. Bake 20 minutes or until a wooden pick inserted in the center comes out clean. *Makes 12 muffins.*

PER MUFFIN: Cal 109 • Carbo 16 gm • Prot 4 gm • Total fat 4 gm • Sat fat 2 gm • Cal from fat 33% • Chol 27 mg

EDUCATION: Add buckwheat flour to baked goods for change-of-pace flavor and vital nutrients. Although it is not a true grain (in fact, it's related to the spring vegetable, rhubarb), buckwheat is high in the amino acid lysine and is rich in magnesium, important to our nerves and normal heartbeat. Manganese, a trace mineral that helps keep our energy level high, is also present in buckwheat. Substitute ¹/₂ cup of buckwheat flour for regular flour next time you make pancakes. Use fresh fruit and honey as toppings.

May 15

INSPIRATION: *My spirituality nurtures all that is uniquely me—it opens me to the enjoyment of just being.*

Chili Non-Carne ✓

❧ No meat needn't mean a boring chili—this vegetable-rich version is delicious. If you want, serve it over rice.

2 cups chopped onions
1 tablespoon olive oil
3 garlic cloves, minced
2 tablespoons chili powder
1 teaspoon ground cumin
¹/₄ teaspoon dried oregano
¹/₄ teaspoon salt
¹/₄ teaspoon freshly ground black pepper

2 cups vegetable stock
4 carrots, peeled and cut into 1-inch slices
4 potatoes, peeled and cut into 1-inch cubes
1 (28-ounce) can tomatoes, drained and chopped
2 cups cooked kidney beans
   (see glossary)
¹/₄ cup minced fresh cilantro
2 tablespoons minced fresh parsley
1 cup nonfat yogurt
Cilantro leaves for garnish

Cook onions in oil in a nonstick Dutch oven over medium heat, stirring frequently, until onions are tender, about 5 minutes. Add garlic, chili powder, cumin, oregano, salt and pepper and cook, stirring constantly, 1 minute more. Add stock, carrots and potatoes to Dutch oven. Bring to a boil, reduce heat, cover and simmer 20 minutes or until vegetables are firm-tender.

Add tomatoes and cooked beans and simmer 5 to 10 minutes more, until vegetables are tender. Remove Dutch oven from heat and stir in minced cilantro and parsley. Serve in large bowls with a dollop of yogurt and garnish with cilantro leaves. *Makes 8 servings.*

PER SERVING: Cal 243 • Carbo 48 gm • Prot 10 gm • Total fat 3 gm • Sat fat trace • Cal from fat 11% • Chol 0 mg

EDUCATION: Make beans in quantity for convenience later. Dried beans are such an excellent low-fat source of protein, it makes good sense to have them on hand. Two easy methods will make quantity cooking a snap. One, place 1 pound of dried beans in a slow-cooker with water to cover generously. Cook on LOW overnight or during working hours. Or, place beans in an oven roasting pan with a generous amount of water. Soak overnight. Bake at 350°F (175°C) 1¹/₂ to 2 hours, depending upon beans, until tender. Drain and refrigerate or freeze beans in pint containers.

INSPIRATION: *I am learning to choose the food, activities and friends that nurture my quest for recovery.*

INSPIRATION: *Discovering myself in terms of new foods I enjoy, new dishes I can prepare and new friends with whom I can share is one of my life's blessings.*

Spinach-Orange Salad

❧ Berry vinegars add a gentle tang to salads, reducing the need for large amounts of oil.

1 pound fresh spinach
2 navel oranges, peeled and sliced crosswise
2 red onion slices, separated into rings
3 tablespoons orange juice
2 tablespoons strawberry vinegar (see glossary)
1 teaspoon olive oil
1/8 teaspoon salt
Dash of freshly ground black pepper

Wash spinach and remove stems. Tear leaves into large, bite-size pieces. Arrange spinach on 4 salad plates. Top with orange slices and onion rings. Combine orange juice, vinegar, oil, salt and pepper in a cup measure. Stir well and spoon over salads.

Makes 4 servings.

PER SERVING: Cal 74 • Carbo 13 gm • Prot 4 gm • Total fat 2 gm • Sat fat trace • Cal from fat 24% • Chol 0 mg

EDUCATION: Create attractive vinegars (see glossary) for healthwise, low-cost gift-giving. Although flavored vinegars are sold in many specialty shops, prices are high. It's easy to make your own while fresh fruits and herbs are in season. Make some extra bottles for gifts throughout the year. Flavored vinegars reduce the need for oil, allowing you to cut back on fats when serving salads.

Curried Tofu & Vegetables

❧ A colorful selection of vegetables makes this meatless main dish pleasing. Serve with a green salad.

1 small head cauliflower (about 1 pound)
1/2 pound green beans
3 carrots
1 onion
1 sweet red bell pepper
1 pound tofu
1 tablespoon olive oil
2 teaspoons Madras curry powder
2 teaspoons unbleached flour
2 teaspoons peeled grated gingerroot
1/2 teaspoon salt
1/8 teaspoon freshly ground black pepper
1 1/2 cups vegetable stock
2 cups cooked brown rice

Trim cauliflower and separate into flowerets. Trim green beans and cut in half. Place cauliflower and beans in 1 inch of boiling water in a nonstick Dutch oven. Return to a boil, reduce heat, cover and simmer 4 minutes or until vegetables are firm-tender. Drain and set aside.

Peel and slice carrots on the diagonal. Chop onion. Cut red pepper into thin, 1-inch strips. Drain tofu and cut into 1-inch cubes.

Cook carrots, onion and red pepper in the oil in the Dutch oven over medium heat, stirring frequently, until vegetables are firm-tender. Add curry, flour, ginger, salt and pepper and cook, stirring, 1 minute.

Add vegetable stock, cauliflower and beans. Stir in tofu and heat through. Serve tofu mixture over rice. *Makes 4 servings.*

PER SERVING: Cal 462 • Carbo 59 gm • Prot 27 gm • Total fat 16 gm • Sat fat 2 gm • Cal from fat 32% • Chol 2 mg

EDUCATION: Be sensitive to your guests. If you invite friends and acquaintances to a meal, be aware of any food allergies or preferences. Have plenty of nonalcoholic beverages available, and don't use alcohol in cooking or desserts without checking beforehand. When serving vegetarian meals, don't slip up and use chicken or beef stock. Also, some vegetarians eat eggs and dairy foods, others don't. Avoid uncomfortable situations by planning ahead.

INSPIRATION: *Today I will eat just the food my body needs, enjoying the pleasure and feeling of contentment it gives me.*

Debbie's Brown Sugar Custard

Top this smooth, rich-tasting dessert with colorful berries or serve it plain.

> 2 cups skim milk
> 3 tablespoons packed brown sugar
> 1/8 teaspoon salt
> 2 eggs, beaten
> 1-inch piece vanilla bean
> Dash of freshly grated nutmeg
> Fresh berries for garnish (optional)

Preheat oven to 300°F (150°C). Beat together milk, sugar, salt, and eggs until well blended. Add the seeds scraped from inside the vanilla bean. Divide custard among 4 custard cups. Dust with nutmeg. Place the cups in a pan of hot water. Bake 20 to 30 minutes or until a knife inserted near the edge comes out clean. The heat contained in the custards will finish cooking the centers. If a knife inserted in the center comes out clean, set the custard cups in ice water to stop further cooking. Garnish with fresh berries, if desired. *Makes 4 servings.*

PER SERVING: Cal 119 • Carbo 16 gm • Prot 7 gm • Total fat 3 gm • Sat fat 1 gm • Cal from fat 23% • Chol 109 mg

EDUCATION: Boost the protein content of a meal with a low-fat, high protein dessert. This custard boasts milk and eggs, two protein-rich sources. Low-fat custards and puddings can be a valuable part of meal planning when serving light meals or certain vegetarian main dishes.

INSPIRATION: *Setting limits for myself in the area of food is part of my recovery. Setting limits helps me maintain good health.*

Sundae Breakfast

❧ Festive, but healthful, a combination of ingredients dresses up low-in-fat ricotta cheese. Select freshly made cheese at an Italian market for best flavor.

> *¹/₂ banana, halved lengthwise*
> *¹/₂ cup part-skim ricotta cheese*
> *¹/₂ cup sliced strawberries*
> *1 tablespoon toasted honey*
>   *wheat germ*
> *1 teaspoon chopped walnuts*

Place banana halves in a dessert bowl. Top with a scoop of ricotta, then strawberries. Sprinkle with wheat germ and walnuts.

Makes 1 serving.

PER SERVING: Cal 303 • Carbo 34 gm • Prot 18 gm • Total fat 12 gm • Sat fat 6 gm • Cal from fat 36% • Chol 38 mg

EDUCATION: Keep your cholesterol intake in balance. We've all heard the bad side about cholesterol, but it's important to realize, too, that cholesterol:

- plays an important part in our body's normal functioning
- is a critical component of all cell walls
- composes part of the bile acids that digest fats
- is a major component of brain and nerve tissue
- is used to help make up the body's hormones
- is so crucial, our bodies are constantly manufacturing it

So, why must we be careful about the cholesterol in our diets? Doctors see a correlation between diet and excess cholesterol in the blood. There's evidence that consuming a high-cholesterol diet, rich in saturated fats and low in fiber contributes to the plaque that clogs arteries. So, while we can have some cholesterol in our diets, it's wise to keep consumption low, as with the recipe above.

INSPIRATION: *What others think of me or my efforts toward recovery is not as important as what I think, myself.*

Oatmeal-Date Muffins

❧ If you don't have oat flour available from your health-food store, place rolled oats in a blender or food processor and process in small batches until powdery. If there are some larger pieces, that's fine, too.

> *1¹/₂ cups oat flour*
> *2 tablespoons brown sugar*
> *2 teaspoons baking powder*
> *¹/₂ teaspoon baking soda*
> *¹/₄ teaspoon salt*
> *12 dates, chopped*
> *²/₃ cup buttermilk*
> *1 egg, separated*
> *2 tablespoons melted butter*
> *1 additional egg white*

Preheat oven to 375°F (190°C). Combine flour, brown sugar, baking powder, soda and salt in a large bowl. Stir in dates. In a medium-size bowl, combine the buttermilk, egg yolk and butter. Stir egg mixture into the dry ingredients just until combined. Stiffly beat egg whites and gently fold into batter. Divide batter among 9 lightly oiled, nonstick muffin cups.

Bake 18 to 20 minutes or until a wooden pick inserted in the center comes out clean.

Makes 9 muffins.

PER MUFFIN: Cal 158 • Carbo 28 gm • Prot 4 gm • Total fat 4 gm • Sat fat 2 gm • Cal from fat 20% • Chol 31 mg

EDUCATION: Line up dates for a Saturday night to gain three major benefits: potassium, iron and dietary fiber. Dates are among the sweetest fruits—up to 70 percent fruit sugar. They add sweetness and flavor to cereals, breads, compotes, salads and desserts. To avoid cracking a tooth, check all dates; even the pitted kind can have the occasional pit. To cut up dates, dip the knife or kitchen scissors frequently in water to keep them from sticking.

May 21

INSPIRATION: *My inner voice, when I pause to hear it, will lead me to satisfying choices in my life.*

Taco Pasta with Salsa

Taco filling in pasta shells topped with salsa and Cheddar offers a change-of-pace meal. The beef filling here is also sufficient for filling 15 tacos. Top tacos with shredded lettuce, salsa, cheese, and sprouts.

2 carrots, cut into large chunks
1 onion, quartered
1 teaspoon olive oil
3 garlic cloves, minced
1 jalapeño chile, minced (see glossary)
1/2 pound lean ground beef
1 tablespoon chili powder
2 teaspoons ground cumin
1 teaspoon ground coriander
1 teaspoon dried oregano
1/2 teaspoon paprika
1/2 teaspoon brown sugar
1/2 teaspoon salt

1/4 teaspoon freshly ground black pepper
1/4 cup split red lentils
3/4 cup beef stock
1 (12-ounce) package large pasta shells
1 cup Sombrero Salsa
    (see February 16) or bottled salsa
1/2 cup shredded Cheddar cheese
1/4 cup thinly sliced green onions
1 tablespoon minced fresh parsley

Place carrots and onion in a food processor and process until finely chopped. Cook in oil in a large nonstick skillet over medium heat, stirring constantly, until vegetables begin to brown. Add garlic, jalapeño and beef, breaking up meat and stirring frequently until meat is browned. Add chili powder, cumin, coriander, oregano, paprika, brown sugar, salt and pepper and cook, stirring, 1 or 2 minutes.

Add red lentils and stock. Bring to a boil, reduce heat, cover and simmer 8 to 10 minutes or until lentils are tender and liquid is absorbed. Let cool slightly.

Meanwhile, preheat oven to 350°F (175°C). Bring a large pot of water to a boil. Add shells and cook 6 or 7 minutes, until firm-tender. Drain. Stuff shells with taco filling, top with salsa and sprinkle with cheese. Place in a baking dish. Bake 20 minutes, until cheese is melted and shells are heated through. Garnish with green onions and parsley. *Makes 6 servings.*

PER SERVING: Cal 408 • Carbo 53 gm • Prot 19 gm • Total fat 14 gm • Sat fat 5 gm • Cal from fat 31% • Chol 38 mg

EDUCATION: Substitute cooked dried beans or lentils for all or part of the ground meat called for in any of your favorite recipes. The stuffing for the shells above adds red lentils to beef for a fiber-rich combination. You'll be cutting back on fats and increasing fiber—both important steps for heart health.

INSPIRATION: *Feeling good about myself is my most important goal. It helps me to treat myself as the special person I am.*

Freda's Broccoli with Garlic

🌺 Available year-round, broccoli is less expensive late fall through May. Choose compact, green heads. Yellowing buds reveal that broccoli is past its prime.

> *1 bunch broccoli (about 1 1/2 pounds)*
> *2 teaspoons olive oil*
> *2 large garlic cloves, minced*

Trim stems from broccoli. Peel stems and cut into 1 1/2-inch lengths. Quarter stem pieces lengthwise. Separate flowerets. Steam broccoli over boiling water until crisp-tender, about 5 minutes. Do not overcook.

Heat oil in a large nonstick skillet. Add garlic and stir 1 minute, just until garlic is softened, not browned. Add broccoli and toss to combine with garlic, cooking until firm-tender.

Makes 4 servings.

PER SERVING: Cal 70 • Carbo 9 gm • Prot 5 gm • Total fat 3 gm • Sat fat trace • Cal from fat 37% • Chol 0 mg

VARIATION
For a colorful addition during winter holidays, toss the broccoli with 1 tablespoon of minced pimiento just before removing from heat.

EDUCATION: Include those little green leaves from the broccoli stems in your meal. Making this one little change can enrich your diet in beta-carotene. The leaves are even richer than the flowerets in that nutrient. If you don't serve them with the broccoli, you may want to add the leaves to soup during the last few minutes of cooking, or add them raw to salads.

INSPIRATION: *I experience a willingness to rid myself of old habits—to resolve old problems by trying new ways.*

Maxine's Frittata with Potatoes & Peas

🌺 Maxine lives in Madrid, has always loved food, and taught me about frittatas when she returned to college after her junior year abroad. Frittatas are thick, flat omelets made with the vegetables cooked right in.

> *1 large baking potato, peeled*
> *   and diced*
> *1/2 cup shelled fresh green peas*
> *1/3 cup chopped onion*
> *1/2 tablespoon olive oil*
> *2 eggs*
> *4 egg whites*
> *Dash of salt*
> *Dash of freshly ground*
> *   black pepper*
> *Paprika for garnish*
> *Parsley sprigs for garnish*

Steam potato and peas over boiling water 8 to 10 minutes, until crisp-tender. Cook onion in oil in a 10- or 12-inch nonstick skillet, stirring frequently, until onion is tender, 4 or 5 minutes. Beat the eggs and additional egg whites until foamy.

Add potatoes and peas to onion in skillet, season with salt and pepper, and cook, stirring, 1 or 2 minutes.

Preheat broiler. Pour eggs over vegetables in pan, tilting pan to distribute the eggs evenly. The eggs should just cover the vegetables. Reduce heat to low, cover and cook 10 to 15 minutes, until eggs are nearly set. Uncover and sprinkle eggs with paprika. Place omelet under the broiler and finish cooking 1 or 2 minutes, until eggs are set. Cut into 4 wedges and serve garnished with parsley.

Makes 4 servings.

PER SERVING: Cal 125 • Carbo 13 gm • Prot 9 gm • Total fat 4 gm • Sat fat 1 gm • Cal from fat 28% • Chol 106 mg

EDUCATION: Count on the versatility of frittatas when you have leftover vegetables. For one thing, you can add 1/2 cup of any leftover cooked vegetable (or combination!), in place of peas. Just add them directly to the pan with the steamed potatoes. Second, frittatas are delicious served hot, at room temperature or chilled. That means they're great for parties and picnics, but also means that any leftovers can be enjoyed without reheating.

May 24

INSPIRATION: *Accepting my feelings as they come, without trying to escape through overeating, drinking or other numbing distractions, is what my recovery is about.*

Avocado, Pink Grapefruit & Jicama Salad

🌱 Contrasts: flavor, color and texture. That's what makes this salad special. The total amount of fat is low even though the percentage looks high.

2 pink grapefruit
1 pound jicama
1 avocado
Juice and a bit of grated peel from 1 lime
2 teaspoons olive oil
1 teaspoon minced fresh cilantro

1/4 teaspoon chili powder
1/8 teaspoon ground cumin

Peel and section the grapefruit over a bowl to catch the juices to use in the dressing. Peel jicama and cut into 1/4-inch-thick slices. Peel avocado and remove pit, then slice lengthwise into 1/4-inch-thick pieces.

Arrange the grapefruit sections, jicama and avocado on a serving plate. Combine juice from grapefruit with 2 tablespoons lime juice, lime peel, olive oil, cilantro, chili powder and cumin. Drizzle dressing over salad.

Makes 6 servings.

PER SERVING: Cal 110 • Carbo 13 gm • Prot 1 gm • Total fat 7 gm • Sat fat 1 gm • Cal from fat 57% • Chol 0 mg

EDUCATION: Discover new vegetables such as jicama (pronounced *HEEK-a-ma*). Popular in Mexico, where slices can be bought on the street sprinkled with lemon or lime juice and chili powder, jicama is a crisp, bland but sweetish root vegetable. A good source of vitamin C, with potassium, iron and calcium, jicama can be added to your diet in many ways. Slivered and added to stir-frys, it is a crisp substitute for water chestnuts. Shred or slice and add to salads, as above, or serve slices with other raw vegetables with dips or salsa. Jicama can also be boiled or baked like a potato. It is less starchy and also contains fewer calories. Choose thin-skinned, silky sheened, unblemished roots for best flavor.

INSPIRATION: *Giving of myself is the only real treasure I have to offer. I become richer as I become more giving.*

INSPIRATION: *When I am obsessed with food, or anything else, I cannot be emotionally available to important people in my life.*

Yvonne's Blushing Rice with Celery

❧ Bob and Yvonne, busy with church activities, enjoy simple, easily prepared dishes. This goes well with most main dishes.

> $^1/_4$ cup minced onion
> $^1/_4$ cup minced celery
> 2 tablespoons unsalted butter or margarine
> 1 cup long-grain brown rice
> 1 cup chicken broth or vegetable stock
> 1 cup tomato juice or vegetable juice
> 1 tablespoon minced parsley

Cook the onions and celery in the butter in a medium-size saucepan over medium heat, stirring frequently, until the onion is translucent, 2 to 3 minutes. Stir in rice until well combined. Add broth and tomato juice.

Bring to a boil, reduce heat to low, cover and simmer 35 to 40 minutes or until liquid is absorbed. Fluff with a fork while adding parsley. Let stand, covered, 5 minutes before serving. *Makes 4 servings.*

PER SERVING: Cal 246 • Carbo 39 gm • Prot 6 gm • Total fat 7 gm • Sat fat 4 gm • Cal from fat 26% • Chol 15 mg

EDUCATION: Be easy on yourself when you give a party. Make a main dish, then have guests bring hors d'oeuvres, a salad or dessert. Even without detailed planning, it seems to work out to a well-rounded meal. Everyone can get to know each other better while discussing what they brought or getting the recipe for a new dish.

Kathy's Raisin Nut Bread

❧ A slice of bread spread with peanut butter makes a filling, protein-rich breakfast.

> 1 egg, beaten
> $^1/_2$ cup medium, unsulfured molasses
> $^1/_2$ cup packed brown sugar
> $1^3/_4$ cups buttermilk
> $^3/_4$ cup raisins
> $^1/_2$ cup toasted walnuts or pecans (see glossary)
> $1^1/_2$ cups whole-wheat pastry flour
> $1^1/_2$ cups unbleached all-purpose flour
> 2 teaspoons baking powder
> $^1/_2$ teaspoon salt

Preheat oven to 350°F (175°C). Lightly oil a nonstick, 9 × 5-inch bread pan. Combine egg, molasses, brown sugar, buttermilk, raisins and nuts in a large bowl. In another bowl, combine flours, baking powder and salt. Add egg mixture to dry ingredients and mix just until combined. Pour batter into loaf pan and bake 1 hour or until a wooden pick inserted in the center comes out clean. *Makes 1 loaf (10 slices).*

PER SLICE: Cal 300 • Carbo 61 gm • Prot 7 gm • Total fat 4 gm • Sat fat 1 gm • Cal from fat 12% • Chol 23 mg

EDUCATION: Add raisins to breads and cereals to enrich your diet with iron. Raisins have nearly as much iron, ounce for ounce, as that contained in ground beef or dried beans. To keep them soft, seal tightly and refrigerate. This will prevent the fruit sugar from crystallizing. Raisins are also a good snack all by themselves.

May 27

INSPIRATION: *I can take risks today because I am not afraid to make mistakes.*

Mushrooms, Asparagus & Green Onions

🌿 Two spring vegetables—asparagus and green onions—combine with mushrooms for an interesting, low-fat side dish.

1 pound asparagus
½ tablespoon unsalted butter
1 cup thinly sliced mushrooms
4 green onions, thinly sliced on the diagonal
⅛ teaspoon salt
⅛ teaspoon freshly ground black pepper

Snap asparagus stems as close to bottoms as possible. Remove scales from stems. Cut diagonally into 3-inch pieces. Cook asparagus in butter in a large nonstick skillet over medium heat 1 or 2 minutes, stirring until coated.

Add mushrooms, green onions, salt and pepper and cook, stirring constantly, until asparagus is crisp-tender, 5 to 7 minutes.

Makes 4 servings.

PER SERVING: Cal 52 • Carbo 6 gm • Prot 3 gm • Total fat 2 gm • Sat fat 1 gm • Cal from fat 43% • Chol 6 mg

EDUCATION: Enjoy asparagus when it's plentiful and affordable. The season is not a long one, and though asparagus is available throughout the year, off-season prices skyrocket. Not only is asparagus tasty, but it contains substantial amounts of three nutrients shown effective in preventing cancer: vitamin C, beta-carotene and selenium.

The microwave is also a wonderful tool for cooking asparagus evenly. Place the more delicate tips toward the center of the plate, the firmer stems toward the outside. Microwave just until asparagus is crisp-tender, 5 to 7 minutes on HIGH for 1 pound. The stems cook without the tips becoming overcooked.

INSPIRATION: *My resources are within me. The foundation on which I am building my recovery already has been laid.*

Cream of Fresh Green Pea Soup

❧ Served with a dollop of minted yogurt, this soup celebrates the season!

1 large baking potato, peeled and diced
2 cups shelled fresh green peas
1 teaspoon fresh marjoram leaves
2 cups vegetable stock
3 cups low-fat (1%) milk
1/3 cup yogurt
1/2 teaspoon minced fresh mint
Marjoram sprigs for garnish

Combine potato, peas, marjoram and stock in a Dutch oven. Bring to a boil, reduce heat, cover and simmer 10 minutes or until vegetables are tender.

Puree vegetables with stock in a blender or food processor. Return to the pot and add milk. Heat through.

Combine yogurt with mint in a small bowl. Serve soup in individual bowls topped with a dollop of minted yogurt and garnished with a sprig of marjoram. *Makes 4 servings.*

PER SERVING: Cal 265 • Carbo 42 gm • Prot 15 gm • Total fat 4 gm • Sat fat 2 gm • Cal from fat 13% • Chol 11 mg

EDUCATION: To avoid messy cleanups, not to mention a nasty scald, use care when processing hot liquids in a blender. Keep the blender less than half full of hot liquid before processing. If you're like me, and try to fit everything in one batch, hold the lid down with a kitchen towel and begin the blender on lowest speed. Gradually increase speed until you reach the desired consistency. Kitchen safety is taking care of yourself, too.

INSPIRATION: *A garden takes the summer to mature; a fruit tree takes years to bear fruit. We all reach our fullest potential with time.*

Adam's Pasta Prima Sauce with Chicken

❧ My son developed this recipe when he decided to make dinner one evening when he was twelve. It's one of my favorites, especially because I get a night off in the kitchen when he decides to serve it! It's rich in vegetables, which makes me hope he'll continue to favor such dishes the rest of his long life.

1 cup chopped onion
1 large carrot, cut into thin, 2-inch sticks
1/2 cup thinly sliced celery
2 teaspoons olive oil
2 cups seeded chopped canned
    Italian plum tomatoes
1 (8-ounce) can tomato sauce
1/2 teaspoon salt
1 boneless skinless chicken breast half
2 tablespoons minced fresh parsley

Cook onion, carrot and celery in the oil in a nonstick Dutch oven over medium heat, stirring frequently, until the vegetables begin to brown, about 10 minutes. Puree the plum tomatoes in a blender or food processor and add to the pan with tomato sauce and salt. Bring to a boil, reduce heat, cover and simmer 10 minutes.

Meanwhile, cut the chicken breast half crosswise into 1/4-inch-wide strips. Stir chicken and parsley into pasta sauce and simmer 5 to 10 minutes, just until the vegetables are tender and the chicken is cooked through. Serve over your choice of pasta. *Makes 4 servings.*

PER SERVING: Cal 124 • Carbo 15 gm • Prot 10 gm • Total fat 4 gm • Sat fat 1 gm • Cal from fat 29% • Chol 21 mg

EDUCATION: Pass on good food habits by getting children involved. Let little ones learn to wash vegetables. As children get older, increase their participation in meal planning and preparation. Young men and women will benefit from knowing how to prepare quick, nutritious, low-fat meals before they go out on their own. It will reduce their reliance on high-fat fast foods and, hopefully, create healthy eaters for life!

May 30

INSPIRATION: *No one knows what is best for me more than I do, with the help of my Higher Power.*

Leah's Lemon Chiffon with Strawberries

🌿 Light as air, lemon chiffon is a tangy counterpoint to ripe strawberries, now in season.

*3 tablespoons fresh
  lemon juice
1 tablespoon water
1 envelope unflavored
  gelatin
1¹/₂ cups skim milk
2 egg yolks
5 tablespoons sugar
3 egg whites
1 teaspoon freshly grated
  lemon peel
1¹/₂ cups sliced strawberries
6 whole strawberries
  for garnish
Mint sprigs for garnish*

Place lemon juice and water in a small bowl. Sprinkle with gelatin and let stand 5 minutes, until gelatin softens. Meanwhile, pour milk into a small saucepan and bring to a boil. Beat egg yolks with 2 tablespoons of the sugar in a medium-size bowl. Beating constantly, gradually add boiling milk to yolks. Return milk mixture to saucepan and cook over medium-low heat, stirring constantly, 5 minutes or until mixture is slightly thickened, but not boiling. Remove from heat and stir in gelatin mixture until dissolved. Return milk mixture to medium-size bowl. Set bowl over a large pan of ice water and let chill, stirring frequently, until mixture is thick, 10 to 15 minutes.

Beat egg whites in a large bowl until soft peaks form. Gradually add remaining 3 tablespoons sugar, beating until stiff. Fold lemon peel and ¹/₃ of the egg whites gently into the chilled lemon mixture. Gently fold the lemon mixture into the remaining egg whites in the large bowl.

Spoon half the lemon chiffon into 6 parfait glasses or dessert dishes. Top with ¹/₄ cup sliced berries. Spoon on remaining lemon chiffon and garnish with whole berries and mint sprigs.

Makes 6 servings.

PER SERVING: Cal 158 • Carbo 31 gm • Prot 6 gm • Total fat 2 gm • Sat fat 1 gm • Cal from fat 11% • Chol 72 mg

EDUCATION: Use low-fat, no cholesterol egg whites to give a light and luscious lift to desserts, cakes and quick breads. All the cholesterol is in the yolk, so cut back on yolks where possible. In recipes calling for 3 whole eggs, you can eliminate 1 yolk without affecting flavor or texture of your finished dish. That easily, you've reduced the fat and cholesterol content from the eggs by one-third!

INSPIRATION: *Life is just a mixture of good and bad, ups and downs, and I'll get my allotment of each, as will everyone.*

Pork Loin Sauté with Bing Cherries

❧ Fruit always complements pork, and here the season's early cherries flavor a low-fat sauce. Serve with noodles, a vegetable and salad.

4 (1-inch-thick) pork chops, trimmed
1/2 teaspoon dried thyme
1/4 teaspoon salt
1/8 teaspoon freshly ground black pepper
1 teaspoon olive oil
1/2 pound fresh or frozen Bing cherries
1/4 cup chicken broth
1/4 cup cranberry-raspberry juice cocktail
2 teaspoons cherry vinegar or cider vinegar
   (see glossary)
2 teaspoons packed brown sugar
1 teaspoon cornstarch

Sprinkle pork chops with thyme, salt and pepper. Cook in oil in a large nonstick skillet over medium heat, turning once, 10 minutes or until juices run clear and meat is cooked throughout.

Meanwhile, cut each cherry in half and remove pits. In a measuring cup, combine broth, juice, vinegar, brown sugar and cornstarch. Remove cooked pork from pan to a warmed platter and keep warm. Stir cherries and broth mixture into drippings in skillet. Bring to a boil, stirring, reduce heat and simmer 3 minutes to blend flavors. Spoon sauce over pork.   *Makes 4 servings.*

PER SERVING: Cal 243 • Carbo 15 gm • Prot 20 gm • Total fat 11 gm • Sat fat 4 gm • Cal from fat 44% • Chol 63 mg

EDUCATION: Make your evening a bowl of cherries. Crisp and sweet, Bing cherries are a delicious 100-calorie–per cup treat from late May to August. Besides fiber, Bings contribute vitamin C. When picking or shopping, select large, firm cherries with stems. Breaking off stems increases the chance of decay and reduces storage time (as if they'll be sitting around, uneaten!). Freezing cherries is an option, especially if they'll be used for cooked dishes like the one above. Rinse and halve cherries and remove pits. Drain well. Freeze on a baking sheet, cut side up, then pack in self-sealing freezer bags. Frozen cherries will keep for up to one year.

INSPIRATION: *Daydreaming about the future is not the same as action: enabling the future to be.*

Strawberry Angel Pie

❧ A sky-high meringue crust tops fresh strawberries. With a light drizzle of melted chocolate completing the picture-pretty presentation.

2 1/2 cups sliced fresh strawberries
2 teaspoons powdered sugar
3 egg whites
1/2 teaspoon baking powder
1/8 teaspoon salt
1 cup vanilla sugar (see glossary)
1 teaspoon cider vinegar mixed with
   1 teaspoon water
1 ounce semisweet chocolate

Preheat oven to 275°F (135°C). Combine sliced strawberries and powdered sugar in a medium-size bowl. Cover and refrigerate. Beat the egg whites, baking powder and salt until whites are stiff, using an electric mixer. Continue beating, adding sugar slowly, 1 teaspoon at a time, alternating with a few drops of the combined vinegar and water. After all ingredients are added, continue beating 2 or 3 minutes. Spoon meringue into a lightly buttered, nonstick, 10-inch pie plate. Swirl surface slightly.

Bake 1 hour, until dry and crisp. Turn off oven and open oven door. Let pie shell cool in oven. To serve pie, melt chocolate in the microwave on LOW 1 or 2 minutes, or in a small saucepan set over hot water, stirring constantly. Arrange strawberries in pie-shaped wedge on each serving plate. Using a serrated knife, cut meringue crust into 8 wedges. Arrange meringue wedges over strawberries and drizzle with chocolate.   *Makes 8 servings.*

PER SERVING: Cal 129 • Carbo 30 gm • Prot 2 gm • Total fat 1 gm • Sat fat trace • Cal from fat 9% • Chol 0 mg

VARIATION

Mound scoops of meringue on a lightly buttered nonstick cookie sheet. Bake until crisp; cool. Gently remove and place meringues over servings of fresh mixed berries or fruit compote.

EDUCATION: Add drama to desserts without resorting to high-fat ingredients. Meringue is elegant, but low in fat—a perfect choice for a smashing but prudent dessert. To get the most volume from egg whites, let them warm to room temperature before beating. Use clean, dry beaters and a glass or metal bowl free of any fat. Plastic can contain fat even after washing. Also, do not let even one particle of yolk, which contains fat, get into the whites, or they cannot be beaten stiff. Beat egg whites until soft peaks form before adding any sugar.

June 2

INSPIRATION: *In always seeking immediate comfort, I may be undermining my progress. Learning to be comfortable within myself is a step toward recovery.*

Macadamia Nut Muffins

❧ Exotic enough for a special occasion, these muffins could also be made with almonds, black walnuts, peanuts or pecans.

> $1/4$ cup unsalted butter, at room
>   temperature
> $1/4$ cup packed brown sugar
> 1 egg, beaten
> 1 cup skim milk
> $1 1/2$ cups unbleached all-purpose flour
> $1/2$ cup whole-wheat pastry flour
> 2 teaspoons baking powder
> $1/2$ teaspoon baking soda
> $1/4$ teaspoon salt
> $1/3$ cup coarsely chopped
>   macadamia nuts

Preheat oven to 375°F (190°C). Lightly oil 9 ($2 3/4$-inch) nonstick muffin cups. Beat butter and sugar together in a large bowl until smooth. Stir in egg, then milk. Combine the flours, baking powder, soda, salt and nuts and stir into the egg mixture just until combined. There can be some lumps. Spoon batter into muffin cups. Bake 18 to 20 minutes or until a wooden pick inserted in the center comes out clean.   *Makes 9 muffins.*

PER MUFFIN: Cal 222 • Carbo 29 gm • Prot 5 gm • Total fat 10 gm • Sat fat 4 gm • Cal from fat 41% • Chol 38 mg

EDUCATION: Use nuts sparingly to add flavor without going overboard. Macadamia nuts are high in fat, like most nuts, but the proportion of monounsaturated fat is higher in macadamias. Monounsaturated fats are believed to aid the "good" cholesterol in our bodies. While it's best to use discretion when adding these or other nuts and nut butters to your diet, macadamias do offer significant amounts of iron, thiamin and magnesium, the latter two of which contribute to a healthy nervous system.

INSPIRATION: *In preparing meals for others, I will seek to welcome and not to impress.*

Candace's Tarragon Mushroom Soup

❧ Portobello and shiitake mushrooms make a delicious broth in this soup, which is flavored with fresh tarragon.

³/₄ cup thinly sliced leeks, white only
2 tablespoons unsalted butter
2 tablespoons unbleached
    all-purpose flour
2 cups chicken broth, heated
3¹/₂ cups low-fat (1%) milk
3 cups diced fresh portobello
    mushroom caps
1 cup thinly sliced fresh shiitake
    mushroom caps
1 teaspoon minced fresh tarragon
    leaves
¹/₄ teaspoon salt
Dash of freshly ground white
    pepper
Dash of freshly grated
    nutmeg
¹/₃ cup nonfat yogurt
6 tarragon sprigs for
    garnish

Cook leeks in the butter in a large saucepan over medium heat, stirring frequently, 5 or 6 minutes, until leeks are tender. Stir in flour and cook slowly, without browning, 2 or 3 minutes. Add hot broth and stir vigorously to combine with flour mixture in saucepan.

Stir in milk, mushrooms, minced tarragon, salt, pepper and nutmeg. Bring to a boil, reduce heat and simmer 10 minutes, stirring frequently. Ladle most of the mushrooms and some liquid into a blender or food processor and puree. Return to the saucepan and stir until blended and heated through. Ladle soup into bowls, add a spoonful of yogurt and top with a sprig of tarragon. *Makes 6 servings.*

PER SERVING: Cal 133 • Carbo 16 gm • Prot 9 gm • Total fat 4 gm • Sat fat 2 gm • Cal from fat 29% • Chol 12 mg

EDUCATION: Set reasonable goals to make life more manageable. Setting unrealistic goals usually ends in defeat. Break down large tasks, such as organizing all your paperwork, to daily or weekly accomplishments. By taking changes a step at a time, we can embrace success more often, giving ourselves the motivation to continue.

INSPIRATION: *Whimsy is a part of my life. With imagination, I create my own enjoyment.*

Baby Squash in a Field of Spinach

❧ A vegetable "still life" adds an artistic note to a summer meal. Double or triple the recipe for parties and serve on a platter.

4 to 8 baby pattypan squash
1 pound fresh spinach leaves
¹/₂ tablespoon unsalted butter
1 garlic clove
1 teaspoon fresh lemon juice
¹/₈ teaspoon salt

Steam baby squash over boiling water just until tender, 4 to 8 minutes, depending on size.

Meanwhile, wash spinach, remove stems and cut leaves into thin strips. Cook spinach in butter in a large skillet over medium heat, stirring frequently, until spinach is wilted, about 5 minutes. Push spinach to one side, press garlic directly into hot pan and add lemon juice. Stir to combine with spinach, cooking 1 or 2 minutes, until spinach is tender. Do not overcook. Spread spinach on a flat serving plate and top with squash.   *Makes 4 servings.*

PER SERVING: Cal 57 • Carbo 8 gm • Prot 5 gm • Total fat 2 gm • Sat fat 2 gm • Cal from fat 31% • Chol 8 mg

EDUCATION: Buy fresh foods in season to maximize taste. Fresh from the field, orchard or home garden, ripe fruits and vegetables are at their peak. The health benefit to you? There's no need for rich sauces to coax some flavor out of a meal. The baby pattypan squashes above, for example, are succulent and moist inside following a simple steaming—a treat for the taste buds without any elaboration.

June 5

INSPIRATION: *Building a healthy life is a positive focus for my energies.*

George's Greek Fish Soup

🌱 Quick and easy, this soup can be made with cod or haddock. Serve with a cabbage salad sprinkled with feta cheese.

1 cup chopped onion
1 tablespoon olive oil
2 garlic cloves, minced
1/4 teaspoon dried thyme
1/4 teaspoon salt

1/8 teaspoon freshly ground black pepper
4 carrots, cut into sticks
3 celery stalks, sliced on the diagonal
2 potatoes, peeled and cubed
4 cups chicken broth or fish stock
1 pound cod or haddock, cut into bite-size pieces
1 (16-ounce) can stewed tomatoes, chopped, with juice
1/4 cup minced fresh parsley

Cook onion in oil in a nonstick Dutch oven over medium heat, stirring frequently, until onion is translucent. Stir in garlic, thyme, salt and pepper and cook, stirring, 1 or 2 minutes more.

Add carrots, celery, potatoes and broth. Bring to a boil, reduce heat, cover and simmer 20 minutes, until vegetables are tender. Add fish, stewed tomatoes and parsley. Simmer 5 minutes or until fish is cooked throughout.

Makes 8 servings.

PER SERVING: Cal 152 • Carbo 17 gm • Prot 14 gm • Total fat 3 gm • Sat fat trace • Cal from fat 18% • Chol 25 mg

EDUCATION: Add seafood to your diet as an important source of iodine. Iodine, needed for normal cell metabolism, is also available in iodized salt (be sure to check the package). If you have cut back or eliminated salt from your diet, seafood could be especially important.

INSPIRATION: *Today I will turn off the constant critic in my head and trade my judgments for moments of acceptance.*

Betsy's Lamb Chops with Mustard Glaze

❧ Garnished with mint, lamb chops are a spring treat. Serve with new potatoes, cooked fresh peas and crusty French bread.

8 rib or loin lamb chops, well trimmed of fat
Dash of salt
Dash of freshly ground black pepper
2 tablespoons apple jelly
2 teaspoons Dijon mustard
Mint sprigs for garnish

Preheat broiler. Sprinkle chops with salt and pepper. Set broiler rack 4 inches from heat. Broil chops 3 or 4 minutes per side for medium-rare. Combine apple jelly and mustard. When chops have nearly reached desired doneness, spread mustard glaze on top of chops and broil 1 minute more. *Makes 4 servings.*

PER SERVING: Cal 293 • Carbo 7 gm • Prot 32 gm • Total fat 15 gm • Sat fat 5 gm • Cal from fat 45% • Chol 104 mg

EDUCATION: If you exercise or drink alcohol, be sure to eat foods rich in zinc, such as lamb, beef or dark-meat turkey. Zinc is the second most popular trace mineral contained in our bodies, next to iron. Our immune system needs zinc, as do cells, as they grow, divide and repair. Alcohol speeds the excretion of zinc from our bodies, as does perspiring. Vegetarians can get zinc in wheat germ, but with the added stress of alcohol and exercise, you may want to include a mineral supplement to be sure of getting a sufficient supply.

INSPIRATION: *Being aware of the wisdom of my body helps me integrate my actions with my body's needs.*

Pineapple-Rhubarb Fruit Compote

❧ Combine rhubarb with pears, pineapple and strawberries for a sweet side dish, or chill and serve for dessert. You can substitute 1 (16-ounce) can crushed pineapple for fresh.

1 fresh pineapple
2 cups thinly sliced rhubarb
2 Granny Smith apples, peeled,
* cored and chopped*
1 tablespoon honey
2 cups halved strawberries
Mint sprigs for garnish

Remove top and bottom from pineapple. Slice crosswise into 1-inch-thick slices. Core, peel and chop slices, catching juice. Add enough water to juice to make ½ cup. Combine liquid, chopped pineapple, rhubarb, apples and honey in a large saucepan and bring to a boil. Reduce heat, cover and simmer 8 to 10 minutes, until the rhubarb is tender. Stir in strawberries and cook 1 minute. Serve warm.
Makes 6 servings.

PER SERVING: Cal 97 • Carbo 24 gm • Prot 1 gm • Total fat 1 gm • Sat fat trace • Cal from fat 7% • Chol 0 mg

EDUCATION: Explore ways to enjoy strawberries without a lot of accompanying fat and sugar. You'll find whipped cream is not the only accompaniment that highlights their flavor. For example, here their traditional pairing with rhubarb gets a new twist with pineapple.

Or, try these: Toss a pint of berries with a splash of balsamic or spicy fruit vinegar. Stir berries into vanilla or lemon-flavored low-fat yogurt. Sprinkle strawberries with orange juice and toss with a little freshly grated orange peel. Slice the berries and dust with a teaspoon or two of sugar. Serve over low-fat frozen yogurt.

INSPIRATION: *Simplicity in my life limits distractions and allows me more easily to be present in the moment.*

Rudy's Lemon Omelet with Strawberries

Omelet with a twist: a lemony tang that complements the fresh herbed strawberry filling.

2 eggs
2 egg whites
2 teaspoons sugar
1 teaspoon fresh lemon juice
$^1/_2$ teaspoon finely grated
    lemon peel
$^1/_2$ teaspoon minced fresh
    tarragon
Dash of salt
$^1/_2$ teaspoon butter
$^1/_2$ cup sliced strawberries
Tarragon sprigs for garnish

Break eggs into a medium-size bowl and add egg whites. Beat with a hand-held mixer 1 minute or until frothy. Add sugar, lemon juice, lemon peel, minced tarragon and salt and beat until combined.

Heat a 10-inch nonstick skillet over medium heat and run a small amount of butter over the bottom of the pan. When butter stops foaming, add egg mixture to pan.

Cook eggs over medium heat, pulling the edge of the omelet toward the center of the pan with a wooden spoon. Swirl the pan to allow uncooked eggs to reach the sides of the pan. Continue to cook over slightly lower heat until the top of the eggs have just set.

Spoon strawberries over half the omelet and fold the remaining half over top. Cut omelet in half, garnish with tarragon sprigs, and serve hot.   *Makes 2 servings.*

PER SERVING: Cal 129 • Carbo 8 gm • Prot 10 gm • Total fat 6 gm • Sat fat 2 gm • Cal from fat 28% • Chol 215 mg

EDUCATION: Move strawberries out of the dessert rut to maximize their healthful benefit. Serve them in a main course, as above, or sliced and added to muffin batters, fruit salads or as a base for fruit soup. When you do serve them as dessert, substitute a glamorous serving bowl or dessert goblets for high-calorie trimmings.

INSPIRATION: *I no longer avoid life's problems with overindulgence. I can work through life's challenges by staying in recovery.*

Daphne's Orange Biscuits

Biscuits with a citrus tang can highlight breakfast, lunch or dinner. Daphne, who has traveled the world and loves to entertain, enjoys flavorful biscuits for brunch.

> 1 1/2 cups unbleached all-purpose flour
> 1/2 cup whole-wheat pastry flour
> 2 teaspoons baking powder
> 1 tablespoon brown sugar
> 1/4 teaspoon salt
> 1/4 cup cold unsalted butter
> 1 orange
> 1 egg, beaten
> 1/2 cup buttermilk

Preheat oven to 400°F (200°C). Lightly oil a nonstick baking sheet. Combine the flours, baking powder, brown sugar and salt in a large bowl. Cut in butter with a pastry blender until the mixture resembles coarse cornmeal.

Finely grate orange peel. Squeeze orange and combine 1/3 cup orange juice with grated peel, egg and buttermilk. Add egg mixture to flour and stir just until combined. Dough should be soft, but firm enough to handle.

Place dough on a floured surface, molding gently into a ball. Handling the dough as little as possible, roll out to a 1/2-inch thickness. Cut out with a 2-inch round cutter. Place biscuits on baking sheet. Bake 12 or 15 minutes or until puffed and browned on bottom.

Makes 12 biscuits.

PER BISCUIT: Cal 130 • Carbo 19 gm • Prot 3 gm • Total fat 5 gm • Sat fat 3 gm • Cal from fat 32% • Chol 29 mg

EDUCATION: Don't try to eliminate all the fat from your diet. Fat-soluble vitamins A, D, E and K can only be absorbed during digestion in the presence of fat, an important reason to have some fat in the diet. Unlike water-soluble vitamins, the vitamins above can be stored in the fatty tissues of our bodies. Relying on food for vitamins and minerals creates its own balance. Unless you are taken to consuming large quantities of polar bear liver, the chances are remote that you will reach toxic levels of vitamin A from food, for example. Eating a balanced diet with lots of grains, fruits and vegetables; a little meat, fish, eggs or dairy; and a small amount of fat satisfies your body's need for nutrients.

INSPIRATION: *Though change is a constant in my life as I get older, healthy life-style choices can mitigate those changes for my benefit.*

Couscous & Any-Bean Salad

❧ Select the cooked beans you like best, or make a new acquaintance. Try the salad several times, using different cooked beans, chick-peas or lentils. A main-dish salad, this is great with soup.

    1 cup couscous
    1 3/4 cups water
    1/4 teaspoon salt
    1 red bell pepper
    1 yellow bell pepper
    6 green onions
    1 1/2 cups cooked dried beans,
        chick-peas or lentils
    1/2 cup finely diced carrots
    1/4 cup diced pitted Greek olives
    1/4 cup crumbled feta cheese
    1/4 cup minced fresh parsley
    1/4 cup minced fresh mint leaves
    2 tablespoons brown rice vinegar
    1 tablespoon balsamic vinegar
    2 tablespoons olive oil
    1 garlic clove, pushed through a press
    1/4 teaspoon brown sugar
    1/4 teaspoon Dijon mustard
    1/4 teaspoon salt
    1/4 teaspoon freshly ground black pepper
    Romaine lettuce leaves for garnish
    Fresh mint or parsley sprigs for garnish

Bring water to a boil in a medium-size saucepan. Stir in couscous and salt. Remove from heat, cover and let stand 5 minutes.

Cut bell peppers into thin, 1-inch strips. Slice green onions on diagonal. Transfer couscous to a large bowl and fluff it with a fork.

Add bell peppers, green onions, beans or lentils, carrots, olives, feta cheese, parsley and mint.

Combine vinegars, oil, garlic, brown sugar, mustard, salt and pepper. Pour over salad and toss to combine. Arrange lettuce leaves around edge of large platter. Mound salad in center and garnish with mint or parsley sprigs.

Makes 4 servings.

PER SERVING: Cal 295 • Carbo 42 gm • Prot 12 gm • Total fat 9 gm • Sat fat 2 gm • Cal from fat 27% • Chol 6 mg

EDUCATION: Choose beans when you want a high-protein, low-fat main-dish salad. Beans are rich in potassium, low in sodium and a good source of iron and thiamin. You can see why adding more of them to your salads can be beneficial. Dried beans generally double in bulk when cooked. Most cook in 1 1/2 to 2 1/2 hours. (Lentils take less time; chick-peas and soy beans take longer.) Store dried beans in a covered jar in a cool, dry, dark place.

INSPIRATION: *I will eat the foods I need for health and focus my energies on making positive changes in my attitudes, relationships and activities.*

Flounder Fillets with Dijon Lemon-Dill Sauce

❧ Flounder may also be sold as "sole." Allow 1/3 pound per person when serving fish fillets.

1/2 cup chicken broth
1 1/3 pounds flounder fillets
1 teaspoon cornstarch
1 teaspoon butter
1 teaspoon Dijon mustard
1 tablespoon fresh lemon juice
1 tablespoon minced
  fresh dill

Bring 1/4 cup of the chicken broth almost to a boil in a large skillet. Add flounder fillets, reduce heat and cook just below a simmer until the fish is opaque, about 10 minutes. Lift out the flounder with wide spatulas and place on a warm platter. Keep warm.

Stir cornstarch into the remaining chicken broth, then stir mixture into the broth in the skillet. Stir in butter, mustard, lemon juice and dill and cook, stirring, until sauce thickens. Spoon over flounder. *Makes 4 servings.*

PER SERVING: Cal 158 • Carbo 1 gm • Prot 29 gm • Total fat 3 gm • Sat fat 1 gm • Cal from fat 17% • Chol 75 mg

EDUCATION: Give fish, like poultry, special handling in the kitchen. To thaw frozen fish, keep in the refrigerator overnight or defrost in the microwave. Cook promptly after defrosting.

Thoroughly wash all utensils used to prepare fish, as well as your hands and any cutting boards or counter surfaces exposed to the raw fish. Do not allow cooked foods to come into contact with raw fish or use utensils on other foods without washing them first in hot, soapy water.

Marinate fish in the refrigerator, not at room temperature where bacteria can multiply. Cook fish sufficiently to destroy harmful organisms, but do not destroy its flavor and texture by overcooking. The flesh of the fish should just be opaque. If it is just slightly translucent at its thickest part, it can be removed from the heat. The temperature of the surrounding flesh will complete cooking. If a fish flakes easily, it is overcooked.

INSPIRATION: *I have the courage to make changes in my life-style in pursuing my growth and healing.*

Rosemary's Vegetable Potpourri with Rice

❧ Colorful enough for special meals, easy enough for everyday, this combination complements chops, fish or poultry.

1 large leek
2 carrots
1 stalk broccoli
1 cup packed spinach leaves
1 tablespoon unsalted butter
1 1/2 cups cooked brown rice
  (see glossary)
Dash of salt
Dash of freshly ground black pepper

Cut leek in half lengthwise about 3 inches from the root end. Fan out leaves and rinse thoroughly to remove dirt. Trim root end and thinly slice leek. Dice carrots. Peel stem and chop broccoli. Wash spinach, remove stems and chop.

Cook leek in butter in a large nonstick skillet over medium heat, stirring frequently, until the leek is translucent, about 10 minutes. Add carrots and cook, stirring frequently, 5 minutes. Add broccoli and cook 2 to 3 minutes. Stir in spinach, rice, salt and pepper and cook, stirring frequently, until rice is heated through and spinach is wilted. *Makes 4 servings.*

PER SERVING: Cal 150 • Carbo 27 gm • Prot 4 gm • Total fat 4 gm • Sat fat 2 gm • Cal from fat 23% • Chol 8 mg

EDUCATION: Add brown rice to vegetable combinations to benefit from its generous supply of B vitamins, which help frayed nerves to heal. Easy for most people to digest, brown rice has a balance of fiber and nutrients (and a pleasing, nutty taste) that makes it a valuable staple.

Stores carry long-grain and short-grain varieties, as well as aromatic brown rice, such as basmati. Generally long-grain rice cooks up with more separate grains, while short-grain tends to stick together slightly. These recipes were tested with short-grain brown rice, my personal preference, but long-grain works equally well.

June 13

INSPIRATION: *Taking good care of my body— accepting it, nurturing it, and enjoying living in it— is part of my self-respect.*

One-Pancake Breakfast

❧ Need a filling, but fast, breakfast? The protein and fiber will keep you on a steady course all morning.

$^1/_2$ cup whole-wheat flour
$^1/_2$ teaspoon baking powder
Dash of salt
1 egg
$^2/_3$ to $^3/_4$ cup buttermilk
  or skim milk
Fresh fruit
Pure maple syrup

Combine flour, baking powder and salt in a medium-size bowl. Beat egg and add to flour with enough milk to make a thin batter.

Lightly oil a medium-size nonstick skillet. Heat over medium heat. Pour batter into skillet and bake until bubbles appear on surface. Turn and bake remaining side until pancake is cooked through. Top with fresh fruit and drizzle lightly with maple syrup. *Makes 1 serving.*

PER SERVING: Cal 371 • Carbo 57 gm • Prot 18 gm • Total fat 7 gm • Sat fat 3 gm • Cal from fat 17% • Chol 219 mg

EDUCATION: When you're treating yourself to a pancake breakfast think whole grains because of their higher mineral content. Minerals play a fundamental role in maintaining the structure, function and balance of our bodies. The calcium, magnesium, manganese, potassium, zinc, copper, chromium and iron in the recipe above all weigh in the direction of healing. Minerals give our bones strength and control the balance of fluids in and around each of our cells. Minerals activate many of the body's enzyme systems and affect the electrical impulses by which cells communicate. Minerals also regulate the pH balance in our bodies. Damage to our bodies as a result of alcohol abuse, addictions, or illness creates an even greater demand for minerals to aid in healing.

INSPIRATION: *I may never become a winning athlete, but I am a winner for doing my healthy best with what I have.*

Spicy Vegetables with Tofu

Bean curd, generally called tofu, is a chameleon of foods, adopting the flavor of whatever it accompanies.

1 onion, halved lengthwise and
  thinly sliced
1 red bell pepper, cut into thin
  2-inch strips
2 celery stalks, thinly sliced on
  the diagonal
4 garlic cloves, minced
1 tablespoon finely minced fresh
  gingerroot
1 tablespoon minced jalapeño
  chile (see glossary)
$^1/_2$ tablespoon canola oil
$^3/_4$ cup sliced broccoli flowerets
$^3/_4$ cup sliced cauliflower flowerets
$^1/_4$ cup thinly sliced mushrooms
$^1/_4$ cup fresh or frozen green peas
$^1/_4$ cup vegetable stock
1 tablespoon fresh lemon juice
1 tablespoon honey
1 cup cubed tofu

Cook onion, bell pepper, celery, garlic, ginger and jalapeño in the oil in a large nonstick skillet over medium heat 5 minutes, stirring constantly. Add broccoli, cauliflower, mushrooms and peas and stir to combine.

Add vegetable stock, lemon juice, honey and cubed tofu to vegetables. Cover and steam 3 or 4 minutes, until vegetables are crisp-tender. Serve over cooked rice.   *Makes 4 servings.*

PER SERVING: Cal 172 • Carbo 18 gm • Prot 13 gm • Total fat 7 gm • Sat fat 1 gm • Cal from fat 35% • Chol 0 mg

EDUCATION: Don't overdo the quest for protein, as protein needs are relatively modest. Roughly 10 to 15 percent of your daily calorie intake should be protein. For a 2,000-calorie daily diet, that amounts to 2 to 3 ounces of pure protein per day. Since protein is mixed in with fiber and other nutrients, you'll really need to eat between 5 and 7 ounces of high-protein foods each day. Besides meat, seafood and poultry, sources include eggs, beans, lentils, grains, vegetables and low-fat dairy products like milk, yogurt and cheese.

Tofu is packed with protein and is super-low in calories, roughly 50 calories per 2-ounce serving. Tofu is ready to eat, with no cooking necessary—a real convenience food. It can be crumbled and seasoned to use as sandwich filling, or cooked, as in the recipe above.

INSPIRATION: *I can receive compliments graciously, moving away from arrogance or false modesty.*

Chocolate Hazelnut Fondue with Fresh Fruits

🌿 Dessert with elegance, but not a lot of fat! A blender or food processor is necessary to achieve a creamy consistency to this luscious chocolate sauce.

1 square (1 ounce) unsweetened
    baking chocolate
1 (15-ounce) container part-skim
    ricotta cheese
1/2 cup strong decaffeinated hazelnut-
    flavored brewed coffee
1/4 cup vanilla sugar (see glossary)
3 tablespoons unsweetened
    cocoa powder
Pinch of salt
1 quart strawberries
1 large, ripe pineapple, peeled, cored
    and cut into chunks
1 large bunch seedless grapes
1 pint sweet cherries, pitted
3 navel oranges, peeled, seeded and
    cut into chunks
2 bananas, cut into chunks and
    tossed with a little lemon juice

Melt chocolate in a small microwave-safe bowl in the microwave on LOW 1 or 2 minutes or in a small saucepan set over hot water, stirring constantly. Place melted chocolate, ricotta, coffee, sugar, cocoa powder and salt in a blender or food processor and process until smooth. Scrape down sides of container as necessary. Transfer sauce to a small serving bowl. Place bowl on a platter and surround with the assortment of fruits. *Makes 10 servings.*

PER SERVING: Cal 216 • Carbo 39 gm • Prot 7 gm • Total fat 6 gm • Sat fat 2 gm • Cal from fat 25% • Chol 13 mg

EDUCATION: Switch to "decaf" to lessen the impact of caffeine on your metabolism. Caffeine is often seen as an innocent pick-me-up. But just 250 milligrams a day—the amount in 2 1/2 cups of "high test"—can cause insomnia, restlessness, irritability, nervousness and anxiety. In addition, some research has shown that caffeine reduces the body's reserves of thiamin—a B vitamin essential for a feeling of tranquillity. Finding caffeine-free alternatives to drinking coffee will help keep nerves on an even keel. Instead of going "cold turkey," gradually substitute decaffeinated varieties and slowly cut back.

INSPIRATION: *When I turn away from my busyness, I find the peace and quiet necessary to commune with my deeper spirit.*

Creamy Carrot Soup with Fresh Herbs

❧ With no cream to add fat, this soup is thickened and textured with potato. A dollop of yogurt adds tang.

$^3/_4$ cup chopped onion
1 tablespoon butter
2 cups diced carrots
$^1/_2$ cup thinly sliced celery
2 garlic cloves, minced
4 cups vegetable stock or
   chicken broth
1 potato, peeled and cubed
$^1/_4$ teaspoon salt
$^1/_8$ teaspoon freshly ground
   white pepper
1 teaspoon minced fresh basil leaves
$^1/_4$ teaspoon minced fresh
   tarragon leaves
$^1/_4$ cup nonfat yogurt
2 tablespoons minced fresh parsley
   for garnish

Cook onion in butter in a nonstick Dutch oven over medium heat, stirring frequently, until the onion is translucent. Add carrots and celery and cook, stirring frequently, 10 minutes. Add garlic and cook, stirring, 1 minute.

Add stock, potato, salt and pepper and bring to a boil. Reduce heat and simmer, uncovered, 30 minutes, stirring occasionally. Add fresh basil and tarragon. Puree soup in batches in the blender. Serve soup in individual bowls with a dollop of yogurt and garnish with minced parsley.   *Makes 4 servings.*

PER SERVING: Cal 144 • Carbo 18 gm • Prot 7 gm • Total fat 4 gm • Sat fat 2 gm • Cal from fat 25% • Chol 4 mg

EDUCATION: Choose fresh herbs instead of excess salt or butter for flavoring. If you have access to a yard, patio, deck or balcony, place a few pots of herbs outside your door or window. The closer you can get them to the kitchen, the more likely you'll reach for them. In the fall, well-established outdoor plants can be brought inside to the kitchen windowsill.

INSPIRATION: *Being honest about my strengths and weaknesses gives me security in knowing the truth about myself.*

Rosy's Quick Barley Pilaf

❧ This quick and easy side dish features a grain you may not be including in your diet on a regular basis. Try it with grilled poultry, lamb chops or shrimp and a green salad.

1 shallot, minced
1 teaspoon butter
1 garlic clove, minced
2 cups chicken broth
1 cup quick-cooking barley
1 zucchini, diced
1 yellow squash, diced
1 tablespoon minced fresh parsley

Cook shallot in butter in a medium-size saucepan over medium heat, stirring frequently, until translucent, 2 to 3 minutes. Add garlic and cook, stirring, 1 minute. Add chicken broth and bring to a boil. Stir in barley. Return to a boil, reduce heat, cover and simmer 5 minutes. Stir in zucchini and yellow squash and return to a boil. Cover and simmer 5 minutes more. Uncover and cook, stirring, until liquid is absorbed and vegetables are tender. Stir in parsley. *Makes 4 servings.*

PER SERVING: Cal 211 • Carbo 38 gm • Prot 9 gm • Total fat 3 gm • Sat fat 1 gm • Cal from fat 13% • Chol 3 mg

EDUCATION: Select easy, quick-cooking grain dishes in summer. While long cooking and oven baking are fine in cold weather, summer calls for quicker, lighter fare. Quick-cooking barley is one option. Besides offering a different slant on a side dish, this barley pilaf is ready in minutes to accompany grilled or broiled main dishes. Its ease of preparation encourages encore appearances at dinner!

INSPIRATION: *I don't have to look to food for excitement if I continue to build a full, rich life through my honest relationships with others.*

Creamy Lemon-Sauced Spaghetti for One

❧ Anne enjoys this as a quick, very low-fat main dish when she has only herself to cook for. For variation, you could add cooked vegetables to the pasta.

¹/₄ pound spaghetti
¹/₃ cup low-fat cottage cheese
1 garlic clove, pushed through a press
2 tablespoons fresh lemon juice
1 teaspoon minced fresh parsley

Bring a large saucepan of water to a boil. Cook spaghetti until firm-tender, 6 to 8 minutes. Heat cottage cheese, garlic and lemon juice in a microwave-safe bowl in the microwave on HIGH 1 minute or in a small saucepan over low heat. Blend until smooth. Drain spaghetti, toss with sauce and sprinkle with parsley. *Makes 1 serving.*

PER SERVING: Cal 486 • Carbo 90 gm • Prot 24 gm • Total fat 3 gm • Sat fat 1 gm • Cal from fat 5% • Chol 3 mg

EDUCATION: Add pasta to your healthy life! Pasta has finally earned the reputation it deserves: a heart-healthy food low in fat and sodium. Pasta also has significant amounts of iron, manganese, copper and phosphorus, plus magnesium and zinc. In addition, some varieties of pasta are high in fiber, such as whole-wheat, spinach and artichoke pastas. For variety you may want to combine these pastas with regular semolina pastas.

INSPIRATION: *Today is a special opportunity to enjoy my self, the people around me and the beauties of nature.*

Lazy Chicken Fajitas

🌿 Fast and easy. Serving chicken fajitas gives everyone the chance to select accompaniments.

12 flour tortillas
1 Spanish onion or other sweet onion
1 red bell pepper
1 tablespoon canola oil
1 garlic clove, minced
$1/4$ teaspoon dried oregano
$1/4$ teaspoon ground cumin
$1/8$ teaspoon paprika
$1/8$ teaspoon hot (cayenne) pepper
$1/2$ cup chicken broth
4 boneless skinless chicken breast halves,
    cut into thin strips
1 tomato, peeled, seeded and chopped
4 green onions, thinly sliced
$1/2$ avocado, peeled and diced
1 cup Sombrero Salsa (see February 16)
    or bottled salsa thinned with tomato juice

Wrap tortillas in foil and place in a preheated warm 300°F (150°) oven.

Halve the onion lengthwise, peel and cut lengthwise into thin strips. Seed bell pepper and thinly slice. Cook onion and bell pepper in oil in a large nonstick skillet over medium heat, stirring frequently, until the onion is translucent. Add garlic, oregano, cumin, paprika and cayenne and cook, stirring, 1 minute. Stir in broth and bring to a boil. Add chicken strips and cook, stirring frequently, 5 minutes or until chicken is cooked through and vegetables are firm-tender. Place fajita filling on a warm serving plate with warm tortillas and serve chopped tomato, green onions, diced avocado and salsa

in separate bowls. Let each person assemble his or her own fajitas.   *Makes 4 servings.*

PER SERVING: Cal 569 • Carbo 65 gm • Prot 39 gm • Total fat 18 gm • Sat fat 2 gm • Cal from fat 28% • Chol 78 mg

EDUCATION: Cut fat in half by removing the skin from chicken breasts before you eat or even before you cook them. High in protein, with just a $3^{1}/_{2}$-ounce serving providing approximately half of the recommended daily allowance, chicken is also versatile, figuring in a wide range of cuisines. Extremely rich in niacin, which helps keep nervous systems healthy, chicken can be a prudent addition to a recovery diet.

INSPIRATION: *I need faith to get on with my life, but I must also be willing to take the next step.*

Brown Rice Salad with Spring Vegetables

🌿 Minted rice salad is terrific as a side dish when grilling outdoors. Add some cooked beans, shrimp or seasoned tofu and you've got a summertime main dish.

$1^{1}/_{2}$ cups brown rice
3 cups water
$1/4$ cup brown rice vinegar
3 tablespoons olive oil
$1/4$ teaspoon salt
$1/4$ teaspoon freshly ground black pepper
$1/4$ teaspoon freshly grated lemon peel
$1/2$ cup chopped red onion
$1/4$ cup minced fresh mint
2 green onions, sliced on the diagonal
1 cup shelled fresh green peas
8 to 10 spinach leaves
$1/2$ cup diced radishes

Lemon slices for garnish
Mint sprigs for garnish

Bring rice and water to a boil in a large saucepan. Reduce heat, cover and simmer 35 to 40 minutes, until rice is tender and liquid is absorbed. Turn rice into a large bowl to cool.

Combine vinegar, oil, salt, pepper and lemon peel. When rice is cool, add dressing, red onion, mint and green onions and toss to combine. Cover and refrigerate several hours or overnight. Remove from refrigerator 1 hour before serving.

Steam peas over boiling water 4 to 5 minutes, until al dente. Run under cold water to cool. Drain and set aside. Wash spinach and remove stems. Cut leaves into thin strips.

Toss peas, spinach and radishes with rice mixture. Garnish with lemon slices and mint sprigs. *Makes 6 servings.*

PER SERVING: Cal 274 • Carbo 44 gm • Prot 7 gm • Total fat 8 gm • Sat fat 1 gm • Cal from fat 28% • Chol 0 mg

EDUCATION: Think "salads" when you are looking for light, nutritious meals as summer approaches. Salads can vary from tossed greens to hearty, main-dish beans and grains, meat and potato, seafood and pasta combinations. Nearly any salad can become a main dish with the addition of a protein source. Try adding sliced, grilled steak to a green salad and serve with grilled potatoes. Add cooked shrimp, lobster or chicken to pasta salad. Look at your favorite salads and mix and match ideas to create some new main-dish enjoyment.

INSPIRATION: *When I totally let go, I give my Higher Power room to meet my needs.*

Summer Grilled Lemon Shrimp

❧ Celebrate the first day of the new season with a cookout!

12 jumbo shrimp
1 tablespoon lemon juice
1/2 teaspoon olive oil
1 teaspoon dried oregano
1 teaspoon dried thyme
1 teaspoon freshly grated lemon peel
1/2 teaspoon salt
1/2 teaspoon freshly ground black pepper
2 tablespoons fresh lemon juice
Lemon wedges for garnish
Parsley sprigs for garnish

Shell and devein shrimp (see glossary). Combine lemon juice, olive oil, oregano, thyme, lemon peel, salt and pepper in a medium-size bowl. Add the shrimp and toss to coat well. Marinate in refrigerator for at least 1 hour or overnight. Add lemon juice and let shrimp stand at room temperature while preparing coals in grill.

Drain shrimp and grill on a rack about 4 inches over hot coals 6 minutes, turning once, or just until opaque throughout. Or broil 4 inches under a preheated broiler about 4 minutes on each side. Garnish with lemon wedges and parsley sprigs. *Makes 4 servings.*

PER SERVING: Cal 34 • Carbo 1 gm • Prot 4 gm • Total fat 1 gm • Sat fat trace • Cal from fat 26% • Chol 32 mg

EDUCATION: Think of the visual appeal of seasonal foods to stimulate interest in healthy eating. Summer vegetables are, by their nature, quick and easy to prepare. To keep yourself and everyone interested in dinner when fun activities beckon, combine colorful vegetables, green salads and fresh fruit desserts with your quick-cooking main dishes.

INSPIRATION: *I will let my body adjust gradually to the healing choices I am making, and not expect great changes overnight.*

Angel Food Cake with Fresh Berry Topping

Delicate white cake and luscious, tart jeweled berries create a delight for the senses, with angelic levels of fat.

1¼ cups cake flour
14 egg whites, at room temperature
1½ teaspoons cream of tartar
¼ teaspoon salt
1⅔ cups vanilla sugar (see glossary)
2 teaspoons fresh lemon juice
¼ teaspoon freshly grated lemon peel
½ cup seedless red raspberry jam
1 pint red raspberries
1 pint blackberries

Preheat oven to 300°F (150°C). Sift cake flour, or put it through a sieve, into a medium-size bowl. With an electric mixer on medium speed, beat egg whites in a large bowl until frothy. Add cream of tartar and salt and continue beating until soft peaks form. Add sugar ⅓ cup at a time, continuing to beat until the whites are stiff but not dry. Fold in lemon juice and peel.

Sift flour over egg whites ¼ cup at a time and gently fold in with a spatula. When all the flour has been folded in, spoon batter into an ungreased 10-inch angel food cake pan.

Bake 1 hour and 10 minutes or until the top is golden and springy to the touch. Remove from the oven and invert the cake pan over the neck of a bottle. Allow to cool completely. Run a knife around the outside edge to loosen the cake, then turn it out onto a waxed-paper–lined plate.

For berry sauce, warm the red raspberry jam in a small saucepan until melted. Toss the warmed jam with the berries. To serve, cut cake with a serrated knife and top each piece with some of the berry mixture.   *Makes 10 servings.*

PER SERVING: Cal 265 • Carbo 61 gm • Prot 7 gm • Total fat trace • Sat fat trace • Cal from fat 1% • Chol 0 mg

EDUCATION: Pick your own to enhance the experience of enjoying fresh fruits. Visiting farms where you can harvest your own fruits can be a soul-satisfying way to improve your health. First, the fruit is as fresh as you'll ever see it. Second, you'll be getting out in the fresh air and having some exercise. Third, if the farm is near you, you'll enhance your sense of connectedness to your community. I always enjoy a chat with my friend Phyllis when I visit her Pryde 'n' Joy farm near my home. If you have to drive, take along a friend or two to enjoy the outing. Cyndi, another friend, used to pick and can fruit once a year with several friends. By working together, they had an enjoyable day, plus plenty of preserves to tuck away for the winter months.

INSPIRATION: *I am willing today to go slowly, to see myself more clearly as I am.*

Lisa's Lemon Tea Bread ✓

 Lightly lemon flavored, this glazed bread is delicious accompanied with sliced, fresh fruits and iced herbal teas—and far less fattening than those lemon bars Lisa made for us in college.

2 lemons
$^1/_4$ cup sugar
1 cup unbleached all-purpose flour
1 cup whole-wheat pastry flour
$1^1/_2$ teaspoons baking powder
$^1/_2$ teaspoon baking soda
2 eggs
$^1/_4$ cup canola oil
$^1/_4$ cup honey
1 cup buttermilk

Preheat oven to 350°F (175°C). Lightly oil a nonstick 9 × 5-inch loaf pan. Finely grate the yellow peels from the lemons. (Use a mushroom brush to remove the grated peel from the grater.) Squeeze $^1/_4$ cup of lemon juice. Combine juice with sugar in a small bowl and stir. Set aside.

In a large bowl, combine flours, baking powder and soda. In a small bowl, beat eggs and stir in oil and honey. Add egg mixture, grated lemon peel and buttermilk to dry ingredients and stir just until combined. Turn batter into prepared loaf pan and bake 35 minutes or until a cake tester or wooden pick comes out clean.

Gently remove bread from pan and place on a plate. With a wooden pick or cake tester, poke holes across the top of the bread. Stir the lemon juice–sugar mixture, then slowly spoon over the surface of the bread. Drain excess syrup off the plate back into the small bowl. Continue to spoon over the bread until all the syrup is absorbed. Carefully transfer bread to a cooling rack. Let cool before slicing.

Makes 1 loaf (10 slices).

PER SLICE: Cal 177 • Carbo 28 gm • Prot 4 gm • Total fat 6 gm • Sat fat 1 gm • Cal from fat 31% • Chol 36 mg

EDUCATION: Incorporate whole-grain flours in your breads to benefit from selenium. Selenium, a trace mineral, is believed to be a cancer preventative. The small amounts needed become clear when we see that selenium is measured in micrograms, one-thousandths of the milligrams used to measure most vitamins and minerals. While liver and kidneys are two of the richest sources of selenium, seafood and whole grains also contain healthful amounts.

INSPIRATION: *My self-worth is not measured as a size.*

White-Bean Dip with Garlic Pita Chips

❧ Similar to the Middle Eastern dip called "hummus," this dip is high in protein. Fresh oregano gives it a special flavor. Raw vegetables are also a good accompaniment.

1 cup dried cannellini beans
    (white kidney beans)
4 whole-wheat pita breads
1 tablespoon unsalted butter
1 teaspoon minced garlic
¹/₈ teaspoon freshly ground black pepper
1 tablespoon fresh lemon juice
1 large garlic clove, crushed
1 teaspoon olive oil
1 teaspoon minced fresh oregano leaves
    or ¹/₄ teaspoon dried
¹/₂ teaspoon ground cumin

Let beans soak overnight, generously covered with water. Drain beans and place in a large saucepan, generously covered with water. Bring to a boil, reduce heat, cover and simmer 1¹/₂ hours or until beans are tender.

While beans are cooking, preheat oven to 400°F (200°C). Cut pita breads into 6 wedges each and separate each wedge at fold. Melt butter in a small saucepan with the minced garlic and pepper. Place pita wedges smooth side up on baking sheets and brush each wedge lightly with butter mixture. Bake 10 minutes or until toasted. Set on racks to cool. Chips can be wrapped and kept at room temperature up to 2 days.

Drain beans. Combine beans, lemon juice, crushed garlic, olive oil, oregano and cumin in a food processor or blender and puree. Turn bean dip into a shallow serving bowl and place on a platter surrounded with pita chips.

Makes 12 servings.

PER SERVING: Cal 66 • Carbo 10 gm • Prot 2 gm • Total fat 2 gm • Sat fat 1 gm • Cal from fat 22% • Chol 3 mg

EDUCATION: Substitute bean dips for dairy dips to add fiber to your diet. Beans, you know by now, are high in fiber. What may come as a surprise is that beans are high in two completely different types of fiber. One, called soluble fiber because it dissolves in water, has shown to be effective in reducing blood-cholesterol levels. Beans also contain insoluble fiber, which helps our digestive system by absorbing water and providing the bulk needed to move food through the entire digestive system.

INSPIRATION: *By building up my inner resources, I can be more resilient in the face of change.*

Broccoli Rabe with Lemon & Garlic

❧ A light cooking mellows the taste of this green that resembles broccoli. Also called Chinese flowering cabbage or rapini, broccoli rabe should not be overcooked.

2 bunches broccoli rabe (about 2 pounds)
2 garlic cloves
2 teaspoons olive oil
¹/₄ teaspoon freshly grated lemon peel
¹/₄ teaspoon salt
Lemon wedges for garnish

Wash broccoli rabe and trim off tough stems. Cut garlic into slivers. Cook garlic in the oil in a Dutch oven over medium heat until tender but not browned. Add broccoli rabe and cook, stirring constantly, just until wilted. Serve with lemon wedges. *Makes 4 servings.*

PER SERVING: Cal 86 • Carbo 12 gm • Prot 7 gm • Total fat 3 gm • Sat fat trace • Cal from fat 32% • Chol 0 mg

EDUCATION: Eat a variety of dark, leafy greens to increase your supply of folate. Familiar with the term "iron deficiency anemia"? You may not know there is another kind of anemia called megaloblastic anemia. It results from an inadequate amount of vitamins B_{12} and folate in the body. Alcohol abuse is closely linked with megaloblastic anemia. Alcohol encourages the body to excrete B vitamins—the very ones we need to stay on an even emotional keel. Add poor nutrition to the picture, and anemia results. Signs of megaloblastic anemia include weight loss, digestive upset, fatigue, depression and irritability. Stoking up on vitamins B_{12} and folate is important to recovery. Almost any animal source of food, such as meat, fish or dairy products, contain B_{12}. For folate, whole grains, beans, peas and lentils, and liver, in addition to the broccoli rabe, above, are sources.

June 26

INSPIRATION: *I know what my limitations are; I am willing to say "no."*

Michelle's Chicken in Parchment

Impressive in appearance, but as easy to make as folding paper! Serve with new potatoes and a salad.

4 boneless skinless chicken breast halves
2 carrots
2 small zucchini
4 green onions
2 tablespoons minced fresh parsley
1/2 teaspoon freshly grated lemon peel
1/2 teaspoon salt
1/8 teaspoon freshly ground black pepper
2 teaspoons unsalted butter

Preheat oven to 375°F (190°C). Cut chicken breast halves crosswise into 1/2-inch-thick slices. Cut carrots and zucchini into thin 2-inch-long slices. Halve green onions lengthwise and cut into 3-inch lengths. Toss together the chicken strips, carrots, zucchini, green onions, parsley, lemon peel, salt and pepper.

Cut 4 (12-inch) squares of parchment, or use aluminum foil. Place one-fourth of the chicken mixture on half of each square. Dot with a small amount of butter. Fold parchment or foil over ingredients and fold edges to seal all around.

Place packets on a jelly roll pan to catch any leakage. Bake 20 minutes, until paper is puffed and browned and chicken is tender. To serve, carefully cut an "X" in the top of each packet, avoiding steam. *Makes 4 servings.*

PER SERVING: Cal 187 • Carbo 6 gm • Prot 28 gm • Total fat 5 gm • Sat fat 2 gm • Cal from fat 24% • Chol 78 mg

EDUCATION: Get out of the mealtime rut by putting a wrap on dinner. All of us get caught in the occasional rut when dinnertime rolls around. Falling back on old favorites that don't take a lot of thought or planning can lead to a boring routine. The recipe above jolts the menu out of a rut, without intense effort. In fact, this simple recipe becomes dramatic with a few folds of paper. Nutritionally, wrapped foods are superior because nutrients are sealed in. Add a little mystery to your meal by wrapping it up!

INSPIRATION: *When I feel well, I have the energy to stick with choices that are in my best interest.*

INSPIRATION: *I am willing to seek my own freedom by relinquishing my stranglehold of control.*

Shell Pasta with Carrots & Spinach

❧ Serve with meat, fish or poultry. This all-in-one side dish can be complemented with a soup appetizer or salad to complete your meal.

> *1 carrot, peeled and diced*
> *2 cups shell pasta*
> *2 cups packed spinach leaves*
> *Dash of salt*
> *Dash of freshly ground pepper*

Bring a large saucepan of water to a boil. Add carrot and pasta. Return to a boil, reduce heat and simmer 7 or 8 minutes, until firm-tender. Tear spinach leaves into small bite-size pieces. Stir into pasta. Bring to a boil, reduce heat and simmer 2 or 3 minutes. Drain. Season with salt and pepper.   *Makes 4 servings.*

> PER SERVING: Cal 208 • Carbo 42 gm • Prot 8 gm • Total fat 1 gm • Sat fat trace • Cal from fat 4% • Chol 0 mg

EDUCATION: When you are cooking pasta, add a vegetable for fun and fiber. While purists might scoff that nutrients are lost in the cooking liquid, the balance is still positive if it encourages us to get more vegetables on the dinner table. Carrots will cook in approximately the same amount of time as noodles, macaroni or shell pasta. Quicker-cooking vegetables, such as frozen peas or fresh spinach, can be added a couple of minutes before the end of cooking time. Combine several vegetables, then add fresh herbs just before removing from heat to add variety.

Cream Cheese Pie with Strawberries

❧ Fat-free cream cheese can be tricky for baking, but this chilled pie offers no problems—only a low-fat, delicious solution!

> *1 (8-inch) Low-Calorie Graham Cracker Crust (see below)*
> *1 (¼-ounce) envelope unflavored gelatin*
> *1 cup cold water*
> *2 (8-ounce) packages nonfat cream cheese, softened*
> *½ cup vanilla sugar (see glossary)*
> *8 strawberries*
> *8 mint leaves for garnish*
>
> LOW-CALORIE GRAHAM CRACKER CRUST
> *¾ cup graham cracker crumbs*
> *3 tablespoons butter, melted*
> *Dash of cinnamon, nutmeg or grated lemon peel*

For crust, combine crumbs, butter and cinnamon in a small bowl. Press the crumb mixture onto the bottom and up the sides of an 8-inch pie plate. Smooth the crumb mixture along the bottom to an even thickness. Chill the crust 10 minutes in the freezer, until it is set, before filling.

In a small saucepan, sprinkle gelatin over ⅓ cup cold water. Let stand 1 minute. Cook over low heat, stirring constantly, until gelatin is completely dissolved. Combine cream cheese and sugar in a food processor and process until smooth. Add dissolved gelatin and remaining water and process until combined. Pour cream cheese mixture into pie crust and chill until firm.

To garnish, remove caps from strawberries and slice in half lengthwise. Evenly arrange strawberry halves on pie, with cap ends toward the outside. Place a mint leaf at the cap end of each strawberry half. Cut pie so that each slice is garnished with 1 strawberry half.

Makes 8 servings.

PER SERVING: Cal 189 • Carbo 26 gm • Prot 9 gm • Total fat 5 gm • Sat fat 3 gm • Cal from fat 24% • Chol 16 mg

EDUCATION: Use a Low-Calorie Graham Cracker Crust as a step toward lighter desserts. If you use graham crackers, you include the benefits of fiber in your dessert. Ready-made graham cracker crusts have less fat than dough crusts.

June 29

INSPIRATION: *When I let go of my self-centeredness, I can grasp the love and support that surrounds me.*

Party Fruit Salad with Strawberry-Garlic Dressing

Party-size; beautiful; scrumptious! This salad is an eyepopper.

Strawberry-Garlic Dressing (see below)
1 head butter lettuce
1 head raddichio
1 cup packed fresh spinach leaves,
*   stems removed, cut into thin strips*
10 romaine lettuce leaves
1 cup red grapes
1 cup blueberries
1 cup halved strawberries
3 slices red onion
2 green onions, sliced on the diagonal
1/2 lemon, thinly sliced

Lemon wedges
STRAWBERRY-GARLIC DRESSING
3/4 cup buttermilk
1/2 cup reduced-fat mayonnaise
2 tablespoons berry vinegar
*   (see glossary)*
1 1/2 teaspoons sugar
1 garlic clove, pushed through a press
5 or 6 strawberries

For dressing, combine buttermilk, mayonnaise, vinegar, sugar, garlic and strawberries in a food processor. Process just until blended.

Separate butter lettuce and raddichio into individual leaves. Remove spinach stems. Wash, dry and tear lettuces, spinach and raddichio into large pieces.

Toss lettuce, raddichio, spinach, grapes, blueberries and strawberries in a large glass bowl. Separate red onion into rings. Arrange over salad with green onions and lemon slices. Toss before serving with dressing and lemon wedges on the side.   *Makes 12 servings.*

PER SERVING: Cal 53 • Carbo 10 gm • Prot 2 gm • Total fat 2 gm • Sat fat trace • Cal from fat 34% • Chol 2 mg

EDUCATION: Combine unexpected flavors to create new interest in healthful foods. Garlic and strawberries, for example, meld in this unusual and delicious dressing which tops off a nutritious melange of fruits and leafy greens. Serving dressing on the side, with optional lemon wedges, allows guests to add prudent amounts to their own servings.

Baby Carrots with Fresh Herbs

Serve chilled, as a salad, for a change-of-pace hot-weather dish. If you don't have a garden, shop at the farmers' market for baby carrots, or halve and carve larger carrots to resemble these.

1 pound baby carrots
2 teaspoons olive oil
2 teaspoons cider vinegar
2 teaspoons fresh lemon juice
1/2 teaspoon dry yellow mustard
1/4 teaspoon paprika
*1/4 teaspoon freshly grated
   lemon peel*
1/8 teaspoon salt
1 tablespoon minced fresh dill
1 teaspoon minced fresh tarragon
1 teaspoon minced fresh mint

Scrub, but do not peel carrots. Trim tops to 1 inch. Cook carrots in a medium-size saucepan in water 4 to 5 minutes or just until the carrots are crisp-tender. Rinse carrots under cold, running water to stop cooking.

Whisk together the oil, vinegar, lemon juice, mustard, paprika, lemon peel and salt in a small bowl. In a large bowl, toss carrots with dressing and fresh herbs. Refrigerate 1 hour before serving, stirring once or twice.

Makes 4 servings.

PER SERVING: Cal 57 • Carbo 8 gm • Prot 1 gm • Total fat 3 gm • Sat fat trace • Cal from fat 47% • Chol 0 mg

VARIATION
Combine two or more cooked vegetables before marinating. Always cook the vegetables separately to maintain flavors.

EDUCATION: Marinate vegetables to change the pace and increase their appeal. Serve the marinated vegetables on a bed of spinach or lettuce, or chop and add to tossed salad. A side dish of marinated vegetables, garnished with fresh herbs, is also attractive. Do not overcook vegetables before marinating, or they will end up soggy, not crisp.

Rainbow Picnic Potato Salad

A real hit at our picnic; several people asked for the recipe. The secret? Garden-fresh herbs in the mayonnaise-free dressing—a colorful counterpoint to the red potatoes, bell pepper and onion.

8 to 10 new red potatoes, halved or quartered
2 celery stalks, thinly sliced on the diagonal
1 medium-size red onion, chopped
1/2 green bell pepper, diced
1/2 red bell pepper, diced
1 green onion, thinly sliced on the diagonal
3 tablespoons olive oil
3 tablespoons brown rice vinegar
1 tablespoon fresh lemon juice
1 garlic clove, pushed through a press
1 tablespoon minced fresh parsley
2 teaspoons minced fresh basil
1 teaspoon dry mustard
1/2 teaspoon minced fresh tarragon
1/4 teaspoon salt
1/8 teaspoon freshly ground black pepper

Cook potatoes in a large saucepan, covered with water, 20 to 25 minutes or until tender, but not soft. Drain and toss hot potatoes with celery, red onion, bell peppers and green onion.

Combine olive oil, vinegar, lemon juice, garlic, parsley, basil, yellow mustard, tarragon, salt and pepper in a small bowl. Pour over salad and toss to combine. Can be served at room temperature or chilled. *Makes 8 servings.*

PER SERVING: Cal 176 • Carbo 30 gm • Prot 3 gm • Total fat 5 gm • Sat fat 1 gm • Cal from fat 27% • Chol 0 mg

EDUCATION: Skip the mayonnaise-based dressings when packing for picnics. You'll not only reduce the cholesterol content of your salads, but lower the risk of foodborne illness when there's no refrigeration. Oil and vinegar, with fresh herbs, above, make a flavorful substitution.

July 2

INSPIRATION: *My enthusiasm is contagious, a gift I can give to everyone around me.*

Hamburger Patties with Fresh Tomato Relish

❧ Lean meat gains fiber and nutrients with the addition of carrot, onion and a touch of bran. Grill or broil, then top with fresh tomato relish.

1 cup Fresh Tomato Relish (see below)
1 carrot
1 onion
1 pound extra-lean ground beef
2 tablespoons unprocessed wheat bran
1 egg white
¼ teaspoon salt

⅛ teaspoon ground black pepper
4 whole-grain rolls
½ cup alfalfa sprouts

FRESH TOMATO RELISH
1 large garden-ripe tomato, peeled,
*   seeded and chopped*
1 green onion, finely minced
1 garlic clove, pushed through a press
1 teaspoon olive oil
1 teaspoon balsamic vinegar
Dash of salt and pepper

For relish, combine tomato, green onion, garlic, olive oil, vinegar, salt and pepper. Cover and set aside.

Preheat grill or broiler. Finely grate carrot and onion or process until finely minced in a food processor fitted with the steel blade. Combine beef with carrot, onion, bran, egg white, salt and pepper. Form into 4 (1-inch-thick) patties. Sear the meat close to the heat to seal in juices, then grill or broil 5 or 6 minutes per side, or according to desired doneness. Serve the patties on rolls topped with relish and sprouts. *Makes 4 servings.*

PER SERVING: Cal 425 • Carbo 31 gm • Prot 27 gm • Total fat 21 gm • Sat fat 8 gm • Cal from fat 44% • Chol 76 mg

EDUCATION: Add relish to your meals with fresh vegetables in season! In summer, when tomatoes are at their peak, this versatile Fresh Tomato Relish can grace any dish: hamburgers, fish, soups, poultry or pasta. One friend loves to stir Fresh Tomato Relish into cottage cheese for a low-fat lunch.

If you want to serve the relish with Mexican-style dishes, add a teaspoon of minced, fresh cilantro and/or a little minced jalapeño chile (see glossary). When you add the relish, you're also adding vitamins C and A with the tomato, important to your immune system.

INSPIRATION: *Holding tightly to events and trying to control them pulls me off balance. Trust and faith can help me to stay centered.*

Gazpacho Soup

❧ One of those wonderful cold soups that take the heat off in summer. This soup boasts a bounty of foods found fresh in local gardens.

> 4 large garden-ripe tomatoes,
>   peeled, seeded and chopped
> 3 mushrooms, chopped
> 1 medium-size cucumber, peeled, seeded
>   and finely chopped
> 1 medium-size green bell pepper, finely diced
> 1 small onion, grated
> 1/4 cup minced fresh parsley
> 1/4 cup minced fresh basil
> 1/4 cup fresh lemon juice
> 1 1/2 tablespoons white vinegar
> 2 green onions, thinly sliced
> 2 garlic cloves, minced
> 3 cups tomato juice
> 1/4 teaspoon salt
> 1/8 teaspoon freshly ground black pepper
> 1/2 cup nonfat yogurt for garnish
> Basil or parsley sprigs for garnish

Combine tomatoes, mushrooms, cucumber, bell pepper, onion, parsley, basil, lemon juice, vinegar, green onions, garlic, tomato juice, salt and pepper in a large bowl. Cover and refrigerate until chilled thoroughly. Serve garnished with a dollop of yogurt and sprigs of fresh herbs. *Makes 6 servings.*

PER SERVING: Cal 115 • Carbo 16 gm • Prot 4 gm • Total fat 0 gm • Sat fat 0 gm • Cal from fat 0% • Chol 1 mg

VARIATION
Stir in some cubes of day-old French or Italian bread before serving.

EDUCATION: Keep healthful foods handy for immediate gratification. Since this soup is served chilled, it is perfect for a quick meal or snack straight out of the refrigerator! And note the range of nutritious, low-fat ingredients that define gazpacho. Rich in variety, this soup is lean where it really counts. Keep melba toast on hand for a contrasting, low-fat crunch.

INSPIRATION: *Making the "right choice" is not as important as having the freedom to make mistakes.*

Fourth of July Almond Meringues

❧ Toasted almonds add a special flavor to low-fat meringue, decked out with red raspberries and blueberries for the holiday!

> 2/3 cup blanched almonds
> 3 egg whites, at room temperature
> 1/8 teaspoon salt
> 1 cup vanilla sugar
>   (see glossary)
> 4 small scoops nonfat vanilla
>   frozen yogurt
> 1 cup red raspberries
> 1 cup blueberries

Preheat oven to 325°F (165°C). Spread almonds in a baking pan and bake 5 minutes, stirring once or twice, or until lightly browned. Set aside to cool. Reduce oven heat to 250°F (120°C). Butter and flour a baking sheet, shaking off excess flour. Mark four 4-inch circles on the floured surface.

Beat egg whites with salt until soft peaks form. Add sugar gradually, beating after each addition, until whites are glossy and form stiff peaks. When almonds are completely cooled, grind in a food processor or grinder just until mealy. Fold ground almonds into the egg whites.

Place meringue in a pastry bag with a ½-inch plain tip and pipe in a spiral to fill each circle, or spoon meringue into circles and swirl surface with the back of the spoon. Bake 45 minutes or until nearly dry. Remove meringues with a spatula and cool on the racks of the turned-off oven.

To serve, place meringues on individual plates. Place a scoop of frozen yogurt on the meringue and arrange some of the raspberries on one side of the meringue, the blueberries on the other. *Makes 4 servings.*

PER SERVING: Cal 335 • Carbo 52 gm • Prot 10 gm • Total fat 11 gm • Sat fat 2 gm • Cal from fat 30% • Chol 0 mg

EDUCATION: Declare your independence from high-fat desserts. Substitute nonfat frozen yogurt for rich ice creams throughout the summer, and enjoy creamy flavor without the fat. Contrasting the crisp texture of meringue lifts this dessert out of the ordinary while colorful berries add a patriotic flair.

July 5

INSPIRATION: *By trying to block bad feelings, I also block the good, which stunts my emotional and spiritual growth and my enjoyment of life.*

Rich's Lemon-Garlic Chicken Salad Bowl

❧ Serve with romaine lettuce and melba toast as a luncheon dish or light supper accompanied by soup.

1 cup diced cooked boneless chicken breast
¼ cup Vidalia or other sweet
    onion, finely chopped
3 tablespoons reduced-fat mayonnaise
2 tablespoons nonfat yogurt
2 tablespoons fresh lemon juice
⅛ teaspoon freshly grated lemon peel
1 garlic clove, pushed through
    a press
¼ teaspoon salt
¼ teaspoon freshly ground
    black pepper
8 romaine lettuce leaves
1 tablespoon minced fresh parsley
6 cucumber slices for garnish
2 lemon slices for garnish

Combine chicken, onion, mayonnaise, yogurt, lemon juice and peel, garlic, salt and pepper in a medium-size bowl. Arrange 4 romaine lettuce leaves in each of 2 bowls and top with a mound of chicken salad. Sprinkle with parsley and garnish with cucumber and lemon slices. *Makes 2 servings.*

PER SERVING: Cal 134 • Carbo 9 gm • Prot 15 gm • Total fat 5 gm • Sat fat 1 gm • Cal from fat 33% • Chol 40 mg

EDUCATION: Cultivate friends who take an interest in what is important to you. It's a plus if they also have a sense of humor. When Rich shared his recipe with me for this book, he offered the following meditation: "Before partaking of this recipe, give a moment of gratitude to the grove of lemon trees for sharing their energies, to the rows of onions for sharing their energies, to the fields of garlic for sharing their energies... and try not to think about the chicken."

INSPIRATION: *Sharing my faith, hope, experience and strengths helps light the way for others on the path to recovery.*

Herbed Summer Squash Sauté with Leeks

🌿 Choose small, sweet, delicate early summer squash. Good with fish, pork or poultry.

1 large leek
2 small zucchini
2 small yellow squash
2 teaspoons butter
1 tablespoon minced fresh
*   parsley*
¹/₂ teaspoon minced fresh basil
¹/₄ teaspoon freshly grated
*   lemon peel*
¹/₈ teaspoon salt
¹/₈ teaspoon freshly ground
*   black pepper*

Trim leek to within 2 inches of white part. Trim root end and cut leek in half lengthwise. Separate leaves and rinse well to remove any dirt. Slice zucchini and squash ¹/₄ inch thick.

Chop leek and cook in the butter in a large, nonstick skillet over medium heat, stirring frequently, about 4 minutes or until tender. Stir in zucchini and yellow squash and cook, stirring frequently, 5 minutes, or until squash is crisp-tender. Stir in parsley, basil, lemon peel, salt and pepper.   *Makes 4 servings.*

PER SERVING: Cal 73 • Carbo 13 gm • Prot 2 gm • Total fat 2 gm • Sat fat 1 gm • Cal from fat 29% • Chol 5 mg

EDUCATION: Eat summer squash in their skins—that's where the beta-carotene is. Choose young, fresh summer squash so the skins are tender. Summer squash are mostly water. If you are adding squash to other dishes, steam or blanch the whole squash 5 to 8 minutes, until slightly tender. This will help remove excess liquid.

INSPIRATION: *My mind is nourished by new activities. Let me be open to new ways of doing things.*

Golden Tomato Soup

🌿 Golden yellow tomatoes give this soup its characteristic color—but the soup is just as delicious with regular red tomatoes.

1 cup chopped onion
1 cup chopped celery
¹/₂ cup chopped carrots
1 tablespoon butter
1 tablespoon unbleached
*   all-purpose flour*
1 teaspoon Madras curry powder
¹/₂ teaspoon paprika
¹/₂ teaspoon salt
¹/₄ teaspoon freshly ground
*   white pepper*
5 cups peeled, seeded and diced
*   yellow tomatoes*
2 cups chicken broth
2 garlic cloves, pushed through
*   a press*
6 large basil leaves or ¹/₂ teaspoon
*   dried basil*
1 teaspoon sugar
¹/₂ cup low-fat (1%) milk

Cook onion, celery and carrots in the butter in a nonstick Dutch oven over medium heat 10 minutes or until vegetables begin to get tender. Stir in flour, curry powder, paprika, salt and pepper and cook 1 minute.

Add tomatoes, chicken broth and garlic and cook 15 minutes, until tomatoes are tender. Stir in basil, sugar and milk. Puree in small batches and return to pan. Heat through before serving. *Makes 8 servings.*

PER SERVING: Cal 78 • Carbo 12 gm • Prot 4 gm • Total fat 3 gm • Sat fat 2 gm • Cal from fat 34% • Chol 8 mg

EDUCATION: Create the unexpected with color. Tomatoes, zucchini and stuffed peppers, for example, get a second glance when they arrive at the table in other than the standard red or green. Visual interest can help stimulate appetites, helping meet your goal of more vegetables on (and eaten from) the dinner table.

July 8

INSPIRATION: *Let me take advantage of the many opportunities I will encounter to learn something today.*

Ricotta Cheesecake with Blueberry Sauce

❧ Lighter than its New York cousins by a country mile!

1 tablespoon unsalted butter, softened
$^1/_3$ cup zwieback or graham
    cracker crumbs
1 (8-ounce) package nonfat cream
    cheese, softened
2 cups nonfat ricotta cheese
$^1/_2$ cup low-fat (1%) creamed cottage
    cheese
$^1/_2$ cup vanilla sugar (see glossary)
2 eggs
2 tablespoons fresh lemon juice
2 cups fresh or frozen blueberries
1 tablespoon pure maple syrup
1 teaspoon cornstarch
$^1/_4$ cup water

Preheat oven to 350°F (175°C). For crust, coat a 9-inch springform pan with the butter. Swirl crumbs in the springform pan, coating bottom and sides. Smooth excess crumbs on bottom of pan, building up in thickness along outside perimeter of the pan. Chill while preparing filling.

Combine cream cheese, ricotta, cottage cheese, vanilla sugar, eggs and lemon juice in a food processor or blender and process until smooth. Pour into prepared springform pan and bake 45 minutes or until cheesecake is semifirm throughout. Turn off oven, open door and allow cheesecake to cool to room temperature. Refrigerate until chilled.

Combine blueberries with maple syrup in a medium-size microwave-safe bowl. Stir cornstarch into water and pour over blueberries. Microwave on HIGH 2 or 3 minutes, until sauce comes to a boil and thickens slightly. To serve, remove outer ring from springform pan. Cut cheesecake into 8 slices. Serve each with blueberry sauce spooned over top.

Makes 8 servings.

PER SERVING: Cal 332 • Carbo 43 gm • Prot 13 gm • Total fat 10 gm • Sat fat 9 gm • Cal from fat 27% • Chol 86 mg

EDUCATION: Keep your potassium intake balanced. When the sodium-potassium ratio is out of whack, many people with vulnerability get high blood pressure. Many processed foods and meat products are high in sodium, increasing the need for potassium-rich foods. For balance, you may want not only to cut back on salty foods, but to enjoy potassium-rich foods like the berries above.

INSPIRATION: *Part of being healthy is the realization that there are always options.*

Hummus-Spread Sandwich Buffet

Let everyone make choices about how to build their own sandwich—with lots of healthful ingredients on hand, they can't go wrong!

> $^1/_4$ cup sesame seeds
> 3 garlic cloves, minced
> 2 tablespoons plus 1 teaspoon
>   olive oil
> 2 cups cooked chick-peas (see note)
> $^2/_3$ cup chick-pea cooking liquid
> 2 or 3 tablespoons fresh lemon juice
> $^1/_4$ teaspoon salt
> 2 cups peeled, seeded and diced
>   ripe tomatoes
> Dash of freshly ground black pepper
> 2 cups shredded romaine lettuce
> 2 cups chopped red or yellow
>   bell peppers
> 1 cup thinly sliced green onions
> 1 cup sliced mushrooms
> 1 cup alfalfa sprouts
> 1 cup nonfat yogurt
> $^1/_2$ cup minced fresh parsley
> $^1/_4$ cup minced fresh cilantro
> Parsley sprigs for garnish
> 20 small or 10 large pocket
>   pita breads

Place sesame seeds in a food processor or blender container with 2 garlic cloves and the 2 tablespoons olive oil and process until combined. Add $^1/_4$ cup of the chick-peas and process until combined. Add remaining chick-peas, the cooking liquid, lemon juice to taste and salt. Process until combined, scraping down the sides of the container as needed. Chill hummus.

Combine tomatoes, remaining clove of garlic, remaining teaspoon oil and pepper. Place in a serving bowl. Place lettuce, bell peppers, green onions, mushrooms, sprouts, yogurt and combined herbs in separate serving dishes. Place hummus in serving dish and garnish with parsley sprigs. Cut breads in half to form 2 pockets for each pita. Let each person select his or her own sandwich ingredients.

Makes 10 servings.

PER SERVING: Cal 242 • Carbo 36 gm • Prot 10 gm • Total fat 7 gm • Sat fat 1 gm • Cal from fat 26% • Chol 0 mg

NOTE: If using canned chick-peas, purchase them without preservatives. To cook your own, begin with 2 cups dried chick-peas, soak overnight or use quick-soak method (see glossary), then simmer 2 to 2$^1/_2$ hours until quite tender. Drain. Use extra chick-peas in soups or salads or freeze for later use.

EDUCATION: Toast chick-peas and eat them in place of high-fat roasted peanuts, cashews or other nuts. Chick-peas have far less than a tenth the fat of peanuts. Heat cooked chick-peas on a baking sheet in a preheated 400°F (200°C) oven 5 to 10 minutes. Season with salt, sesame salt, chili powder or hot (cayenne) pepper, according to your taste.

INSPIRATION: *By keeping my mind open to life's pos-sibilities, I make room for the unknown and invite change.*

Salmon Grilled with Brown Sugar Glaze

❧ Anne discovered and re-created this recipe after a trip to Alaska, where the salmon is plen-tiful and fresh-from-the-water delicious!

> *4 small salmon fillets (about*
> *   1 1/2 pounds total)*
> *1 tablespoon unsalted butter*
> *2 tablespoons fresh lemon juice*
> *1 tablespoon brown sugar*
> *1/4 teaspoon salt*
> *Lemon slices for garnish*

Prepare grill. Grill salmon fillets skin side up over medium coals 4 minutes. While fillets are grilling, melt butter in a small saucepan and stir in lemon juice, brown sugar and salt. Turn salmon fillets and grill, brushing frequently with glaze, 4 or 5 minutes, or until cooked through. Garnish with lemon slices.

Makes 4 servings.

PER SERVING: Cal 261 • Carbo 4 gm • Prot 34 gm • Total fat 11 gm • Sat fat 2 gm • Cal from fat 39% • Chol 95 mg

EDUCATION: Try different flavors to create new interest in nutritious foods such as fish. You've probably not combined salmon with brown sugar before, but, enhanced by the smoky taste of the grill, you'll find it an inspired combination. If it encourages you to eat more salmon, you're ahead. Salmon is super-rich in vitamin B_{12}, important to help maintain your central nervous system. Just 3 1/2 ounces offers three times the recommended daily allowance.

INSPIRATION: *I am willing to take actions today that are in my own best interest.*

Dusty's Curried Mixed Summer Vegetables

🍴 Hearty and robustly flavored, this main dish can persuade even dyed-in-the-wool meat-eaters that eating "vegetarian" has its good points.

1 1/2 cups brown rice

3 cups water

2 onions, chopped

2 celery stalks, thinly sliced

1 tablespoon canola oil

2 garlic cloves, minced

2 tablespoons Madras curry powder

1 teaspoon minced gingerroot

1/4 teaspoon salt

1/4 teaspoon freshly ground black pepper

1/8 teaspoon hot (cayenne) pepper

1 large potato, unpeeled, diced

1 small head cauliflower, separated
   into flowerets

1 cup fresh or frozen green peas

1/2 cup vegetable stock or water

5 large tomatoes, peeled, seeded
   and diced

1 cup tomato juice

1 teaspoon brown sugar

1 teaspoon sesame seeds

Bring rice and water to a boil in a large saucepan and boil 1 minute. Reduce heat, cover and simmer 35 to 40 minutes, until the water is absorbed and the rice is tender. Remove from heat and keep covered.

Cook onions and celery in the oil in a non-stick Dutch oven over medium heat, stirring frequently, until onions are translucent. Add the garlic, curry powder, gingerroot, salt, pep-per and cayenne and cook, stirring, 1 minute. Add potato, cauliflower, peas, if using fresh, and vegetable stock or water. Bring to a boil, reduce heat, cover and simmer 5 minutes, until vegetables are crisp-tender.

Add tomatoes, tomato juice, and brown sugar. Bring to a boil, reduce heat, cover and simmer 15 minutes, stirring occasionally. Add peas and cook 3 to 5 minutes more, until vegetables are tender. Toast sesame seeds in a small dry skillet over low heat 3 or 4 minutes, stirring frequently, until golden brown.

Serve curried vegetables over rice. Sprinkle with toasted sesame seeds.   *Makes 4 servings.*

PER SERVING: Cal 505 • Carbo 99 gm • Prot 15 gm • Total fat 8 gm • Sat fat 1 gm • Cal from fat 14% • Chol 0 mg

EDUCATION: Explore cuisines that feature tasty, low-fat vegetarian main dishes. In many parts of the world, meat is absent or infrequent on the dinner table. Cultures have survived by selecting (probably hit or miss) vegetable sources of protein that sustained them. Families making the right choices thrived, passing their food selections on to their offspring. Twentieth-century scientists have found these selections to contain complementary pro-teins—one food compensating for another's lack of an essential amino acid. Rice and bean curd in the Far East and beans and corn or flour tortillas in Mexico are two examples of cuisines based on complementing beans and grain. This Indian-style combination features vegetables, seeds and rice for a protein-rich main dish.

INSPIRATION: *Sensitivity, understanding and healing are born of the process of recovery, everything happening in its own time.*

Ratatouille with Pasta

❧ When my son was small, we called this "ratatat-touey." But even he was charmed by the traditional French dish of eggplant and summer vegetables, served here over pasta.

1 onion, chopped
1 tablespoon olive oil
2 garlic cloves, minced
1 medium-size eggplant, diced
3 medium-size zucchini, diced
¹/₂ green bell pepper, cut into
    2-inch strips
¹/₂ red bell pepper, cut into
    2-inch strips
¹/₂ cup water
1 teaspoon minced fresh oregano
    leaves or ¹/₂ teaspoon dried
1 teaspoon minced fresh thyme leaves
    or ¹/₂ teaspoon dried
8 fresh basil leaves, minced, or
    ¹/₂ teaspoon dried
¹/₂ teaspoon salt
¹/₄ teaspoon freshly ground
    black pepper
8 ounces penne pasta
2 large tomatoes, cut into wedges
1 tablespoon minced fresh parsley
¹/₄ cup freshly grated Parmesan cheese

Cook onion in the oil in a nonstick Dutch oven over medium heat, stirring frequently, until onion is tender, about 5 minutes. Add garlic and cook, stirring, 1 minute. Add diced eggplant, zucchini, bell peppers, water, herbs, if using dried, salt and pepper. Bring to a boil, reduce heat, cover and simmer 20 minutes or until vegetables are tender, stirring occasionally.

Meanwhile, bring a large pot of water to a boil. Cook pasta 7 to 10 minutes or until firm-tender. Drain. Add herbs, if using fresh, tomato wedges and parsley to vegetable mixture and heat through. Serve over pasta, sprinkled with Parmesan cheese. *Makes 4 servings.*

PER SERVING: Cal 343 • Carbo 59 gm • Prot 13 gm • Total fat 7 gm • Sat fat 2 gm • Cal from fat 18% • Chol 5 mg

EDUCATION: Change the way you think about fat and cut it from familiar favorite recipes. Time was, we used ¹/₃ cup of oil to cook the vegetables separately. Now, with the help of a nonstick Dutch oven, and a slight change in the recipe, the entire dish features just 1 tablespoon of oil. By using fresh herbs and garden-fresh vegetables for the dish, no one misses the fat.

INSPIRATION: *Giving up the predictability of the old is the only way of finding out what the new can be for me.*

Garlic Bruschetta

🌿 Crusty bread oven-baked with garlic is complemented by a ripe tomato topping—great as an appetizer before an Italian-style meal. Try the mozzarella version and serve with soups.

> 5 large garlic cloves
> 8 diagonally cut slices day-old
>   Italian bread
> 2 cups peeled, seeded and
>   chopped tomatoes
> 1 tablespoon extra-virgin olive oil
> 1 tablespoon minced fresh parsley
> 1 teaspoon minced fresh basil leaves
> 1/4 teaspoon salt
> 1/8 teaspoon freshly ground
>   black pepper

Preheat oven to 400°F (200°C). Peel and halve 4 of the garlic cloves. Rub a cut edge thoroughly over both sides of each bread slice. Arrange the bread on an ungreased baking sheet and bake 5 to 8 minutes, until golden brown.

Meanwhile, combine tomatoes, oil, parsley, basil, salt, pepper and the remaining garlic clove, pushed through a press, in a small bowl. Let stand at room temperature. To serve, allow each person to spoon tomato topping on bread slices.   *Makes 4 servings.*

PER SERVING: Cal 230 • Carbo 41 gm • Prot 7 gm • Total fat 3 gm • Sat fat trace • Cal from fat 12% • Chol 0 mg

VARIATION
Garlic Bruschetta with Mozzarella Shred 4 ounces (1 cup) part-skim mozzarella cheese. Top garlic bread with tomato topping. Sprinkle with cheese and place under a preheated broiler until cheese is melted.

EDUCATION: Don't let oil- and butter-rich garlic bread ruin an otherwise healthy low-fat Italian meal. The version above, dry-baked, provides the appealing flavor of garlic bread without adding a drop of fat. For plain garlic bread, just eliminate the topping. Day-old Italian bread holds up better as you rub in the freshly sliced garlic.

INSPIRATION: *I am learning to eat for my health, not for the numbers on my scale or the size rack where I shop.*

Linguini with Scallops & Shrimp

🌿 A pasta dish for entertaining: serve this seafood extravaganza with a big, tossed green salad made with a variety of ingredients, such as the salad featured July 25.

> 1 pound linguini
> 1/4 cup diced red bell pepper
> 1 shallot, minced
> 3 garlic cloves, minced
> Dash of red pepper flakes
> 1 tablespoon olive oil
> 1 pound sea scallops, halved crosswise
> 1 pound medium-size shrimp, shelled
>   and deveined (see glossary)
> Juice and grated peel of 1 lemon
> 3 large Italian plum tomatoes, peeled
>   and diced
> 4 cups packed chopped spinach leaves

¹/₄ cup minced fresh basil
2 tablespoons minced fresh parsley
¹/₂ teaspoon salt

Bring a large pot of water to a boil. Cook linguini 9 to 11 minutes, or until firm-tender. Drain.

Meanwhile, cook bell pepper, shallot, garlic and pepper flakes in the oil in a large nonstick Dutch oven over medium heat, stirring frequently, 2 or 3 minutes or until vegetables are crisp-tender. Add the scallops, shrimp, lemon juice and lemon peel and cook, stirring, 1 minute. Add remaining ingredients and cook, stirring frequently, 2 or 3 minutes or until spinach is tender. Toss with linguini in a large serving bowl.   *Makes 6 servings.*

PER SERVING: Cal 301 • Carbo 29 gm • Prot 34 gm • Total fat 5 gm • Sat fat 1 gm • Cal from fat 16% • Chol 167 mg

EDUCATION: Measure oil or butter into a heated pan when sautéing foods. If you add oil without measuring, chances are you'll use more than asked for in your recipes. And each extra *tablespoon* adds an extra 120 calories! A heated pan will let a little oil go a long way as you swirl the hot oil to cover the bottom of the pan.

July 15

INSPIRATION: *I know that if I cannot discover peace and tranquillity within myself, I will not find it elsewhere.*

Blueberry Pie with Red Currants

🌿 Blueberries and currants, vibrant in color and in taste, nestle like jewels in a crumb crust.

1 Low-Calorie Graham Cracker
   Crust (see June 28)
4 cups blueberries
¹/₄ cup red currants
¹/₂ cup water
¹/₄ cup pure maple syrup
2 tablespoons cornstarch
¹/₈ teaspoon salt

Prepare crust.

Combine blueberries, currants, water, maple syrup, cornstarch and salt in a medium-size saucepan. Cook over medium heat, stirring, until the mixture is thickened and clear, 7 to 8 minutes. Let filling cool, but not set. Pour into the pie shell and chill before serving.

Makes 8 servings.

PER SERVING: Cal 156 • Carbo 28 gm • Prot 1 gm • Total fat 5 gm • Sat fat 3 gm • Cal from fat 29% • Chol 11 mg

EDUCATION: Extend the healthful berry and currant season by freezing your own area's ripe-picked. There's very little in life that's easier. Don't wash berries; save that for when you're defrosting them for use. Spread berries out on a baking sheet and place the sheet in your freezer. When berries are hard-frozen, put them in heavy, self-sealing plastic bags or containers with lids. The berries will stay separated and you can use as many or as few as you like throughout the year. Small, red currants are especially attractive in baked goods and fruit salads as Thanksgiving and Christmas holidays approach.

INSPIRATION: *Creating an attractive dish, adding music or flowers to a meal nurtures my spirit in the same way good foods nurture my body.*

INSPIRATION: *Part of being a functional person is making good choices—in what I eat, what I say and what I do.*

Melon Breakfast Bowl with Berries

❧ The fruits of summer: melons, berries, nectarines. Indulge in a bountiful assortment of fruits and berries for luxurious flavor, parsimonious fats.

1/2 cantaloupe, seeded
1/2 cup part-skim ricotta cheese
1/2 nectarine, thinly sliced
1 tablespoon honey-toasted wheat germ
1/2 cup red raspberries, blueberries
    or blackberries
Mint sprig for garnish

Place the melon half on a plate and place half the nectarine slices in the center. Add ricotta cheese. Sprinkle with wheat germ and top with remaining nectarine slices and berries. Garnish with mint. *Makes 1 serving.*

PER SERVING: Cal 343 • Carbo 45 gm • Prot 19 gm • Total fat 12 gm • Sat fat 6 gm • Cal from fat 31% • Chol 38 mg

EDUCATION: Mellow out with summer melons. High in potassium, which is vital for nerve function, melons are a sweet and juicy source of this important mineral. There is evidence that a high-potassium diet can reduce your risk of hypertension and stroke. Melons offer a pleasant means to that healthy end.

Cherry-Ginger Chicken Breasts

❧ Like berries, cherries can be easily frozen to extend enjoyment throughout the year. Simply halve, pit and freeze, cut side up, on a baking sheet. Store in heavy, self-sealing bags when frozen.

2 boneless skinless chicken breasts, halved
1 garlic clove, minced
1/4 teaspoon salt
1/4 teaspoon ground ginger
1 small onion, finely chopped
1/2 tablespoon unsalted butter
1 teaspoon minced gingerroot
1 1/2 cups fresh sweet cherries, halved
    and pitted
2/3 cup chicken broth
1/4 teaspoon ground cinnamon
1 tablespoon cornstarch
2 tablespoons water
2 tablespoons fresh lemon juice
1/4 teaspoon freshly grated lemon peel

Preheat oven to 375°F (190°C). Rub chicken breasts with a mixture of the garlic, salt and ginger. Bake in a shallow casserole dish, skin side up, 40 to 50 minutes, or until chicken is tender.

Cook onion in the butter in a medium-size nonstick skillet over medium heat, stirring frequently, until onion is translucent. Add gingerroot and cook, stirring, 1 minute. Add cherries, broth and cinnamon and bring to a boil.

Stir cornstarch into water. Add with lemon juice and peel to cherry mixture and cook, stirring, 2 or 3 minutes, or just until mixture is thickened.

Remove skin from chicken, and place chicken on a warmed platter. Top with cherry sauce.   *Makes 4 servings.*

PER SERVING: Cal 303 • Carbo 33 gm • Prot 30 gm • Total fat 6 gm • Sat fat 2 gm • Cal from fat 18% • Chol 77 mg

EDUCATION: Replace fantasy with nutritious reality. Though we've all seen the pitfalls of trying to live the fantasy that "life is just a bowl of cherries," it's easy to see why this fruit inspired such a euphoric declaration. Cherries are jolly: sweet, juicy, colorful, convenient, nutritious and low in calories. The only preparation needed is to remove the stem and pit. Easy! An inexpensive cherry pitter can help you prepare cherries in quantity for freezing cherries whole or for preparing dishes like the one above.

July 18

INSPIRATION: *In trying something new, I can eliminate self-defeating beliefs and affirm my worth: "I may not be doing this perfectly, but I am learning."*

Curried Broccoli Soup
with Watercress

❧ Served chilled, this soup can be refreshing on a warm summer evening.

1 cup thinly sliced leeks (see glossary)
2 teaspoons olive oil
2 garlic cloves, minced
1 teaspoon Madras curry powder
1/2 teaspoon ground coriander
1/4 teaspoon ground cumin
3 cups chicken broth
1 large carrot, halved across

1 large stalk broccoli
1 cup trimmed watercress
1/2 cup skim milk
1/4 teaspoon salt

Cook leeks in the oil over medium heat, stirring frequently, until the leeks are wilted. Add the garlic, curry powder, coriander and cumin and cook, stirring, 2 minutes. Add broth and carrot and bring to a boil. Reduce heat, cover and simmer, 5 to 8 minutes, or until carrot is firm-tender. Remove carrot and set aside.

Meanwhile, trim, peel and slice broccoli stem and separate head into flowerets. Add to broth and return to a boil. Reduce heat, cover and simmer 10 to 12 minutes, just until firm-tender. Stir in watercress and simmer 4 to 5 minutes, until watercress is wilted.

Puree soup in batches in a blender or food processor until smooth. Place in large bowl and thin with milk. Dice carrot and add to soup. Season with salt. Cover and chill 2 hours or more before serving.   *Makes 4 servings.*

PER SERVING: Cal 125 • Carbo 16 gm • Prot 7 gm • Total fat 4 gm • Sat fat trace • Cal from fat 28% • Chol trace

EDUCATION: Explore many different ways to enjoy broccoli, one of the healthiest foods you can eat (if you avoid that sauce). A member of the cruciferous vegetables, and therefore considered to be effective against cancer, broccoli is also a powerhouse of vitamin C, vitamin A and folic acid. Versatile broccoli can be added to main dishes, side dishes, soups or salads—or served raw with a low-calorie dip.

INSPIRATION: *To ensure the best possible future, all I can do is to live as well as I am able, today.*

Chunky Marinated Vegetable Salad

❦ Make ahead and chill before serving. Unlike green salads that wilt, leftovers of this salad are great the next day. For a great party look, line the serving bowl with large red cabbage leaves.

> 1/2 small head cabbage
> 2 yellow summer squash
> 1 zucchini
> 1 cucumber
> 1 purple or orange bell pepper
> 1 red bell pepper
> 2 green onions
> 1/2 cup cider vinegar
> 1/4 cup honey
> 2 tablespoons canola oil
> 1 teaspoon dry yellow mustard
> 1/2 teaspoon salt
> 1/4 teaspoon freshly ground black pepper

Coarsely shred cabbage with a knife. Cut summer squash and zucchini into bite-size pieces. If cucumber is waxed, peel then halve lengthwise, remove seeds and cut into bite-size pieces. Remove seeds from bell peppers and cut into bite-size pieces. Slice green onions on the diagonal into 1-inch lengths. Place vegetables in a large glass or stainless steel bowl.

Bring vinegar, honey, oil, dry mustard, salt and pepper to a boil in a small saucepan and cook 1 minute. Pour the hot dressing over the vegetables and toss gently to mix well. Cover and refrigerate 6 hours or longer, stirring occasionally. *Makes 8 servings.*

PER SERVING: Cal 93 • Carbo 16 gm • Prot 2 gm • Total fat 3 gm • Sat fat trace • Cal from fat 37% • Chol 0 mg

EDUCATION: Remove the "burp" from low-calorie cucumbers to increase their popularity. The Pennsylvania Dutch have used the following technique for taming cucumbers: cut about 1/2 inch off the blossom end of the cucumber. Rub the cut edges of the cucumber together in a circular motion for about a minute. Rinse away the white foam and discard the end. Cucumbers are a cooling, practically nonfat addition to summer soups, salads and dressings.

INSPIRATION: *Being satisfied with the progress I have made so far and having patience that the rest will come in time free me to have new joy in living.*

Skillet Spaghetti with Garden Tomatoes

❦ Garden tomatoes, green onions, zucchini and basil add fresh flavor to this easy dinner. Serve with bread and a green salad.

> 1/2 pound lean ground beef
> 2 green onions, sliced
> 2 garlic cloves, minced
> 1 1/2 cups peeled, seeded and chopped
>   ripe tomatoes
> 1 medium-size zucchini, diced
> 2 1/4 cups water
> 1 (15-ounce) can tomato sauce
> 1/2 pound uncooked spaghetti
> 2 tablespoons minced fresh basil or
>   1/2 teaspoon dried
> 1 teaspoon fresh marjoram leaves or
>   1/4 teaspoon dried
> 1/4 teaspoon salt
> 1/4 teaspoon freshly ground
>   black pepper

Brown beef over medium heat with the green onions and garlic, breaking up beef as it cooks and stirring frequently. Stir in tomatoes, zucchini and ½ cup of water and simmer over low heat, uncovered, 5 minutes or until zucchini begins to get tender. Add remaining water, tomato sauce, pasta and seasonings. Bring to a boil, cover, reduce heat and simmer 12 to 15 minutes, stirring 3 or 4 times, until pasta is firm-tender. *Makes 4 servings.*

PER SERVING: Cal 303 • Carbo 32 gm • Prot 16 gm • Total fat 12 gm • Sat fat 5 gm • Cal from fat 36% • Chol 42 mg

EDUCATION: Make life easier by cooking one-pan, stove-top meals. This dish calls for the spaghetti to be cooked right in the skillet, eliminating the additional pot for pasta water. You'll simplify cleanup and avoid steaming up the kitchen on hot summer days, making it easier to "keep your cool." Substitute a variety of pastas to vary this easy skillet dinner.

July 21

INSPIRATION: *Affirming my good qualities helps them become stronger.*

Grilled Tuna with Orzo, Red Pepper & Basil

❧ Serve with grill-baked potatoes, corn-on-the-cob and a green salad for a summer-style feast!

1 lime
4 tuna steaks (about 1½ pounds)
1 red bell pepper
1¼ cups orzo pasta
1 small shallot

1 small tomato
8 to 12 fresh basil leaves
1 tablespoon olive oil
1 tablespoon brown rice vinegar
¼ teaspoon salt
Dash of hot (cayenne) pepper

Preheat grill or broiler. Grate zest from lime and squeeze juice. Combine zest and lime juice and brush over tuna steaks. Cover and refrigerate.

Roast bell pepper on the grill or under a broiler until the skin blackens and blisters on all sides. Wrap in a wet paper towel and set aside. Bring a large saucepan of water to a boil. Add orzo and cook 8 to 10 minutes or until firm-tender.

Meanwhile, peel and coarsely chop shallot. Peel and seed tomato.

When bell pepper has cooled enough to handle, remove skin, stem and seeds. Place bell pepper, shallot, tomato, basil leaves, oil, vinegar, salt and hot pepper in a food processor or blender and process until smooth.

Grill tuna steaks 2 or 3 minutes per side or just until cooked through. Do not overcook. Drain orzo. Place orzo on a serving plate, top with grilled tuna and spoon sauce over top.

Makes 4 servings.

PER SERVING: Cal 352 • Carbo 29 gm • Prot 46 gm • Total fat 6 gm • Sat fat 1 gm • Cal from fat 15% • Chol 77 mg

EDUCATION: Replace high-fat sauces with low-fat alternatives. Cooked red bell pepper creates a creamy, flavorful sauce base with almost no fat. Flavoring sauces with fresh herbs also maximizes their ability to enhance dishes without packing a high-fat punch to your good intentions.

INSPIRATION: *My eyes are open to all the opportunities and blessings that help to support my recovery.*

INSPIRATION: *Q. What can you do when your pancake is only done on one side? A. Turn it over. Q. What style of humor would you call this? A. Flippant!*

Mango-Strawberry Frozen Yogurt Ice

❧ Except for occasional stirring, this sherbet-like dessert is almost no work. Put it into the freezer before starting dinner.

> 2 ripe mangoes
> 1 cup halved strawberries
> 1/4 cup nonfat yogurt

Peel mangoes and cut flesh from pits. Chop mangoes and place in a blender or food processor with the strawberries and yogurt. Process until smooth.

Spoon the mixture into a medium-size bowl. Cover with foil or plastic wrap and place the bowl in the freezer. Freeze 1 1/2 to 2 1/2 hours, until nearly firm, stirring every 20 to 30 minutes to prevent ice crystals from forming.

Makes 4 servings.

PER SERVING: Cal 88 • Carbo 21 gm • Prot 1 gm • Total fat trace • Sat fat trace • Cal from fat 0% • Chol 0 mg

EDUCATION: Use your freezer to create appealing low-fat, fresh fruit desserts. Although the recipe above is easy, here are some even easier freezer desserts:

- Freeze bananas in their skin, or peel and wrap in plastic. Puree in a food processor for a rich-tasting banana sherbet with all the nutrition of the fresh fruit and zero added fat.
- Process frozen banana with some skim milk, an ice cube and a teaspoon of sugar for a fast, nutritious shake.
- Freeze grapes and enjoy their refreshing icy sweetness unadorned.

New England Blueberry Buttermilk Pancakes

❧ Sunday mornings in Massachusetts, with fresh blueberry pancakes in the late summer, were a treat. Serve at the hammock on the back porch for best results.

> 1 cup whole-wheat flour
> 1 cup unbleached all-purpose flour
> 1 teaspoon baking powder
> 1/2 teaspoon baking soda
> 1/4 teaspoon salt
> 2 eggs
> 1 1/2 to 2 cups buttermilk
> 1 tablespoon canola oil
> 2 pints (4 cups) blueberries
> 1 tablespoon brown sugar
> 1/4 cup maple syrup
> 2 teaspoons cornstarch

Combine flours, baking powder, baking soda and salt in a medium-size bowl. In a small bowl, beat eggs, add buttermilk and oil. Add liquid ingredients to dry ingredients with 1 cup blueberries and brown sugar. Stir just until combined.

Heat a large skillet and brush lightly with unsalted butter. Pour 1/4 cup batter into pan to form each pancake. Cook pancakes until bottoms are brown and tops are bubbly. Turn and brown remaining sides. Repeat with remaining batter, keeping pancakes warm.

Combine remaining blueberries with maple syrup and cornstarch in a medium-size saucepan. Bring to a boil and cook, stirring,

until sauce is thickened. Serve hot over pancakes.   *Makes 4 servings.*

PER SERVING: Cal 487 • Carbo 92 gm • Prot 14
gm • Total fat 8 gm • Sat fat 2 gm • Cal from fat
15% • Chol 110 mg

EDUCATION: Have your own nutritious pancake mix (see glossary) on hand when you are
in more of a hurry, or just want to sit down with
the Sunday morning paper. Select the best
ingredients and still enjoy convenience.

July 24

INSPIRATION: *To be present in the moment and to
contribute my best are two ways to make the most of
my situation.*

Seafood Tabbouleh
with Cilantro

A variety of vegetables and herbs topped
with shrimp and bay scallops varies the traditional recipe. A bonus? The bulgur just needs
to be soaked, not cooked. Soaking the bulgur
with some lemon juice intensifies the flavor.

1 cup hot tap water
²/₃ cup fresh lemon juice
1 cup bulgur
1 pound medium-size shrimp,
    peeled and deveined (see glossary)
¹/₂ pound bay scallops
3 garden-ripe tomatoes,
    peeled, seeded and diced
3 green onions, thinly sliced
1 carrot, shredded
1 cucumber, peeled, seeded, halved
    lengthwise and thinly sliced
¹/₂ cup minced fresh parsley
¹/₄ cup minced fresh cilantro

1 tablespoon minced fresh mint
3 tablespoons olive oil
2 teaspoons minced garlic
¹/₂ teaspoon salt
¹/₄ teaspoon freshly ground
    black pepper
Cherry tomatoes for garnish

Combine hot water, lemon juice and bulgur
in a medium-size bowl. Set aside 20 minutes.

Bring a medium-size saucepan of water to a
boil. Add shrimp and scallops, return to a boil
and cook 1 or 2 minutes, just until the seafood
is opaque. Drain and immediately run seafood
under cold water to stop cooking.

Drain any excess liquid from bulgur.
Combine bulgur, seafood, tomatoes, green
onions, carrot, cucumber, parsley, cilantro,
mint, oil, garlic, salt and pepper in a large bowl,
toss and serve, garnished with cherry tomatoes.
                                Makes 6 servings.

PER SERVING: Cal 288 • Carbo 28 gm • Prot 26
gm • Total fat 9 gm • Sat fat 1 gm • Cal from fat
28% • Chol 129 mg

EDUCATION: Take the best from traditional
cuisines. Made with grain, vegetables and
herbs, tabbouleh scores high. It remains a popular dish because of its flavor. But it abounds in
healthful nutrients: vitamins C, A, E; folacin
and magnesium. And that is good reason to
keep including tabbouleh in your diet.

July 25

INSPIRATION: *I will pay attention to the messages my body sends me today, and use the information as a guide to self-care and self-nurturing.*

Mixed Greens Salad with Fresh Tomato Dressing

Radicchio lends color to a combination of crisp greens. Add your own garden greens, if you've grown some.

1/2 pound spinach
1 small head romaine lettuce
1 small head radicchio
1 small head red-leaf lettuce
1 cup broccoli flowerets
1 carrot, thinly sliced on the diagonal
1 celery stalk, thinly sliced on the diagonal
3 green onions, thinly sliced on the diagonal
1/2 cup shredded red cabbage
1/4 cup diced red bell pepper
1/4 cup minced fresh parsley
1/4 cup minced fresh dill
1 tablespoon minced fresh basil
1 medium-size garden-ripe tomato, peeled, seeded and chopped
1 large shallot
1/2 garlic clove
3 tablespoons brown rice vinegar
1 tablespoon extra-virgin olive oil
1/2 teaspoon salt
1/4 teaspoon freshly ground black pepper

GARNISHES
Red bell pepper rings
Purple basil leaves
Dill sprigs
Thin lemon slices

Thoroughly wash spinach in lukewarm water. Remove tough stems and thinly slice leaves. Wash and separate romaine, radicchio and red-leaf lettuce leaves and tear into large pieces. Place spinach, lettuces and radicchio in a large glass serving bowl. Add broccoli flowerets, broken up into bite-size pieces, carrot, celery and green onions, cabbage, bell pepper, parsley, dill and basil. Toss to combine.

In a blender or food processor, combine tomato, shallot, garlic, vinegar, oil, salt and pepper and process until smooth. Garnish salad with red bell pepper rings, basil, dill sprigs and lemon slices. Serve dressing separately.

Makes 8 servings.

PER SERVING: Cal 57 • Carbo 11 gm • Prot 3 gm • Total fat 2 gm • Sat fat trace • Cal from fat 31% • Chol 0 mg

EDUCATION: Compensate for using less oil in salad dressings by choosing highly flavorful varieties of oil. For example, a small bottle of extra-virgin olive oil, walnut, hazelnut or macadamia nut oil, reserved for salads, will impart more flavor than highly refined oils, which are more appropriate for cooking.

INSPIRATION: *I can center myself in my commitment to continue making choices that enhance my well-being.*

New-Fangled Meat Loaf

Cook in the microwave to avoid steaming up the kitchen with a hot oven. Serve with boiled new potatoes and fresh green beans.

$^1/_2$ cup rolled oats
$^1/_2$ cup shredded zucchini
$^1/_3$ cup finely chopped onion
$^1/_4$ cup minced fresh parsley
1 garlic clove, minced
2 tablespoons tomato paste
$^1/_4$ teaspoon dried thyme
$^1/_4$ teaspoon salt
$^1/_4$ teaspoon freshly ground black pepper
1 pound extra-lean ground beef
$^1/_2$ pound ground skinless turkey breast
$^1/_2$ cup tomato sauce

Combine oats, zucchini, onion, 3 table-spoons of the parsley, garlic, 1 tablespoon of the tomato paste, thyme, salt and pepper in a large bowl. Add the meats and mix until combined.

Pat meat into a medium-size microwave-safe soufflé dish. Microwave on HIGH 5 minutes, rotating once. Combine remaining parsley and tomato paste with tomato sauce and pour over meat-loaf. Microwave on MEDIUM 20 to 25 minutes, or until cooked through, rotating once. *Makes 6 servings.*

PER SERVING: Cal 231 • Carbo 8 gm • Prot 25 gm • Total fat 11 gm • Sat fat 6 gm • Cal from fat 43% • Chol 77 mg

VARIATION
Bake 1 hour in a preheated 350°F (175°C) oven if you prefer.

EDUCATION: Let your microwave take the heat off. Cooking on top of the stove or hour-long oven baking can flood the kitchen with heat when that is the last thing you need more of! Save yourself the discomfort and, perhaps, the expense of extra air conditioning, by using your microwave on hot days. Many books are available to help you learn the basics of simple microwave cooking, including my own *Low-Fat Microwave Cooking* (Rodale Press, 1992).

INSPIRATION: *I can free myself from the need to impress others when my success is self-motivated.*

Chilled Avocado Soup with Tomato-Cucumber Salsa

For sheer appearance value this soup is worth creating. As a bonus, it's also delicious and rich in nutrients.

1 avocado
1 1/2 tablespoons fresh
*   lemon juice*
1 1/2 tablespoons fresh lime juice
2 cups chicken broth
1 1/2 cups skim milk
1/4 teaspoon ground cumin
1/4 teaspoon salt
1 large, ripe tomato, peeled,
*   seeded and finely diced*
2 green onions, thinly sliced on the
*   diagonal*
1 jalapeño chile, seeded and minced
*   (see glossary)*
1 garlic clove, minced
1/2 red bell pepper, seeded and
*   finely diced*
1/2 cucumber, peeled, seeded and
*   finely diced*
1 tablespoon minced fresh
*   cilantro*
1 tablespoon minced fresh parsley
Garlic melba toast rounds

Peel and pit avocado. Place in a food processor with lemon and lime juices and process until smooth. Add broth, milk, cumin and salt and process until combined. Place soup in a bowl and chill.

For salsa, combine tomato, green onions, jalapeño, garlic, bell pepper, cucumber, cilantro and parsley in a small bowl. To serve, divide soup among 4 bowls. Sprinkle some of the salsa in the center of each serving. Serve remaining salsa and garlic rounds with soup.

Makes 4 servings.

PER SERVING: Cal 173 • Carbo 20 gm • Prot 8 gm • Total fat 9 gm • Sat fat 1 gm • Cal from fat 46% • Chol 1 mg

EDUCATION: Tame higher-fat ingredients with low-fat additions. Above, we use chicken broth and skim milk with a salsa to "stretch" the avocado. While avocados are higher in fat than most other fruits and vegetables, they are worth occasional inclusion in our diets.

Avocados contain substantially more potassium than bananas and more beta-carotene than many other fruits. High in fiber, low in sodium and with significant amounts of vitamin B_6, vitamin C and folic acid, avocados carry their own weight. Though their fat content is high, the fat is mostly monounsaturated (the kind shown to lower blood cholesterol) and there's no cholesterol.

INSPIRATION: *Instead of spending energy to complain, I will find ways to make things better for myself.*

Oriental Pilaf with Mango

 Colorful rice pilaf features tantalizing aroma, delicate flavor and the added crunch of almonds.

1 lime
2 garlic cloves, minced
1 1/2 teaspoons minced gingerroot
1 tablespoon unsalted butter
1 cup brown basmati or brown long-grain rice
   (see below)
2 cups water
1/4 teaspoon salt
2 tablespoons slivered almonds
12 snow peas
2 green onions, thinly sliced on diagonal
1/2 mango, peeled and diced
1 teaspoon minced fresh cilantro
Lime slices for garnish
Cilantro leaves for garnish

Grate zest from lime and squeeze 2 tablespoons juice. Cook garlic and gingerroot in 2 teaspoons of the butter in a large saucepan over medium heat 1 minute. Add rice and cook, stirring, 1 minute. Add the water, salt, lime peel and lime juice. Bring to a boil, reduce heat, cover and simmer 35 to 40 minutes, until the liquid is absorbed and the rice is tender.

While the rice is cooking, toast the almond slivers in a large skillet over medium-low heat, stirring frequently, until the almonds are lightly browned, or spread almonds in a baking pan and toast 5 minutes in a preheated 325°F (165°C) oven.

Trim stems and remove strings from snow peas and cook in boiling water in a small saucepan 1 minute or until crisp-tender. Run under cold water to stop cooking. Drain and cut diagonally into 1/2-inch pieces.

Cook green onions in remaining teaspoon of butter in a large skillet over low heat, stirring frequently, until wilted, about 2 minutes. Add snow peas, diced mango, cilantro and toasted almonds and heat through, stirring, 1 or 2 minutes. Stir in cooked rice. Garnish with lime slices and cilantro leaves. *Makes 4 servings.*

PER SERVING: Cal 261 • Carbo 46 gm • Prot 6 gm • Total fat 6 gm • Sat fat 2 gm • Cal from fat 23% • Chol 8 mg

VARIATION
Substitute 1 cup low-fat or fresh coconut milk (see glossary) for water when cooking rice for a more exotic flavor.

EDUCATION: Add an extra dimension to your cooking as you expand the role of grains in your meals. With no extra effort, you can enhance your meals with the aroma of basmati, jasmine or even popcorn rice! Any brown rice will take twice as long to cook as white rice, but remember, brown rices are far higher in fiber and nutrition. Substitute a small portion of wild rice for the brown specialty rices (they cook in the same amount of time) for an even more elegant result.

INSPIRATION: *Today I will not try to change people and situations to meet my expectations, but I will be open to things as they are (which may, in fact, change me!).*

Peachy Fruit Cup with Cream Sauce

❧ Oh, these glorious summer days with fresh fruits abounding! And better, still, delicious recipes that require minimal effort to create!

3 peaches
1 cup strawberries
1 kiwi fruit
1 cup blueberries
³/₄ cup low-fat cottage cheese
¹/₃ cup orange juice
1 tablespoon fresh lemon juice
1 tablespoon brown sugar
¹/₄ teaspoon freshly grated
    orange peel
¹/₈ teaspoon freshly grated
    lemon peel

Halve, remove pits and cut unpeeled peaches into slices. Remove caps from strawberries and cut in half. Peel, quarter and slice kiwi fruit. Combine peaches, strawberries, kiwi and blueberries in a medium-size bowl.

Combine cottage cheese, orange and lemon juices, sugar, orange and lemon peel in a blender and process until smooth, scraping down the sides of the container as needed. To serve, spoon fruit into dessert cups and top with cream sauce. *Makes 6 servings.*

PER SERVING: Cal 88 • Carbo 17 gm • Prot 5 gm • Total fat 1 gm • Sat fat trace • Cal from fat 9% • Chol 2 mg

EDUCATION: Expand cottage cheese beyond a boring "diet" routine. Cottage cheese can be a versatile part of a low-fat diet. Use it as a base for savory or, as above, sweet sauces. Process cottage cheese in a blender until creamy; use in place of sour cream on baked potatoes. Substitute a bagel, spread with sweetened, spiced cottage cheese with raisins, instead of a high-fat doughnut or sweet roll. The protein will also help keep blood-sugar levels in line.

INSPIRATION: *Each day is a new opportunity to choose life.*

INSPIRATION: *Sharing our experiences is a way for me, and others, to stay with the process of recovery.*

French Toast with Blueberry-Peach Sauce

The first time I made this, I thought it *almost* looked too good to eat!

2 eggs
2 tablespoons skim milk
$^1/_2$ teaspoon ground cinnamon
4 to 6 thick slices day-old whole-grain French bread
1 cup blueberries
1 tablespoon maple syrup
1 teaspoon cornstarch
$^1/_2$ peach, pitted, peeled and diced

Beat the eggs in a pie pan. Beat in the milk and cinnamon. Soak the bread slices in the egg mixture, turning several times, until eggs are absorbed.

Cook French toast on a lightly buttered nonstick griddle, turning to brown both sides, until cooked through.

Meanwhile, combine blueberries, maple syrup and cornstarch in a small saucepan. Bring to a boil, reduce heat and simmer, stirring, until sauce thickens slightly. Remove from heat and stir in diced peach. Place French toast on warmed plates and top with sauce.   *Makes 2 servings.*

PER SERVING: Cal 360 • Carbo 58 gm • Prot 14 gm • Total fat 8 gm • Sat fat 2 gm • Cal from fat 20% • Chol 213 mg

EDUCATION: Switch to whole-grain breads when you're making French toast. The heartiness of whole wheat (or even pumpernickel) gives substance and satisfaction to the morning meal. The fiber helps prevent snacking before lunch by keeping blood-sugar levels on an even keel.

Dilled Creamy Tomato Soup

Serve with a green salad and Garlic Bruschetta with Mozzarella (see July 13).

2 cups quartered onions
2 garlic cloves
4 cups chicken broth
5 cups peeled, seeded, chopped ripe tomatoes
1$^1/_2$ cups buttermilk
$^1/_4$ cup minced fresh dill
$^1/_2$ teaspoon salt
$^1/_8$ teaspoon freshly ground black pepper
Lemon slices for garnish
Dill sprigs for garnish

Bring the onions, garlic and broth to a boil in a Dutch oven. Reduce heat, cover and simmer 10 minutes. Add tomatoes and return to a boil. Reduce heat, cover and simmer 10 to 15 minutes, until vegetables are tender. With a slotted spoon, remove vegetables from broth and process in a blender or food processor until smooth. Pour broth into a large bowl, add pureed vegetables, buttermilk, dill, salt and pepper. Cover and refrigerate until chilled. Serve garnished with lemon slices and dill sprigs.   *Makes 8 servings.*

PER SERVING: Cal 85 • Carbo 13 gm • Prot 6 gm • Total fat 1 gm • Sat fat trace • Cal from fat 16% • Chol 2 mg

EDUCATION: Substitute low-fat buttermilk for heavy cream in cold soups. The tangy, tart taste of buttermilk is a nice complement to a variety of vegetable and fruit soups. In the soup above, no oil or butter is used to cook the onions, further insuring a low fat content.

INSPIRATION: *My body is a gift to me, and I have the responsibility to take good care of it!*

Fresh Fruit Plate with Minted Ricotta Dip

❧ Part-skim ricotta cheese makes a dip that is rich-tasting and versatile as well as low in fat.

1 pound red seedless grapes
1 pound green seedless grapes
2 ripe mangoes, peeled and cubed
2 kiwi fruit, peeled and cut into wedges
1 ripe papaya, peeled, seeded and cubed
1¹/₂ cups part-skim ricotta cheese
3 tablespoons powdered sugar
2 teaspoons fresh lemon juice
2 tablespoons minced fresh mint leaves
Fresh mint sprigs for garnish
Lemon slices for garnish

Arrange fruit attractively on a large platter. For ricotta sauce, place ricotta in a blender or food processor and process with sugar and lemon juice. Stir in mint. Place in a small bowl and arrange on the platter with the fruit.

Makes 8 servings.

PER SERVING: Cal 212 • Carbo 40 gm • Prot 7 gm • Total fat 5 gm • Sat fat 2 gm • Cal from fat 21% • Chol 14 mg

EDUCATION: Be aware of your nutrient status when you are taking prescribed medicine to avoid deficiencies. Medications can be vital to our healing. But some may interfere with our body's ability to maintain a proper state of nutrition. For example, folic acid stored in the body can be adversely affected by anticancer drugs, anticonvulsant drugs, birth control pills, cortisone, sulfa drugs and sleeping pills. A simple blood test can reveal any problems with folic acid if you are taking the medications.

Meanwhile, eat folic acid–rich foods, such as the papaya above, dark green leafy vegetables, citrus fruits, beans, whole grains, poultry, pork and shellfish.

INSPIRATION: *As I recover, I can begin reaching out to others. I can become an agent of healing.*

Linda's Cheddar-Tomato Soup

❧ After sampling a similar soup on a trip to Massachusetts, Linda spent a lot of time re-creating it, much to her and Rob's delight. Garden-fresh tomato flavor shines in this simple preparation. Serve with a pasta salad for a light lunch.

1 onion, chopped
¹/₂ tablespoon butter
4 cups peeled, seeded and chopped
    garden-ripe tomatoes
2 cups tomato juice
1 garlic clove, pushed through
    a press
¹/₄ teaspoon salt
¹/₂ cup shredded sharp
    Cheddar cheese
2 tablespoons minced fresh
    parsley

In a large saucepan over medium heat, cook onion in the butter until translucent but not browned, 4 or 5 minutes. Add tomatoes, juice, garlic and salt. Bring soup to a boil, reduce heat, cover and simmer 10 minutes. Puree half the soup in a food processor or blender and return to the pan. Turn off heat. Stir in cheese until melted. Serve immediately, topped with minced parsley. *Makes 4 servings.*

PER SERVING: Cal 150 • Carbo 19 gm • Prot 7 gm • Total fat 6 gm • Sat fat 4 gm • Cal from fat 36% • Chol 17 mg

EDUCATION: Eat more tomatoes to reduce your risk of cancer. Tomatoes are rich in vitamin C, believed to be a cancer-fighter. Also, researchers have found that tomatoes contain at least two chemicals that seem to neutralize cancer-causing agents in the body. To enjoy the taste and nutrients of garden-ripe tomatoes all year, quarter tomatoes and freeze on a baking sheet. When frozen, slip into heavy, self-sealing plastic bags and freeze up to 1 year. When defrosted, tomatoes will lose their shape, but they are delicious in soups, stews and pasta sauces.

August 3

INSPIRATION: *Integrating my thoughts, feelings and actions through trust in my Higher Power moves me, each day, toward wholeness.*

Fruit Basket Granola Crisp

❧ Sprinkle low-fat granola over seasonal fruits any time of year for a delicious dessert.

2 cups old-fashioned rolled oats
1/2 cup sliced almonds
1/2 cup raisins
3 tablespoons pure maple syrup
1 tablespoon canola oil
1/2 teaspoon ground cinnamon
2 cups halved strawberries
3/4 cup blueberries
2 nectarines, pitted and thinly sliced
3 plums, pitted and thinly sliced
1/4 cup fresh orange juice
1/4 teaspoon freshly grated
*   orange peel*

Preheat oven to 350°F (175°C). Combine oats, almonds and raisins in a 13 × 9-inch baking pan. Combine maple syrup, oil and cinnamon in a small saucepan, and, stirring constantly, bring to a boil. Pour over oat mixture and stir until oat mixture is evenly moistened.

Bake granola 15 to 18 minutes, stirring frequently, or until golden. Cool, then crumble granola in pan.

Meanwhile, combine strawberries, blueberries, nectarines, plums, orange juice and grated peel in a medium-size bowl. Let stand up to 1/2 hour at room temperature, or chill. To serve, divide fruit among dishes and spoon on some of the fruit liquid. Top each serving with 3 tablespoons granola. *Makes 6 servings.*

PER SERVING: Cal 314 • Carbo 53 gm • Prot 6 gm • Total fat 10 gm • Sat fat 1 gm • Cal from fat 29% • Chol 0 mg

EDUCATION: Go easy on packaged granola to avoid hidden fat. Many granolas are high in oil, packed with nuts and studded with seeds. While such granolas can be rich in nutrients, these are available at the cost of high fat. The granola above contains a modest amount of nuts and a small portion of oil. Flavor is added with real maple syrup, though honey could be substituted. With low-fat goodness, it provides beneficial amounts of thiamin, folacin, magnesium, phosphorus, vitamins A and E, iron, calcium, riboflavin and zinc.

INSPIRATION: *My future is hidden. I can only see and respond to today as I travel to that destination.*

Puffed German Pancake with Plum Filling

🌱 Time to pull out that cast-iron skillet, though any ovenproof skillet will do. This makes an attractive brunch dish.

1 tablespoon unsalted butter
4 eggs
1 cup milk
1/2 cup whole-wheat pastry flour
1/2 cup unbleached all-purpose flour
2 teaspoons brown sugar
2 cups quartered, pitted plums
1/4 cup orange juice
2 teaspoons cornstarch
1 tablespoon red raspberry jam

Preheat oven to 425°F (220°C). Melt butter in a 12-inch ovenproof skillet. Combine eggs, milk, flours and sugar in a blender and process until smooth. Swirl butter to coat bottom and sides of pan. Pour in batter. Bake 20 minutes or until puffy.

Combine plums and 2 tablespoons of the orange juice in a medium-size saucepan and bring to a boil. Reduce heat and cook, stirring, about 15 minutes, or until tender. Stir cornstarch into remaining orange juice until dissolved. Stir cornstarch mixture and jam into plums. Cook, stirring, until mixture is slightly thickened. Spoon filling into pancake. Cut into wedges to serve. *Makes 4 servings.*

PER SERVING: Cal 359 • Carbo 60 gm • Prot 12 gm • Total fat 9 gm • Sat fat 4 gm • Cal from fat 24% • Chol 225 mg

EDUCATION: Make yourself plum healthy with this low-fat, low-calorie fruit. Raw, succulent plums are a juicy, vitamin C–rich treat.

Plums also make a delicious soup. Combine peeled, pitted plums with apple juice, a dash of nutmeg and cinnamon and cook until tender. Puree in a blender, thinning as needed with additional juice. Chill; serve with a dollop of Low-Fat Crème Fraîche (see May 12).

INSPIRATION: *I will spend time cultivating loving relationships in my life with the knowledge that relationships are more fulfilling than anything the material world offers.*

Stuffed Tortillas with Garden Vegetables

🌱 Tortillas bursting with garden-ripe goodness get a finishing touch in the microwave, keeping your kitchen cooler.

1/2 cup chopped broccoli flowerets
1/4 cup chopped green onions
1 cup loosely packed chopped fresh spinach
1/2 cup peeled, seeded and diced garden-
    ripe tomatoes
1/2 cup diced zucchini
1/2 cup diced red bell pepper
1/2 cup whole-kernel corn
2 tablespoons water
4 flour tortillas
1/2 cup (2 ounces) shredded sharp
    Cheddar cheese
3/4 cup Sombrero Salsa (see February 16)
    or bottled salsa thinned with
    tomato juice

Place vegetables in a saucepan with 2 tablespoons water. Cook over medium heat until boiling. Cover, reduce heat to low and cook 2 or 3 minutes or until crisp-tender; remove from heat.

Heat flour tortillas in a microwave on MEDIUM 30 seconds or until warm and pliable.

To assemble, sprinkle each tortilla with ¼ cup cheese. Arrange one-fourth of the vegetable mixture down the center of each tortilla. Fold two sides of the tortilla over filling and place seam side down in a shallow, microwave-safe casserole dish. Spoon salsa over tortillas and heat in a microwave on MEDIUM 2 minutes or until heated through.   *Makes 4 servings.*

PER SERVING: Cal 208 • Carbo 28 gm • Prot 9 gm • Total fat 8 gm • Sat fat 3 gm • Cal from fat 34% • Chol 15 mg

EDUCATION: Increase intake of foods high in the B vitamins to fight depression. Deprived of adequate thiamin, our bodies may show a variety of symptoms: inability to concentrate, forgetfulness, anxiety, loss of appetite and dizziness. Inadequate niacin, another B vitamin, also may lead to mental and emotional problems. Vitamin B₆ and folate are also important to serene nerves and sharp mental processes. Increasing our B vitamin intake is as simple as eating poultry and fish, whole grains, beans, dark green leafy vegetables, nuts, seeds, and liver.

INSPIRATION: *Today I will welcome new opportunities and let go of the past.*

Summer Squash with Couscous

A quick and easy side dish, delicious with poultry or fish. Serve a tossed salad and whole-grain French bread, too.

1½ cups coarsely shredded yellow
  summer squash
1½ cups coarsely shredded zucchini
1½ cups chicken broth
1¼ cups couscous
¼ cup minced fresh parsley
1 tablespoon minced fresh basil
1 tablespoon fresh lemon juice
¼ teaspoon freshly ground black pepper

Combine squash, zucchini and broth in a large saucepan. Bring to a boil, reduce heat, cover and simmer 3 or 4 minutes, stirring occasionally or until squash is firm-tender. Stir in couscous, parsley, basil, lemon juice and pepper. Remove from heat, cover and let stand 5 minutes, until couscous is tender.

Makes 4 servings.

PER SERVING: Cal 152 • Carbo 28 gm • Prot 7 gm • Total fat 1 gm • Sat fat trace • Cal from fat 7% • Chol 0 mg

EDUCATION: Get fresh with lemon juice to obtain the best flavor while seasoning low-fat foods. Lemon juice tickles the taste buds, reducing the perceived need for salt in dishes it flavors. Bottled lemon juice lacks some of the zesty flavor, and since it must be heat-processed, loses a good measure of its vitamin C. Whole lemons keep well under refrigeration and so are easy to keep on hand.

INSPIRATION: *It is important for me to replenish myself, to find small ways to "recharge" during the day.*

Diane's Broiled Chicken Kabobs

Diane and Bill enjoy these on the deck with Matthew. Broiled until browned and juicy, these chicken kabobs are served with brown rice studded with colorful vegetables.

1 1/2 cups brown rice
3 cups chicken broth
1/2 red bell pepper, finely diced
1 1/4 cups sliced green onions
2 tablespoons minced
   fresh parsley
1 tablespoon honey
1 tablespoon Worcestershire sauce
1 tablespoon canola oil
2 teaspoons grated peeled gingerroot
1 teaspoon salt
1/2 teaspoon ground allspice
1/4 teaspoon red pepper flakes
6 boneless skinless chicken
   breast halves

Soak 12 (8-inch) bamboo skewers in water 1 hour to prevent charring under the broiler. Bring rice and chicken broth to a boil in a large saucepan. Reduce heat, cover and simmer 30 minutes. Remove lid and quickly add diced bell pepper and 1/2 cup of the green onions without stirring. Replace lid and steam 10 minutes or until all liquid is absorbed. Remove from heat, add parsley and stir. Cover and set aside.

While rice is cooking, combine remaining 3/4 cup green onions, honey, Worcestershire sauce, oil, gingerroot, salt, allspice and red pepper flakes in a blender and process until smooth. Cut chicken breasts into 1 1/2-inch chunks.

Preheat broiler. Toss chicken with sauce in a medium-size bowl. Thread the chicken pieces onto presoaked bamboo skewers. Place kabobs on a rack in a broiling pan and brush with any remaining sauce.

With oven rack at closest position to heat, broil kabobs 10 minutes, turning once, or just until chicken is cooked through. Place rice mixture in a large, warmed serving dish. Top with chicken kabobs. *Makes 6 servings.*

PER SERVING: Cal 371 • Carbo 41 gm • Prot 33 gm • Total fat 7 gm • Sat fat 1 gm • Cal from fat 17% • Chol 73 mg

EDUCATION: Skewer vegetables and the fish, poultry or meats they accompany separately when making kabobs so cooking is completed at the same time. You may be setting yourself up for frustration by combining foods that need different heats or cooking times. By cooking vegetables and meats separately, you have more control over the finished product—and you know how good that sounds!

INSPIRATION: *By setting daily priorities for myself, I am able to do what is truly important to me and enhances my well-being.*

Radiatore with Ricotta & Sautéed Vegetables

Garden-fresh vegetables, tasty basil and garlic bring raves for this simple pasta creation.

1 pound radiatore or corkscrew pasta
1/2 cup part-skim ricotta cheese
4 large garden-ripe tomatoes, peeled, seeded and chopped
1 green onion, thinly sliced
2 tablespoons olive oil
1 tablespoon thinly sliced fresh basil
1/4 teaspoon salt
1/8 teaspoon freshly ground black pepper
1 small onion, chopped
2 small zucchini, halved lengthwise and sliced
2 garlic cloves, minced
2 tablespoons minced fresh parsley for garnish
2 tablespoons freshly grated Parmesan cheese for garnish

Bring a large pot of water to a boil. Add pasta and cook 7 to 9 minutes or until firm-tender. While pasta is cooking, place ricotta in a food processor or blender and process until smooth. Drain pasta, return to pot and toss with the ricotta cheese. Cover and keep warm.

Combine chopped tomatoes, green onion, 1 tablespoon of the oil, basil, salt and pepper in a large serving bowl. Set aside. Cook chopped onion in the remaining oil in a large nonstick skillet over medium heat, stirring frequently, until onion is very tender, 7 or 8 minutes. Stir in zucchini and cook, stirring frequently, 4 or 5 minutes or until zucchini is tender and beginning to brown. Add garlic and cook, stirring, 1 minute.

Stir pasta and zucchini mixture into tomatoes. Toss well and serve garnished with minced parsley and grated Parmesan.

Makes 6 servings.

PER SERVING: Cal 520 • Carbo 66 gm • Prot 28 gm • Total fat 16 gm • Sat fat 8 gm • Cal from fat 28% • Chol 33 mg

EDUCATION: Substitute blended part-skim ricotta for heavy cream in pasta recipes to cut fat. Heavy cream contains 36 percent or more milk fat. Just 1/2 cup of heavy cream has 345 calories, 37 grams of fat and 65 milligrams of cholesterol. The same amount of part-skim ricotta has 138 calories, 8 grams of fat and less than half the cholesterol, but enough flavor to create a tasty dish.

INSPIRATION: *I am becoming aware of my connection to those around me, and giving up my illusions of isolation.*

Ruth's Pickled Beets & Eggs

❧ The mom of one of my oldest friends is a wonderful Pennsylvania Dutch cook. This classic dish can make a colorful appetizer. Follow the boiling method below for perfect hard-cooked eggs without those greenish yolks.

6 eggs
1 (16-ounce) jar sliced red beets, with liquid
¹/₂ cup cider vinegar
¹/₃ cup sugar
8 whole black peppercorns
8 whole allspice berries
1 small onion, thinly sliced
Parsley sprigs for garnish
Lemon slices for garnish

Prick shell at the large end of each egg with a pin or egg pricker. This prevents the eggs from cracking as they heat. Place the eggs in a large saucepan and cover generously with cold water. Bring just to a boil over high heat. Cover pan, remove from heat and let stand 17 minutes. Remove eggs from pan and place in a large bowl of cold water with ice cubes. Chill 15 to 20 minutes. Crack the shells all over by hitting on a flat surface, and peel eggs. Return peeled eggs to ice water to continue chilling.

Meanwhile, combine liquid from beets, cider vinegar, sugar, peppercorns and allspice in a medium-size glass or stainless steel pan. Bring to a boil, stirring, until sugar dissolves. Add eggs and sliced onion. Turn eggs to coat. Add beets. Cover and refrigerate, turning eggs occasionally, until eggs are deep pink, about 8 hours. Drain juices. Place beets and onions on serving plate. Cut eggs in half lengthwise and arrange on top of beets. Garnish with parsley and lemon slices. *Makes 6 servings.*

PER SERVING: Cal 132 • Carbo 14 gm • Prot 7 gm • Total fat 5 gm • Sat fat 1 gm • Cal from fat 34% • Chol 213 mg

EDUCATION: Avoid using aluminum cookware with acidic foods to minimize your exposure to this metal. Aluminum can react with acid ingredients. There is evidence that ingested aluminum accumulates in the brain and may, over time, cause memory loss and brain deterioration. Also use care when broiling or grilling foods on aluminum when using acidic marinades.

INSPIRATION: *I am blessed with experiences of growth and healing, and delight in recognizing these important events.*

Whole-Wheat Cheddar Popovers

❧ Popovers are steaming, hollow, flavorful creations to serve in place of bread or muffins. With the addition of cheese, there's no need for butter when they pop out hot from the oven.

¹/₂ cup whole-wheat pastry flour
¹/₂ cup unbleached flour
¹/₄ teaspoon salt
1¹/₄ cups skim milk
2 eggs at room temperature
1 egg white at room temperature
2 teaspoons freshly grated
    Parmesan cheese
¹/₃ cup shredded sharp Cheddar cheese

Preheat oven to 375°F (190°C). Butter 11 cast-iron popover forms or 12 (2³/₄-inch) muffin cups. Combine the flours, salt and milk in a large bowl and beat together until smooth. Beat the eggs and egg white together until they are very light. Beat eggs into the flour mixture along with the two cheeses until well combined. Fill cups two-thirds full with batter. Bake 50 minutes, not opening the oven door until the last 10 minutes. If popovers seem to be browning too quickly, reduce heat to 325°F (165°C) for the final 10 minutes. Popovers should be puffed but can be moist inside, though cooked through. *Makes 11 to 12 popovers.*

PER SERVING: Cal 73 • Carbo 9 gm • Prot 4 gm • Total fat 2 gm • Sat fat 1 gm • Cal from fat 25% • Chol 39 mg

EDUCATION: Use "eggs-acting" care when handling raw eggs and foods made with them to avoid foodborne illness. Never use cracked or dirty eggs since damaged or contaminated shells can allow harmful bacteria to penetrate. Keep raw eggs and egg dishes in the refrigerator. Serve cooked egg dishes immediately after cooking. And wash your hands, utensils and work surfaces in hot soapy water whenever using raw eggs. Do not allow cooked food, or food that will be eaten raw, to come in contact with raw eggs.

To most effectively kill all possible salmonella bacteria, both egg whites and yolks should be cooked until firm, as should all dishes—such as custards or French toast—containing eggs. Small children and those individuals with illnesses or immune deficiencies should be particularly cautioned against eating raw egg. (And that means no tasting the cookie or cake batter once eggs have been added!)

August 11

INSPIRATION: *By focusing on the essentials, I avoid distractions and get closer to my goal of healing.*

Shrimp & Zucchini with Feta Cheese

Serve with pasta, Quick Cherry Tomatoes (see below) and a tossed salad.

> 2 medium-size zucchini
> 1/2 tablespoon olive oil
> 1 pound large shrimp, shelled and
>   deveined (see glossary)
> 1 garlic clove, minced
> 1/4 teaspoon dried basil
> 1/4 teaspoon salt
> 1/8 teaspoon freshly ground black pepper
> 2 tablespoons minced fresh parsley
> 1 tablespoon finely crumbled feta cheese

Cut zucchini diagonally into 1/2-inch-thick slices. Cook zucchini in the oil in a large non-stick skillet over medium heat, stirring frequently, until zucchini is crisp-tender. Remove to a warm bowl with a slotted spoon.

Add shrimp, garlic, basil, salt and pepper to the same skillet and cook over medium heat, stirring, about 5 minutes or just until the shrimp are opaque throughout. Return zucchini to the skillet with the parsley and heat through. Toss with feta and serve.

Makes 4 servings.

PER SERVING: Cal 198 • Carbo 4 gm • Prot 25 gm • Total fat 8 gm • Sat fat 2 gm • Cal from fat 36% • Chol 181 mg

EDUCATION: Take advantage of bite-sized cherry tomatoes as a nutritious, easy and colorful side dish. Just rinse off these little babies, and they're ready to go. Heat a pint of cherry tomatoes in a small amount of butter or oil in a medium-size skillet. Toss with minced fresh herbs or, for a twist, a teaspoon of honey. Colorful cherry tomatoes pack a powerful supply of vitamins A, C and E in that small package, and they dress up any meal in minutes.

INSPIRATION: *I will balance my activities today: work and play, time with people and time alone, activity and rest.*

Olé Mexican Chicken Salad

❧ A combination of spicy and sweet, this south-of-the-border salad can be served with warmed tortillas or corn bread. A light soup would complete a delightful outdoor meal.

3 boneless and skinless chicken breast halves
1 teaspoon ground cumin
1/2 teaspoon ground cinnamon
Dash of ground cloves
Dash of hot (cayenne) pepper
1 tablespoon fresh lime juice
1 tablespoon chicken broth or water
1 tablespoon canola oil
1/4 teaspoon salt
1/4 teaspoon freshly grated lime peel
1/2 cup finely diced celery
1/2 cup finely diced jicama (see May 24)
1/2 cup thinly sliced green onions
1/2 fresh jalapeño chile, seeded and minced
* (see glossary)*
Red-leaf lettuce leaves

GARNISHES
Minced fresh cilantro leaves
Lime wedges
Tomato wedges

Using a mallet or heavy pan, slightly flatten breast halves between two layers of waxed paper. Arrange chicken breasts in a single layer in a large skillet. Add a small amount of water. Bring to a boil, reduce heat, cover and simmer chicken breasts just until cooked through, 2 or 3 minutes. Remove chicken and set aside to cool.

Combine cumin, cinnamon, cloves and cayenne in a small saucepan. Stir over low heat until fragrant, about 30 seconds. Place spices in a large bowl. Add lime juice, broth or water, oil, salt and lime peel and stir until combined.

Dice chicken and add with celery, jicama, green onions and jalapeño to spice mixture. Toss to coat evenly. Arrange lettuce leaves on a serving plate. Top with chicken salad. Sprinkle with cilantro and garnish with lime and tomato wedges. *Makes 4 servings.*

PER SERVING: Cal 142 • Carbo 2 gm • Prot 20 gm • Total fat 6 gm • Sat fat 1 gm • Cal from fat 36% • Chol 55 mg

EDUCATION: Eat outdoors for a change of pace. A change of scenery can do wonders to lift sagging spirits. If you don't have a patio, balcony or backyard, pack up a picnic dinner and head for a park. Many communities combine picnic pavilions with athletic areas, so you can work off some stress before sitting down to a meal.

INSPIRATION: *I will accept what I must, and change what I can in seeking my health and healing.*

Ravioli & Broccoli with Fresh Tomato Sauce

❧ The colors of the Italian flag provide this satisfying main-dish meal with visual appeal.

2 cups chopped garden-
* ripe tomatoes*
4 teaspoons olive oil
2 tablespoons minced fresh parsley
1 tablespoon minced fresh basil
1/2 teaspoon salt
1/8 teaspoon freshly ground
* black pepper*

2 (8-ounce) packages frozen
    cheese-stuffed mini ravioli
1 bunch broccoli
1 garlic clove, minced
1 tablesppon freshly grated
    Parmesan cheese

Combine tomatoes, half the olive oil, the parsley, basil, salt and pepper in a large bowl. Set aside.

Bring a large pot of water to a boil and cook ravioli until firm-tender, 6 to 8 minutes or according to package directions.

While pasta is cooking, peel broccoli stems and thinly slice. Separate broccoli into bite-size flowerets. Place remaining oil in a medium-size nonstick skillet, add broccoli and stir until coated. Add 1/4 cup water, bring to a boil, reduce heat, cover and simmer 3 or 4 minutes. Remove cover, add garlic and cook, stirring, until broccoli is crisp-tender, 3 to 4 minutes.

Drain ravioli and place in the large bowl with tomato mixture. Add hot broccoli and toss until combined. Top with Parmesan cheese. *Makes 4 servings.*

PER SERVING: Cal 258 • Carbo 36 gm • Prot 13 gm • Total fat 8 gm • Sat fat trace • Cal from fat 28% • Chol 5 mg

EDUCATION: When eating out Italian, go low-fat by choosing pastas with tomato sauce and those made with small amounts of cheese or meat. Many Northern Italian specialties, made with heavy cream or with garlic-and-oil and bacon-based toppings, weigh in too heavy with fats to be healthy. Tomato-based sauces are leaner, allowing you a hearty meal and a clear conscience. Skip the high-fat garlic breads in favor of the plain, sliced Italian-style bread; it's great to help pick up those last bits of your flavorful meal.

INSPIRATION: *As I release the need for conflict in my life, I will become more aware of serenity, charity and love.*

Anita's Green Beans with Dill & Mustard

Green beans get a zesty touch of mustard-vinegar sauce. Don't overcook beans or they'll lose flavor and nutrients.

1 pound green beans
2 teaspoons olive oil
2 teaspoons brown rice vinegar
1/2 teaspoon Dijon mustard
1 tablespoon minced fresh dill

Bring a large pot of water to a boil. Snap or trim both ends of beans, leaving beans whole. Drop beans slowly into boiling water so that water continues to boil. Cook beans 5 minutes or until bright green and crisp-tender.

Place oil in a hot large nonstick skillet. Add drained beans and cook 1 or 2 minutes, stirring constantly. Combine vinegar, mustard and dill in a cup. Add to beans and stir until combined. Serve hot. *Makes 4 servings.*

PER SERVING: Cal 60 • Carbo 9 gm • Prot 2 gm • Total fat 3 gm • Sat fat 1 gm • Cal from fat 45% • Chol 0 mg

EDUCATION: Eat more fresh beans, as well as dried, to get a variety of nutrients. Familiar green beans and yellow wax beans grow up to become dried beans if they are left on the plant. By picking while the bean pod is immature, and edible, you can enjoy healthful amounts of vitamin C and beta-carotene. Once mature, the dried beans contain mostly protein and starch.

INSPIRATION: *I am able to forge new, healthful behavior patterns as I become more aware of my physical, emotional and spiritual needs.*

French Hero-style Roast Beef Sandwiches

❦ Deli roast beef and a delicious blue-cheese sauce on French bread takes these sandwiches a step above the ordinary. They make a delicious, no-cooking-needed dinner.

> $^1/_3$ cup crumbled blue cheese
> $1^1/_2$ tablespoons skim milk
> 2 medium-size garden-ripe tomatoes
> $^1/_2$ small red onion
> 1 bunch watercress, washed,
>   large stems removed
> $^1/_4$ cup Niçoise or small, pitted ripe olives
> 1 large loaf French bread or 2 baguettes
> $^1/_2$ pound sliced deli roast beef
> 8 small romaine lettuce leaves
> 4 thin slices cantaloupe or honeydew
>   melon for garnish
> 4 small bunches red grapes for garnish

Combine blue cheese and skim milk with a fork in a small bowl.

Cut tomatoes into 4 slices each. Cut onion into 8 thin slices. Chop enough watercress to make $^1/_2$ cup. Mince olives.

Cut bread loaf into 4 equal pieces or each baguette into 2 equal pieces. Slice lengthwise in half. Arrange the bottom halves of the bread pieces on serving plates. Divide the roast beef and loosely fold across bottom of each sandwich. Spread with blue cheese sauce. Top with romaine lettuce, onion slices, chopped watercress, and tomato slices and sprinkle with minced olives. Top with remaining bread. Garnish plates with a slice of melon and some grapes. *Makes 4 servings.*

PER SERVING: Cal 535 • Carbo 64 gm • Prot 33 gm • Total fat 16 gm • Sat fat 5 gm • Cal from fat 27% • Chol 62 mg

EDUCATION: Include no more than three 3-ounce servings of red meat in your diet each week. A healthy diet change does not have to mean eliminating meat, but just learning ways to cut back. Here, for example, $^1/_2$ pound of roast beef is sufficient to provide hearty taste for 4 in these layered sandwiches. The fiber, iron, vitamins A and C, beta-carotene and calcium also present in this meal create a healthful balance with the small amount of meat.

INSPIRATION: *Accepting people just as they are is the greatest gift I can give them.*

Stir-fried Garden Vegetables

❦ Garlic and ginger give Oriental flavor to a trio of fresh garden vegetables. Serve as a side dish with grilled poultry or shrimp.

> 1 teaspoon grated gingerroot
> 1 teaspoon minced garlic
> 2 teaspoons canola oil
> 3 cups sliced green beans
> 2 cups julienned carrots
> $^1/_2$ cup thinly sliced green onions
> 3 tablespoons chicken broth or
>   orange juice
> 1 tablespoon minced fresh parsley
> $^1/_2$ teaspoon salt
> Dash of hot (cayenne) pepper

Cook gingerroot and garlic in the oil in a nonstick Dutch oven over medium heat, stirring constantly, 30 seconds. Add beans, carrots and green onions and cook, stirring, 2 minutes. Add broth or juice and bring to a boil. Reduce heat, cover and simmer 4 or 5 minutes or until vegetables are crisp-tender. Stir in parsley, salt and cayenne to taste and cook, stirring, 1 minute. *Makes 6 servings.*

PER SERVING: Cal 54 • Carbo 9 gm • Prot 2 gm • Total fat 2 gm • Sat fat trace • Cal from fat 30% • Chol 0 mg

VARIATION
Make this a main-dish meal for four by adding 1 pound cooked shrimp and serving over cooked brown rice.

EDUCATION: Use high-quality nonstick cookware to reduce the need for oil. When wok cookery was at its peak some years ago, recipes routinely used ¼ or ½ cup oil for stir-frying. Today, with increasing knowledge of the benefits of a low-fat diet, it's important to find ways to cut back. A good nonstick pan (some have 20-year warranties and can be used with metal utensils) will help you cook foods evenly with a minimum of fat.

INSPIRATION: *"As within, so without." I am learning that the only changes needed are those inside of me.*

Creamy Scrambled Eggs with Cheese

❧ The creamy surprise here is cottage cheese, which adds a delicious flavor to the eggs with not a hint of "diet food" taste. Serve with fresh fruit and whole-grain toast.

1 egg
1 egg white
1 tablespoon skim milk
1 teaspoon unsalted butter
2 tablespoons low-fat cottage cheese
Dash of salt
Dash of freshly ground black pepper
2 slices whole-grain bread, toasted

In a small bowl, beat egg and egg white, add milk and beat until combined. Melt butter in a small nonstick skillet over medium heat, and when foam subsides, pour in egg mixture. As eggs begin to set, draw in toward center of pan with a wooden spoon. Continue cooking about 2 minutes or until eggs are nearly set. Add cottage cheese and sprinkle with a little salt and pepper. Stir until heated through and eggs are set. Serve with toast. *Makes 1 serving.*

PER SERVING: Cal 275 • Carbo 28 gm • Prot 19 gm • Total fat 10 gm • Sat fat 3 gm • Cal from fat 32% • Chol 22 mg

EDUCATION: Serve fiber-filled foods to balance low-fiber meat, poultry, fish, eggs and dairy foods. While the latter foods are high in protein, their fiber content is low to nonexistent. Even beef, which can appear stringy, is not a fiber source. By balancing protein sources with fruits, whole grains and vegetables, you can help balance your digestive tract with needed fiber. Vegetarian sources of protein, such as beans, nuts and grains, have fiber built right in.

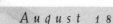

August 18

INSPIRATION: *Accepting exactly where I am is what enables me to move forward from this point.*

Whole-Grain Blueberry Muffins

One of the happiest ways to enjoy blueberries—nestled in a tasty muffin warm from the oven.

2¼ cups whole-wheat pastry flour
¼ cup ground yellow cornmeal
1¼ teaspoons baking powder
½ teaspoon baking soda
¼ teaspoon ground cinnamon
¼ teaspoon salt
⅔ cup pure maple syrup
½ cup buttermilk
¼ cup canola oil
4 eggs, beaten
2 cups fresh or frozen blueberries

Preheat oven to 375°F (190°C). Lightly butter 18 (2¾-inch) nonstick muffin cups. Combine pastry flour, cornmeal, baking powder, baking soda, cinnamon and salt in a large bowl until well blended. Make a well in the center of the dry ingredients and add maple syrup, buttermilk, oil, beaten eggs and blueberries. Stir into dry ingredients just until combined.

Spoon batter into muffin cups. Bake 20 to 25 minutes or until a wooden pick inserted in the centers comes out clean. Remove from pans and cool on a wire rack.   *Makes 18 muffins.*

PER SERVING: Cal 152 • Carbo 25 gm • Prot 3 gm • Total fat 4 gm • Sat fat 1 gm • Cal from fat 26% • Chol 48 mg

EDUCATION: Shop a natural-food store for baking powder made without aluminum salts or make your own (see glossary). Preliminary research shows aluminum may accumulate in the brain where it could lead to mental deterioration.

August 19

INSPIRATION: *If I am willing to learn, the events of each day become the teachers on my road to recovery.*

Broccoli & Bell Pepper Curried Rice Salad

Using mild brown rice vinegar calls for less oil to balance this colorful side dish.

¾ cup basmati or other long-
    grain white rice
1½ cups water
2 stalks broccoli
1 red bell pepper
4 green onions
2 tablespoons canola oil
2 teaspoons Madras curry powder
½ teaspoon salt
¼ teaspoon freshly ground black pepper
3 tablespoons brown rice vinegar
½ teaspoon packed brown sugar
2 tablespoons minced fresh parsley

Bring rice and water to a boil in a medium-size saucepan. Reduce heat, cover and simmer 20 minutes or until rice is tender and liquid is absorbed. Spread rice out in a large bowl to cool.

Meanwhile, peel broccoli stalks and cut stalks into 1½-inch sticks. Separate flowerets into bite-size pieces. Seed bell pepper and cut into 1-inch pieces. Slice green onions on the diagonal.

Steam broccoli in a vegetable steamer over boiling water 4 or 5 minutes, just until crisp-tender. Immediately run under cold water to stop cooking. When cool, set aside. Cook bell pepper and green onions in the oil in a small skillet over medium heat, stirring frequently, 1 or 2 minutes, just until crisp-tender. Stir in curry powder, salt and pepper and cook, stirring, 1 minute. Remove from heat and stir in vinegar and sugar.

Combine broccoli, curry mixture and parsley with rice in large bowl and stir until well combined. *Makes 4 servings.*

PER SERVING: Cal 211 • Carbo 33 gm • Prot 4 gm • Total fat 7 gm • Sat fat trace • Cal from fat 30% • Chol 0 mg

EDUCATION: Pepper your diet with vitamin C to reduce your cancer risk. Surprisingly, red bell peppers, ounce for ounce, contain three times the vitamin C found in citrus fruits! Bell peppers are also rich in beta-carotene. All are potent cancer-fighters. Add diced red bell peppers to green salads, soups, rice pilafs, pasta sauces and raw vegetable trays.

INSPIRATION: *I can take care of myself by learning to do things the easy way.*

Rollover Lazy Corn-on-the-Cob

The easiest-ever recipe awaits, and you won't steam up the kitchen! The corn flavor is intensified, the silk keeps the corn moist, and it stays hot until it's ready to eat. If you don't have a garden, buy corn from a farmers' market or roadside stand for peak freshness. Choose ears with entire husks intact.

4 garden-fresh ears of sweet corn, with husks

Arrange ears with husks on the floor of your microwave. Microwave on HIGH 10 to 12 minutes, until corn is just tender, turning and rotating corn once. Remove husk and corn silk and serve hot. If corn is served outdoors, put unhusked corn on a serving plate. Let each person husk his or her own. This keeps corn piping hot until eaten. Provide a trash container for husks. *Makes 4 servings.*

PER SERVING: Cal 83 • Carbo 19 gm • Prot 3 gm • Total fat 1 gm • Sat fat trace • Cal from fat 11% • Chol 0 mg

EDUCATION: Go light when flavoring corn so you don't wind up with a high-fat side dish. Corn is a naturally low-fat, high-carbohydrate food—an excellent addition to any diet. Add a tablespoon of butter and a liberal sprinkling of salt, and fat and sodium levels soar. Try some of the newer "supersweet" varieties of corn, so tasty no topping is necessary. If you do want to dress up corn, sprinkle with pepper, minced fresh herbs, a squeeze of lemon or lime wedge or a light vinaigrette dressing.

INSPIRATION: *I am becoming aware of a sense of purpose in my life.*

Summer Beef Vegetable Soup

❧ Light and refreshing, this soup is based on inexpensive shin beef and fresh garden produce. Serve with whole-grain rolls.

> 1 pound sliced beef shin, trimmed of fat
> 1 teaspoon olive oil
> 1 large onion, thinly sliced
> 1 garlic clove, minced
> 5 cups beef stock or chicken broth
> 1 cup peeled, seeded and chopped tomatoes
> 1 potato, peeled and cubed
> 2 carrots, diced
> 1 cup green beans, trimmed and snapped in half
> 2 ears corn
> ¹/2 small zucchini, sliced
> ¹/2 cup packed fresh spinach leaves, stems
>   removed and thinly sliced
> 2 tablespoons minced fresh parsley
> 1 tablespoon minced fresh basil
> ¹/2 teaspoon fresh marjoram

Brown the beef shins in the oil in a nonstick Dutch oven over medium heat. Add onion and cook, stirring frequently, until the onion is translucent. Add garlic and cook, stirring, 1 minute.

Add stock and tomatoes and bring to a boil. Reduce heat, cover and simmer 1¹/2 hours, until meat is very tender. Remove meat from bones and shred meat. Return meat to pan with potato, carrots and beans. Bring to a boil, reduce heat, cover and simmer 10 minutes. Cut kernels off ears of corn with a sharp knife. Add with zucchini, spinach and fresh herbs. Simmer 5 minutes or until vegetables are tender.

Makes 6 servings.

PER SERVING: Cal 193 • Carbo 20 gm • Prot 11 gm • Total fat 8 gm • Sat fat 3 gm • Cal from fat 37% • Chol 23 mg

EDUCATION: If you don't have a garden, buy fresh produce from a reliable local grower to obtain maximum nutrients. The sooner vegetables are eaten after picking, the more nutrients they retain. In winter, choose frozen vegetables over fresh when they are not in season. Frozen vegetables are frozen almost immediately after picking and can be far higher in nutrients than vegetables picked halfway around the world, stored, shipped, then purchased "fresh" from the supermarket.

INSPIRATION: *I will seek clarity today, to see the world around me and in me without illusions.*

Jean's Flaky Country Biscuits

❧ Made with some whole-wheat flour, these biscuits have a hearty flavor and light texture.

> 1 cup unbleached all-purpose flour
> ³/4 cup whole-wheat pastry flour
> 1 tablespoon baking powder
> ¹/2 teaspoon baking soda
> 2 teaspoons brown sugar
> ¹/4 teaspoon salt
> 4 tablespoons unsalted butter
> ²/3 to ³/4 cup buttermilk

Preheat oven to 450°F (230°C). Combine the flours, baking powder, baking soda, sugar and salt in a large bowl. Cut in butter with a pastry blender until the mixture resembles coarse meal. Stir in enough buttermilk to form a soft dough.

Turn dough out onto a floured surface and knead 1 minute. Pat dough out to ½-inch thickness. Cut out into 2-inch rounds. Place on an ungreased baking pan. Bake 10 to 12 minutes or until nicely browned.

Makes about 12 biscuits.

PER SERVING: Cal 110 • Carbo 16 gm • Prot 2 gm • Total fat 4 gm • Sat fat 2 gm • Cal from fat 34% • Chol 11 mg

EDUCATION: Increase the proportion of whole-grain flour in your baking for more taste, nutrition, and fiber. Gradually increase the amount of whole-wheat pastry flour and reduce white flour by an equal amount. The texture of the baked goods will become more dense and firm as you increase whole-grain flours. Find the proportion that satisfies your personal taste and provides you with whole-grain nutrition. Remember, even enriched flours lack most of the vitamins and minerals of whole-grain flours and contain just a small fraction of the fiber.

INSPIRATION: *I grant myself the freedom to use my power and my resources wisely.*

Grilled Turkey Tenderloin Steaks

❧ Bottled salsa makes this delicious, attractive and low-fat main dish a simple creation. Serve with grilled vegetables (see below), noodles and a salad.

6 (4- to 6-ounce) turkey breast
    tenderloin steaks
½ cup bottled salsa
1 tablespoon fresh lime juice
¼ teaspoon ground coriander

Prepare grill. Grill turkey steaks over medium coals 10 to 12 minutes, turning once. Combine salsa, lime juice and coriander. Brush turkey steaks with marinade and continue grilling 5 minutes or just until cooked throughout.

Makes 6 servings.

PER SERVING: Cal 110 • Carbo 2 gm • Prot 23 gm • Total fat 1 gm • Sat fat trace • Cal from fat 8% • Chol 63 mg

EDUCATION: Heighten interest in summer vegetables by cooking them on the grill. Who can resist the hearty outdoor flavor? Prior preparation will prevent vegetables charring on the outside before the inside is tender.

Vegetables can be steamed, cooked in a saucepan in a small amount of boiling water or microwaved on HIGH in a single layer on a plate. Microwave times are in parentheses. After precooking, brush vegetables lightly with olive oil and arrange crosswise on wire rack so they don't fall through. Grill over medium-hot coals.

- New potato halves 8 to 10 (5) minutes and grill 8 to 10 minutes
- Carrots 3 to 5 (2) minutes and grill 3 to 5 minutes
- Fennel bulb halves 7 to 8 (4) minutes and grill 7 to 8 minutes
- Leeks 10 (4) minutes and grill 5 minutes
- Eggplant and bell pepper slices grill 8 to 10 minutes
- Zucchini slices grill 5 to 6 minutes

INSPIRATION: *I am able to participate fully in the reality that surrounds me.*

Frozen Yogurt & Mixed Fruit Parfaits

❧ Peaches and blueberries meet with a hint of raspberry to create an attractive dessert that's great for hot-weather dining.

> 2 large peaches, peeled
> 1 pint low-fat vanilla frozen yogurt
> $^1/_4$ cup seedless red raspberry
>   preserves
> $^1/_2$ cup blueberries
> Mint sprigs for garnish

Coarsely cut up peaches. Place in a food processor or blender with 1 cup frozen yogurt and process until smooth. Divide blended peach mixture among 6 parfait glasses.

Warm raspberry preserves in the microwave on MEDIUM 30 to 45 seconds or until liquid.

Spoon remaining frozen yogurt over peach mixture and top with warmed raspberry preserves. Sprinkle with blueberries and garnish with mint. *Makes 6 servings.*

> PER SERVING: Cal 133 • Carbo 29 gm • Prot 4 gm • Total fat 1 gm • Sat fat trace • Cal from fat 6% • Chol 3 mg

EDUCATION: Learn to laugh at yourself and discover the healing effects of humor. While walking in a cemetery one day, a friend and I happened across an example of healing humor. On the tombstone before us was the name of a local man, the dates of his birth and death, and beneath a question that must have been repeated often and hopefully throughout his marriage: "What's for dessert?" On his wife's stone, beneath her name and dates, was the obviously unwavering reply: "Nothing." This couple, who appreciated the humorous in the mundane, continues to share their amusement with others long after their own laughter has faded.

INSPIRATION: *Letting go of old patterns gives me access to more effective ways of coping and advancing my recovery.*

Garden Lima Bean & Corn Soup

❧ Hearty and flavorful, this colorful soup is complemented by biscuits and a salad for a light but satisfying meal.

> 1 cup chopped onion
> 1 cup chopped red bell pepper
> 1 tablespoon olive oil
> 4 cups chicken broth
> 2 cups fresh shelled lima beans
> 1 small potato, peeled and diced
> 2 teaspoons fresh marjoram leaves or
> $^1/_2$ teaspoon dried
> 1 garlic clove, minced
> $^1/_8$ teaspoon ground allspice
> $^1/_8$ teaspoon salt
> $^1/_8$ teaspoon freshly ground white pepper
> 1 cup fresh or frozen whole-kernel corn
> 1 cup cooked brown rice

Cook onion and bell pepper in the oil in a large nonstick pot over medium heat until onion is translucent. Add broth, lima beans, potato, marjoram, garlic, allspice, salt and pepper. Bring to a boil, reduce heat, cover and simmer 10 to 12 minutes, until lima beans are firm-tender. Stir in corn, return soup to a simmer and cook 2 or 3 minutes, until the beans and corn are tender. Stir in rice, heat through and serve. *Makes 8 servings.*

PER SERVING: Cal 156 • Carbo 26 gm • Prot 7 gm • Total fat 3 gm • Sat fat trace • Cal from fat 16% • Chol 0 mg

EDUCATION: Play the shell game with beans; you'll come out a low-fat protein winner! Shelled green mature beans—lima beans are the most familiar—are a good source of protein with a nice supply of vitamin C and iron, two nutrients that work together to supply your blood with red cell–building material. Shelled beans, including soybeans, fava and cranberry beans, are also rich in potassium. To use shelled beans, split the pods open and remove beans by hand. Discard shells and cook beans just until tender. To avoid mealiness, do not over-cook.

A u g u s t   2 6

INSPIRATION: *The inner satisfaction I receive through my loving responses to others nurtures my recovery.*

Lenore's Vegetable, Walnut & Raisin Salad

Lenore, an ardent dog lover active in all-breed rescue, chooses organic foods for her happy dogs. A cancer survivor, she's also careful to eat well herself. Here a mix of summer vegetables—cool cucumbers, a bit of carrot and green onions—is made tangy with a minted yogurt dressing.

2 medium-size garden cucumbers
1 teaspoon salt
2 medium-size carrots
2 green onions
1/4 cup chopped walnuts
1/4 cup golden raisins
1/3 cup nonfat yogurt
1 tablespoon minced fresh mint
1 tablespoon minced fresh parsley
2 teaspoons lemon juice
1/4 teaspoon grated lemon peel

Thinly slice cucumbers. Toss with salt in a large bowl. Cover and let stand 1/2 hour. Scrub, trim and coarsely shred carrots. Thinly slice green onions on the diagonal. In a small saucepan, toast chopped walnuts over medium heat until lightly browned, stirring frequently. Set walnuts aside.

Drain cucumbers in a colander, rinsing with cold running water to remove salt. Wipe out bowl. Place cucumbers, carrots, green onions, walnuts and raisins in bowl. Combine yogurt, mint, parsley, lemon juice and peel in a small bowl. Add to cucumber salad and toss until combined. *Makes 4 servings.*

PER SERVING: Cal 110 • Carbo 19 gm • Prot 4 gm • Total fat 3 gm • Sat fat trace • Cal from fat 25% • Chol 1 mg

EDUCATION: To avoid excess pesticide residues, peel any produce you suspect is waxed. Better yet, peel any produce unless you are certain it has not been waxed. Vegetables are often waxed before being sent to market. The wax improves their appearance and, by slowing moisture loss, extends their shelf life. While the waxes themselves are not harmful, waxes can seal in pesticide residues and other chemicals. Washing, even scrubbing, will not remove these surface chemicals. Only by peeling the vegetables will you be certain to remove them. Although wax is often visible on rutabagas and cucumbers, it may not be visible or suspected on tomatoes, bell peppers, beets, squashes, potatoes and sweet potatoes. Apples, peaches and pears may also be waxed. Unless you know the fruit or vegetable grower personally, don't eat it without peeling.

INSPIRATION: *I will learn to accept the gifts of the day and, more importantly, to let go gracefully what is not meant for me.*

Broiled Eggplant & Bell Peppers

❧ Picture-perfect and a great hearty accompaniment to grilled meat, poultry or fish.

1 medium-size eggplant (about 1 1/2 pounds), cut into 1/2-inch cubes
1 onion, cut lengthwise into thin wedges
1/2 teaspoon salt
2 red bell peppers
2 yellow bell peppers
1 cup loosely packed fresh basil, thinly sliced
1/4 cup minced fresh parsley
1 tablespoon olive oil
1 tablespoon fresh lemon juice
1/4 teaspoon freshly ground black pepper

Preheat broiler. Combine eggplant, onion and salt in a large bowl and toss together until combined. Place eggplant mixture on the rack of a nonstick broiling pan. Broil vegetables, stirring occasionally, about 20 minutes or until eggplant and onion are browned on all sides. Return eggplant mixture to bowl and keep warm.

Meanwhile, cut bell peppers into 1/4-inch strips. Place pepper strips on rack of broiling pan. Broil peppers, stirring occasionally, about 15 minutes or until browned on all sides.

Add bell peppers, basil, parsley, oil, lemon juice and pepper to eggplant mixture and toss until combined. *Makes 8 servings.*

PER SERVING: Cal 47 • Carbo 8 gm • Prot 1 gm • Total fat 2 gm • Sat fat trace • Cal from fat 38% • Chol 0 mg

EDUCATION: Use nonfat cooking methods with eggplant to enjoy its low-fat goodness.

Eggplant is notorious for soaking up oil as it cooks. One Iranian dish, called "Imam Biyaldi," translates as "The Imam Fainted" when he saw how much expensive oil was consumed in preparing his favorite dish. Steaming, grilling, broiling and baking are some cooking possibilities. Also, you might add eggplant to stews, soups and casseroles.

INSPIRATION: *Perfectionism is a self-made fence that prevents me from moving on. Let me do a good job today, and be done.*

Melon Balls with Kiwi Fruit

❧ Use a handy little instrument called a "melon baller" to create this attractive dessert. As a variation, add fruit sherbet, scooped with the melon baller, and toss together at the last minute.

2 cups honeydew melon balls
2 cups cantaloupe balls
1 cup watermelon balls
2 kiwi fruit, peeled
1/2 cup pineapple juice
1 tablespoon fresh lime juice
1/8 teaspoon freshly grated lime peel
Mint sprigs for garnish

Combine honeydew, cantaloupe and watermelon balls in a large serving bowl. Quarter kiwi fruit lengthwise and slice 1/2 inch thick. Add to melons with pineapple and lime juice and lime peel. Toss and serve in dessert dishes garnished with mint sprigs. *Makes 8 servings.*

PER SERVING: Cal 57 • Carbo 14 gm • Prot 1 gm • Total fat trace • Sat fat trace • Cal from fat 5% • Chol 0 mg

EDUCATION: Eat 2 to 4 servings of fruit each day. Fruit—packed with two types of fiber to keep blood-cholesterol levels in check *and* digestion running smoothly—also contains a wealth of vitamins, minerals and other essential nutrients. The fruits above are no exception. Melons are a good source of potassium and vitamin C, while cantaloupe and other orange-fleshed melons abound in beta-carotene. Kiwi fruit, ounce for ounce, outshine oranges in vitamin C content, and are rich in cholesterol-lowering soluble fiber.

August 29

INSPIRATION: *Fulfilling my whims and desires never brings lasting happiness—that is happiness I can only find within me.*

Jesse's Tuna Linguini with Tomatoes

Quick top-of-the-stove dinner is a pleasing marriage of flavors, colors and textures. Serve with crusty Italian-style bread.

1 pound linguini
1 onion, chopped
1 tablespoon olive oil
2 medium-size zucchini, cut into
   ³/₄-inch cubes
2 teaspoons minced garlic
1 (28-ounce) can crushed tomatoes
¹/₂ teaspoon freshly grated orange peel
¹/₄ teaspoon dried oregano
¹/₄ teaspoon salt
¹/₈ teaspoon freshly ground black pepper
1 (6¹/₂-ounce) can water-packed,
white meat tuna, drained
2 tablespoons minced fresh parsley
2 tablespoons freshly grated
   Parmesan cheese

Bring a large pot of water to a boil. Add pasta and cook until firm-tender, 7 to 9 minutes.

While water is heating, cook onion in the oil in a large nonstick skillet over medium heat, stirring frequently, until the onion is translucent. Add zucchini and garlic and cook, stirring, until zucchini is crisp-tender, about 5 minutes. Stir in tomatoes, orange peel, oregano, salt and pepper. Bring to a boil, reduce heat, cover and simmer 5 minutes. Flake tuna and add to skillet. Simmer 3 minutes, until vegetables are tender. Stir in parsley.

Drain linguini and place in a serving bowl. Top with tomato sauce and sprinkle with cheese. Toss together before serving.

Makes 4 servings.

PER SERVING: Cal 589 • Carbo 100 gm • Prot 32 gm • Total fat 7 gm • Sat fat 2 gm • Cal from fat 10% • Chol 22 mg

EDUCATION: Select canned tuna packed in water to get the most benefit from this low-fat, high-protein fish. Oil-packed varieties can add up to ten times the fat found in the fish itself. Some 15 percent of calories come from fat in water-packed tuna, compared to over 60 percent calories from fat for the same fish packed in oil. Also, draining the oil can remove up to one-fourth of the healthful omega-3 fatty acids from the tuna, while the loss from draining water-packed tuna is negligible.

INSPIRATION: *Today I will look at things I can do differently to get myself out of a rut.*

Tex-Mex Succotash

Succotash goes south-of-the-border for an unexpected combination that livens up any summer meal.

    4 ears corn, in husks
    1 cup fresh baby lima beans
    1/2 cup fresh green peas
    1 cup sliced yellow wax beans
    1/4 cup thinly sliced green onions
    2 teaspoons canola oil
    1 tablespoon nonfat yogurt
    1 teaspoon minced fresh cilantro
    1 teaspoon chili powder
    1/4 teaspoon ground cumin
    1/4 teaspoon salt
    1/8 teaspoon freshly ground
       black pepper
    Dash of hot (cayenne) pepper
    1/4 cup minced fresh parsley
    1 bacon slice, cooked and crumbled

Microwave corn, in husks, on HIGH 10 minutes. Set aside. (Corn can also be husked, then steamed 7 minutes.)

Meanwhile, bring a large saucepan of water to a boil. Add lima beans and peas, reduce heat and cook 5 minutes. Add wax beans, return to a boil and cook 3 or 4 minutes, until the vegetables are crisp-tender. Add green onions and cook 1 minute. Drain.

While vegetables are cooking, cut corn kernels from cobs. Combine oil, yogurt, cilantro, chili powder, cumin, salt, pepper and cayenne in a small bowl. Combine corn kernels, beans, peas and green onions in a medium-size bowl. Stir in yogurt-chili mixture and parsley. Garnish with crumbled bacon. *Makes 4 servings.*

PER SERVING: Cal 203 • Carbo 36 gm • Prot 8 gm • Total fat 5 gm • Sat fat 1 gm • Cal from fat 22% • Chol 2 mg

EDUCATION: To cut back on fat, use bacon as flavoring, rather than as part of your meals. Savory bacon flavor comes at the expense of high fat. You don't have to exclude it entirely, if you stick to ways to keep intake to a minimum. Here, each person gets one-fourth of one piece of bacon, just enough to taste. Remember, when serving such small quantities, it's best to buy slices individually at your butcher or supermarket deli. That way there's no temptation to "finish off" the package.

INSPIRATION: *Being strong is seeing the truth about myself in an accepting, loving light. It means treating myself and others with kindness and respect.*

Tomato Salad with Arugula

🌿 It's hard to go wrong with tomatoes in the summer; nearly everything you do with them turns out to be delicious!

5 garden-ripe tomatoes
1 small zucchini
1 small yellow bell pepper, seeded
2 tablespoons minced fresh parsley
1 teaspoon minced fresh basil
3 tablespoons brown rice vinegar
2 tablespoons olive oil
1 teaspoon sugar
$^1/_2$ teaspoon salt
$^1/_8$ teaspoon freshly ground black pepper
1 bunch arugula or watercress, trimmed and rinsed

Core tomatoes and cut tomatoes, zucchini and bell pepper into 1-inch pieces. Combine in a large bowl with minced parsley and basil. Stir together vinegar, oil, sugar, salt and pepper in a small bowl. Pour over vegetables and toss.

Arrange arugula or watercress on a serving platter. Top with the tomato salad.

Makes 8 servings.

PER SERVING: Cal 59 • Carbo 8 gm • Prot 1 gm • Total fat 4 gm • Sat fat trace • Cal from fat 56% • Chol 0 mg

EDUCATION: Add arugula and other dark greens to your salads. Arugula may twist your tongue (especially if you say it three times, fast), but this green is incredibly rich in three important nutrients for you to sink your teeth into. Arugula contains about four times the vitamin C of romaine lettuce (which in turn has six times the amount found in iceberg!) and three times as much beta-carotene as romaine. That's twenty times what you'll find in iceberg. Arugula is also bursting with calcium. It has a peppery taste with young leaves being mildest. A small amount can add zest—and plenty of nutrition—to any green salad.

INSPIRATION: *In building a satisfying relationship, I have to discover an honest and true individual—inside myself.*

Grilled Pizza

🌱 Combining my son's fondness for pizza and grilling makes this a perfect choice for his birthday. If you don't want to fire up the grill, bake in a preheated 500°F (260°C) oven about 10 minutes or until cheeses are melted and crust is browned. For a quicker dish, buy a prepared crust (see variation, below).

> 1 cup lukewarm water
> 1 tablespoon brown sugar
> 1 tablespoon active dry yeast
> 2 cups unbleached all-purpose flour
> 1 cup stone-ground yellow cornmeal
> 1/4 cup whole-wheat pastry flour
> 1 teaspoon salt
> 3 tablespoons olive oil
> 1 cup chopped onions
> 1 tablespoon canola oil
> 2 tomatoes, peeled, seeded and chopped
> 3 garlic cloves, minced
> 1/4 cup thinly sliced fresh basil
> 1 1/2 cups (6 ounces) shredded part-skim mozzarella cheese
> 1/4 cup freshly grated Parmesan cheese
> Minced fresh basil for garnish

For crust, combine water and sugar in a small bowl. Sprinkle yeast over top and set aside until foamy, about 5 minutes.

Combine 1 3/4 cups of the unbleached flour, cornmeal, pastry flour and salt in a large bowl. Make a well in the center of the flour mixture and pour in the yeast mixture and olive oil. Beat the mixture with a wooden spoon until the dough begins to hold together.

Turn the dough out on a lightly floured surface, dust your hands with flour and knead the dough, adding the remaining 1/4 cup unbleached flour, until the dough is no longer sticky. Knead the dough about 10 minutes, until it feels smooth and springy.

Place dough in a well-oiled bowl, turning to coat with oil. Cover bowl tightly with plastic wrap and set in a draft-free warm [75° to 85°F (25° to 30°C)] place until doubled in bulk, 45 to 60 minutes.

While dough is rising, cook onions in the canola oil in a large nonstick skillet over medium heat, stirring frequently, until firm-tender, 6 to 7 minutes. Stir in tomatoes and garlic and cook, stirring frequently, until liquid evaporates, about 10 minutes. Stir in basil.

Preheat grill or oven. Punch down dough and flatten. Roll out on a floured surface to a 14-inch round. Sprinkle a baking sheet with cornmeal and transfer dough to baking sheet. Cover with a towel and let rise 20 minutes. Spread sauce over dough, leaving a 1/2-inch border. Top with cheeses.

Place a pizza stone on the grill and heat for 5 minutes. Slide pizza off baking sheet and onto pizza stone. Cover grill and cook until cheeses melt and crust is crisp, about 10 minutes. Sprinkle with basil and serve.

Makes 6 servings.

PER SERVING: Cal 458 • Carbo 62 gm • Prot 17 gm • Total fat 16 gm • Sat fat 5 gm • Cal from fat 31% • Chol 19 mg

VARIATION

If you want a quicker, easier grilled pizza, purchase a prepared, thin 12-inch pizza crust. Grill over low coals, top side down, about 4 minutes. Top with sauce and cheeses. Grill, covered, 4 minutes or until cheeses are melted and crust is crisp.

EDUCATION: Exchange favorite low-fat recipes with friends to expand your low-fat repertoire.

We tend to repeat what works: easy-to-prepare main dishes. But that can lead to a rut. By seeing what friends are doing for their meals, you get kitchen-tested results and personalized pointers. Your friends will benefit, too, with the sharing of your meal ideas.

September 2

INSPIRATION: *Today I will make a conscious effort to be good to the people I care about.*

Blueberry-Peach Dessert Crisps

Seasonal fresh fruits, a simple addition of ingredients plus quick baking equal a summer-style company dessert without too much fuss. Serve with fat-free frozen yogurt, if desired.

8 large peaches
1/2 cup blueberries
1/4 cup granulated sugar
2 tablespoons unbleached all-
    purpose flour
1/3 cup whole-wheat pastry flour
3 tablespoons unsalted butter, at
    room temperature
3 tablespoons brown sugar
1/4 teaspoon ground cinnamon

Preheat oven to 400°F (200°C). Peel and pit peaches. Cut into thin slices. Combine sliced peaches and blueberries with granulated sugar and unbleached flour in a large bowl. Spoon peach mixture into 8 ramekins or custard cups. In a small bowl, combine pastry flour, butter, brown sugar and cinnamon with a fork until the mixture resembles coarse meal. Sprinkle cinnamon mixture on fruit in ramekins.

Place ramekins on a jelly roll pan or baking sheet. Bake 25 to 30 minutes or until mixture is bubbly and topping is golden. Serve warm.

Makes 8 servings.

PER SERVING: Cal 148 • Carbo 27 gm • Prot 1 gm • Total fat 4 gm • Sat fat 3 gm • Cal from fat 27% • Chol 11 mg

EDUCATION: Include seven or more servings of fruits and vegetables every day. That doesn't mean you have to have a raw carrot followed by celery sticks and a shiny, plain apple. Though that is certainly a healthy choice, you can also count vegetables and fruits used in salads, soups, main dishes and desserts. Keeping your intake varied helps to sustain your interest. Variety, in addition to being the spice of life, can help us stick to a healthy diet.

INSPIRATION: *Avoiding my difficulties is not the same thing as learning to resolve them.*

Linguini with Fresh Basil-Tomato Sauce

❦ Take advantage of garden-ripe tomatoes to make a tasty sauce that requires no cooking.

> 3 cups peeled, seeded and diced garden-ripe
>   tomatoes
> $^1/_4$ cup thinly sliced fresh basil
> 2 tablespoons minced fresh parsley
> 1 tablespoon extra-virgin olive oil
> 1 small garlic clove, pushed through a press
> $^1/_4$ teaspoon salt
> $^1/_8$ teaspoon freshly ground black pepper
> 1 pound linguini, broken in half
> $^1/_4$ cup shredded part-skim mozzarella cheese

Combine tomatoes, basil, parsley, oil, garlic, salt and pepper in a large serving bowl. Set aside for flavors to blend.

Bring a large pot of water to a boil. Cook linguini 7 to 9 minutes or just until firm-tender. Drain and toss with tomato mixture until well combined. Serve topped with mozzarella.

Makes 4 servings.

PER SERVING: Cal 504 • Carbo 93 gm • Prot 18 gm • Total fat 7 gm • Sat fat 1 gm • Cal from fat 12% • Chol 4 mg

EDUCATION: Cut back on cheeses to reduce cholesterol intake. While cheeses are high in protein and calcium, most pack a wallop with fat and cholesterol. Even switching to part-skim cheeses, like ricotta or the mozzarella above is only a partial solution. Most cheeses derive 60 to 90 percent of their total calories from fat. Even part-skim mozzarella weighs in at over 50 percent fat calories. However, because cheese is so richly flavorful, you can make a little go a long way. Shredding or grating cheeses, for example, allows cheese flavor to be distributed throughout a dish, maximizing taste and minimizing fat intake.

INSPIRATION: *To join the path set out for me by my Higher Power frees me to live with energy and love.*

Beet, Mandarin Orange & Asian Pear Salad

❦ In late fall, you can make this salad with fresh tangerines (use three) as long as you refrigerate some Asian pears now to serve then. They will keep up to three months under refrigeration. Select ripe Asian pears by their sweet aroma.

> 4 medium-size beets
> 1 tablespoon brown rice vinegar
> 1 tablespoon olive oil
> 1 tablespoon brown sugar
> 1 tablespoon fresh orange juice
> 2 teaspoons Dijon mustard
> $^1/_4$ teaspoon salt
> 2 Asian pears
> 1 (6-ounce) can mandarin oranges, drained
> 1 tablespoon minced fresh parsley
> 1 small head red-leaf lettuce

Scrub beets and trim leaves, leaving 2 inches of stems. Bring beets to a boil in a large saucepan with enough water to cover. Reduce heat, cover and simmer 30 minutes or until beets are tender. Drain and allow beets to cool.

Meanwhile, whisk together vinegar, oil, brown sugar, orange juice, mustard and salt in a large bowl. Peel beets and cut into small cubes. Peel pears and cut into thin wedges. Toss beets, pears, mandarin oranges and parsley with the dressing in the large bowl. To serve, wash and dry lettuce leaves and arrange on a serving plate. Top with the beet mixture.

Makes 4 servings.

PER SERVING: Cal 153 • Carbo 31 gm • Prot 1 gm • Total fat 4 gm • Sat fat trace • Cal from fat 24% • Chol 0 mg

EDUCATION: Serve fruits and vegetables together to increase your servings of each. Many vegetables and fruits have complementary flavors and textures, creating a whole more satisfying than its parts. In addition to the salad combination above, you might try salads featuring pears and green beans; cabbage and crushed pineapple; celery, apples and raisins; spinach and grapefruit or combinations of your own invention. Serve with a low-fat salad dressing to complete the healthful package.

September 5

INSPIRATION: *I may not be able to control events, but by staying healthy in mind, body and spirit, I can be prepared to respond sanely to the unexpected.*

Chilled Minted Zucchini Soup

❧ Pick garden zucchini while they're small and tender, or purchase small, firm zucchini for this easy soup.

¹/₂ cup chopped onion
1 teaspoon olive oil
3 small zucchini, diced
2 cups chicken broth
³/₄ cup nonfat yogurt

¹/₄ cup buttermilk
2 teaspoons fresh lime juice
1 teaspoon minced fresh mint
¹/₄ teaspoon salt
¹/₄ teaspoon freshly grated lime peel
Mint sprigs for garnish

Cook onion in the oil in a nonstick Dutch oven over medium heat, stirring frequently, 2 or 3 minutes. Add zucchini and cook, stirring frequently, 5 minutes. Add chicken broth and bring to a boil. Reduce heat, cover and simmer 8 minutes or until zucchini is tender. Cool to lukewarm.

Place zucchini mixture, ¹/₂ cup of the yogurt, buttermilk, lime juice, mint and salt in a blender or food processor and process until smooth. Cover and refrigerate until chilled.

To serve, divide soup among 4 bowls. Stir grated lime peel into remaining ¹/₄ cup yogurt. Swirl yogurt-lime mixture into each bowl of soup. Garnish with mint. *Makes 4 servings.*

PER SERVING: Cal 366 • Carbo 36 gm • Prot 26 gm • Total fat 14 gm • Sat fat 4 gm • Cal from fat 34% • Chol 13 mg

EDUCATION: Keep the blender running for lightning-quick, nutritious beverages and desserts! Choose a large, extra-ripe peach, remove pit and peel, and blend until smooth. Stir in a dollop of honey-sweetened yogurt and voilá, dessert peach soup! For a melon beverage, place 2 cups peeled, seeded and diced watermelon or cantaloupe (or try a combination of the two) and blend until smooth. Serve over ice. Of course, you really won't want to serve a blender dessert or beverage following a blender soup. Remember to vary tastes and textures at meals to keep them interesting.

INSPIRATION: *The vibrant flow of energy that is my life can be channeled in positive directions each day.*

Turkey Cutlets with Snow Peas

❧ Frozen snow peas will work just fine for this dish, though in spring, fresh snow peas are preferable.

> 1 pound turkey breast cutlets
> 4 teaspoons unsalted butter
> 2 tablespoons sliced almonds
> 2 garlic cloves, minced
> ³/₄ pound frozen snow peas,
>   thawed and
>   halved diagonally
> 2 teaspoons minced fresh tarragon
> ¹/₄ cup chicken broth
> ¹/₄ teaspoon salt
> ¹/₈ teaspoon freshly ground
>   black pepper

Cook turkey breast cutlets in half the butter in a large nonstick skillet over medium heat 2 or 3 minutes, turning once or until lightly browned and cooked through. Remove to a warm platter and cover with foil. Keep warm.

Add almonds to same pan and cook over medium heat, stirring constantly, about 30 seconds or until lightly browned. Remove almonds to a small bowl.

Melt remaining butter in skillet. Stir in garlic, then add snow peas and tarragon. Cook over medium heat, stirring constantly, about 2 minutes or just until snow peas are firm-tender. Arrange snow peas and almonds over turkey and cover with foil. Add broth, salt and pepper to skillet and boil, stirring constantly, 3 minutes or until stock is slightly reduced. Pour sauce over turkey and snow peas and serve.

Makes 4 servings.

PER SERVING: Cal 217 • Carbo 9 gm • Prot 28 gm • Total fat 7 gm • Sat fat 3 gm • Cal from fat 29% • Chol 76 mg

EDUCATION: Serve low-fat turkey more often than just at Thanksgiving. Turkey breast cutlets can be served year-round. Take advantage of this low-fat, delicious protein source. White meat turkey has less than 1 gram of saturated fat per serving, but is high in vitamin B_6 (important because it helps maintain normal brain function), phosphorus, vitamin B_{12} and zinc, which is rapidly depleted with the consumption of alcohol.

INSPIRATION: *My spiritual growth is worth the time, attention and energy I focus on making it a priority in my life.*

Garden Vegetable Summer Pasta

❧ Pasta Primavera has become synonymous with pasta and vegetables. And though *primavera* is Italian for "spring," most often the vegetables called for are of the late summer harvest. This pasta dish highlights a variety of summer's fresh produce and is served chilled.

> 2 ears corn, with husks
> 2 cups peeled, seeded and
>   diced tomatoes
> ¹/₂ cup peeled, seeded and diced cucumber
> ¹/₂ cup diced yellow or orange
>   bell pepper
> ¹/₃ cup sliced green onions
> 3 tablespoons olive oil
> 2 tablespoons fresh lime juice

2 tablespoons minced fresh cilantro
2 tablespoons minced fresh parsley
1 garlic clove, minced
$^1/_2$ teaspoon ground cumin
$^1/_4$ teaspoon salt
$^1/_8$ teaspoon freshly ground
    black pepper
$^3/_4$ pound penne pasta

Microwave corn with husks on HIGH 6 minutes, or husk and steam 2 or 3 minutes. Set aside to cool. Combine tomatoes, cucumber, bell pepper, green onions, oil, lime juice, cilantro, parsley, garlic, cumin, salt and pepper in a large bowl. Cover and refrigerate.

Bring a large pot of water to a boil. Add pasta and boil 7 to 9 minutes or just until firm-tender. Drain and run under cold running water until cooled. Cut corn from ears. Toss corn and pasta with tomato mixture. Serve chilled.

Makes 4 servings.

PER SERVING: Cal 478 • Carbo 80 gm • Prot 14 gm • Total fat 12 gm • Sat fat 2 gm • Cal from fat 22% • Chol 0 mg

EDUCATION: Eliminate oil from the cooking water for pasta to keep calories low. Although adding oil is touted as a method to keep pasta from sticking, a few simple steps will keep pasta separate. First, cook pasta in plenty of rapidly boiling water, stirring frequently, especially right after pasta is added. If you are chilling pasta, run under cold water to eliminate excess starch and to cool pasta. Adding oil to cooking pasta will prevent sauces from adhering to the pasta, and add unwanted fat and calories to your dish.

September 8

INSPIRATION: *I will focus on the things I can do, not regret those I cannot, as I make my way along the path of recovery.*

Grain & Fruit Breakfast Cereal

You can use all brown rice, if there's no cooked bulgur on hand, or substitute cooked steel-cut oats, cooked barley or couscous.

    1 cup cooked brown rice
    $^1/_2$ cup cooked bulgur
    $^3/_4$ cup skim milk
    2 tablespoons raisins
    1 tablespoon honey
    1 tablespoon chopped toasted
        walnuts
    $^1/_2$ teaspoon ground cinnamon
    Skim milk
    Sliced fresh peaches, apples
        or bananas
    Blueberries

Combine rice, bulgur, milk, raisins, honey, walnuts and cinnamon in a medium-size saucepan. Cook over low heat 5 to 7 minutes, stirring occasionally, or until heated through. Serve with milk, sliced fruit and blueberries.

Makes 4 servings.

PER SERVING WITHOUT EXTRA MILK AND FRESH FRUIT: Cal 132 • Carbo 26 gm • Prot 4 gm • Total fat 2 gm • Sat fat trace • Cal from fat 14% • Chol trace

EDUCATION: Switch from whole milk to skim or low-fat (at most, 1 percent) milk to cut out dietary fat. Calcium, important to bone health, blood pressure and cancer resistance, stays the same. In recipes, you may not even notice a change in taste. And as drinking lower-fat milk becomes a habit, you may wonder how you drank whole milk. To continue getting the benefits of calcium without suffering the drawbacks of high fat, use low-fat milk in place of whole milk or cream in soups, puddings and desserts, baked goods and main dishes.

INSPIRATION: *I am able to decide what is worth doing and what isn't, and to set my own priorities.*

Irmina's Vinegar Cucumber Salad

❧ A cool refresher for spicy foods or for hot days.

>4 medium-size cucumbers
>1 teaspoon salt
>1 small red onion
>$1/4$ cup apple juice
>2 tablespoons cider vinegar
>1 teaspoon sweet
>	Hungarian paprika
>1 teaspoon sugar
>1 tablespoon minced fresh parsley

Peel cucumbers, halve lengthwise, seed and slice thinly. Place cucumber slices in a large bowl, sprinkle with salt and toss to coat. Set aside 30 minutes.

Peel, halve lengthwise and thinly slice red onion. Place in a medium-size bowl with half a dozen ice cubes and cold water to cover. Set aside 30 minutes. Combine apple juice, vinegar, paprika and sugar in a medium-size bowl. Rinse cucumbers, squeeze and discard excess liquid. Drain onion and pat dry.

Add cucumbers, onion and parsley to dressing; toss to combine. Cover and chill before serving.　　　　*Makes 6 servings.*

PER SERVING: Cal 40 • Carbo 9 gm • Prot 1 gm • Total fat trace • Sat fat trace • Cal from fat 6% • Chol 0 mg

EDUCATION: To keep salads slimming, find alternatives to sour cream and mayonnaise in your dressings. A healthful salad can become a high-fat disaster with the simple addition of the wrong dressing. Here a vinegar-based dressing keeps low-fat cucumber salad lean.

INSPIRATION: *I am discarding old feelings of inadequacy as I discover more of my inner worth.*

Red Bell Peppers with Millet Stuffing

❧ Stuffed peppers are a favorite with many. Serve with soup and salad for a satisfying summer meal. You can substitute $1 1/2$ cups cooked brown rice for the cooked millet.

>$1/2$ cup millet
>$1 1/2$ cups chicken broth
>4 red bell peppers, halved lengthwise
>	and cored
>$1/2$ cup chopped onion
>2 teaspoons olive oil
>$1/2$ pound extra-lean ground beef
>3 tablespoons minced fresh parsley
>1 tablespoon minced fresh basil or
>	$1/2$ teaspoon dried
>$1/4$ teaspoon salt
>$1/8$ teaspoon freshly ground black pepper
>$1/2$ cup shredded part-skim
>	mozzarella cheese
>1 cup tomato sauce, heated

Combine millet and chicken broth in a medium-size saucepan. Bring to a boil, reduce heat, cover and simmer 25 to 30 minutes or until liquid is absorbed and grain is tender.

Preheat oven to 350°F (175°C). Steam pepper halves in a vegetable steamer over boiling water 5 minutes. Meanwhile, cook onion in the oil in a medium-size nonstick skillet over medium heat, stirring frequently, until the onion is translucent. Add beef, stirring to brown meat evenly.

Combine cooked millet, beef mixture, parsley, basil, salt and pepper. Mound into pepper halves and sprinkle each with shredded mozzarella. Arrange stuffed peppers in a large, shallow baking pan. Bake 20 minutes, until peppers are tender. Top with hot tomato sauce.

Makes 4 servings.

PER SERVING: Cal 343 • Carbo 30 gm • Prot 19 gm • Total fat 15 gm • Sat fat 6 gm • Cal from fat 41% • Chol 46 mg

EDUCATION: Make millet a part of your diet to help you keep your cool. This grain, a staple in Northern Africa and Asia, is among the richest in nerve-soothing B vitamins. This hulled, whole grain is available from natural-food stores and some supermarkets. As with other grains, do not stir millet as it cooks if you want your final product fluffy and separate. Add cooked millet to meat loaves and casseroles, or use cooked millet in recipes calling for cooked brown rice. Simmer in skim milk for a hot breakfast cereal, flavored with spices.

September 11

INSPIRATION: *If I am open and accepting of others just as they are, they will more likely be as open and accepting of me.*

Jerry's Curried Squash Soup

The delicate curry flavor complements this soup whether it's served hot or cold.

*¹/₄ cup minced green onions, white
    part only*
¹/₂ tablespoon unsalted butter
1 garlic clove, minced
*1¹/₂ teaspoons Madras
    curry powder*
¹/₄ teaspoon ground coriander
*4 yellow crookneck squash (about
    1 to 1¹/₄ pounds), diced*

2 to 2¹/₂ cups chicken broth
¹/₄ cup nonfat yogurt
¹/₄ cup buttermilk
*2 tablespoons minced fresh
    parsley*

Cook green onions in butter in a nonstick Dutch oven over medium heat, stirring frequently, 1 to 2 minutes or until translucent. Add garlic, curry powder and coriander and cook, stirring, 1 minute. Add squash and cook, stirring, 2 to 3 minutes. Add 2 cups broth and bring to a boil. Reduce heat, cover and simmer 15 to 20 minutes, until squash is tender. Puree in batches in a blender or food processor. Thin with additional broth, if necessary. Serve hot or cover and chill.

Ladle soup into bowls. Stir together yogurt and buttermilk. Swirl 2 tablespoons of the yogurt mixture into each serving. Garnish with minced parsley. *Makes 4 servings.*

PER SERVING: Cal 55 • Carbo 6 gm • Prot 5 gm • Total fat 2 gm • Sat fat 1 gm • Cal from fat 32% • Chol 8 mg

EDUCATION: Develop your expertise with seasonings by exploring varieties of curry powder in flavoring low-fat foods. "Curry" powder is not a single ground spice, but a combination of spices used to flavor foods. The Indian subcontinent is rich in curries—each one blended individually to season a particular dish.

To make your own curry powder, combine 1 teaspoon ground coriander, 1 teaspoon ground cumin, ¹/₂ teaspoon ground ginger, ¹/₄ teaspoon ground hot red (cayenne) pepper and ¹/₄ teaspoon freshly ground black pepper. Vary the proportions according to your taste. Begin seasoning dishes lightly with curry, then next time you prepare the dish, add more, if you wish. Stirring curry powder into hot oil and cooking briefly helps to develop the flavors of the spices.

INSPIRATION: *Believing I am capable of change is a basic step on my road to recovery.*

Fruit-Studded Applesauce Cake

A moist confection with no need for icing. A sprinkle of confectioners' sugar is all the adornment this simple dessert needs.

1 $1/3$ cups unbleached all-
  purpose flour
$1/3$ cup whole-wheat pastry flour
$3/4$ cup packed brown sugar
1 teaspoon baking soda
$1/2$ teaspoon ground allspice
$1/2$ teaspoon ground cinnamon
$1/4$ teaspoon salt
$1/2$ cup applesauce
$1/4$ cup buttermilk
$1/4$ cup canola oil
1 tablespoon unsalted butter,
  melted
1 teaspoon fresh lemon juice
$1/2$ cup diced pitted prunes
Powdered sugar for garnish

Preheat oven to 400°F (200°C). Butter a 9-inch-square baking pan. Combine flours, sugar, baking soda, spices and salt in a large bowl.

In a small bowl, combine applesauce, buttermilk, oil, melted butter and lemon juice. Stir into dry ingredients just until combined. Pour batter into pan and sprinkle with the diced prunes. Bake 20 to 22 minutes or until a wooden pick inserted in the center comes out clean.

Makes 9 servings.

PER SERVING: Cal 256 • Carbo 45 gm • Prot 3 gm • Total fat 8 gm • Sat fat 1 gm • Cal from fat 27% • Chol 4 mg

EDUCATION: Cut fat and calories from baked goods by substituting applesauce for part of the butter, oil or shortening called for. Start by substituting only half or less of the fat or oil called for. Increase that proportion with subsequent baking. Some recipes will remain delectable with all of the fat replaced. Adding buttermilk helps ensure a tender crumb in low-fat baked goods.

INSPIRATION: *In recovery, I can use my energy to connect with friends and family, allowing my trust and intimacy to grow.*

Company's Coming Low-Fat Nachos

❧ Use nonfat tortilla chips, or make your own. Top with low-fat refried beans and cheese, broil, then serve with salsa. For a spicy lift, top with bottled, sliced jalapeño chiles. Easy and fun to eat!

    8 corn tortillas
    ¹/₂ cup finely chopped onion
    2 teaspoons canola oil
    2 garlic cloves, minced
    ¹/₂ teaspoon ground coriander
    ¹/₂ teaspoon ground cumin
    ¹/₈ teaspoon hot (cayenne) pepper
    2 cups cooked or canned pinto beans,
       drained
    ¹/₄ cup water
    1¹/₂ cups Sombrero Salsa (see February 16) or
       bottled salsa, thinned with tomato juice
    1 tablespoon minced fresh cilantro
    2 teaspoons fresh lemon or lime juice
    ¹/₂ cup shredded sharp Cheddar cheese
    Bottled jalapeño chiles for garnish (optional)

Preheat oven to 450°F (230°C). Cut each tortilla into 8 wedges and spread in a single layer on 2 baking sheets. Bake 5 to 7 minutes, until crisp.

Meanwhile, cook onion in the oil in a large nonstick skillet over medium heat, stirring frequently, until the onion is tender, about 5 minutes. Add garlic, coriander, cumin and cayenne and cook, stirring, 1 minute. Add beans and heat through, mashing beans with the back of a spoon. Stir in water, and cook, stirring, until water is absorbed. Stir in ¹/₄ cup of the salsa, minced cilantro and lemon or lime juice. Remove from heat. Preheat broiler.

Place all of the tortilla wedges on 1 baking sheet. Top with hot bean mixture and sprinkle with cheese. Run under broiler about 1 minute or until cheese is melted. Transfer to a heated platter and garnish with jalapeños, if using. Serve remaining salsa in a small bowl.

Makes 4 servings.

PER SERVING: Cal 371 • Carbo 56 gm • Prot 16 gm • Total fat 12 gm • Sat fat 3 gm • Cal from fat 29% • Chol 15 mg

EDUCATION: Treat your friends like family and your family like friends. Sometimes we can get so uptight about "entertaining" that we make everyone, including our guests, feel uncomfortable. By serving relaxed meals in relaxed surroundings, we can welcome in our friends to the family setting. On the other hand, it's possible to get too relaxed with family. If you find yourself serving attractive dishes or putting candles on the table only when guests appear, you may want to put some effort into making the occasional family meal special.

INSPIRATION: *All of my feelings have something to teach me; I can be open to the feelings and their lessons.*

Cocoa Coconut Cupcakes with White Frosting

🌿 Bananas add moisture and flavor to cocoa-flavored cupcakes. A touch of low-fat cream cheese icing tops each.

1 1/2 cups unbleached all-purpose flour
1/2 cup whole-wheat pastry flour
1/2 cup packed brown sugar
1/2 cup unsweetened cocoa powder
3 tablespoons shredded coconut
1 teaspoon baking powder
1 teaspoon baking soda
1/4 teaspoon salt
1 1/4 cups low-fat (1%) milk
1 cup mashed ripe bananas
2 eggs, beaten
2 tablespoons canola oil
1 (3-ounce) package nonfat cream cheese, softened
3/4 cup powdered sugar
1 1/2 teaspoons skim milk

Preheat oven to 375°F (190°C). Line 18 (2 3/4-inch) muffin pan cups with paper liners. Combine the flours, brown sugar, cocoa, coconut, baking powder, baking soda and salt in a large bowl. Stir together low-fat milk, mashed bananas, eggs and oil in a medium-size bowl. Beat with an electric mixer at medium speed until blended. Add to flour mixture and stir just until combined.

Spoon batter into prepared cups. Bake 18 to 20 minutes, until a wooden pick inserted in the center comes out clean. Cool in pan on wire rack.

Prepare icing by working cream cheese in a medium-size bowl to make it soft and fluffy. Beat in powdered sugar gradually with milk. When cupcakes are cooled, put a swirl of icing on top of each cupcake. *Makes 18 cupcakes.*

PER CUPCAKE: Cal 141 • Carbo 25 gm • Prot 4 gm • Total fat 4 gm • Sat fat 1 gm • Cal from fat 25% • Chol 25 mg

EDUCATION: Indulge in your love for chocolate without sabotaging yourself with high fat. There are many chocolate-flavored foods and beverages you can enjoy without overdoing the fat calories. For example, cocoa powder is far lower in fat than unsweetened chocolate squares, and can be used in baking. Other low-fat ways to enjoy chocolate are: low-fat or non-fat chocolate frozen yogurt, low-fat (1%) chocolate milk, cocoa rice crispy cereal, hot cocoa, chocolate-flavored coffee and low-fat frozen chocolate desserts.

INSPIRATION: *A connection with nature releases the creative energies of seeds, plants, roots and, of course, people.*

Crunchy Baked Buttermilk Chicken

A low-fat blue cheese–cucumber dipping sauce adds zest to baked, crusty chicken. Add a purchased hot pepper sauce, if desired, for delicious double-dipping.

2 (3¹/₂-pound) frying chickens
1 large egg
¹/₂ cup buttermilk
1 (7-ounce) package corn
    flakes cereal, coarsely crushed
¹/₄ cup sesame seeds
¹/₂ cup unbleached all-purpose flour
1 teaspoon salt
¹/₂ teaspoon freshly ground black pepper
Blue Cheese–Cucumber Dipping
    Sauce (see below)
Picante sauce (optional)

BLUE CHEESE–CUCUMBER DIPPING
SAUCE
1 cup nonfat yogurt
¹/₂ cup peeled, seeded and shredded
    cucumber
1 thinly sliced green onion
2 tablespoons crumbled blue cheese
¹/₄ teaspoon salt

Preheat oven to 350°F (175°C). Rinse chicken and pat dry with paper towels. Beat egg in a pie pan; stir in buttermilk. Combine cereal and sesame seeds in another pie pan. Combine flour, salt and pepper in another pie pan. Dip chicken pieces into flour mixture, then into egg mixture. Coat well with corn flakes mixture. Place the coated chicken pieces in 2 (15 × 10-inch) nonstick jelly roll pans. Bake 50 to 60 minutes or until fork-tender and juices run clear when chicken is pierced with a knife. Switch pans between upper and lower oven racks halfway through cooking time so chicken cooks evenly.

While chicken is baking, make cucumber sauce by combining all ingredients in a small bowl. Serve chicken hot or cold with cucumber sauce and picante sauce, if desired.

Makes 8 servings.

PER SERVING: Cal 486 • Carbo 31 gm • Prot 42 gm • Total fat 20 gm • Sat fat 6 gm • Cal from fat 37% • Chol 143 mg

EDUCATION: Make two meals at once to save time and effort. This chicken is delicious hot, but just as tasty cold. For a gathering of four, you could enjoy the hot chicken, then two days later, an al fresco meal on the patio or a picnic. Refrigerate any extra dipping sauce.

INSPIRATION: *If I judge myself or my body by unrealistic standards, I am setting myself up for failure.*

Gai's Wheat-Berry Salad

Living in Africa, Gai learned easy ways to cook simple foods. This is a more intricate recipe she would only try stateside. Great-tasting whole-wheat berries distinguish this hearty late-summer salad. This recipe includes extra cooked grain for adding to casseroles, meat loaf, soups or homemade breads, or to serve hot with milk and maple syrup as breakfast cereal.

1 cup wheat berries (see note)
3 cups water
1 cup blueberries
3/4 cup thinly sliced celery
1/3 cup diced red onion
1/4 cup finely diced red bell pepper
2 tablespoons finely chopped walnuts
2 tablespoons minced fresh parsley
2 tablespoons olive oil
2 tablespoons fresh lemon juice
1 tablespoon honey
1/4 teaspoon dry yellow mustard
1/4 teaspoon freshly grated lemon peel
1/8 teaspoon paprika
1/8 teaspoon ground coriander
1/8 teaspoon salt
12 large spinach leaves, stems removed

Combine wheat berries and water in a large saucepan. Bring to a boil, reduce heat, cover and simmer 2 hours or until wheat berries are tender. Set aside to cool.

Combine 1 cup cooked cooled wheat berries with blueberries, celery, red onion, bell pepper, walnuts and parsley in a serving bowl. Whisk together the olive oil, lemon juice, honey, dry mustard, lemon peel, paprika, coriander and salt in a small bowl. Toss salad mixture with dressing. Serve salad on spinach leaves.   *Makes 4 servings.*

PER SERVING: Cal 298 • Carbo 48 gm • Prot 8 gm • Total fat 10 gm • Sat fat 1 gm • Cal from fat 30% • Chol 0 mg

NOTE: Whole-wheat berries can be found at natural-food stores.

EDUCATION: Find your own most convenient way (see glossary) to cook grains so that you eat them more often.

INSPIRATION: *I am moving from being my own worst critic to becoming my most loyal supporter.*

Louisa's Creamy Cauliflower Soup

Colorful vegetables liven up this creamy cauliflower soup.

1 sweet Spanish onion, finely chopped
2 tablespoons unsalted butter
4 cups chicken broth or vegetable stock
1/2 cup basmati or other long-grain white rice
1/4 teaspoon dried thyme
1 large head cauliflower (about 2 pounds)
1/2 red bell pepper, diced
1 carrot, cut into matchsticks
1/2 cup frozen green peas
3 cups low-fat (1%) milk
2 tablespoons minced fresh parsley

Cook onion in the butter in a nonstick Dutch oven over medium heat, stirring frequently, until tender, 5 to 7 minutes. Add broth, rice and thyme and bring to a boil. Reduce heat, cover and simmer 20 minutes or until the rice is soft.

Meanwhile, divide cauliflower into flowerets. Peel and trim cauliflower stem and chop.

Place cauliflower in a vegetable steamer in a large saucepan over ½ inch of water. Steam cauliflower 4 or 5 minutes or until firm-tender.

Remove the steamer from the pan. Over high heat, boil down the water to about ¾ cup liquid. Add the bell pepper, carrot and peas and cook 1 or 2 minutes, just until the vegetables are crisp-tender. Remove from heat.

Blend steamed cauliflower in batches with rice mixture. Return to the Dutch oven and add carrot mixture, with cooking liquid, and milk. Heat just to boiling, stir in parsley and serve.

Makes 8 servings.

PER SERVING: Cal 177 • Carbo 25 gm • Prot 10 gm • Total fat 5 gm • Sat fat 3 gm • Cal from fat 25% • Chol 12 mg

EDUCATION: Cook cauliflower quickly in a stainless steel or other nonreactive cooking utensil to maximize its flavor and appearance. Prolonged cooking transforms plant acids found in cauliflower, Brussels sprouts and broccoli into odorous sulfur compounds. Other chemical compounds will cause cauliflower to turn yellow if cooked in aluminum and an unattractive bluish-green or brown when cooked in unenameled iron pans.

September 18

INSPIRATION: *Taking the time to dive deep into myself helps me stay centered amid currents of change.*

Jean's Sea Vegetable Sauté with Carrots

Nori or hiziki are two varieties of sea vegetables that blend deliciously with carrots, parsnips and other root vegetables.

3 carrots, cut into matchsticks
2 teaspoons sesame oil
1 garlic clove, minced
¼ teaspoon minced gingerroot
1 tablespoon water
½ teaspoon brown rice vinegar
½ sheet nori (see note, below)
1 tablespoon minced fresh parsley

Cook carrots in the oil in a large nonstick skillet, stirring constantly, until crisp-tender, 3 or 4 minutes. Stir in garlic, gingerroot, water and vinegar. Cover pan and steam carrots 2 or 3 minutes, just until firm-tender.

Meanwhile, toast nori by holding it over a stove burner until sheet turns slightly brown and begins to curl. Do not allow seaweed to burn. Crumble the nori into the skillet with the carrots, add parsley and stir until combined.

Makes 4 servings.

PER SERVING: Cal 45 • Carbo 6 gm • Prot 1 gm • Total fat 2 gm • Sat fat trace • Cal from fat 40% • Chol 0 mg

NOTE: Sheets of nori seaweed are available at some Asian markets and at natural-food stores. Hiziki, another tasty seaweed, can be substituted for the nori. Use 1 tablespoon hiziki in place of nori.

EDUCATION: Look to the sea for nutritious vegetables to increase your vitamin and mineral intake. Ounce for ounce, nori, for example, contains as much vitamin C as lemons and more vitamin A than chicken livers. Though seaweeds contain some sodium (eliminate salt when using them), they are rich in calcium, phosphorus, and iodine—important if you've cut out salt, the most common source of iodine. Also found in seaweeds are magnesium, potassium, iron, copper, sulfur, and vitamins E, B₁, B₁₂, niacin, folate and pantothenate. Discover what coastal dwellers from Asia to Hawaii, Ireland to Canada have known for centuries: Nutritious, tasty sea vegetables add a wave of flavor and nutrition to meals.

INSPIRATION: *I will be open today to sources of support in my life, wherever they are present.*

Sesame Wheat Sandwich Rolls

Hearty rolls add flavor and fiber to any sandwich. Freeze extra rolls until needed.

3 tablespoons honey
½ cup lukewarm water
2 tablespoons active dry yeast
1½ cups water
1¼ cups buttermilk
⅓ cup canola oil
1 teaspoon salt
3½ cups whole-wheat flour
3½ to 4 cups unbleached all-purpose flour
¼ cup skim milk
2 tablespoons sesame seeds

In a large bowl, dissolve honey in the lukewarm water. Sprinkle yeast on the water and set the bowl aside.

Heat the water, buttermilk and oil in a small saucepan until lukewarm. When the yeast mixture is foamy, stir in the buttermilk mixture, salt, whole-wheat flour, and enough of the unbleached flour to make a moderately stiff dough.

Knead dough on a lightly floured surface until smooth, then form it into 18 balls. Knead each ball until smooth, then place the balls about 2 inches apart on 2 large nonstick baking sheets.

Preheat oven to 400°F (200°C). Cover rolls and let rise until they are nearly doubled in bulk, about 20 minutes. Brush lightly with skim milk and sprinkle with sesame seeds. Bake 10 minutes. Reduce heat to 350°F (175°C) and bake 15 to 20 minutes or until the rolls are lightly browned and sound hollow when tapped.

Cool the rolls on wire racks, covered loosely with a cloth. *Makes 18 rolls.*

PER ROLL : Cal 233 • Carbo 41 gm • Prot 6 gm • Total fat 5 gm • Sat fat trace • Cal from fat 18% • Chol 1 mg

EDUCATION: Pyramid your sandwiches by reflecting nutritional guidelines in your choice of fillings. Start with whole-grain bread or rolls, then select a variety of vegetables. Dark green lettuce or spinach, grated carrots, slices of onion, tomato and bell pepper, chopped green onions and alfalfa sprouts are some possibilities. At the top of the pyramid, to be used sparingly, are sliced meat or cheese.

INSPIRATION: *I will start to deal creatively with things in my life that cannot be changed.*

Cheddar-Corn Pudding with Cherry Tomatoes

❧ Individual ramekins make a dramatic presentation of this delicious side dish.

1 tablespoon unsalted butter
1 tablespoon whole-wheat pastry flour
³/₄ cup skim milk
²/₃ cup fresh or thawed frozen whole-
    kernel corn
2 tablespoons grated sharp Cheddar cheese
¹/₄ teaspoon salt
Dash of freshly grated nutmeg
1 egg
1 egg white
6 cherry tomatoes
Dash of paprika for garnish
Parsley sprigs for garnish

Preheat oven to 350°F (175°C). Lightly butter 4 ramekins or custard cups. Melt butter in a medium-size saucepan. Stir in flour and cook, stirring, 1 minute. Add milk and stir until sauce is slightly thickened and just begins to boil.

Place the sauce, corn, cheese, salt and nutmeg in a food processor or blender and process until smooth. Add egg and egg white and process several seconds, just until combined.

Divide the blended mixture among ramekins or custard cups. Center a cherry tomato in each. Place the cups in a shallow baking pan. Add ¹/₂ inch boiling water around cups. Bake 30 minutes or until the corn pudding is golden and a wooden pick inserted off-center comes out clean. Dust with paprika and garnish with parsley sprigs.   *Makes 4 servings.*

PER SERVING: Cal 114 • Carbo 11 gm • Prot 6 gm • Total fat 5 gm • Sat fat 2 gm • Cal from fat 39% • Chol 65 mg

EDUCATION: Use unsalted butter in your cooking to increase flavor while using conservative amounts of fat. Since you're only going to use a little, you want to get the best flavor. Dairy producers are particularly fussy about the quality of unsalted butters, since there's no disguising possible off-flavors with salt. It also leaves you in control of the salt content in any dish. As you cut down or even eliminate salt completely from your cooking, your taste buds will adjust to the natural flavors of foods.

INSPIRATION: *Listening, and really hearing, lets me know I am not on this journey alone.*

All-American Apple Pie

Take advantage of the variety of baking apples available in fall. Jonathan, Cortland, Northern Spy, Granny Smith, Stayman and Crispin alone or in combination can be used for this pie.

3/4 *cup unbleached all-purpose flour*
1/4 *cup whole-wheat pastry flour*
1/4 *teaspoon baking powder*
1/4 *teaspoon salt*
1/4 *cup cold unsalted butter*
1 *teaspoon white vinegar*
2 or 3 *tablespoons ice water*
3 *pounds baking apples, peeled, cored*
and thinly sliced
1/2 *cup sugar*
1 *teaspoon ground cinnamon*
Dash of freshly grated nutmeg

Combine flours, baking powder and salt in a large bowl. With a pastry blender, cut in butter until the mixture resembles coarse meal. Sprinkle with vinegar, then water, 1 tablespoon at a time, tossing with a fork just until the pastry holds together. Shape into a ball, flatten, wrap in plastic wrap and refrigerate at least 1 hour.

Preheat oven to 400°F (200°C). On a floured surface, roll out pastry into a 12-inch circle. Fit into a 9-inch pie pan; trim and flute edge.

Place apples in a large bowl. Combine sugar and spices and toss with the apples until apples are evenly coated. Spoon apples into pie shell. Bake 15 minutes. Reduce heat to 375°F (190°C) and bake 50 to 55 minutes, until apples are tender. If crust browns too quickly, cover loosely with foil. Cool on a wire rack.

Makes 8 servings.

PER SERVING: Cal 251 • Carbo 50 gm • Prot 2 gm • Total fat 6 gm • Sat fat 4 gm • Cal from fat 23% • Chol 16 mg

EDUCATION: Make fruit pies when you have the time, then freeze them for future entertaining. Freezing unbaked pies preserves the freshest flavor. For freezing, add a tablespoon of flour to the fruit pie filling. Wrap pie well in freezer wrap and freeze up to 3 months. To bake, do not thaw. Follow directions above, adding 15 to 20 minutes to the baking time.

INSPIRATION: *Serenity comes with my acceptance of who I am, a trust in my place in the universe.*

Audrey's Harvest Cabbage-Corn Soup

Audrey grows her own vegetables and helps at the family's dairy farm store. Her love of good cooking spills over for her customers' enjoyment at the country restaurant in rural Neffs, Pennsylvania.

> 1 pound shin beef with bone
> 1 teaspoon canola oil
> 1 onion, chopped
> 1 garlic clove, minced
> 6 cups beef stock
> 1 tomato, peeled, seeded
>   and chopped
> 1 bay leaf
> 1/4 teaspoon salt
> 1/4 teaspoon dried basil
> 1/8 teaspoon dried thyme
> 1/8 teaspoon freshly ground
>   black pepper
> 2 cups coarsely shredded cabbage
> 4 ears of corn or 1 cup frozen
>   shoepeg or
>   yellow corn
> 1/4 cup minced fresh parsley

Brown the beef in the oil over medium heat in a nonstick Dutch oven. Add onion and cook, stirring frequently, until translucent. Add garlic and cook, stirring, 1 minute.

Add beef stock, tomato, bay leaf, salt, basil, thyme and pepper and bring to a boil. Reduce heat, cover and simmer 1 1/2 to 2 hours or until beef is fork-tender. Remove beef and bones and set aside to cool.

Add cabbage to soup and return to a boil. Reduce heat, cover and simmer 15 minutes or until cabbage is tender. Add corn and simmer 5 minutes. Remove meat from bones and shred into small pieces. Add meat and parsley to soup, heat through and serve.   *Makes 4 servings.*

PER SERVING: Cal 268 • Carbo 28 gm • Prot 17 gm • Total fat 11 gm • Sat fat 5 gm • Cal from fat 37% • Chol 34 mg

EDUCATION: Soup it up for fall, giving vegetables the starring role to allow a cutback on meats. Make soups and stews with a small amount of meat for flavoring, instead of beef stews with incidental carrots and potatoes. Instead of 1 1/2 pounds stewing beef for four, cut the amount of meat in half. In the soup recipe above the weight is greater because of the bones.

INSPIRATION: *I am no different than others. Understanding that we all struggle keeps me from isolating myself with my "unique" problems.*

Lentil-Walnut Salad with Cilantro Chicken

🌿 Lentils make a great accompaniment to chicken. Serve with a small bunch of grapes and sliced fruit.

1 cup lentils
6 whole cloves
6 cardamom pods
2¹/₂ cups water
1 small carrot
1 garlic clove, peeled
10 parsley sprigs
2 tablespoons olive oil
3 tablespoons fresh lemon juice
¹/₄ teaspoon salt
¹/₈ teaspoon freshly ground black pepper
4 boneless, skinless chicken breast halves
¹/₄ cup chopped walnuts
¹/₂ cup thinly sliced celery
¹/₄ cup thinly sliced green onions
2 tablespoons minced fresh parsley
²/₃ cup nonfat yogurt
¹/₃ cup reduced-fat sour cream
¹/₂ cup chopped fresh cilantro
¹/₄ teaspoon freshly grated lemon peel
¹/₈ teaspoon hot (cayenne) pepper

GARNISHES:
4 small bunches red grapes
1 red apple, quartered, seeded and thinly sliced
1 pear, quartered, seeded and thinly sliced

Pick over and rinse lentils. Tie cloves and cardamom in a piece of cheesecloth. Combine spices, lentils, water, carrot, garlic and parsley sprigs in a large saucepan and bring to a boil.

Reduce heat, cover and simmer 20 or 25 minutes or until lentils are just tender. Drain and place lentils in a medium-size bowl. Remove carrot, spices and parsley sprigs. Add olive oil, 2 tablespoons of the lemon juice, salt and pepper and toss until lentils are coated. Set aside.

Place chicken breasts in a medium-size saucepan with water to cover. Bring almost to a boil, reduce heat and simmer gently 10 minutes. Drain and set aside to cool. Toast walnuts in a small, heavy skillet over medium heat, stirring constantly, until nuts are fragrant. Toss nuts, celery, green onions and minced parsley with lentils until combined.

Divide lentil salad among 4 individual plates. Thinly slice chicken breast halves and arrange on plates. Combine yogurt, sour cream, cilantro, remaining tablespoon of lemon juice, lemon peel and cayenne and drizzle a small amount over chicken. Garnish plates with grapes and apple and pear slices. Serve remaining cilantro sauce on the side.

Makes 4 servings.

PER SERVING: Cal 588 • Carbo 71 gm • Prot 38 gm • Total fat 20 gm • Sat fat 5 gm • Cal from fat 31% • Chol 75 mg

EDUCATION: When eating out, make low-fat choices at the salad bar. Lettuces, spinach, carrots, cucumbers, onion rings, mushrooms, diced bell peppers, broccoli and cauliflower are excellent choices. Be sparing in selecting seeds, hard-boiled eggs or shredded cheeses. Avoid bacon bits and high-fat dressings.

INSPIRATION: *Today I give the child within me permission to play and have fun.*

Peanut Butter Blender Breakfast

🌿 When you need something on-the-run, or

you're trying to get kids to eat something nutritious to start the day, try the occasional blender drink.

> 1 banana, cut up
> 3/4 cup skim milk
> 1 tablespoon natural peanut butter
> 1 teaspoon honey
> 2 ice cubes
> Dash of cinnamon

Combine ingredients in a blender. Process on high speed until ingredients are smooth and ice cubes are dissolved. *Makes 1 serving.*

PER SERVING: Cal 286 • Carbo 44 gm • Prot 12 gm • Total fat 9 gm • Sat fat 2 gm • Cal from fat 28% • Chol 3 mg

VARIATION
Omit peanut butter and use 1/2 banana. Add 1/2 cup fresh or frozen strawberries and 1/4 cup honeyed wheat germ cereal.

EDUCATION: Eat nut butters in moderation to control your fat intake. Though peanut butter is a good source of fiber, thiamin, niacin, folacin, iron and magnesium, it also contains 78 percent of calories from fat. Peanuts provide more protein than any other nuts, however, so that moderate amounts combined with other foods can be an important protein source.

September 25

INSPIRATION: *Being unaware of what I'm doing doesn't provide me with the opportunity for change. Sharing with others helps me become self-aware.*

Mexican Meatballs & Brown Rice

Delicious and colorful, flavorful meatballs simmer in a spicy jalapeño-tomato sauce studded with corn.

> 1 pound extra-lean ground beef
> 1/2 cup stone-ground cornmeal
> 1 egg, beaten
> 1 tablespoon tomato paste
> 1 tablespoon minced fresh parsley
> 1/2 teaspoon dried oregano
> 2 teaspoons olive oil
> 6 tomatoes, peeled, seeded and chopped
> 1 jalapeño chile, seeded and
>   minced (see glossary)
> 1 cup tomato juice
> 1 tablespoon chili powder
> 2 garlic cloves, pushed through
>   a garlic press
> 1/2 teaspoon ground cumin
> 1 1/2 cups whole-kernel corn
> 1 cup chopped spinach leaves
> 4 cups cooked brown rice

In a medium-size bowl, combine beef, cornmeal, egg, tomato paste, parsley and oregano. Form into 24 small meatballs.

In a large nonstick skillet, heat oil, then add the meatballs and brown over medium heat. When the meatballs have browned on all sides, add the tomatoes, jalapeño, tomato juice, chili powder, garlic and cumin. Bring to a boil, reduce heat, cover and simmer 20 minutes, stirring occasionally.

Add corn and simmer 10 minutes. Add spinach and stir just until the spinach is wilted. Serve over rice. *Makes 6 servings.*

PER SERVING: Cal 465 • Carbo 57 gm • Prot 23 gm • Total fat 17 gm • Sat fat 17 gm • Cal from fat 34% • Chol 86 mg

EDUCATION: Eat complex carbohydrates instead of simple sugars. They keep our metabolism in healthy balance, and offer more, besides. That's because complex carbohydrates—such as potatoes, whole grains, beans and peas—are rich in fiber, protein, starch, vitamins and minerals.

INSPIRATION: *I am free to speak the truth, without fear or self-censorship.*

Green-Bean Salad with Tarragon

Tarragon highlights the garden-fresh flavor of beans. Mix green and yellow wax beans for visual impact.

$^1/_2$ *pound green beans*
$^1/_2$ *pound yellow wax beans*
1 tablespoon olive oil
4 teaspoons minced shallots
1 tablespoon brown rice vinegar
2 teaspoons minced fresh tarragon
$^1/_4$ *teaspoon salt*
$^1/_8$ *teaspoon freshly ground*
    black pepper

Trim stem ends from beans; leave beans whole. Bring a large saucepan of water to a boil. Add beans, cover, and return to a boil. Uncover and cook beans 2 or 3 minutes, just until crisp-tender. Drain and rinse under cold water until cooled.

Combine oil, shallots, vinegar, tarragon, salt and pepper in a cup measure. Toss dressing with beans and serve.   *Makes 4 servings.*

PER SERVING: Cal 136 • Carbo 20 gm • Prot 6 gm • Total fat 4 gm • Sat fat 1 gm • Cal from fat 26% • Chol 0 mg

EDUCATION: Choose calorie-free drinks between and with meals. Calories we eat are more satisfying than those we drink, so save them up for food enjoyment. For best health-enhancement, forego artificially sweetened soft drinks and stick with club soda with slices of lemon and lime, herbal teas, hot or over ice, and plain water. Check labels on flavored sparkling water: some are high in sugar and/or sodium.

INSPIRATION: *With proper, sustaining food and moderate exercise, I find myself with sufficient energy and the stamina I need to deal effectively with my life.*

Lydia's Pasta & Vegetable Chili

An array of fresh vegetables distinguishes this pasta-chili dish. Use cooked red kidney beans or purchased canned beans without additives, available at health-food stores.

1 cup elbow macaroni
2 carrots, diced
1 cup chopped onions
2 tablespoons olive oil
1 zucchini, diced
1 yellow squash, diced
3 tablespoons chili powder
$^1/_2$ teaspoon ground cumin
$^1/_4$ teaspoon dried oregano
3 cups peeled, seeded and
    chopped tomatoes
3 cups tomato juice
$^1/_3$ cup tomato paste
$^1/_4$ teaspoon hot pepper sauce
$^1/_4$ teaspoon salt
$^1/_8$ teaspoon freshly ground
    black pepper
2 cups frozen whole-kernel corn
4 cups cooked drained red
    kidney beans
    (see glossary)
1 (4-ounce) can chopped mild
    green chiles

Bring a large saucepan of water to a boil. Add macaroni and cook 7 to 10 minutes or just until firm-tender. Drain and run under cold water. Set aside.

Cook carrots and onions in the oil in a nonstick Dutch oven over medium heat, stirring frequently, until vegetables begin to brown, 5 to 7 minutes. Add zucchini and yellow squash and cook, stirring frequently, until all vegetables are crisp-tender. Add chili powder, cumin and oregano and cook, stirring, 1 minute. Add tomatoes, tomato juice, tomato paste, hot pepper sauce, salt and pepper and stir until combined. Bring to a boil, reduce heat, cover and simmer 15 minutes. Stir in corn, kidney beans and chiles and return to a boil. Stir in cooked macaroni, heat through and serve.

Makes 6 servings.

PER SERVING: Cal 408 • Carbo 75 gm • Prot 19 gm • Total fat 7 gm • Sat fat 1 gm • Cal from fat 15% • Chol 0 mg

EDUCATION: Round out meals with low-fat carbohydrates to bring down the percentage of fat in your diet. Pasta, as above, rice, potatoes and other vegetables provide complex carbohydrates and next to no fat. That means if part of the meal, such as meat, contains fat, it will be balanced with leaner foods—and your meal, as a whole, will be healthier.

INSPIRATION: *I can operate best as my true self, instead of the person others expect me to be...as a real person rather than a role.*

Carob Cake with Carob Icing

Carob, ground from a pod and sometimes called St. John's bread, is naturally sweet. This cake features a tart orange counterpoint to highlight carob's chocolatelike taste.

¹/₂ cup carob powder, sifted

¹/₄ cup canola oil

¹/₂ cup maple syrup

1 egg

2¹/₄ teaspoons grated orange peel

¹/₂ cup buttermilk

1¹/₂ cups unbleached all-purpose flour

¹/₄ cup ground almonds

1 teaspoon baking soda

¹/₂ teaspoon ground cinnamon

¹/₈ teaspoon ground allspice

¹/₈ teaspoon ground cloves

³/₄ cup apricot preserves

3 tablespoons orange juice

ICING:

3 tablespoons butter

¹/₄ cup carob powder, sifted

3 tablespoons maple syrup

1 tablespoon light unsulfured molasses

1 tablespoon orange juice

Preheat oven to 350°F (175°C). Butter and flour an 8-inch-round nonstick cake pan. Place carob, oil and maple syrup in a large bowl and stir together until smooth. Beat in the egg and 2 teaspoons of the orange peel. Stir in the buttermilk.

In a smaller bowl, combine the flour, ground almonds, baking soda, cinnamon, allspice and cloves. Add the dry ingredients to the wet ingredients and stir just until combined.

Spread the batter evenly in pan. Bake 25 to 30 minutes or until a wooden pick inserted in the center comes out clean. Do not overbake or the cake will be dry.

Place the apricot preserves, orange juice and remaining orange peel in a blender. Process on low to medium speed until smooth, stopping to stir the mixture, if necessary, so that all the apricot is well blended.

Turn cake upside down in the cake pan on a cake rack to cool. When the cake has cooled, remove it from the pan. Using a long, serrated knife, cut the cake in half horizontally. Remove the upper round of cake and place it top down on a serving plate. Spread with apricot filling. Cover with the bottom half of the cake, smooth side up.

To prepare the icing, melt the butter in a small saucepan. Stir in the carob, then the maple syrup, molasses and the orange juice. Spread the icing over the cake, allowing it to drip down the sides. *Makes 8 servings.*

PER SERVING: Cal 391 • Carbo 79 gm • Prot 6 gm • Total fat 14 gm • Sat fat 4 gm • Cal from fat 33% • Chol 39 mg

EDUCATION: Explore the possibilities of carob confections for dessert if you're allergic to chocolate. Carob tastes somewhat like chocolate and cocoa, but has several advantages over them. Unlike cocoa, carob is naturally sweet (which means adding less sugar), and it's low in fat and high in fiber.

Carob has about four times the calcium of chocolate or cocoa and none of the oxalic acid present in chocolate, which binds calcium and prevents its absorption. Carob also is free of caffeine and theobromine, two powerful stimulants. Carob has the added benefit of causing fewer allergic reactions than either cocoa or chocolate.

INSPIRATION: *Today I will start with one thing, done just for the fun of it!*

Double-Apple Cinnamon Pancakes

Apples blended in the batter and sliced and baked right on the griddle distinguish these moist, flavorful pancakes. Top with fruit topping, maple syrup or dust with confectioners' sugar.

> 1 cup diced tart red apples
> 2 eggs
> 1 cup skim milk
> 1 cup apple juice or cider
> 1 tablespoon canola oil
> 2 cups whole-wheat flour
> 2 teaspoons baking powder
> 1 teaspoon ground cinnamon
> 1 tart red apple, peeled and
>   thinly sliced

Place diced apples, eggs, milk, apple juice and oil in a blender. Process on medium speed until smooth.

Combine flour, baking powder and cinnamon in a medium bowl. Stir in the apple mixture just until combined.

For each pancake, pour about ¼ cup of batter onto a lightly oiled, nonstick griddle. Top each pancake with a few slices of apple before the top has a chance to set.

When the bubbles that form on the top of the pancake have burst and the bottom is browned, turn the pancake and cook until the second side is browned.   *Makes 6 servings.*

PER SERVING: Cal 258 • Carbo 46 gm • Prot 8 gm • Total fat 5 gm • Sat fat 1 gm • Cal from fat 16% • Chol 72 mg

EDUCATION: To reduce your risk of cancer, use care when cooking so you don't burn foods. There's evidence that cancer-causing chemicals form when food is charred. Choose low to moderate heat for most stove-top cooking, use low amounts of fat in pans and check foods often.

INSPIRATION: *Making sure I take care of myself is part of a healthy giving of myself to others.*

Herbed Mushroom-Stuffed Chicken Legs

Boned, skinned chicken drumsticks prove tasty morsels when filled with herbed mushrooms. To cut costs, substitute regular mushrooms for portobello.

8 chicken drumsticks
1 tablespoon butter
4 green onions, finely chopped
1 small garlic clove, minced
1 1/2 cups chopped portobello mushrooms
1/3 cup dried whole-wheat bread crumbs
1/4 teaspoon dried marjoram
1/2 cup chicken broth
3 tablespoons minced fresh parsley
2 cups cooked brown rice
Orange slices for garnish
Parsley sprigs for garnish

Remove and discard skin from chicken. With a boning knife or other small sharp knife, separate the chicken from the bone at the thigh end. Using the knife, gently scrape down the bone to separate the chicken, without cutting into the meat. (This process will turn the leg meat inside out.) Cut around the bone at the bottom to separate the meat from the bone. Turn the drumstick right side out.

To prepare the stuffing, melt butter in a medium-size skillet. Add the green onions and cook over low heat until wilted. Stir in garlic and mushrooms. Cook until the mushrooms have released their liquid and it has evaporated. Stir in the bread crumbs and marjoram. Remove from heat.

Preheat oven to 350°F (175°C). Divide the stuffing among the boned drumsticks. Fill the openings of the chicken with stuffing, closing the meat around it.

Arrange the stuffed drumsticks in a shallow 9-inch baking dish. Pour broth over stuffed drumsticks.

Bake 1 hour, basting several times. When the drumsticks are done, carefully remove the cheesecloth. Stir parsley into cooked rice. Serve drumsticks with drippings over rice.

Makes 4 servings.

PER SERVING: Cal 246 • Carbo 31 gm • Prot 16 gm • Total fat 7 gm • Sat fat 3 gm • Cal from fat 22% • Chol 43 mg

EDUCATION: Get selenium from foods in your diet such as the chicken, mushrooms and garlic above to avoid overdoses. Selenium in large doses, such as in some supplements, can be extremely toxic. The balanced amount found in foods, however, is important for proper immune response and heart muscle function. Evidence also shows selenium may protect against certain cancers. Grains, fish, shellfish, eggs and liver are other good sources of selenium.

INSPIRATION: *I promise to be gentle to myself, one day at a time.*

Delicious Basic Chicken Broth

Because so many fall and winter soups are based on chicken broth, enjoy the pleasure of creating your own. The technique is simple and creates a wonderful aroma in your kitchen. The result gives flavor and character to each soup you create.

5 to 6 pounds chicken parts (wings, necks, backs, feet or raw bones)
3 celery stalks, with leaves
1 large onion

1 large carrot
4 1/2 quarts water
10 parsley sprigs
1 fresh thyme sprig
1 small bay leaf

Preheat oven to 450°F (230°C). Place the chicken in one layer in the bottom of a large roasting pan. Coarsely chop the celery, setting aside 4 to 6 leaves. Coarsely chop the onion and carrot. Arrange the chopped vegetables over the chicken and bake 1 hour, until chicken is well browned.

Remove chicken and vegetables from the roasting pan and place in a large Dutch oven or stock pot. Pour off any fat from the roasting pan. Set the roasting pan over high heat, stir in 2 cups water and scrape up browned bits from the bottom of the pan. Pour into the stockpot and add the remaining water, celery leaves, parsley, thyme and bay leaf.

Bring ingredients just to a simmer. Reduce heat slightly and continue to simmer 3 hours, skimming off foam every 20 minutes for the first hour.

Line a colander with cheesecloth and through it pour the broth into a large bowl. Chill the broth in smaller containers immediately. When chilled, freeze any broth not to be used within a day or two. Skim off fat before using broth (the fat will help preserve the flavor of the broth while it is stored).   *Makes 3 quarts.*

PER SERVING: Cal 15 • Carbo 1 gm • Prot 3 gm
• Total fat trace • Sat fat trace • Cal from fat 0%
• Chol 0 mg

EDUCATION: Make your own broth to control your sodium intake. Many canned or packaged, prepared soups are exceedingly high in sodium. Start from scratch and your low-fat, low-sodium soups will be blessed with fabulous flavor.

INSPIRATION: *Every day that I choose what is good for me is a day spent strengthening my recovery.*

Balsamic Eggplant with Basil Sauce

Select smaller eggplants for tenderness and flavor. Large, overly mature eggplant tend to be overly seedy. Serve with poultry or seafood, or serve as a main dish sprinkled with toasted pine nuts.

1 small white eggplant (about 1/2 pound)
1 small purple eggplant (about 1/2 pound)
1/4 teaspoon salt
2 garlic cloves, pushed through a press
1 1/2 tablespoons balsamic vinegar
2 teaspoons extra-virgin olive oil
1/2 cup thinly sliced fresh basil leaves

Steam eggplants in a tightly covered pan over boiling water 20 to 25 minutes or until eggplants are soft throughout. Combine salt and garlic puree in a small bowl and slowly add vinegar, stirring after each addition. Stir in olive oil.

When eggplants are soft, cut off stem end and slice eggplants into quarters lengthwise. Cut slashes in the eggplant flesh and spoon sauce over each. Arrange on serving plate, sprinkled with basil.   *Makes 8 servings.*

PER SERVING: Cal 30 • Carbo 5 gm • Prot trace
• Total fat 1 gm • Sat fat trace • Cal from fat 30%
• Chol 0 mg

EDUCATION: Employ balsamic vinegar as a flavor-enhancer to keep your dishes high in flavor while low in fat. Splash it on cooked vegetables, meat, poultry—even fruits! Completely fat-free, balsamic vinegar is more flavorful and less tart than most vinegars. It can be used in sauces and salad dressings where less fat is required to offset its milder pungency.

INSPIRATION: *By sharing my experience and my gifts with others, and allowing them to do the same with me, we all move toward the goal of fulfilling our potential.*

Carolyn's New Carrot Soup

❧ Buttermilk adds a tangy freshness to this comforting soup.

³/₄ pound carrots with tops
1 onion, chopped
1 teaspoon butter
1 shallot, minced
2 cups chicken broth
1 tablespoon fresh parsley
1 teaspoon minced fresh chervil or basil
¹/₄ teaspoon freshly grated lemon peel
1 to 1¹/₂ cups buttermilk
Dash of freshly grated nutmeg

Remove carrot tops and mince ¹/₄ cup to use as a garnish. Trim, scrub and slice carrots.

Cook onion in the butter in a nonstick Dutch oven over medium heat, stirring frequently, until onion is translucent. Add shallot and cook, stirring, 1 minute.

Add chicken broth and sliced carrots to pan and bring to a boil. Reduce heat, cover and simmer 10 to 12 minutes or just until carrots are tender.

Place carrots and some of the liquid in a blender or food processor and puree. Return to pan with parsley, chervil or basil, grated lemon peel, and enough buttermilk to reach the desired consistency. Heat through, but do not boil. Garnish with minced carrot tops and a dash of nutmeg.   *Makes 4 servings.*

PER SERVING: Cal 107 • Carbo 16 gm • Prot 6 gm • Total fat 2 gm • Sat fat 1 gm • Cal from fat 20% • Chol 5 mg

EDUCATION: Do your blood pressure a favor and put a nutmeg grater on the table in place of the salt shaker. Freshly grated nutmeg gives a surprising lift to many dishes, both sweet and savory. In the bargain you'll be cutting down on sodium, implicated in high blood pressure.

INSPIRATION: *My self-approval depends upon appreciating myself as a capable and loving individual, not on pleasing others.*

Jambalaya

❧ Jambalaya can be made with just vegetables and rice, or with shellfish, meat, or chicken, or a combination.

1 cup brown rice
2 cups chicken broth
1 cup chopped onion
¹/₄ cup diced celery
1 tablespoon butter
³/₄ pound boneless, skinless chicken breasts,
*   cut into 2-inch pieces*
¹/₂ pound fresh okra, cut into 1-inch pieces
1 green bell pepper, cored, seeded
*   and cut into 1-inch pieces*
2 garlic cloves, minced
¹/₂ pound medium-size shrimp,
*   peeled and deveined (see glossary)*
¹/₂ cup sliced mushrooms
1¹/₂ cups peeled, seeded and chopped tomatoes
¹/₄ cup thinly sliced green onions
2 tablespoons minced fresh parsley
¹/₂ teaspoon salt
¹/₈ teaspoon freshly ground black pepper
¹/₈ teaspoon ground red pepper

Combine rice and broth in a medium-size saucepan and bring to a boil. Reduce heat, cover and simmer 35 minutes. Set aside.

Cook onion and celery in the butter in a

nonstick Dutch oven over medium heat, stirring frequently, until translucent, 3 to 4 minutes. Add the chicken, okra, pepper and garlic and cook, stirring, until chicken is lightly browned and pepper is firm-tender, 5 to 7 minutes. Add shrimp and mushrooms and stir just until the shrimp is nearly opaque throughout, about 3 minutes.

Add tomatoes and green onions and cook, stirring, 5 minutes until shrimp are cooked through and vegetables are tender. Stir in parsley, salt, pepper and red pepper. Combine with rice and serve. *Makes 4 servings.*

PER SERVING: Cal 435 • Carbo 51 gm • Prot 38 gm • Total fat 8 gm • Sat fat 3 gm • Cal from fat 17% • Chol 143 mg

VARIATION
Omit shrimp and stir in 1/4 pound diced smoked ham.

EDUCATION: Add okra to your vegetable menu to increase your fiber. Okra is also a good source of vitamin C; B vitamins, including folacin; magnesium; potassium and calcium. Special handling will keep okra appetizing. Don't wash and store okra or the pods will become slimy from the moisture. Wash just before using and use a vegetable brush to remove excess fuzz. Don't cook in iron or aluminum or the okra will discolor.

October 5

INSPIRATION: *Taking good care of myself frees new energy for me to focus on my interests and relationships.*

Pat's Date & Nut Oatmeal Squares

Dates add a sweet richness to these dessert squares, which are flavored with toasted walnuts.

1 1/2 cups chopped pitted dates
1 cup water
1/2 teaspoon freshly grated orange peel
1/2 cup unbleached all-purpose flour
1/4 cup whole-wheat pastry flour
1/2 teaspoon baking soda
1/8 teaspoon salt
1/2 cup packed brown sugar
1/4 cup unsalted butter, softened
2 tablespoons buttermilk
1 1/4 cups rolled oats
1/4 cup chopped toasted walnuts (see glossary)

Bring dates and water to a boil in a small saucepan. Reduce heat, cover and simmer 6 to 8 minutes or until thickened. Stir in orange peel. Set aside to cool.

Preheat oven to 350°F (175°C). Lightly butter a 9-inch-square nonstick baking pan. Combine flours, baking soda and salt in a small bowl.

Beat sugar and butter together in a medium-size bowl with a mixer. On low speed, add buttermilk, then dry ingredients, just until blended. Stir in rolled oats.

Firmly pat 2 cups of the oat mixture evenly on the bottom of the pan. Spread date mixture evenly on top. Sprinkle with remaining oat mixture. Bake 35 to 40 minutes, until topping is golden brown. Cool in the pan on a wire rack. Cut into squares. *Makes 16 servings.*

PER SERVING: Cal 111 • Carbo 16 gm • Prot 2 gm • Total fat 4 gm • Sat fat 2 gm • Cal from fat 36% • Chol 8 mg

EDUCATION: Include healthful whole grains in desserts to help meet your daily quota. Keeping fat and sugar levels in line ensures that these desserts offer a nutritional bonus. For picky eaters, it is an appealing way to introduce whole grains.

October 6

INSPIRATION: *I am as strong, as competent and as powerful as I allow myself to be.*

Microwaved Flounder with Vegetables

Quick and easy, this delicious low-fat dish features cherry tomatoes and zucchini. Serve with orzo pasta or couscous and a salad.

1 zucchini, cut into 1/4-inch slices
1 green onion, thinly sliced
1 teaspoon unsalted butter, softened
1/2 teaspoon freshly grated lemon peel
1/4 teaspoon salt
1/8 teaspoon freshly ground black pepper
1 pint cherry tomatoes, halved
4 (4- to 6-ounce) flounder or sole fillets
1 tablespoon fresh lemon juice
1 tablespoon minced fresh parsley
1 tablespoon thinly sliced fresh basil

Combine zucchini, green onion, butter, lemon peel, salt and pepper in an 11 × 7-inch microwave-safe baking dish. Microwave on HIGH 2 minutes. Stir in tomatoes and microwave on HIGH 1 minute more.

Fold fillets crosswise in half. Place folded fillets on top of the vegetables, open ends toward the center of the dish. Sprinkle with lemon juice. Cover with waxed paper and microwave on HIGH 5 to 7 minutes, rotating dish once or until fish is just opaque throughout. Let stand, covered, 2 minutes. Sprinkle with parsley and basil. *Makes 4 servings.*

PER SERVING: Cal 135 • Carbo 5 gm • Prot 22 gm • Total fat 3 gm • Sat fat 1 gm • Cal from fat 17% • Chol 57 mg

VARIATION

Cook zucchini with butter and seasonings in a large nonstick skillet over medium heat, stirring frequently, until zucchini is firm-tender. Stir in cherry tomatoes and cook, stirring, 3 minutes. Lay fish fillets over vegetables and add lemon juice. Cover and simmer 5 to 7 minutes or until fish is just opaque throughout. Sprinkle with parsley and basil and serve.

EDUCATION: When cooking in a low-fat way, keep fish succulent and appetizing by cooking it correctly. Fish will cook unevenly if it is cold when placed in a baking dish or on the stove. If the fish is cold, the outside or thinner areas of fillets will be overcooked when the insides, or thicker areas, are done. Fish will cook perfectly if brought to room temperature before cooking.

October 7

INSPIRATION: *What I put out into the world helps create the reality I must live with.*

Barb's Chicken with Tiny Pasta

Serve with a medley of mixed vegetables and a light soup for an appetizer. Crusty bread completes this meal.

1 cup orzo pasta
4 boneless, skinless chicken breast halves
1/2 teaspoon salt
1/4 teaspoon freshly ground white pepper
2 teaspoons olive oil
1/4 cup minced green onions
1/2 cup chicken broth
3 tablespoons balsamic vinegar
1 teaspoon packed brown sugar
1 teaspoon unsalted butter
2 tablespoons minced fresh parsley

Bring a large saucepan of water to a boil. Add orzo and cook 9 to 10 minutes or until tender. Drain and keep warm.

Meanwhile, place chicken breasts between

2 sheets of waxed paper. Pound to ½-inch thickness with a rubber mallet or rolling pin. Season with salt and pepper. Cook breasts in the olive oil in a large, nonstick skillet over medium heat, 4 minutes per side, or just until lightly browned and cooked throughout.

Place chicken on a warmed serving plate and cover with foil. Add green onions to skillet and cook, stirring, 1 minute. Add stock, vinegar and sugar. Bring to a boil and cook 4 minutes or until liquid is reduced by about one-third. Stir butter into liquid until melted. Pour sauce over chicken. Toss parsley with cooked orzo and serve. *Makes 4 servings.*

PER SERVING: Cal 291 • Carbo 24 gm • Prot 31 gm • Total fat 7 gm • Sat fat 2 gm • Cal from fat 21% • Chol 76 mg

EDUCATION: Eat three well-balanced meals and two healthy snacks each day to stabilize your metabolic rate. A regular intake of low-fat foods will help to burn off calories and reduce cravings for less healthful food choices.

INSPIRATION: *My life is notable not for what I own, but for what I give of myself.*

Pearl Barley with Curried Vegetables

Similar in cooking time to brown rice, pearl barley makes a delicious-tasting side dish. The grain is complemented here by shredded vegetables and a light touch of curry. This dish makes a fine accompaniment to pork.

¹/₂ cup finely chopped onion
1 tablespoon canola oil
1 teaspoon Madras curry powder
2¹/₂ cups chicken broth
1 cup pearl barley
1 cup shredded carrots
1 cup shredded zucchini
2 tablespoons minced fresh parsley

Cook onion in the oil in a large saucepan over medium heat, stirring frequently, until onion is translucent. Add curry powder and cook, stirring, 1 minute. Add broth and barley and bring to a boil. Reduce heat, cover and simmer 45 minutes, or until barley is tender.

Stir in carrots and zucchini, cover and steam 2 or 3 minutes. Stir in parsley and serve. *Makes 6 servings.*

PER SERVING: Cal 171 • Carbo 30 gm • Prot 6 gm • Total fat 3 gm • Sat fat trace • Cal from fat 18% • Chol 0 mg

EDUCATION: Pay attention to serving sizes when calculating fats and calories. If a recipe or container lists 4 servings, and two of you polish it off entirely, you must double the amount of calories and fat grams listed when figuring your day's allowances. Remember, eating lower-fat dishes allows you to eat more in general without getting too much fat or calories.

INSPIRATION: *I am overcoming my impatience to better accept and rejoice in the small signs of my healing and recovery.*

Minestrone

❧ A classic soup to enjoy when cooler weather visits. Serve with Italian bread and a mixed greens salad.

1/2 pound Great Northern beans
4 slices (about 1/4 pound) slab bacon
1 cup chopped onion
1 cup diced carrot
1 cup diced celery
3 garlic cloves, minced
2 zucchini, diced
2 cups sliced green beans
2 cups cubed potatoes
4 cups shredded Savoy cabbage
4 cups chopped kale leaves
1 (28-ounce) can whole tomatoes, drained
  and chopped
4 to 5 cups chicken broth
1/4 cup minced fresh parsley
1/2 teaspoon salt
1/4 teaspoon freshly ground black pepper
1/4 cup freshly grated Parmesan cheese
  for garnish

Pick over and rinse beans. Soak overnight in enough water to cover generously, or use the quick-soak method (see glossary). Drain beans and place in a large saucepan with enough water to cover them by 2 inches. Bring to a boil, reduce heat and simmer, uncovered, 45 minutes to 1 hour or until tender, adding water, as needed. Remove pan from heat, but do not drain beans.

Cook the bacon in a nonstick Dutch oven, stirring, until golden brown. Pour off half the rendered fat and break up bacon. Add onion and cook over medium heat, stirring frequently, until translucent. Add carrot, celery and gar-lic and cook, stirring, 4 minutes. Add zucchini, green beans, potatoes, cabbage and kale and cook, stirring, until cabbage is wilted.

Add tomatoes and 4 cups broth and bring to a boil. Reduce heat, cover and simmer 1 hour. Reserving the liquid, drain the beans. Puree half the beans in a blender or food processor with 1 cup of the reserved cooking liquid. Stir remaining beans and pureed mixture into soup and simmer, uncovered, 15 minutes. Stir in parsley, salt and pepper and thin soup, if desired, with remaining bean liquid and/or chicken broth. Serve garnished with a sprinkling of Parmesan.   *Makes 8 servings.*

PER SERVING: Cal 213 • Carbo 34 gm • Prot 12 gm • Total fat 4 gm • Sat fat 1 gm • Cal from fat 18% • Chol 5 mg

EDUCATION: Buy the best knives you can afford, and keep them sharp to make cooking less of a chore. Eating low-fat, high-fiber foods means lots of chopping, dicing and slicing. High-carbon stainless steel with handles that feel comfortable in your hand, is your best bet. Wash knives by hand, not in the dishwasher, where they will bump against other utensils and become dull.

INSPIRATION: *I am in a continuous process of growth: each day flowering and pruning, changing and becoming . . .*

Honeydew-Kiwi-Avocado Salad with Spicy Dressing

❧ Flavor, texture, color, contrast—this salad has it all! A real change-of-pace salad for autumn.

6 cups packed red-leaf lettuce
1 1/2 cups diced honeydew melon

¹/₂ avocado, pitted, peeled and diced
2 kiwi fruit, peeled, halved lengthwise
*   and thinly sliced*
2 tablespoons brown rice vinegar
1 tablespoon fresh lime juice
1 tablespoon water
1 teaspoon brown sugar
¹/₂ teaspoon salt
¹/₄ teaspoon freshly ground white pepper
¹/₄ teaspoon hot pepper sauce

Combine lettuce, honeydew, avocado and kiwi fruit in a serving bowl and toss gently.

Combine vinegar, lime juice, water, brown sugar, salt, pepper and hot sauce in a cup for dressing. Pour dressing over the salad just before serving. *Makes 6 servings.*

PER SERVING: Cal 79 • Carbo 12 gm • Prot 1 gm • Total fat 3 gm • Sat fat trace • Cal from fat 33% • Chol 0 mg

EDUCATION: When including avocado in a salad, balance it with nonfat dressing. Avocado, while higher in fat than almost all other fruits, can still be a healthy salad ingredient, if you provide balance. Use the pit for a winter growing project. Suspend the pit, flat side down, over a jar by pushing sharp wooden picks into the top third of the pit on 4 sides. Fill the jar with water just touching the avocado pit. Set in a sunny window. Wait patiently for your avocado tree in the making!

October 11

INSPIRATION: *Fighting my feelings is what disturbs my peace. Serenity is allowing them to pass without a battle.*

Penne Pasta with Cauliflower & Tomatoes

❧ Quick and easy, the tomato sauce is simply heated through before serving.

2 cups peeled, seeded and finely chopped
*   plum tomatoes*
¹/₂ cup thinly sliced green onions
¹/₄ cup minced fresh basil
1 tablespoon minced fresh parsley
1 tablespoon chopped pitted ripe olives
1 tablespoon olive oil
2 garlic cloves, minced
2 cups penne pasta or fusilli
3 cups chopped cauliflower flowerets
¹/₄ teaspoon salt
¹/₈ teaspoon freshly ground black pepper
1 tablespoon toasted pine nuts (see glossary)

Combine tomatoes, green onions, basil, parsley, olives, olive oil and garlic in a medium-size bowl and set aside.

Bring a large pot of water to a boil and add pasta. Cook 7 to 9 minutes or until nearly tender. Add cauliflower and return to a boil. Cook cauliflower about 3 minutes or until tender. Drain well and return pasta and cauliflower to pot. Stir in tomato mixture and heat through. Season with salt and pepper. Stir in pine nuts and serve.

Makes 4 servings.

PER SERVING: Cal 300 • Carbo 52 gm • Prot 10 gm • Total fat 6 gm • Sat fat 1 gm • Cal from fat 18% • Chol 0 mg

EDUCATION: Say "C" for cauliflower when you include it in your meals, to remind you that cauliflower is a rich source of vitamin C. One cup provides 100 percent of the RDA for this vitamin. In addition, cauliflower is rich in potassium and a good source of fiber, yet low in sodium and calories. With any of the cabbage family, you'll want to avoid overcooking. In addition to the dish above, you may want to increase healthy benefits in your diet by adding chopped fresh cauliflower to salads.

INSPIRATION: *The fewer "things" I desire, the more freedom I can experience.*

Black Walnut–Pumpkin Bread

🌿 Black walnuts are a native nut. They are usually available from locals who gather them for sale or from specialty markets and some natural-food stores.

1 cup apple cider
1 cup canned pumpkin puree
1 egg
1 egg white
1 tablespoon buttermilk
3 tablespoons canola oil
³/₄ cup packed light brown sugar
1 teaspoon freshly grated orange peel
2 cups whole-wheat pastry flour
2 teaspoons baking powder
¹/₄ teaspoon baking soda
¹/₄ teaspoon salt
¹/₄ teaspoon ground cinnamon
¹/₄ teaspoon ground mace
¹/₈ teaspoon ground cloves
¹/₂ cup chopped black walnuts or
*   English walnuts*

Preheat oven to 350°F (175°C). Lightly butter a 9 × 5-inch loaf pan. In a small saucepan, boil cider until reduced to ¹/₄ cup. Allow to cool. In a large bowl, stir pumpkin, egg, egg white, buttermilk, oil, brown sugar, peel and reduced cider until combined.

In another bowl, combine flour, baking powder, baking soda, salt, cinnamon, mace, cloves and black walnuts. Combine with cider mixture and stir just until combined.

Spoon batter into loaf pan. Bake 50 to 60 minutes or until a wooden pick inserted in the center comes out clean.   *Makes 1 loaf, 10 slices.*

PER SLICE: Cal 257 • Carbo 41 gm • Prot 5 gm • Total fat 9 gm • Sat fat 1 gm • Cal from fat 32% • Chol 21 mg

EDUCATION: Make muffins and quick breads more nutritious by using squash, pumpkin, carrots or sweet potatoes. In addition to the fiber of whole grains, you'll receive a significant amount of vitamins C and A, beta-carotene and other vitamins and minerals. An added bonus: these flavorful quick breads don't require a high-fat spread to make a tasty, healthful snack.

INSPIRATION: *Honesty is a key to recovery. Therefore, being honest with others—and with myself—is necessary today and every day.*

Swordfish with Raisins, Olives & Mint

🌿 Aromatic and intricately flavored, this swordfish goes well with a fresh pasta topped with fresh tomato sauce, and crusty Italian bread.

4 (6- to 8-ounce) swordfish steaks
3 teaspoons olive oil
1 onion, finely chopped
¹/₂ cup pitted green Spanish olives, quartered
¹/₃ cup golden raisins
2 tablespoons drained capers
2 tablespoons brown rice vinegar
2 tablespoons minced fresh mint leaves
2 tablespoons minced fresh parsley
Mint sprigs for garnish

Cook the swordfish steaks in 2 teaspoons of the oil in a large, nonstick skillet over medium heat about 2 minutes per side or until lightly browned but not cooked through. Remove steaks and set on a warmed plate.

Add remaining oil and cook onion in the same skillet over medium heat, stirring frequently, until golden, about 4 minutes. Add olives, raisins and capers and stir over low heat 2 minutes. Push olive mixture to one side of pan, return swordfish steaks and spoon ingredients over top. Add vinegar, mint and parsley. Cover pan and cook 2 minutes, until swordfish steaks are opaque throughout. Place steaks topped with olive mixture on individual plates and garnish with mint sprigs.   *Makes 4 servings.*

PER SERVING: Cal 332 • Carbo 15 gm • Prot 35 gm • Total fat 14 gm • Sat fat 3 gm • Cal from fat 39% • Chol 66 mg

EDUCATION: Treat yourself to gourmet food items that are rich in taste but low in fat. Coarse-ground or Dijon-style mustards, fruited or herbed vinegars, capers and fresh herbs pack intense flavor. Adding one of these ingredients or a combination can add taste appeal to many low-fat dishes.

INSPIRATION: *Avoiding impulsiveness lets me work toward long-term satisfactions without self-inflicted distractions.*

Quinoa Muffins with Apples & Raisins

Egg whites lighten a low-fat muffin with an added touch—moist, cooked grain.

1 cup unbleached all-purpose flour
2/3 cup whole-wheat pastry flour
1/2 cup packed dark brown sugar

1 teaspoon baking powder
1/2 teaspoon baking soda
1/2 teaspoon ground cinnamon
1/2 teaspoon salt
3/4 cup buttermilk
1/3 cup unsweetened applesauce
1/3 cup cooked quinoa (see below)
     or cooked bulgur
2 egg whites
2 tablespoons canola oil
1 cup peeled, seeded and chopped apple
1/3 cup raisins

Preheat oven to 400°F (200°C). Lightly butter 12 (2¾-inch) nonstick muffin cups. Combine flours, brown sugar, baking powder, baking soda, cinnamon and salt in a large bowl.

In a medium-size bowl, combine buttermilk, applesauce, cooked quinoa or bulgur, egg whites, oil, apple and raisins. Pour buttermilk mixture into dry ingredients and stir just until combined. Divide batter among muffin cups. Bake 25 minutes or until a wooden pick inserted in the center comes out clean.

Makes 12 muffins.

PER MUFFIN: Cal 152 • Carbo 30 gm • Prot 3 gm • Total fat 3 gm • Sat fat trace • Cal from fat 16% • Chol trace

EDUCATION: Get keen about quinoa for its iron and lysine. Pronounced *Keen-wa*, this grainlike food is not a true grain, but looks like one and can be used similarly. Quinoa is high in protein and the amino acid lysine, which is lacking in most grains and vegetables. Adding quinoa to these foods creates a complete vegetarian protein. It also supplies more iron than grains and is rich in potassium, magnesium, zinc, copper, manganese and morale-boosting B vitamins.

INSPIRATION: *Believing in myself and my ability to change is foundational to my goal of recovery.*

Saffron Rice with Cumin

❧ When you want rice to have a special presence on the dinner table, this recipe fits the bill. Attractive and fragrant, it can be served with meat, fish or poultry; curried dishes; or plain.

2 teaspoons cumin seeds
4 teaspoons olive oil
$^1/_4$ teaspoon crumbled saffron threads
2 cups brown basmati or brown
    long-grain rice
4 cups chicken broth
$^1/_2$ teaspoon salt
2 tablespoons minced fresh parsley
    for garnish

Cook the cumin seeds in the oil in a saucepan over medium heat about 10 seconds or until fragrant. Stir in the saffron until combined, then add the rice, stirring until the rice is evenly coated with oil.

Stir in broth and salt, bring to a boil and boil 2 minutes. Reduce heat, cover and simmer rice on lowest heat 35 minutes. Remove from heat and let stand, covered, 5 minutes. Fluff with a fork as rice is put into a serving bowl. Garnish with parsley.   *Makes 8 servings.*

PER SERVING: Cal 213 • Carbo 36 gm • Prot 6 gm • Total fat 4 gm • Sat fat 1 gm • Cal from fat 17% • Chol 0 mg

EDUCATION: Eat 6 to 11 servings of rice, breads, cereals and pastas daily. This may seem like a daunting goal, but servings add up quickly. One bread slice, 1 ounce of cereal, $^1/_2$ cup of cooked pasta, rice, other grain or cereal equals 1 serving. A plate of pasta often contains 1 to 2 cups; that's 2 to 4 servings. A sandwich or 2 pieces of toast or a bagel equals 2 servings, and most of us wind up with 2 ounces of cereal in our bowls, another 2 servings. Add crackers, air-popped popcorn or pretzels for snacks, and you've easily achieved this dietary goal.

INSPIRATION: *Finding happiness inside myself may not be easy, but it's downright impossible to find it somewhere else.*

Creamy Corn & Potato Chowder

❧ Red pepper dots this rich-tasting soup with color. Fresh herbs add a satisfying flavor and attractive garnish. A great soup to eat while reading a good book in your pajamas!

1 slice slab bacon
$^1/_2$ cup finely chopped onion
1 baking potato, peeled and cubed
$^1/_2$ sweet red bell pepper, diced
1 tablespoon fresh thyme leaves or
    1 teaspoon dried thyme
2 to 2$^1/_2$ cups low-fat (1%) milk
1 cup fresh or frozen whole-kernel corn
1 (15-ounce) can creamed corn
2 tablespoons minced fresh parsley
Fresh thyme sprigs for garnish

Cook bacon in a large saucepan over medium heat, stirring frequently, 3 minutes or until crisp. Remove bacon and set aside. Pour off half the fat. Add onion to the pan and cook, stirring frequently, until translucent. Add cubed potato and red pepper and cook, stirring, 1 minute. Add 2 cups milk and bring to a boil. Reduce heat, cover and simmer 13 to 15 minutes, stirring occasionally or until vegetables are tender and soup is slightly thickened.

Add corn and creamed corn to soup and simmer 2 or 3 minutes or until corn is tender. Add extra milk, if necessary, to reach desired consistency. Serve sprinkled with minced parsley and garnished with thyme sprigs.

Makes 4 servings.

PER SERVING: Cal 218 • Carbo 45 gm • Prot 9 gm • Total fat 3 gm • Sat fat 1 gm • Cal from fat 11% • Chol 6 mg

EDUCATION: In soup recipes, replace whole milk, half-and-half or cream with low-fat (1%) or skim milk to reduce fat. If the recipe is a family favorite, you may want to cut down gradually. Begin by substituting low-fat milk for half the higher-fat ingredient called for. Eventually everyone will become accustomed to the healthier, lower-fat version.

October 17

INSPIRATION: *When I tell my own truth as I know it, it makes it easier for those around me to be truthful.*

Brian's Black Bean Tostadas

A protein-rich meatless meal features an assortment of vegetable toppings.

6 corn tortillas
1 onion, chopped
1 tablespoon olive oil
2 garlic cloves, minced
1 (15-ounce) can black beans,
    rinsed and drained
¼ cup Sombrero Salsa (see February 16)
    or bottled salsa thinned with tomato juice
¼ cup minced fresh parsley
¼ teaspoon salt
⅛ teaspoon ground cumin
⅛ teaspoon ground coriander
⅛ teaspoon freshly ground black pepper

Dash of ground red pepper
⅓ cup low-fat (1%) cottage cheese
    or yogurt cheese (see glossary)
⅓ cup nonfat sour cream
1 tablespoon fresh lemon juice
2 cups thinly sliced fresh spinach leaves
2 cups peeled, seeded and diced tomatoes
1 zucchini, quartered lengthwise and
    thinly sliced
½ cup thinly sliced green onions
¼ cup minced fresh cilantro
Cherry tomatoes for garnish
Parsley sprigs for garnish

Preheat oven to 350°F (175°C). Arrange tortillas on a baking sheet and bake 6 minutes per side, until crisp.

Cook the onion in the oil in a large, non-stick skillet over medium heat, stirring frequently, until the onion is translucent. Add the garlic and cook, stirring, 1 minute. Add beans and mash them lightly with a potato masher or fork. Stir in salsa, parsley, salt, cumin, coriander, pepper and red pepper and heat through.

Combine the cottage cheese, sour cream and lemon juice in a blender or food processor and process until smooth. Divide the bean mixture among the warm tortillas, spreading evenly. Top with spinach, diced tomatoes, sliced zucchini, and green onions. Top each with a dollop of sour cream mixture and a sprinkle of fresh cilantro. Garnish with cherry tomatoes and parsley sprigs. *Makes 6 servings.*

PER SERVING: Cal 291 • Carbo 45 gm • Prot 14 gm • Total fat 7 gm • Sat fat 2 gm • Cal from fat 22% • Chol trace

EDUCATION: Use prepared flavor enhancers to perk up the flavor of low-fat, low-salt foods. Salsa is a natural for Mexican-style dishes, but try it, too, on fish, chicken, burgers, rice, eggs and baked potatoes. Try chutney on pork, chicken and rice dishes.

INSPIRATION: *Being able to relieve stress without reaching for food is another measure of my recovery.*

Belgian Endive Salad with Fennel

🌿 Contrasting flavors distinguish this elegant salad, suitable for entertaining.

2 medium-size fennel bulbs, with feathery tops
4 Belgian endive
1/2 small red onion, thinly sliced
1 tablespoon finely crumbled feta cheese
2 tablespoons minced fresh parsley
2 tablespoons extra-virgin olive oil
2 tablespoons nonfat yogurt
2 tablespoons fresh lemon juice
1 garlic clove, pushed through a press
1/4 teaspoon freshly ground white pepper
1/8 teaspoon dried marjoram

Trim fennel, discarding cores and saving feathery tops. Thinly slice fennel bulbs lengthwise. Chop enough of the tops to measure 1 tablespoon and set aside. Trim endive, discarding cores, and thinly slice lengthwise. Toss fennel and endive together in a wide salad bowl. Separate red onion slices into rings, and arrange over top of salad. Sprinkle salad with feta, minced parsley, and chopped fennel tops.

For dressing, combine oil, yogurt, lemon juice, garlic, pepper and marjoram in a cup measure. Drizzle dressing over salad just before serving. *Makes 6 servings.*

PER SERVING: Cal 64 • Carbo 4 gm • Prot 1 gm • Total fat 4 gm • Sat fat 0 gm • Cal from fat 56% • Chol 3 mg

EDUCATION: Substitute nonfat yogurt for half the oil to trim salad dressings. The creamy, tangy dressing will give a lift to salads while cutting fat calories in half! Add dressings just before serving so salads remain crisp and attractive, or serve dressing on the side so folks can add it when they like.

INSPIRATION: *My relationships with others can become one of the most fulfilling areas of my life.*

Peter's Pumpkin Bread Pudding

🌿 An easy dessert for two, made easier with use of a microwave. Place the puddings in the microwave before dinner, and they'll be warm and ready for dessert.

3/4 cup canned pumpkin puree
3/4 cup low-fat (1%) milk
1 egg
1 additional egg white
1/4 cup packed brown sugar
2 tablespoons raisins or dried currants
1/4 teaspoon salt
1/4 teaspoon ground cinnamon
Dash of freshly grated nutmeg
4 slices lightly toasted cinnamon-
   raisin bread

Combine the pumpkin puree and milk in a large bowl. Lightly beat the egg and additional white and add to pumpkin mixture with the brown sugar, raisins or currants, salt, cinnamon and nutmeg. Whisk until mixture is smooth. Cut toast into 1/2-inch cubes. Gently stir into pumpkin mixture and let stand 5 minutes.

Lightly butter 2 (1-cup) microwave-safe ramekins or custard cups. Cut 2 pieces of waxed paper long enough to fit around ramekins and overlap by 1 inch. Fold the waxed paper to make a collar extending 2 inches above the top of the ramekins. Tie the collars around the ramekins with string.

Divide the pumpkin mixture between the ramekins. Microwave on HIGH 15 to 18 minutes, turning once or until a wooden pick inserted in the center comes out clean. Let stand 5 minutes, remove collars and serve.

Makes 2 servings.

PER SERVING: Cal 385 • Carbo 73 gm • Prot 13 gm • Total fat 6 gm • Sat fat 2 gm • Cal from fat 14% • Chol 110 mg

EDUCATION: Use your microwave to save time when you're in a hurry. You'll also save money. Microwave ovens use only one-third to one-half as much energy as conventional ovens. They make particularly good sense for those of us who live alone. Knowing a meal can be on the table in minutes makes it more likely we'll eat nutritiously.

October 20

INSPIRATION: *In order to receive love, I must learn to give it. To improve my ability to give love, I continue seeking my growth and healing.*

Gingerbread Pancakes with Ginger-Pear Sauce

🍃 Enjoy a dessert twist to breakfast, with gingerbread flapjacks. Fresh ginger juice adds zest to the pear sauce.

3 pears, peeled, cored and quartered
1/4 cup pure maple syrup
1/4 cup shredded gingerroot
1 teaspoon fresh lemon juice
1/4 teaspoon freshly grated lemon peel
1/2 cup whole-wheat pastry flour
1/2 cup unbleached all-purpose flour
1 teaspoon ground ginger
1/2 teaspoon ground cinnamon
1/2 teaspoon baking soda
1/4 teaspoon salt
Dash of freshly grated nutmeg
Dash of ground cloves
2 eggs
1/3 cup medium unsulfured molasses
1 cup buttermilk
1 tablespoon butter, melted
1/4 cup nonfat sour cream

Place pears and syrup in a blender container or food processor. Squeeze juice from gingerroot and add to pears with the lemon juice and lemon peel. Process until smooth. Heat in a small saucepan just to boiling, stirring frequently. Cover and set aside.

Combine flours, ginger, cinnamon, baking soda, salt, nutmeg and cloves in a large bowl. In a medium-size bowl, beat the eggs and combine with the molasses. Stir in buttermilk and melted butter. Add egg mixture to dry ingredients and stir just until combined.

Cook pancakes on a lightly oiled nonstick griddle over medium heat. Pour batter by 1/4-cupfuls onto the griddle and cook pancakes 1 or 2 minutes per side or until golden brown and cooked through. Keep pancakes on an oven-proof plate, covered loosely with foil, in a warm oven until pancakes are all cooked. Serve with a tablespoon of sour cream and warm pear sauce. *Makes 4 servings.*

PER SERVING: Cal 426 • Carbo 80 gm • Prot 9 gm • Total fat 9 gm • Sat fat 5 gm • Cal from fat 19% • Chol 116 mg

EDUCATION: Throw a breakfast party for low-cost fun! Most people throw dinner parties, which can add up to great expense. Breakfast is a more economical meal. Besides, it can be followed by some wholesome, shared, outdoor activity as simple as a walk in the park.

INSPIRATION: *As I let go of resentments from the past, I feel the burden of tension and negative energy lifting.*

Kathy's Stir-fried Pork, Vegetables & Noodles

Richly flavored with teriyaki sauce and Oriental sesame oil, this mixture of vegetables and pork combines deliciously with wheat noodles.

¹/₂ pound linguini, broken in half

¹/₂ pound lean pork tenderloin

2 teaspoons canola oil

1 teaspoon dark Oriental sesame oil

1 small onion, chopped

1 medium-size red bell pepper, seeded and diced

1 carrot, cut in matchstick strips

1 celery stalk, thinly sliced on diagonal

4 green onions, thinly sliced on diagonal

2 garlic cloves, minced

²/₃ cup chicken broth

¹/₄ cup teriyaki sauce

2 teaspoons cornstarch

Dash of hot (cayenne) pepper

Bring a large saucepan of water to a boil. Add linguini and cook 7 to 9 minutes or until firm-tender. Drain and run under cold water until cooled. Drain and return to saucepan.

Cut the tenderloin into thin strips. Cook in half of the canola oil and half of the sesame oil in a large, nonstick skillet over medium heat, stirring frequently, until pork is cooked through and begins to brown. Remove pork and add to linguini.

Add remaining oil to skillet and cook onion, stirring frequently, until translucent. Add pepper, carrot and celery and cook, stirring, 2 to 3 minutes, until vegetables are crisp-tender. Add green onions and garlic and stir until combined.

Mix broth, teriyaki sauce, cornstarch and cayenne and pour into skillet. Bring to a boil, stirring, and boil 30 seconds or until thickened and clear. Stir in pork and noodles and heat through. *Makes 4 servings.*

PER SERVING: Cal 386 • Carbo 53 gm • Prot 26 gm • Total fat 7 gm • Sat fat 2 gm • Cal from fat 16% • Chol 53 mg

EDUCATION: Use your microwave to defrost frozen pork, beef, poultry, other meats or fish to save time and ensure food safety. Defrosting foods at room temperature can allow bacteria to grow. Quickly thawing foods in the microwave, then cooking, means more vitamins and minerals are retained.

INSPIRATION: *To enjoy living, to have enthusiasm for the beauty of the world and an appreciation of the gifts I have received are ways of "giving back" to life.*

Paella

A Spanish dish combining chicken, seafood and sometimes sausage, paella is a colorful, hearty main course.

$^1/_4$ *teaspoon saffron*
$^1/_4$ *cup hot chicken broth or water*
4 chicken drumsticks
4 chicken thighs
1 tablespoon olive oil
1 onion, chopped
1 green bell pepper, diced
2 garlic cloves, minced
1 (28-ounce) can Italian plum tomatoes
1$^1/_2$ cups brown rice
$^1/_2$ teaspoon salt
$^1/_4$ teaspoon freshly ground black pepper
$^1/_4$ teaspoon ground cinnamon
1 pound medium-size shrimp, shelled
    and deveined (see glossary)
1 (10-ounce) package frozen green peas,
    thawed
1 (2-ounce) jar pimientos, drained and
    chopped
12 mussels in shells, scrubbed

In a cup, mix saffron with stock or water. Set aside. Cook chicken in the oil in a nonstick Dutch oven over medium heat until browned on all sides. Add onion, bell pepper and garlic and cook, stirring frequently, 2 minutes.

Add saffron mixture, tomatoes and their liquid, brown rice, salt, pepper and cinnamon and bring to a boil. Reduce heat, cover and simmer 35 to 40 minutes, until chicken is tender and liquid is nearly absorbed. Stir in shrimp, peas and pimientos. Place mussels on top, cover and simmer 5 to 10 minutes, until mussels open, rice is tender and all liquid is absorbed. Discard any mussels that do not open. *Makes 8 servings.*

PER SERVING: Cal 400 • Carbo 41 gm • Prot 37 gm • Total fat 9 gm • Sat fat 2 gm • Cal from fat 20% • Chol 150 mg

EDUCATION: Change the battery in your smoke detector to protect yourself from fire. Working smoke detectors increase your chance of escaping from a fire unharmed by 50 percent. Carry your own portable smoke detector if you do a lot of traveling.

INSPIRATION: *I recognize myself on the road to recovery when I reach out to those I care about, fearlessly.*

Turkey-Stuffed Mushroom Caps

❧ Serve as an appetizer or convenient bite-sized party fare. For a more impressive presentation, line a plate with radicchio leaves or kale before arranging mushrooms.

16 medium-size mushrooms
1/2 cup ground skinless turkey breast
1/2 cup fresh bread crumbs
2 tablespoons minced fresh parsley
1 tablespoon minced Greek olives
1 garlic clove, pushed through a press
1/4 teaspoon salt
1/4 teaspoon ground coriander
1/4 teaspoon paprika
1/4 teaspoon freshly ground black pepper
Dash of hot (cayenne) pepper
Parsley sprigs for garnish
Lemon slices for garnish

Brush any dirt off mushrooms and remove and trim stems. Finely chop stems and place in a medium-size bowl. Add the turkey, bread crumbs, parsley, olives, garlic, salt, coriander, paprika, pepper and cayenne.

Stuff mushroom caps generously with the turkey mixture. Place in a shallow casserole and cover with waxed paper. Microwave on HIGH 3 minutes. Rotate the dish a half turn and microwave on HIGH 2 or 3 minutes or until the turkey is cooked through and the mushrooms are tender. Garnish with parsley sprigs and lemon slices. *Makes 8 servings.*

PER SERVING: Cal 46 • Carbo 2 gm • Prot 4 gm • Total fat 2 gm • Sat fat trace • Cal from fat 38% • Chol 9 mg

EDUCATION: Get an early start on holiday entertaining, and bring people together before holiday preparations and stepped-up social obligations have everyone frazzled. In developing a menu, use small amounts of the leanest meats or poultry available and cook fat free, as above. Set out trays of raw, cut-up vegetables and fruits. For dip, stir Mexican herbs and spices into nonfat yogurt cheese (see glossary). Dip fruits in yogurt cheese flavored with fruit preserves.

INSPIRATION: *By unraveling my self-deceptions I discover the fabric of my own truth.*

Golden Basmati Split-Pea Pilaf

❧ An East Indian–style side dish, this pilaf is protein-rich and could serve as a main course. Turmeric gives it a golden hue.

1 bay leaf
4 teaspoons canola oil
1 cup finely chopped onion
2 teaspoons minced garlic
1 teaspoon ground cinnamon
1/2 teaspoon ground coriander
1/2 teaspoon ground cumin
1/4 teaspoon ground cloves
1/4 teaspoon turmeric
1/4 teaspoon salt
1/4 teaspoon freshly ground black pepper
1 1/2 cups brown basmati rice or long-grain brown rice
3 cups chicken broth
2/3 cup dried yellow split peas
4 cups water
1 cup nonfat yogurt cheese (see glossary)

Cook bay leaf in the oil in a large saucepan over medium heat about 5 minutes, stirring occasionally, until the bay leaf is golden. Add onions and cook, stirring frequently, until onion is tender, 5 to 7 minutes. Add garlic, cinnamon, coriander, cumin, cloves, turmeric, salt and pepper and cook, stirring, 1 minute. Add rice and stir until combined with onion mixture. Add broth, bring to a boil and boil 2 minutes. Reduce heat, cover and simmer on lowest heat 35 minutes. Set aside rice, covered.

While the rice cooks, place the split peas and water in a large saucepan. Bring to a boil, reduce heat and simmer, uncovered, 30 to 35 minutes, until tender but not falling apart. Stir the cooked split peas into the rice, heat through and serve with yogurt cheese.

Makes 4 servings.

PER SERVING: Cal 514 • Carbo 85 gm • Prot 25 gm • Total fat 8 gm • Sat fat 1 gm • Cal from fat 14% • Chol trace

EDUCATION: For an alternative to high-fat cheeses, make your own tart and tangy, creamy, nonfat cheese from yogurt. Useful as a garnish, as a base for dips or spreads, or to top baked potatoes, yogurt cheese is simple to make (see glossary).

October 25

INSPIRATION: *Getting on with the business of living means accepting myself where I am, accepting others where they are, and moving forward from there.*

Bluefish with Onions & Ginger Rice

❧ Ginger rice is also a tasty side dish for poultry. The delicious flavor comes from low-fat seasonings, so it's a healthy addition to your meal.

1 1/2 pounds bluefish fillets
3 tablespoons fresh lemon juice
2 tablespoons water
1 teaspoon olive oil
1/3 cup minced green onions
3 tablespoons minced gingerroot
1 cup basmati or regular long-grain rice
2 cups water
2 green onions, sliced on diagonal
   for garnish
2 tablespoons minced fresh
   parsley for garnish

Place the fish fillets skin side up in a flameproof, shallow casserole dish. Add lemon juice, water and oil. Allow to marinate 10 minutes, turning once. Combine minced green onions with 2 tablespoons of the gingerroot and press over surface of bluefish. Let stand 5 minutes.

Combine rice, remaining tablespoon of gingerroot, and water in a large saucepan. Bring to a boil, reduce heat, cover and simmer 15 minutes. Turn off heat and let stand.

Place casserole dish with the fish over medium heat. Bring to a boil, reduce heat, cover and simmer 10 minutes or until fish is cooked through. Serve with ginger rice garnished with sliced green onions and parsley.

Makes 4 servings.

PER SERVING: Cal 399 • Carbo 38 gm • Prot 39 gm • Total fat 10 gm • Sat fat 2 gm • Cal from fat 22% • Chol 100 mg

EDUCATION: Choose fresh fish instead of fish sticks and other prepared products that may be far higher in salt and fat. High fat is often nestling in that innocent-looking bread coating. Other products are sky-high in sodium. To highlight the advantages of fish—a low-fat source of protein, B vitamins and omega-3 fatty acids—buy it fresh and prepare in a low-fat, low-sodium way, as above.

INSPIRATION: *I have no greater sense of well-being and joy than that found in treating myself with love.*

Glazed Pumpkin Spice Bars

A great autumn dessert. Serve with hot cider in front of a roaring fire.

$^3/_4$ cup unbleached all-purpose flour
$^1/_2$ cup whole-wheat pastry flour
1 teaspoon baking powder
1 teaspoon baking soda
$^1/_2$ teaspoon salt
$1^1/_2$ teaspoons ground cinnamon
$^1/_2$ teaspoon ground ginger
$^1/_8$ teaspoon ground cardamom
$^1/_8$ teaspoon freshly grated nutmeg
1 egg
$^1/_2$ cup packed brown sugar
1 cup canned pumpkin
$^1/_4$ cup canola oil
2 tablespoons buttermilk
$^1/_2$ cup raisins
1 (8-ounce) can crushed pineapple
    with juice
$^3/_4$ cup vanilla powdered sugar
    (see glossary)
1 to $1^1/_2$ tablespoons skim milk
$^1/_4$ teaspoon freshly grated
    orange peel

Preheat oven to 350°F (175°C). Lightly butter a nonstick 13 × 9-inch baking pan. Combine flours, baking powder and soda, salt, cinnamon, ginger, cardamom and nutmeg in a medium-size bowl.

Beat egg and brown sugar together in a large bowl. Beat in pumpkin, oil and buttermilk. Stir in raisins and pineapple with juice. Stir in dry ingredients just until combined.

Spread pumpkin mixture in baking pan. Bake 30 to 35 minutes or until a wooden pick inserted in the center comes out clean. Cool to room temperature in the pan on a wire rack.

Combine powdered sugar, enough milk to thin to desired consistency, and grated orange peel. Spread over cooled pumpkin bars. Cut into 24 (3 x 1½-inch) bars.   *Makes 24 bars.*

PER BAR: Cal 104 • Carbo 20 gm • Prot 1 gm • Total fat 3 gm • Sat fat trace • Cal from fat 23% • Chol 9 mg

EDUCATION: Add moist ingredients, such as the pineapple above, to counteract dryness in low-fat baked goods. Plumping raisins in liquid before adding to low-fat baked items is another way to add moisture. These tricks create a satisfying texture to such desserts without increasing fat.

INSPIRATION: *The knowledge of how to live my life comes not from books or other people, but from deep within myself.*

Thom's Spicy Black Bean Soup

Cold-weather satisfying—hot and spicy, thick and tasty. Serve over cooked brown rice for a hearty main dish, perfect for Thom before he takes the dogs for a run.

2 pounds dried black beans
4 slices slab bacon, diced
2 cups chopped onions
1 red bell pepper, seeded and diced
1 green bell pepper, seeded and diced
3 garlic cloves, sliced
10 cups chicken broth
1 bay leaf
2 teaspoons dried oregano
$1/2$ teaspoon ground cumin
$1/2$ teaspoon ground coriander
$1/2$ teaspoon salt
$1/2$ teaspoon freshly ground
    black pepper
$1/4$ teaspoon hot (cayenne) pepper
$1/2$ cup tomato paste
$1/4$ cup minced fresh parsley
$1/2$ cup nonfat sour cream
$1/2$ cup thinly sliced green onions

Pick over and rinse beans. Soak overnight in enough water to cover generously, or use the quick-soak method (see glossary).

Cook bacon in a nonstick Dutch oven over medium heat, stirring frequently, until crisp. Pour off half the rendered fat. Add onions, peppers and garlic to the pan and cook over medium heat, stirring frequently, until onions are translucent. Drain soaked beans and add to pan with broth, bay leaf, oregano, cumin, coriander, salt, pepper and cayenne and bring to a boil. Reduce heat and simmer, uncovered, $1 1/2$ to 2 hours, stirring occasionally, until beans are tender.

Puree 4 cups of soup in a blender or food processor with the tomato paste. Return to pan and stir into soup with parsley. Simmer 10 minutes. Serve soup in bowls garnished with a dollop of sour cream and sprinkled with sliced green onions. *Makes 8 servings.*

PER SERVING: Cal 283 • Carbo 38 gm • Prot 19 gm • Total fat 7 gm • Sat fat 3 gm • Cal from fat 22% • Chol 3 mg

EDUCATION: Eat beans and unrefined rice once a week to offset higher-fat fare on other days. The majority of people in the world eat like this every day, if they're lucky. We can gain not only an appreciation for the simplicity of such sustaining fare, but gratitude for the abundance and variety of foods that surround us. Nutritionally, in addition to balancing even moderately higher-fat meals of the week, beans and rice provide a hearty boost of soluble and insoluble fiber. Seasonings can be varied to reflect a host of international cuisines.

INSPIRATION: *Comparing myself to others blinds me to my unique gifts and individuality.*

Tex-Mex Veggie Rice

❧ A colorful side dish for any Mexican meal, brown rice shines with south-of-the-border flavor and a bonus of vegetables.

> 1/4 cup finely chopped onion
> 2 teaspoons olive oil
> 2 teaspoons cumin seeds
> 1 teaspoon minced garlic
> 1/4 teaspoon salt
> 1/8 teaspoon freshly ground
>   black pepper
> Dash of turmeric
> 1 cup brown rice
> 2 cups chicken broth
> 1 cup diced zucchini
> 1 plum tomato, peeled, seeded and
>   finely chopped
> 1/2 cup frozen whole-kernel corn
> 2 tablespoons minced fresh
>   parsley
> 1 tablespoon minced fresh
>   cilantro

Cook onion in the oil in a large saucepan over medium heat, stirring frequently, until translucent, about 3 minutes. Add cumin seeds, garlic, salt, pepper and turmeric and cook, stirring, 1 minute. Stir in rice until combined with seasonings.

Add chicken broth and bring to a boil. Reduce heat, cover and simmer 30 minutes. Gently stir in zucchini, tomato and corn. Cover and simmer 10 minutes or until rice and vegetables are tender and liquid is absorbed. Add parsley and cilantro and fluff rice with a fork. *Makes 4 servings.*

PER SERVING: Cal 248 • Carbo 44 gm • Prot 8 gm • Total fat 5 gm • Sat fat 1 gm • Cal from fat 17% • Chol 0 mg

EDUCATION: Counteract irritability and depression with complex carbohydrates, abundant in the recipe above. Complex carbohydrates boost brain levels of serotonin, a calming chemical. Carbohydrates encourage tryptophan, an amino acid building block of serotonin, to enter the brain. Antidepressant medications also work by keeping serotonin levels high, but sometimes with the expense of disturbing side effects.

INSPIRATION: *Finding people who support the positive changes I am making in my life is a part of my recovery.*

Scallops Cappadocia

❧ An elegant, but easy, seafood main dish. Serve with cooked spinach, rice or couscous and a mixed salad.

> 1 1/2 pounds sea scallops
> 1 tablespoon unsalted butter, melted
> 2 tablespoons dried whole-wheat
>   bread crumbs
> 1/2 teaspoon dried marjoram
> 1/2 teaspoon dried basil
> 1/8 teaspoon freshly ground
>   black pepper
> Lemon wedges for garnish
> Parsley sprigs for garnish

Preheat broiler. Rinse scallops thoroughly and pat dry with paper towels. Toss scallops with butter in a medium-size bowl. Combine the bread crumbs, marjoram, basil, salt and pepper in a pie pan. Dip flat top of each scallop into the bread-crumb mixture. Place scallops breaded side up on a rack in a broiling pan.

Broil 5 minutes, just until bread-crumb topping is golden brown and scallops are opaque throughout. Serve garnished with lemon wedges and parsley sprigs.   *Makes 4 servings.*

PER SERVING: Cal 188 • Carbo 7 gm • Prot 29 gm • Total fat 4 gm • Sat fat 2 gm • Cal from fat 21% • Chol 64 mg

EDUCATION: To reduce hypertension, cut down on salt without making foods taste dull and uninteresting. A few tricks will perk up your taste buds so you'll never miss the salt. Try a sprinkling of grated lemon peel or lemon juice to give a lift to seafood and vegetables. Become familiar with a variety of herbs, and add them regularly to your cooking. Combine flavors, such as fruits with vegetables, to create more interest without salt.

INSPIRATION: *Truly believing that whatever I am is enough adds balance to my life and enjoyment to living.*

Bran Bread with Raisins

If you don't have time to make a yeast bread, this quick loaf is a convenient alternative.

2 tablespoons unsalted butter, softened
$^3/_4$ cup packed brown sugar
2 eggs, beaten
1 cup buttermilk
$1^1/_2$ cups unbleached all-purpose flour
$1^1/_4$ cups unprocessed wheat bran
1 teaspoon baking soda
$^1/_4$ teaspoon salt
$^1/_3$ cup raisins
$^1/_3$ cup chopped walnuts

Preheat oven to 350°F (175°C). Lightly oil a 9 × 5-inch nonstick loaf pan. Cream together butter and sugar in a large bowl. Beat in eggs. Add buttermilk and stir until combined.

Combine flour, bran, baking soda, salt, raisins and nuts in a medium-size bowl. Stir dry ingredients into the egg mixture just until combined.

Spoon batter into loaf pan. Bake 30 minutes. Reduce heat to 300°F (150°C) and bake another 20 to 30 minutes or until a wooden pick inserted in the center comes out clean.

Makes 1 loaf, 10 slices.

PER SLICE: Cal 231 • Carbo 41 gm • Prot 6 gm • Total fat 6 gm • Sat fat 2 gm • Cal from fat 23% • Chol 50 mg

EDUCATION: When looking for a low-fat snack, turn to grain foods like a slice of the bread above. Toast the bread, but skip the butter. Try a thin spread of all-fruit jam, instead. Other good low-fat grain choices: air-popped popcorn, low-salt pretzels, bagels and bread sticks.

INSPIRATION: *Today I will flaunt my uniqueness—be enthusiastically the one and only "me!"*

Mini-Pumpkin Cups with Green Pea Puree

Those tiny pumpkins used as autumn decorations are actually edible squashes. Sold as "Jack-Be-Little" pumpkins, these squashes are just the right size for individual servings, especially attractive when stuffed with a second vegetable, as they are in this recipe, a bright puree of peas.

> 4 Jack-Be-Little pumpkin squashes, about
> 3 to 4 inches in diameter
> 1 1/4 cups frozen green peas
> 1 fresh mint leaf
> 1 tablespoon skim milk
> 1 teaspoon unsalted butter
> Dash of salt
> Dash of freshly ground
> black pepper
> Mint sprigs for garnish

Pierce the tops of each pumpkin squash and microwave them on HIGH 8 to 10 minutes, until tender. Keep warm.

Cook peas with mint in a small amount of water in a small saucepan, covered, 3 to 4 minutes, just until tender. Drain and rinse under cold running water, then drain again. Discard mint leaf.

Puree peas in a food processor or blender, with the milk, until smooth, scraping down the sides of the container as necessary. Return pea puree to saucepan and heat through with butter, salt and pepper.

Cut tops from mini-pumpkins and scoop out seeds and stringy portion. Fill each with pureed peas and garnish with mint sprigs.

Makes 4 servings.

VARIATIONS
Mini-pumpkins can also be filled with lightly seasoned pureed pumpkin, cooked corn, hot chunky applesauce, or even soup.

PER SERVING: Cal 74 • Carbo 13 gm • Prot 4 gm • Total fat 1 gm • Sat fat 1 gm • Cal from fat 12% • Chol 3 mg

EDUCATION: Have fun with vegetables! Sure, nutrition should be taken seriously. But a light approach can encourage even reluctant vegetable-eaters to give it a try.

INSPIRATION: *I am learning to draw on my own resources to find comfort and peace.*

Spaghetti Squash with Garden Sauce

Stored harvest from the garden (or from a roadside stand) creates a winning dish with pastalike spaghetti squash as a base.

> 1 spaghetti squash
> 1/2 cup chopped onion
> 1/4 cup diced green bell pepper
> 1 tablespoon olive oil
> 2 garlic cloves, minced
> 2 cups peeled, seeded and chopped tomatoes
> 1/2 cup tomato sauce
> 1/2 cup fresh or frozen whole-kernel corn
> 1/4 cup diced bottled roasted
> red bell peppers
> 1/4 cup minced fresh parsley
> 1/4 cup pine nuts, toasted
> Freshly grated Parmesan cheese for garnish

Pierce the spaghetti squash with a sharp knife in several places, through to the hollow cavity inside. Place on a paper towel directly on the floor of the microwave and cook on HIGH 11 to 15 minutes, turning once, or until tender. Let stand 5 to 10 minutes.

While the squash is cooking, cook the onion and bell pepper in the oil in a large, nonstick skillet over medium heat, stirring frequently, until the onion is translucent, 3 to 4 minutes. Add garlic and cook, stirring, 1 minute more.

Add tomatoes and sauce and bring to a boil. Reduce heat, cover and simmer 5 to 8 minutes or until tomatoes are tender. Stir in corn and simmer, covered, 2 or 3 minutes. Add roasted red pepper and parsley and heat through.

Cut squash in half lengthwise, remove seeds, and with 2 forks, gently pull out strands and place on a warm platter. Top with the tomato sauce, sprinkle with pine nuts and garnish with Parmesan. *Makes 4 servings.*

PER SERVING: Cal 227 • Carbo 36 gm • Prot 9 gm • Total fat 9 gm • Sat fat 1 gm • Cal from fat 34% • Chol 0 mg

EDUCATION: Substitute spaghetti squash for pasta, occasionally, for valuable vegetable fiber. When cooked, the flesh of this squash can be pulled apart to resemble spaghetti. Although pasta is a perfectly healthy ingredient, flavorful spaghetti squash is even lower in calories as well as higher in fiber content than pasta. If you choose not to microwave the squash, it can be pierced and baked 1 to 1³/₄ hours in a 350°F (175°C) oven until slightly soft, or pierced and placed in a large pot of boiling water, then simmered about 45 minutes or until tender.

November 2

INSPIRATION: *The value of the lessons I learn in life depends upon my attitude.*

Maryann's Risotto

Creamy arborio rice is a delicious side dish for special meals. Oven baking makes this dish easy, which Maryann loves. Who wouldn't? Homemade stock really brings out the flavor.

¹/₂ cup finely chopped onion
2 tablespoons unsalted butter
1¹/₂ cups arborio or other white,
*   short-grain rice*
3 cups Basic Homemade Chicken Stock (see
*   October 1) or canned chicken broth*
¹/₂ teaspoon salt
¹/₈ teaspoon freshly ground white pepper
2 sprigs fresh parsley
1 sprig fresh thyme or ¹/₄ teaspoon dried thyme
¹/₂ small bay leaf

Preheat oven to 350°F (175°). Slowly cook the onion in the butter in a flameproof, ovenproof casserole over medium heat, stirring frequently, until onion is tender. Do not brown. Add rice and stir until the grains are translucent, then turn milky white.

Bring the stock, salt and pepper to a boil. Tie the parsley, thyme and bay leaf in a small square of cheesecloth. Pour the boiling stock over the rice and stir. Add the herb bouquet. Bake, uncovered, 20 to 25 minutes or until liquid is absorbed and rice is tender. Remove herb bouquet, fluff rice with a fork and cover casserole. Rice can stand up to 20 minutes before serving. *Makes 4 servings.*

PER SERVING: Cal 352 • Carbo 61 gm • Prot 9 gm • Total fat 7 gm • Sat fat 4 gm • Cal from fat 18% • Chol 16 mg

EDUCATION: When doubling a recipe, add only one-third as much oil as is called for. The oil will be sufficient to cook the added ingredients, and you will have less fat grams in the finished dish. When using stocks or broths, as above, chill first and skim off fats.

INSPIRATION: *I can meet the needs and accept the limitations of my body.*

INSPIRATION: *The compassion I show others gently heals me as well.*

Broiled Glazed Bananas with Maple Yogurt-Cream

❧ A warming, easy-to-create dessert with a low-fat yogurt–sour cream dressing.

3 tablespoons packed brown sugar
1 tablespoon lime juice
4 firm, ripe bananas
1/3 cup nonfat yogurt
1/4 cup reduced-fat sour cream
1 teaspoon maple syrup
1/8 teaspoon freshly grated lime peel
Mint leaves for garnish

Preheat broiler. Combine brown sugar and lime juice in a medium-size bowl. Peel bananas and slice 1/2 inch thick. Add to brown sugar mixture and toss to coat.

Spread bananas in a shallow baking dish. Broil about 4 inches from heat 3 to 5 minutes or until sugar syrup has melted into a glaze.

While bananas are cooking, combine yogurt, sour cream, maple syrup and grated lime peel. Serve hot bananas with a dollop of the maple cream. Garnish with mint leaves.

Makes 4 servings.

PER SERVING: Cal 187 • Carbo 40 gm • Prot 3 gm • Total fat 3 gm • Sat fat 2 gm • Cal from fat 16% • Chol 1 mg

EDUCATION: Go for a walk for overall health. In addition to eating low-fat, nutritious meals and desserts, choosing moderate aerobic exercise is essential to good physical (and mental) health. Twenty minutes a day (or at least three times a week) is all it takes. Exercise tones the body, reduces stress, and relaxes the mind.

Vegetarian Navy Bean & Corn Soup

❧ A delicious vegetarian broth is made with kombu, a rich-tasting kelp. You'll be amazed at the mild flavor of this very light soup.

1 (4-inch) piece kombu (see below)
6 cups water
1/3 cup dried navy beans
1 celery stalk, thinly sliced
1 onion, chopped
2 cups frozen whole-kernel corn
1/4 teaspoon salt
1/8 teaspoon freshly ground white pepper
1/4 cup minced fresh parsley

Bring the kombu and water to a boil. Reduce heat and simmer 5 minutes. Remove kombu.

Add navy beans to water and return to a boil. Reduce heat, cover and simmer 1 hour or until beans are tender. Add celery and onion and simmer 15 minutes. Add corn, salt, pepper and parsley and simmer 5 minutes more.

Makes 4 servings.

PER SERVING: Cal 104 • Carbo 24 gm • Prot 4 gm • Total fat trace • Sat fat trace • Cal from fat 2% • Chol 0 mg

EDUCATION: Get minerals safely from foods. Because there is a danger of overdosing on some minerals in supplement form, the best way to ensure an adequate supply is through a varied and balanced diet. Kombu, like other sea vegetables, is a rich source of minerals. Calcium, potassium, magnesium, iron and iodine are abundant in kelp and seaweeds. When they are used to make flavorful stocks, the minerals they contain are leached out into the cooking liquid.

INSPIRATION: *Today I will resist getting lost in activities, finding time and space to nurture my spirit.*

Mat's Lentil–Beef–Taco Buffet

🌿 Studded with raisins and pecans, the lentil-beef filling is complemented by a range of taco topping choices. Mat enjoys crisp taco shells, an alternative, though slightly higher in fat.

1/3 cup lentils

2 cups water

1 bay leaf

1/2 cup chopped onion

1/2 cup diced green bell pepper

2 teaspoons canola oil

3 garlic cloves, minced

4 teaspoons ground cumin

1 teaspoon chili powder

1/2 pound extra-lean ground beef

1/2 cup tomato sauce

1/4 cup raisins

2 tablespoons chopped pecans

2 tablespoons minced fresh cilantro

1/2 teaspoon salt

1/4 teaspoon freshly ground black pepper

12 (6-inch) soft corn tortillas

2 cups thinly sliced romaine lettuce

2 cups peeled, seeded and chopped tomatoes

1 cup Sombrero Salsa (see February 16) or bottled salsa thinned with tomato juice

1/2 cup nonfat yogurt cheese (see glossary)

1/2 cup shredded sharp Cheddar cheese

1/4 cup minced fresh parsley

Combine the lentils, water and bay leaf in a medium-size saucepan and bring to a boil. Reduce heat, cover and simmer 30 minutes or until lentils are tender. Remove bay leaf, drain and coarsely mash lentils with a potato masher.

While lentils are cooking, cook onion and green pepper in the oil in a large, nonstick skillet over medium heat, stirring frequently, until onion is translucent. Add garlic, cumin and chili powder and cook, stirring, 1 minute. Add beef and cook, breaking up beef with a fork, about 10 minutes or until meat is browned. Spoon off fat from pan. Add cooked lentils, tomato sauce, raisins and pecans and cook about 5 minutes, stirring frequently, until mixture is heated through. Stir in cilantro, salt and pepper.

Warm tortillas on a plate, four at a time, for 30 seconds on HIGH in the microwave. Keep warm. Place filling, tortillas, lettuce, tomatoes, salsa, cheeses and parsley on the table. Have each person assemble his or her own, spooning 1/4 to 1/3 cup filling on each tortilla, rolling it up and placing seam side down on the plate. Pass toppings.   *Makes 4 servings.*

PER SERVING: Cal 591 • Carbo 73 gm • Prot 33 gm • Total fat 24 gm • Sat fat 7 gm • Cal from fat 36% • Chol 52 mg

EDUCATION: Read labels at the meat counter. Choose ground beef that's at least 90 percent lean. Look for ground turkey or chicken that contains breast meat and not skin. Even lean meat can be made a leaner protein source by combining with beans or lentils, as above.

INSPIRATION: *Today I will risk trying something new without worrying about the outcome.*

Stuffed Eggplant

A meatless meal can still have visual impact and satisfying taste.

> 4 small to medium-size eggplants
> 1 cup cooked brown rice
> ¼ cup finely diced green bell pepper
> ¼ cup grated onion, lightly pressed in a sieve to remove excess liquid
> 2 tablespoons finely chopped ripe olives
> 2 tablespoons minced fresh parsley
> ¼ teaspoon dried marjoram
> ⅛ teaspoon dried thyme
> ⅛ teaspoon salt
> Dash of freshly ground pepper
> ¾ cup tomato sauce
> ¼ cup water
> ½ cup shredded part-skim mozzarella cheese

Remove stem ends and pierce the eggplants in several places. Microwave on HIGH, turning the eggplants twice during cooking, 10 minutes or until slightly tender. (Eggplants can also be boiled in a large pot of water until slightly tender.) With eggplant on its side, cut a slice off the top surface. Keep eggplant slice. Hollow out the eggplants, leaving about ½ inch of flesh all around.

Preheat oven to 350°F (175°). Finely chop the scooped out eggplant flesh and combine with the rice, bell pepper, onion, olives, parsley, marjoram, thyme, salt, pepper and ¼ cup tomato sauce. Spoon the filling into the eggplants and cover with the eggplant slices. Place the stuffed eggplants in a shallow casserole dish. Combine the remaining ½ cup tomato sauce with water and pour over the stuffed eggplants.

Cover casserole and bake 30 minutes. Uncover casserole, sprinkle eggplants with mozzarella and bake an additional 15 minutes or until eggplants are tender.   *Makes 4 servings.*

PER SERVING: Cal 312 • Carbo 58 gm • Prot 10 gm • Total fat 6 gm • Sat fat 2 gm • Cal from fat 17% • Chol 8 mg

EDUCATION: Egg yourself on to include eggplant in your diet for several health-related benefits. Some studies suggest eggplant itself contains substances that can help lower cholesterol. Also, a serving of eggplant contains almost as much fiber as a serving of oat bran. Its high potassium content helps fight high blood pressure.

INSPIRATION: *Day by day, small step by small step, I will continue to grow and to heal.*

Thirty-Minute Chicken Stew

🌿 Chicken thighs give delicious flavor to this low-fat, economical dinner. Serve with a salad and biscuits.

6 boneless, skinless chicken thighs

1 tablespoon unbleached all-purpose flour

¹/₄ teaspoon salt

¹/₈ teaspoon freshly ground black pepper

1 tablespoon olive oil

1 onion, halved lengthwise and sliced

1 celery stalk, thinly sliced

¹/₂ red bell pepper, seeded and diced

2 garlic cloves, minced

6 small new red potatoes, quartered

2 cups chicken broth

¹/₂ teaspoon dried basil

¹/₄ teaspoon dried thyme

1 (14-ounce) can whole tomatoes, chopped, with liquid

1 tablespoon chopped pimiento-stuffed green olives

Cut chicken thighs into bite-size pieces. Combine flour, salt and pepper on a plate and dredge chicken pieces. Cook chicken in the oil in a nonstick Dutch oven over medium heat, about 4 minutes, turning once, or until lightly browned.

Add onion, celery and bell pepper and cook, stirring frequently, until vegetables are crisp-tender. Add garlic and stir 1 minute.

Add potatoes, broth, basil and thyme and bring to a boil. Reduce heat, cover and simmer 15 minutes or until potatoes are firm-tender. Add tomatoes and olives and simmer 5 minutes more.   *Makes 4 servings.*

PER SERVING: Cal 441 • Carbo 52 gm • Prot 28 gm • Total fat 13 gm • Sat fat 3 gm • Cal from fat 27% • Chol 73 mg

EDUCATION: Limit meats and protein foods to 2 to 3 servings per day. A recipe like the stew above helps achieve the balance. Four ounces of chicken per serving is accompanied by a healthy selection of vegetables in a low-fat stew. Since protein for the day should total 5 to 7 ounces, this stew would provide slightly more than half of the recommended daily protein.

INSPIRATION: *I will open myself to experiences today without jumping to judgments or comparisons.*

Sweet & Sour Tofu with Vegetables

🌿 Tofu takes on the succulent flavor of sweet and sour sauce. Serve over brown rice.

1 (16-ounce) container firm tofu
1/3 cup brown rice vinegar
1/4 cup orange juice
1/4 cup pineapple juice
1/4 cup tomato paste
2 tablespoons honey
1/2 teaspoon salt
1 onion, halved lengthwise and thinly sliced
1 tablespoon canola oil
3 garlic cloves, minced
1 tablespoon minced gingerroot
1 jalapeño chile, seeded and minced
1/2 cup thinly sliced carrots
1 cup diced yellow or green bell pepper
1 cup diced red bell pepper
1 1/2 cups diced zucchini
1 cup diced yellow summer squash
3 1/2 cups cooked brown rice

Drain tofu and pat dry. Cut into bite-size pieces and place in a medium-size bowl. Combine the vinegar, orange and pineapple juice, tomato paste, honey and salt. Pour half over the tofu and stir to combine. Let tofu marinate 15 minutes, stirring once or twice.

Meanwhile, cook onion in the oil in a large, nonstick skillet over medium heat, stirring frequently, until the onion is translucent. Add the garlic, gingerroot and jalapeño and cook, stirring, 1 minute. Add the carrots and bell peppers and cook, stirring, 1 minute. Add the zucchini and squash and cook, stirring, 3 or 4 minutes, until the vegetables are firm-tender.

Add remaining sweet and sour sauce and marinated tofu. Heat through and serve over brown rice.

Makes 4 servings.

PER SERVING: Cal 504 • Carbo 72 gm • Prot 25 gm • Total fat 15 gm • Sat fat 8 gm • Cal from fat 27% • Chol 0 mg

EDUCATION: Help reduce your blood-cholesterol levels by eating more tofu. Soybeans—which form the basis for this vegetarian bean curd—have shown a remarkable cholesterol-lowering effect. Substituting tofu for cheese protein has also shown to beneficially reduce blood cholesterol. Bland tofu can be livened up with any number of herbs and spices, including the sweet and sour sauce above.

INSPIRATION: *Taking proper care of my body gives my spirit a more stable home in which to be renewed.*

Bonita's Chocolate Pecan Brownies

🌿 A home economics teacher, Bonnie appreciates the value of an easy dessert with reduced fat.

2 tablespoons canola oil
2 tablespoons unsalted butter, at room temperature
3/4 cup vanilla sugar (see glossary)
1/4 teaspoon salt
1 egg
2 egg whites
1/2 cup whole-wheat pastry flour
1/2 cup unsweetened cocoa powder
1/4 cup chopped pecans

Preheat oven to 350°F (175°). Cream together oil, butter, sugar and salt in a medium-size bowl.

In a small bowl, beat together the egg and egg whites. Stir into butter mixture until combined. Stir together flour, cocoa and pecans. Stir into batter in bowl. Pour into an 8-inch-square lightly buttered nonstick baking pan. Bake 25 minutes or until the edges begin to pull away from the sides of the pan. Cool in pan on a wire rack. Cut into 16 squares.

Makes 16 brownies.

PER BROWNIE: Cal 100 • Carbo 3 gm • Prot 2 gm • Total fat 4 gm • Sat fat 1 gm • Cal from fat 53% • Chol 17 mg

EDUCATION: If you don't feel well, rest. Trying to push on with work, appointments and social life can compromise your immune system even more. Taking the time you need to recover at the beginning of an illness may significantly shorten the time you are ill by avoiding complications.

INSPIRATION: *Making room for those around me to just "be," without trying to change them, is a generous act of caring.*

Linda's French Onion Soup with Cheese

❧ Linda loves playing with soups, coming up with just the right combination of flavors, with Rob a willing tester. A combination of beef and chicken broth is used for this hearty main-course soup. However, using either alone will produce an equally good result.

3 pounds onions, sliced
2 tablespoons unsalted butter
1/2 teaspoon brown sugar
2 tablespoons unbleached all-purpose flour
2 1/4 cups chicken broth
2 cups beef broth
1/2 teaspoon Dijon mustard
1/4 teaspoon salt
1/8 teaspoon freshly ground black pepper
4 (1/2-inch-thick) slices French
    bread, toasted
2 slices Swiss cheese, halved

Cook the onions slowly in the butter in a covered nonstick Dutch oven over low heat, stirring occasionally, about 20 minutes or until the onions are very soft. Sprinkle with brown sugar, increase the heat to medium and cook, stirring occasionally, about 10 minutes or until the onions are golden brown. Sprinkle with flour and cook, stirring, 2 minutes.

Add chicken broth, beef broth, mustard, salt and pepper and bring to a boil, stirring frequently. Reduce heat, cover and simmer 10 minutes.

Preheat broiler. Ladle soup into four heat-proof bowls. Top with toasted bread slices and then cheese. Broil until cheese melts and begins to brown.   *Makes 4 servings.*

PER SERVING: Cal 379 • Carbo 52 gm • Prot 16 gm • Total fat 12 gm • Sat fat 7 gm • Cal from fat 30% • Chol 29 mg

EDUCATION: Reduce your chance of stroke by eating more onions. Onions have been discovered to have a protective effect against excess blood clotting, which can block vessels. According to researchers, onions offset the excess platelet aggregation that can occur after a high-fat meal and lead to heart attack or stroke. And onions do the job whether eaten raw, boiled or fried.

INSPIRATION: *Today is a treasure so rare and fleeting, it can only happen once. Let me appreciate its joys and challenges by being present and doing the best I can.*

Mary's Stuffed Cabbage Rolls

🌱 A classic, this skillet dinner has the hearty flavor of brown rice. Mary's little boy, Nathaniel, loves to help in the kitchen. Soon he may be making this dish on his own.

8 large green cabbage leaves
¹/₂ pound extra-lean ground pork
¹/₄ pound extra-lean ground beef
1¹/₂ cups cooked brown rice
1 cup finely chopped onion
1 egg, beaten
¹/₄ cup minced fresh parsley
¹/₄ teaspoon dried thyme
¹/₄ teaspoon salt
¹/₈ teaspoon freshly ground
    black pepper
1 cup tomato juice
¹/₂ cup tomato sauce
¹/₂ cup beef broth
1 large onion, halved lengthwise
    and thinly sliced

Bring a large saucepan of water to a boil and cook cabbage leaves 5 minutes or until slightly tender. Drain. Combine ground pork and beef, rice, chopped onion, egg, half the parsley, thyme, salt and pepper.

Divide filling among cabbage leaves. Beginning at the base of the leaf, roll each to enclose filling. (You can trim out part of the thick center rib, if necessary.) Tie rolls with kitchen string.

Combine the tomato juice, sauce, broth, sliced onion and remaining parsley in a large skillet. Add cabbage rolls and bring to a boil.

Reduce heat, cover and simmer, turning occasionally, 1 hour or until tender. Discard string and serve cabbage rolls with sauce.

Makes 4 servings.

PER SERVING: Cal 328 • Carbo 30 gm • Prot 24 gm • Total fat 12 gm • Sat fat 4 gm • Cal from fat 33% • Chol 116 mg

EDUCATION: Choose friends who listen with their hearts. Few things in life are as deeply satisfying as being heard. Even if a friend cannot assuage the pain or experience the triumph, really being there to hear your experience is his or her valuable gift. The willingness to listen, to remember and share things that are important to you, are signs you've found an irreplaceable friend.

INSPIRATION: *Recovery affords me the power of choice. I can choose to eat well, choose to honor my limits and choose how to spend my time and energy.*

Carrot & Barley Pilaf

🌱 Crisp-cooked vegetables provide the texture for this grain side dish.

¹/₂ cup chopped onion
2 teaspoons canola oil
¹/₂ teaspoon salt
¹/₂ teaspoon Madras curry
    powder
¹/₄ teaspoon ground coriander
Dash of freshly grated nutmeg
2¹/₂ cups chicken broth
1 cup pearl barley
¹/₂ cup finely chopped celery
³/₄ cup shredded carrot
³/₄ cup shredded zucchini

Cook the onion in the oil in a large saucepan over medium heat, stirring frequently, until the onion is translucent. Add the salt, curry powder, coriander and nutmeg and stir 1 minute more.

Add broth and bring to a boil. Stir in barley and return to a boil. Reduce heat, cover and simmer 45 minutes or until barley is tender. Stir in celery and simmer 1 minute. Stir in carrots and zucchini and simmer 1 or 2 minutes, until vegetables are crisp-tender and broth is absorbed. *Makes 6 servings.*

PER SERVING: Cal 162 • Carbo 30 gm • Prot 6 gm • Total fat 2 gm • Sat fat trace • Cal from fat 14% • Chol 0 mg

EDUCATION: Remember to use the three As to reduce your stress: *Avoid* vexing people or situations when possible. Hate crowded highways? Start earlier or take a less-busy route. *Alter* the situation or relationship by trying to change it or talk it out. Sometimes others want to change the situation as much as you do, but fear making the first move. *Adapt* to stresses you can't change by using techniques such as meditation, exercise and following a healthful diet.

November 13

INSPIRATION: *I will take advantage of the opportunities I have today to change, to grow and allow healing into my life.*

Italian-style Pork Tenderloin

❧ Orzo pasta complements the rosemary-scented sauce that dresses the pork slices.

¹/₂ cup orzo pasta
1 pound pork tenderloin, trimmed of fat
1 tablespoon olive oil
1 small onion, thinly sliced
1 (16-ounce) can whole tomatoes, chopped, with juice
2 (9-ounce) packages frozen artichoke hearts
1 tablespoon tomato paste
¹/₂ teaspoon salt
¹/₂ teaspoon brown sugar
¹/₄ teaspoon dried rosemary
1 cup frozen green peas
¹/₄ cup chopped pitted ripe olives
¹/₄ cup minced fresh parsley

Bring a large pot of water to a boil. Cook orzo 7 to 9 minutes or until firm-tender. Drain and keep warm.

Meanwhile, thinly slice the pork tenderloin on the diagonal. Cook in the oil in a large non-stick skillet over medium heat about 5 minutes, turning until browned on both sides. Remove the pork to a plate. Add the onion to the skillet and cook, stirring, 1 minute.

Add chopped tomatoes with juice, artichoke hearts, tomato paste, salt, sugar and rosemary and bring to a boil. Reduce heat, cover and simmer 10 minutes or until artichoke hearts are tender. Stir in peas, pork, olives and parsley and heat through. Serve with orzo.

Makes 4 servings.

PER SERVING: Cal 415 • Carbo 39 gm • Prot 43 gm • Total fat 11 gm • Sat fat 3 gm • Cal from fat 24% • Chol 105 mg

EDUCATION: For low-fat meat meals, explore the possibilities of pork. Pork has been streamlined. With less fat, lean pork is now considered a respectable source of meat protein. Pork is especially high in zinc and thiamin. Also, like other meats, a small amount of pork will enhance iron absorption from vegetable sources, such as the artichoke hearts above.

INSPIRATION: *I am learning to get out of my own way so that I can accept and enjoy my share of life's blessings.*

Super Stuffed Baked Potatoes

❧ Make potatoes a main dish with a variety of stuffings and toppings. The microwave speeds preparation.

> *4 large baking potatoes*
> *2 cups low-fat (1%) cottage cheese*
> *1/2 cup finely diced cooked ham*
> *1/2 cup shredded Cheddar cheese*
> *1/2 cup finely chopped green onions*
> *2 tablespoons nonfat sour cream*
> *1/4 teaspoon salt*
> *1/8 teaspoon freshly ground white pepper*
> *Dash of freshly grated nutmeg*
> *2 tablespoons minced fresh*
>   *parsley*

Prick potatoes with a fork. Arrange on a microwave-safe plate and microwave on HIGH, 8 minutes. Turn and microwave 7 to 10 minutes, or until potatoes are tender.

Preheat oven to 400°F (200°C). Cut potatoes in half, lengthwise, and scoop out flesh, leaving a 1/4-inch shell. Mash cooked potato with cottage cheese in a medium-size bowl. Stir in ham, Cheddar, green onions, sour cream, salt, pepper and nutmeg.

Spoon mixture into shells. Bake 20 minutes. Sprinkle with parsley.   *Makes 4 servings.*

PER SERVING: Cal 375 • Carbo 38 gm • Prot 26 gm • Total fat 13 gm • Sat fat 7 gm • Cal from fat 31% • Chol 38 mg

NOTE: For small amounts of cooked ham, purchase 1 slice, thick-cut, at your supermarket deli.

EDUCATION: Keep potatoes low-fat with judicious choices of toppings. Nonfat yogurt, chili, creamed corn (made without cream), steamed fresh vegetables, chipped smoked salmon, canned mushrooms, sauerkraut and Swiss cheese, creamed spinach, or flaked tuna with minced pimiento are delicious on baked potatoes. When dining out, choose such low-fat selections as barbecue sauce, prepared horseradish, salsa or steak sauce.

INSPIRATION: *Serenity comes closer as I take responsibility for myself and realize I am the only one I can change.*

Celebration Citrus Salad with Lime Vinaigrette

❧ Avocados, oranges and pink grapefruit create a centerpiece salad when arranged over watercress and Belgian endive.

> *1 tablespoon extra-virgin*
>   *olive oil*
> *1 tablespoon fresh lime juice*
> *1 teaspoon honey*
> *1 teaspoon poppy seeds*
> *1/4 teaspoon dry yellow*
>   *mustard*
> *1/4 teaspoon salt*
> *1/8 teaspoon freshly grated*
>   *lime peel*
> *2 Belgian endive*
> *1 large bunch watercress*
> *2 pink grapefruit*
> *2 navel oranges*
> *1 small avocado*

Combine the oil, lime juice, honey, poppy seeds, mustard, salt and grated lime peel in a small bowl. Set aside.

Trim and core Belgian endive and separate into leaves. Remove tough stems from watercress and wash. Line a large serving plate with the endive and watercress.

Peel grapefruit and oranges and section each, removing membranes and saving juices to add to dressing. Arrange grapefruit and orange sections over top of salad greens. Cover and chill, if desired. Just before serving, peel, pit and halve avocado lengthwise. Cut each half crosswise into thin slices and arrange over greens. Whisk dressing until well combined, then drizzle over salad. *Makes 6 servings.*

PER SERVING: Cal 172 • Carbo 15 gm • Prot 3 gm • Total fat 12 gm • Sat fat 2 gm • Cal from fat 45% • Chol 0 mg

EDUCATION: Begin your own illness-prevention program by taking a health inventory. Make note of your health habits: exercise, diet, tobacco or alcohol use, caffeine consumption, stress management. Write down any symptoms you may have experienced lately. Discuss these observations with your doctor.

November 16

INSPIRATION: *Change changes things. I respect the mystery of where my new way of thinking and being will eventually lead me.*

Cranberry-Apple Fruit Conserve

❧ Made with half the sugar in half the time of conventional recipes, with the help of your microwave. Prepare before the holidays get busy. It will keep a couple of weeks in the refrigerator. Stir into yogurt cheese (see glossary) for a party spread, or serve on Thanksgiving or with leftover turkey.

1 small orange with peel, scrubbed,
   cut into cubes and seeded
1 1/4 cups sugar
3/4 cup water
3/4 pound cranberries, rinsed
3 Granny Smith apples, peeled, cored and diced
1 cup zante currants or raisins
1/4 teaspoon ground allspice

Place orange cubes in a food processor and process on high speed until finely chopped. Place in a large bowl with 1/2 cup sugar and 1/4 cup water and stir until combined. Microwave on HIGH 5 to 7 minutes, until orange appears translucent. Stir in cranberries, diced apples, currants or raisins, allspice and remaining 3/4 cup sugar and 1/2 cup water.

Microwave on HIGH, rotating dish twice, 10 minutes. Stir thoroughly. Microwave an additional 10 minutes, rotating dish twice. Stir well, then microwave on HIGH 5 minutes more or until thickened. Cool, then pack in sterile jars, cap and refrigerate. *Makes 5 cups.*

PER 1/4 CUP: Cal 47 • Carbo 12 gm • Prot trace • Total fat trace • Sat fat trace • Cal from fat 0% • Chol 0 mg

EDUCATION: Stock up on cranberries for a low-cost year of uses. As the holidays approach, the price of cranberries generally rises substantially. Buying them when they first come on the market, when prices are often lowest, saves money. And cranberries keep well. Unwashed, in their bag, they will last 2 weeks or more in the refrigerator, up to a year in the freezer. Remove what you need from the bag and rinse when it's time to use them.

INSPIRATION: *Contentment is not a gift someone else can bestow on me, but a creation of peace and harmony that comes of knowing myself and discovering what I need.*

Martha's Molasses Anadama Muffins

❦ My friend Martha, a New England cook, enjoys a mix of flours punctuated with a hint of molasses to make these muffins a hearty treat.

1 cup unbleached all-purpose flour
1/2 cup whole-wheat pastry flour
*1/2 cup stone-ground yellow
    cornmeal*
*2 tablespoons packed brown
    sugar*
1 tablespoon baking powder
1/2 teaspoon baking soda
1/4 teaspoon salt
Dash of freshly grated nutmeg
1 egg, beaten
1 cup buttermilk
3 tablespoons canola oil
*3 tablespoons medium
    unsulfured molasses*

Preheat oven to 425°F (220°C). Lightly butter 12 (2³/₄-inch) muffin cups. Combine flours, cornmeal, brown sugar, baking powder and soda, salt and nutmeg in a large bowl. Combine egg, buttermilk, oil and molasses in a medium-size bowl. Add to dry ingredients and stir just until combined. Spoon batter into muffin cups. Bake 20 minutes or until a wooden pick inserted in the center comes out clean. Remove from pan and cool on a wire rack.

Makes 1 dozen.

PER SERVING: Cal 144 • Carbo 23 gm • Prot 3 gm • Total fat 4 gm • Sat fat trace • Cal from fat 27% • Chol 18 mg

EDUCATION: Compute good health by remembering the formula "30 plus 40 plus 50." That reminds you to include a minimum of 30 grams of fiber in your diet daily. It also means no more than 40 grams of fat and 50 grams of protein daily for maximum health.

INSPIRATION: *Nourishing communication happens when I let down my guard, speak from my heart and risk being myself.*

Autumn Root Vegetable Soup

❦ Enjoy a perfect combination: chill weather and a satisfying, creamy soup. One big plus comes from using rice as a thickener, adding the feel of richness without extra fat.

2 leeks
1 celery stalk
1 tablespoon unsalted butter
5 or 6 carrots
2 or 3 parsnips
6 cups chicken broth
1/4 cup long-grain white rice
1/2 teaspoon salt
Dash of freshly grated nutmeg
1/2 cup low-fat (1%) milk

Clean leeks (see glossary) and trim to include 2 inches of green leaves. Chop leeks and celery. Cook in the butter in a nonstick Dutch oven over medium heat, stirring frequently, until tender, 6 or 7 minutes.

Trim and cut carrots and parsnips into thick slices. Add with broth, rice, salt and nutmeg to the pan and bring to a boil. Reduce heat, cover and simmer 40 minutes, stirring occasionally, or until vegetables and rice are tender. Puree the soup in batches in a blender or food processor and return to the pan. Add milk and heat through, but do not boil, before serving.

Makes 8 servings.

PER SERVING: Cal 140 • Carbo 23 gm • Prot 6 gm • Total fat 3 gm • Sat fat 1 gm • Cal from fat 19% • Chol 4 mg

EDUCATION: To keep soups lean, thicken with pureed rice or vegetables. There's no need to add cream to enjoy a creamy soup. Rice can be cooked with soup, as above, or separately. Blend with broth and stir into soup for a creamy texture. Or, using a slotted spoon, remove some vegetables from soup, blend and return to the pan.

N o v e m b e r   1 9

INSPIRATION: *I will continue to challenge myself today to get over any option-limiting fears.*

Brussels Sprouts with Sliced Apples

Compact Brussels sprouts require a little extra care to cook evenly. An easy answer is shredding the sprouts before cooking to create an attractive and evenly cooked side dish.

2 pints fresh Brussels sprouts or 2 (10-ounce) packages frozen, thawed
1/2 cup finely chopped onion
1 teaspoon unsalted butter
1/4 cup apple juice or water
2 small, tart apples, peeled, cored and thinly sliced
1 tablespoon fresh lemon juice
1/8 teaspoon freshly grated lemon peel
1/8 teaspoon salt
Dash of freshly grated nutmeg

Trim bottoms from Brussels sprouts and shred by finely slicing with a knife. Cook the onion in the butter in a large nonstick skillet over medium heat, stirring frequently, until translucent. Add the shredded Brussels sprouts and apple juice or water and bring to a boil. Reduce heat, cover and simmer 10 minutes (2 or 3 minutes for frozen, thawed sprouts) or until nearly tender. Stir in apple slices and cook, covered, an additional 4 or 5 minutes, until the sprouts and apple slices are tender. Toss the mixture with lemon juice, peel, salt and nutmeg.

Makes 6 servings.

PER SERVING: Cal 78 • Carbo 17 gm • Prot 3 gm • Total fat 1 gm • Sat fat trace • Cal from fat 15% • Chol 2 mg

EDUCATION: Reduce your risk of cancer by eating more Brussels sprouts. Cruciferous vegetables (which include broccoli, cabbage, cauliflower, collard greens, kale, radishes, turnips and watercress) contain substances that help the body destroy carcinogens. Some studies show that the fiber in these vegetables may also help lower estrogen levels in the bloodstream, helping reduce the risk of breast and uterine cancer.

INSPIRATION: *The ultimate goal of my recovery is to discover my soul and reunite with it.*

Mary Ruth's Turkey Chili

🌿 Using turkey breast fillets, this chili features a delicious combination of ingredients, including mild green chiles and roasted pimiento.

1 1/2 cups brown rice

3 cups water

1 1/4 pounds turkey breast fillet

4 teaspoons olive oil

1/2 cup chopped onion

1 tablespoon minced garlic

1/2 teaspoon salt

1/2 teaspoon ground cumin

1/4 teaspoon ground cinnamon

1/4 teaspoon chili powder

1/4 teaspoon red pepper flakes

1/4 teaspoon rubbed sage

1/4 teaspoon dried marjoram

1/8 teaspoon freshly ground
    black pepper

4 cups cooked black or red beans
    (see glossary)

2 cups chicken broth

1 cup frozen whole-kernel corn

1 (7-ounce) jar roasted pimiento, rinsed,
    drained and chopped

1 (4-ounce) can chopped mild green
    chiles, rinsed and drained

Combine rice and water in a large saucepan and bring to a boil. Reduce heat, cover and simmer 35 minutes. Remove from heat and let stand 10 minutes.

Meanwhile, cut the turkey fillets into 1-inch cubes. Cook the turkey in half of the oil in 2 batches in a nonstick Dutch oven over medium heat, stirring frequently, about 4 minutes or until turkey is golden brown. Remove turkey to a plate, cover and keep warm.

Cook onion in the remaining oil in the Dutch oven, stirring frequently, until tender, about 5 minutes. Add garlic, salt, cumin, cinnamon, chili powder, pepper flakes, sage, marjoram and pepper and cook, stirring, 1 minute.

Puree half the beans with the chicken broth in a blender or food processor. Add to the onion mixture with the remaining beans, corn, chiles and chopped pimiento and bring to a boil. Reduce heat, cover, and simmer 5 minutes.

Return turkey to pot and simmer 1 or 2 minutes, until heated through. Serve turkey chili over brown rice. *Makes 4 servings.*

PER SERVING: Cal 740 • Carbo 108 gm • Prot 55 gm • Total fat 9 gm • Sat fat 2 gm • Cal from fat 11% • Chol 82 mg

EDUCATION: When possible, choose foods that contain a spark of life. The life force is so powerful that it can create 600 times the vitamin C contained in a dormant seed with the simple addition of water. Many common foods contain that life energy. Potatoes, cabbage, turnips and carrots sprout roots if kept too long in cool, damp conditions. Dried beans and seeds will re-create themselves if planted in a garden. Though much is known about the foods we eat, not all food elements have been identified. Eating life-charged foods connects us with our ancestors, who ate little else, and may provide vital health-sustaining elements that science has yet to discover.

INSPIRATION: *Yesterday is gone. Today offers me a new chance. I can profit from mistakes of the past by making wiser choices as I move toward tomorrow.*

Fruit & Bran
Breakfast Farina

❧ Bran adds fiber to a tasty farina breakfast studded with chopped, dried fruit instead of sweeteners.

1 ¹/₂ cups apple juice
¹/₄ teaspoon salt
3 tablespoons farina
1 tablespoon oat bran or unprocessed
    wheat bran
2 tablespoons diced pitted prunes
1 tablespoon diced dried apricots
1 tablespoon raisins
Skim milk or apple juice

Bring apple juice and salt to a boil in a medium-size saucepan. Gradually add farina, stirring constantly, then add bran. Reduce heat, add fruit and simmer, stirring occasionally, 2 or 3 minutes or until cereal is thickened. Serve with skim milk or apple juice. *Makes 2 servings.*

PER SERVING: Cal 202 • Carbo 49 gm • Prot 3 gm • Total fat 1 gm • Sat fat trace • Cal from fat 3% • Chol 0 mg

EDUCATION: Get enough sleep and have a good breakfast, especially when life gets rushed. When most of us get busy, cutting back on sleep is one of the first ways we find extra time. Sleep deprivation combined with additional stress sets us up for illness by impairing our immune system. Making time for proper rest and fueling our bodies for the busy day ahead are two caretaking steps that lay the groundwork for a healthy, if busy, holiday season.

INSPIRATION: *My spiritual core, when nurtured, provides peace and strength to get through the troubles of the day.*

Spicy Skillet Pork with Sweet Potatoes

Cajun-style flavor permeates this pork and sweet potato dish. Served over brown rice or pasta, it makes a delicious meal.

1 pound pork tenderloin

2 tablespoons unbleached all-purpose flour

1 teaspoon ground cumin

1/2 teaspoon ground ginger

1/2 teaspoon salt

1/4 teaspoon paprika

1/8 teaspoon hot (cayenne) pepper

1/8 teaspoon ground cinnamon

1/2 cup chopped onion

2 tablespoons canola oil

1 large sweet potato, peeled, halved lengthwise and thinly sliced

1/4 cup finely chopped apricots

1/2 cup chicken broth

1 (14 1/2-ounce) can Cajun-style or plain stewed tomatoes

1/4 cup minced fresh parsley

3 1/2 cups cooked brown rice

Trim off fat and cut the pork tenderloin into 1-inch cubes. In a shallow bowl, combine the flour, cumin, ginger, salt, paprika, hot pepper and cinnamon. Toss pork cubes with flour mixture to coat.

Cook the onion in the oil in a large non-stick skillet, stirring frequently, until translucent. Add the pork and sweet potato and cook, stirring frequently, 5 minutes. Stir in apricots and broth and bring to a boil. Reduce heat, cover and simmer 2 or 3 minutes until apricots are plump. Add stewed tomatoes and return to a boil. Reduce heat, cover and simmer 5 to 7 minutes, until pork and sweet potatoes are tender. Stir in parsley and serve over brown rice.

Makes 4 servings.

PER SERVING: Cal 532 • Carbo 60 gm • Prot 40 gm • Total fat 14 gm • Sat fat 3 gm • Cal from fat 24% • Chol 105 mg

EDUCATION: To keep your diet lean, order creatively when you dine out. If the entree you want is breaded and fried, request it broiled or steamed. Ask for salad dressings on the side so you can add them sparingly to salads and vegetables. If a rich dessert is accompanied by a low-fat fruit sauce, see if you can get the sauce served over low-fat frozen yogurt, fresh fruit or angel food cake.

INSPIRATION: *I will no longer sit on the sidelines, but join others at life's banquet.*

Peggy & Charlie's Seafood Cioppino

A West Coast classic fish stew, indigenous to my friends' favorite city of San Francisco, cioppino features a mixture of seafood. Try it served over linguini with a touch of Parmesan.

1 cup chopped onion
1 cup chopped green bell pepper
1 tablespoon extra-virgin olive oil
2 garlic cloves, minced
2 (28-ounce) cans whole tomatoes
    with liquid
1 cup chicken broth
1 bay leaf
1/2 teaspoon dried basil
1/2 teaspoon salt
1/4 teaspoon freshly ground
    black pepper
1/4 teaspoon dried thyme
1/8 teaspoon hot (cayenne) pepper
24 littleneck clams
1 pound medium-size shrimp, shelled
    and deveined (see glossary)
1 pound cod or haddock fillets, cut into
    2-inch pieces
1 pound bay scallops
2 (12-ounce) packages frozen Alaska
    King Crab split legs, thawed and
    cut into chunks
1/4 cup minced fresh parsley
1 1/2 pounds linguini, cooked (optional)
1/4 cup freshly grated Parmesan
    cheese

Cook onion and bell pepper in the oil in a nonstick Dutch oven over medium heat, stirring frequently, until the onion is tender, 5 or 7 minutes. Add the garlic and cook, stirring, 1 minute more.

Coarsely chop tomatoes and add, with their liquid, broth, bay leaf, basil, salt, black pepper, thyme and cayenne and bring to a boil. Reduce heat, cover and simmer 15 minutes.

Add clams, return stew to a gentle boil and cook 10 minutes, stirring occasionally. Add shrimp, cod or haddock, crab and parsley and continue to cook 5 minutes, stirring occasionally, or until the shrimp turn pink and the scallops and fish are opaque. Remove bay leaf. Serve stew over linguini, if desired, garnished with a sprinkle of Parmesan.   *Makes 8 servings.*

PER SERVING: Cal 509 • Carbo 40 gm • Prot 67 gm • Total fat 8 gm • Sat fat 1 gm • Cal from fat 14% • Chol 203 mg

EDUCATION: Eat a variety of foods to ensure you get all the nutrients your body needs to regain or maintain good health. One way to do this is to select dishes that incorporate a range of low-fat ingredients, like the dish above. When you visit the fish monger or produce aisles of your supermarket, regularly select items different from the ones you've chosen before. Select fewer processed, commercially prepared foods and more fresh foods.

INSPIRATION: *My true appetite, which I am learning to trust, is a positive force, motivating me to nourish my body in healthy ways.*

Bob's Chestnut Soup

Growing up with chestnut trees on the East Coast, Bob and I learned to appreciate the subtle flavor of their bounty. Roasted or boiled, chestnuts said "autumn" in a way no other food could. This soup highlights the comforting flavor of chestnuts. Buy chestnuts in Italian or Asian markets, and pick out the ones that feel heavy and solid.

1/2 cup finely chopped onion
1/4 cup minced shallots or green onions
    (white part only)
2 teaspoons unsalted butter
1/2 teaspoon dried thyme leaves
3 cups peeled, roasted chestnuts (see glossary)
6 cups chicken broth
1/3 cup low-fat (1%) milk or chicken
    broth (optional)
2 tablespoons nonfat sour cream
2 tablespoons nonfat yogurt

Cook the onion and shallots or green onions in the butter in a nonstick Dutch oven over medium heat, stirring frequently, until tender, 4 or 5 minutes. Add thyme and cook, stirring, 1 minute.

Add chestnuts and broth and bring to a boil. Reduce heat, cover and simmer 30 minutes, stirring occasionally, or until chestnuts are quite tender. With a slotted spoon, remove chestnuts and puree in a blender or food processor, with a little of the liquid, until smooth. Return soup to Dutch oven and thin, if desired, with milk or additional broth.

Combine sour cream and yogurt and serve soup garnished with a dollop of the mixture.

Makes 4 servings.

PER SERVING: Cal 185 • Carbo 22 gm • Prot 10 gm • Total fat 6 gm • Sat fat 3 gm • Cal from fat 29% • Chol 7 mg

EDUCATION: For a low-fat treat, lean toward chestnuts. Most nuts derive 70 to 95 percent of calories from fat and should be used sparingly. Chestnuts, with only 8 percent fat calories, can be enjoyed with abandon. Chestnuts are, unlike all other nuts, rich in vitamin C and also contain rich supplies of nerve-soothing B vitamins.

INSPIRATION: *I will no longer seek in food what I must find in myself and my relationships with other people.*

Mashed Apples & Sweet Potatoes

 This holiday dish serves twelve, and can be made up to 3 days ahead and reheated in the oven. Cut ingredients in half for smaller gatherings.

> 4 pounds sweet potatoes,
>   peeled and cubed
> 1 cup chopped onion
> 1 tablespoon unsalted butter
> 5 cups peeled, cored and chopped
>   tart apples
> 2/3 cup apple juice
> 1/2 teaspoon salt
> 1/4 teaspoon freshly ground
>   nutmeg

Place sweet potatoes in a large pot of water and bring to a boil. Cook 20 to 25 minutes, until tender.

Meanwhile, cook onion in the butter in a large skillet over medium heat, stirring frequently, about 6 to 8 minutes or until onion is golden brown. Add apples and apple juice and bring to a boil. Reduce heat, cover and simmer 10 to 15 minutes, stirring occasionally, until apples are tender.

Drain sweet potatoes and return to pot. Add apple mixture, salt and nutmeg. Mash until smooth and serve, or place in a baking dish and refrigerate overnight.

Reheat in a preheated 375°F (190°C) oven 25 to 30 minutes, or if baking immediately, 15 to 20 minutes. *Makes 12 servings.*

PER SERVING: Cal 188 • Carbo 43 gm • Prot 3 gm • Total fat 1 gm • Sat fat trace • Cal from fat 6% • Chol 2 mg

EDUCATION: Cook ahead to make holidays less frantic. Some side dishes, conserves, desserts and breads can be made days, or even weeks, ahead of a big meal. Refrigerate or freeze, as appropriate, for holiday meals and parties. By planning ahead, you'll have more time to visit with friends and family when they gather to celebrate.

INSPIRATION: Q. *Why is a Higher Power so important when baking bread? A. It guarantees our kneads are met.*

Thanksgiving Cranberry Bread

A most delicious yeast bread. Whole wheat provides a hearty addition to holiday meals, with a delicious hint of tart sweetness so characteristic of cranberry dishes ever popular at Thanksgiving.

1 cup cranberries, halved
1/3 cup packed brown sugar
1/3 cup medium unsulfured molasses
1 tablespoon dry yeast
1/2 cup lukewarm water
1 tablespoon honey
1 cup boiling water
2 tablespoons unsalted butter
2 1/2 cups whole-wheat flour
1 to 1 1/2 cups unbleached all-purpose flour
1 teaspoon salt
1/4 teaspoon ground allspice

Combine the cranberries, brown sugar and molasses in a medium-size bowl and set aside 1 hour, or refrigerate overnight or longer.

Place yeast, warm water and honey in a small bowl and set aside until foamy. Combine the boiling water with the butter, and when the butter is melted, stir the mixture into the cranberries.

Combine whole-wheat flour, 1 cup of unbleached flour, salt and allspice in a large bowl. Add the yeast and cranberry mixtures to the flours and beat together with a wooden spoon. Add enough additional unbleached flour to make a soft dough.

Knead the dough on a floured surface until smooth. Return the dough to the large bowl, cover tightly with plastic wrap and set it in a warm place to rise until doubled in size. Lightly oil a 9 × 5-inch bread pan. Punch down the dough, knead until smooth and shape into a loaf. Place dough in pan, cover and let the dough rise in a warm place about 45 minutes, until dough is even with the pan.

To complete the rising, put the pan in a cold oven, and turn the oven to 400°F (200°C). After 15 minutes, reduce heat to 325°F (165°C) and bake 35 minutes. Remove the bread from the pan and cover bread with a kitchen towel as it cools. *Makes 1 loaf, 12 slices.*

PER SLICE: Cal 206 • Carbo 42 gm • Prot 4 gm • Total fat 2 gm • Sat fat 1 gm • Cal from fat 8% • Chol 5 mg

EDUCATION: Get the "feel" of creating whole-grain bread dough so you are encouraged to bake more often. Notice how the dough feels as you knead, then observe the finished loaf. If the bread dips in the middle, not enough flour was used; if the bread is too dense, too much flour is the cause.

INSPIRATION: *Being unreasonable with my body—giving it much more or much less than it needs to properly function—is a form of abuse I can live without.*

Kae's Mashed Potatoes Dressed for Dinner

Special-occasion mashed potatoes are succulent, without too much fat. Have the cream cheese, sour cream, yogurt and butter at room temperature for best results. The finished product can be spooned into a casserole dish and baked at 350°F (175°) for 20 minutes to reheat, if necessary.

5 or 6 large potatoes (about 2 pounds),
    peeled and quartered
1/4 cup reduced-fat cream cheese
1/4 cup nonfat sour cream
2 tablespoons nonfat yogurt
2 tablespoons unsalted butter
2 tablespoons minced fresh chives
1/2 garlic clove, pushed through a press
    (optional)
Dash of salt
Dash of freshly ground white pepper
Dash of paprika

Combine potatoes and enough salted water to cover in a large saucepan and bring to a boil. Reduce heat and simmer 15 to 20 minutes or until fork-tender. Drain in a colander then return to the saucepan.

Mash potatoes with cream cheese, sour cream, yogurt and butter. Stir in chives and garlic, if desired. Season with salt, pepper and paprika and serve. *Makes 6 servings.*

PER SERVING: Cal 213 • Carbo 31 gm • Prot 4 gm • Total fat 8 gm • Sat fat 5 gm • Cal from fat 33% • Chol 20 mg

EDUCATION: On a regular basis, use nonfat yogurt and skim milk in place of butter and cream in mashed potatoes. You'll cut fat while enjoying rich flavor. Use about 1/3 cup or more skim milk, scalded, and beat in 1 or 2 tablespoons nonfat yogurt. Make sure potatoes are cooked until very tender to avoid unpleasant lumps.

November 28

INSPIRATION: *Give me the courage it takes today to be purely and simply myself.*

Grilled Thanksgiving Turkey Breast

❧ Ready for a small break with tradition? Don't pack away the grill at summer's end—instead, give a light, smoky flavor to your holiday poultry by grilling a meaty and delicious turkey breast over hot coals. Precooking in the microwave allows you to grill and brown in just minutes, yielding a succulent flavor without charring. Grill immediately after microwaving.

1 (4 1/2- to 5-pound) bone-in turkey breast

If turkey breast has a backbone, remove it and save for making gravy or stock.

Preheat coals. Place the turkey breast, skin side down, in an 11 × 7-inch microwave-safe dish. Microwave on HIGH 9 minutes. Turn the breast so it rests on one side. Microwave on MEDIUM 15 minutes. Turn the breast on the other side, and microwave on MEDIUM 15 minutes. Turn the turkey skin side up, and microwave on MEDIUM 15 minutes.

Transfer the turkey to a hot grill. Cook 20 to 30 minutes or until the skin is brown and the juices run clear when the turkey is pierced with a fork. *Makes 8 servings.*

PER SERVING: Cal 266 • Carbo 0 gm • Prot 51 gm • Total fat 5 gm • Sat fat 2 gm • Cal from fat 17% • Chol 118 mg

EDUCATION: If you can't be with family on the "family" holiday, create your own. Chances are many members of your church, synagogue, or other religious group might be spending the holiday alone. If your house of worship has a large kitchen, round up a few folks to prepare the main dishes, then have pot-luck for the rest. Invite everyone for the meal and show a family movie afterward. It will be a day young and old can enjoy, with renewed contacts and newly forged friendships.

INSPIRATION: *Food is meant to nourish my body, not change my mood or distract me from problems. By putting food in perspective, I can gain more satisfaction from life.*

Apple-Walnut Bread Dressing

Making dressing from scratch adds a fresh note when serving leftover sliced turkey, lamb, beef or ham. Serve slimmed dressings and stuffings to keep post-holiday meals low-fat.

1 cup chopped onion
1 1/2 cups diced celery
1 tablespoon unsalted butter
1 teaspoon minced fresh garlic
1/2 teaspoon ground coriander
1/8 teaspoon freshly grated nutmeg
2 Granny Smith apples, peeled,
    cored and diced
1/2 cup chopped dried apricots
1/2 cup chopped pitted dried prunes
1/2 cup apple juice
1/2 cup fresh orange juice
1/4 teaspoon freshly grated orange peel
1 (1-pound) package bread stuffing
1/2 cup chopped walnuts, toasted
1/4 cup minced fresh parsley
1 teaspoon salt
1/4 teaspoon freshly ground black pepper

Cook onion and celery in the butter in a nonstick Dutch oven over medium heat, stirring frequently, until tender, about 5 minutes. Stir in garlic, coriander and nutmeg and cook, stirring, 1 minute.

Add diced apple, apricots, prunes, apple and orange juices and orange peel and bring to a boil. Reduce heat, cover and simmer 5 minutes. Remove from heat.

Stir in bread stuffing, walnuts, parsley, salt and pepper until well combined. Cover with foil and let stand 5 minutes. Meanwhile preheat oven to 350°F (175°C). Bake dressing 30 to 45 minutes or until heated through, removing foil for final 10 minutes of baking.

Makes 10 servings.

PER SERVING: Cal 288 • Carbo 52 gm • Prot 8 gm • Total fat 7 gm • Sat fat 1 gm • Cal from fat 21% • Chol 3 mg

EDUCATION: Slim your favorite stuffings to help keep meals low-fat. Many dressings and stuffings call for cooking vegetables in as much as 1/2 cup butter. You can reduce the amount of butter called for by using nonstick cookware as above, or you can eliminate fat altogether and microwave the vegetables. Sprinkle onion and celery with a few drops of water and microwave on HIGH 4 or 5 minutes, stirring once, until crisp-tender. Add garlic and microwave 30 seconds. Place in Dutch oven with next eight ingredients and continue as above.

INSPIRATION: *I can accept my imperfections and enjoy a full, rewarding life in spite of them.*

Mark's Rice Salad

Mark, who loves salads, gave me my first chance to really learn about food writing. For this salad, cut the pineapple in slices before removing core and skin for ease of preparation.

1 cup long-grain brown rice
1 cup apple juice
1 cup chicken broth
1/2 small pineapple
1/2 sweet yellow bell pepper, seeded and
*   finely diced*
2 green onions, thinly sliced on the diagonal
2 tablespoons minced fresh parsley
2 tablespoons olive oil
1 tablespoon brown rice vinegar
Dash of ground coriander
Dash of paprika
Pomegranate for garnish
Mint sprigs for garnish

Combine rice, apple juice and broth in a medium-size saucepan and bring to a boil. Reduce heat to low, cover and simmer 35 to 40 minutes. Turn off heat and let stand 5 minutes.

Core, peel and cut pineapple into small chunks over a bowl, saving any liquid. Combine pineapple, bell pepper, green onions and parsley in a serving bowl. In a small jar with lid, combine oil, vinegar, and brown sugar. Cover and shake until well combined. Toss rice with pineapple mixture and dressing. Chill before serving, if desired. Peel pomegranate and remove seeds. Sprinkle some of the seeds over the salad and add mint sprigs for garnish.   *Makes 4 servings.*

VARIATION

You can substitute 2 1/2 cups cooked rice and eliminate the first three ingredients.

PER SERVING: Cal 311 • Carbo 54 gm • Prot 5 gm • Total fat 9 gm • Sat fat 1 gm • Cal from fat 23% • Chol 0 mg

EDUCATION: Keep time in your busier holiday schedule for exercise and relaxation. Caloric intake is usually higher during the holidays, so moderate exercise becomes even more important to avoid lethargy. Relaxation can help to keep your mind clear, so that you are more able to tackle tasks without distraction.

INSPIRATION: *I can change my life one step at a time to become healthier in body, more peaceful in spirit.*

Donna's Roast Capon with Millet

❧ "Necessity is the mother of invention" was the guiding force for the creation of this delicious stuffing from a nearly bare pantry.

1 cup millet
$^1/_4$ cup dried lentils
$4^1/_2$ cups water
1 bay leaf
8 dried apricot halves
$^1/_4$ cup raisins
$^1/_4$ cup chopped onion
1 celery stalk, diced
$^1/_2$ tablespoon unsalted butter
1 tablespoon minced fresh parsley
$^1/_2$ teaspoon dried rosemary, crumbled
$^1/_8$ teaspoon celery seeds
1 egg, beaten
1 (6- to 7-pound) capon or
   roasting chicken

Combine millet, lentils, $3^1/_2$ cups of the water and bay leaf in a medium-size saucepan and bring to a boil. Reduce heat, cover and simmer 35 minutes or until nearly tender. Drain, remove bay leaf, cover, and set aside.

While millet is cooking, chop the apricot halves and place in a small bowl with the raisins and remaining cup water. Set aside to soak.

Preheat oven to 450°F (230°C). Cook the onion and celery in the butter over medium heat in a medium-size, nonstick skillet, stirring frequently, until the onion is translucent. Add parsley, rosemary and celery seeds and cook, stirring, 1 minute more.

Drain apricots and raisins. Combine in a large bowl with the millet and the onion mix-

ture. Let cool thoroughly, then stir in beaten egg.

Rinse capon and pat dry. Stuff body cavity with cooled stuffing. Arrange on a rack in a large roasting pan. Place the bird in the oven and turn heat down to 350°F (175°C). Roast 2 hours (about 20 minutes per pound) or until capon is quite tender. [If using a meat thermometer, the center of the stuffing should reach 165°F (75°C).] Baste frequently with pan juices. *Makes 10 servings.*

PER SERVING: Cal 483 • Carbo 26 gm • Prot 44 gm • Total fat 21 gm • Sat fat 7 gm • Cal from fat 39% • Chol 179 mg

EDUCATION: Expand your familiarity with grains and get added iron with millet. Richer in iron than rice and barley, millet is also high in protective fiber and carbohydrates. Millet can be used in stuffings as above, or substituted for rice in side dishes, soups and salads.

INSPIRATION: *The less time I spend trying to impress others, the more time I can spend in understanding them and engaging in real dialogue.*

Broiler-Grilled Cheese Sandwiches

Broiling instead of pan-grilling these sandwiches cuts down substantially on fat. Use a hearty, hearth-baked loaf of bread for best flavor. Serve with soup and a simple tossed salad.

4 thick slices whole-grain bread
2 garlic slices, halved
4 tomato slices
1/2 cup (2 ounces) shredded longhorn,
  provolone or Monterey Jack cheese
4 red onion slices (optional)
1/2 cup alfalfa sprouts

Preheat broiler. Toast bread and place on a baking sheet. Rub each toast slice with a garlic half and top toast with a tomato slice. Sprinkle equal amount of cheese over each toast slice. Broil until cheese is melted and lightly browned.

Top with onion slices, if desired, and alfalfa sprouts. *Makes 4 servings.*

PER SERVING: Cal 197 • Carbo 18 gm • Prot 11 gm • Total fat 9 gm • Sat fat 5 gm • Cal from fat 41% • Chol 20 mg

EDUCATION: Have some extra-quick and easy dinner ideas at the ready to save you time during the busy holiday season. You might resort to frozen soups or stews prepared during less hectic times of the year, or try some of the following ideas.

Make a quick pasta dish with vegetables by adding a bag of frozen mixed vegetables to a pound of boiling pasta just before the pasta is done. Toss with a cup of heated tomato sauce. Drain canned beans and heat in a chunky spaghetti sauce. Toss with cooked pasta spirals. Defrost frozen chopped spinach, sauté in a little olive oil and garlic, then stir in ricotta or cottage cheese. Serve over cooked rice or noodles. Top a frozen pizza with thawed, frozen mixed vegetables before baking.

INSPIRATION: *I am learning to ask for what I want, knowing sometimes the answer will be "no."*

Artichoke Pasta with Seafood Sauce

🌿 Vegetable pastas, such as this one made with artichokes, are available both fresh and dried.

> 1 pound artichoke linguini
>   (see note)
> 1/3 cup finely chopped onion
> 1 tablespoon olive oil
> 3 garlic cloves, minced
> 1/4 teaspoon dried red pepper flakes
> 1 (28-ounce) can Italian plum
>   tomatoes, with juice
> 1 (10-ounce) can baby clams,
>   with juice
> 1/4 cup minced fresh parsley
> 1 tablespoon tomato paste
> 1/2 teaspoon dried basil
> 1/4 teaspoon dried marjoram
> 1/4 teaspoon dried thyme
> 1/4 teaspoon salt
> 1/8 teaspoon freshly ground
>   black pepper
> 3/4 pound medium-size shrimp, peeled
>   and deveined (see glossary)
> 1/4 cup freshly grated Parmesan cheese

Bring a large pot of water to a boil. Add pasta and cook 7 to 9 minutes or until firm-tender. Drain, rinse under warm water and set aside.

Meanwhile, cook the onion in the oil in a nonstick Dutch oven over medium heat, stirring frequently, until tender, 3 or 4 minutes. Add the garlic and pepper flakes and cook, stirring, 1 minute more.

Coarsely chop the tomatoes and add with their juice, the juice drained from the clams, parsley, tomato paste, basil, marjoram, thyme, salt and pepper. Stir until combined and bring to a boil. Reduce heat, cover and simmer 15 minutes. Uncover and simmer an additional 15 minutes, stirring occasionally, until the sauce thickens.

Add clams and shrimp and continue to simmer 3 or 4 minutes or until shrimp are just cooked through. Add drained pasta to seafood sauce and toss until combined. Serve garnished with Parmesan cheese.   *Makes 4 servings.*

PER SERVING: Cal 630 • Carbo 103 gm • Prot 37 gm • Total fat 8 gm • Sat fat 2 gm • Cal from fat 12% • Chol 137 mg

NOTE: Made from wheat and flour of Jerusalem artichokes, this pasta is available from health-food stores and some supermarkets. It is slightly higher in protein than regular pastas, and has a similarly mild flavor.

EDUCATION: Keep hot foods hot and cold foods cold when taking a potluck dish to parties. Transport cold or frozen food in an insulated cooler with an ice pack. Hot foods can also be transported in insulated chests. The zone between 40° and 140°F (5° and 60°C) is the perfect temperature for bacteria to grow in foods. When reheating, bring sauces, soups and gravies to a boil, and heat foods to 165°F (75°C).

INSPIRATION: *A lot goes on in the world besides my life. By paying attention to what goes on around me and putting my energies to constructive use, I can avoid self-absorption and the isolation it creates.*

Red Beans & Rice

New Orleans–style beans and rice feature Cajun seasonings for a warming, spicy winter meal.

 1 1/2 cups dried red beans
 1 bay leaf
 1 1/2 cups brown rice
 3 cups water
 1 cup chopped onion
 1 cup diced green bell pepper
 1 tablespoon olive oil
 1/2 jalapeño chile, seeded and minced
     (see glossary)
 4 garlic cloves, minced
 1/2 teaspoon salt
 1/4 teaspoon freshly ground black pepper
 1/4 teaspoon dried oregano
 1/4 teaspoon dried thyme
 1/4 teaspoon paprika
 1/4 teaspoon chili powder
 1/8 teaspoon hot (cayenne) pepper
 2 tablespoons minced fresh parsley

Pick over and rinse beans. Soak the beans overnight in water to cover generously, or use the quick-soak method (see glossary). Bring beans, soaking water and bay leaf to a boil. Reduce heat, cover and simmer 45 minutes or until tender.

While beans are cooking, combine the rice and water in a large saucepan and bring to a boil. Reduce heat, cover and simmer 35 minutes. Remove from heat and let stand 10 minutes.

Cook the onion and bell pepper in the oil in a nonstick Dutch oven over medium heat, stirring frequently, until the vegetables are tender, about 10 minutes. Add the jalapeño, garlic, salt, pepper, oregano, thyme, paprika, chili powder and cayenne and cook, stirring, 1 minute more.

Remove bay leaf from beans. Add beans and 1 cup of their cooking liquid to the onion mixture and bring to a boil. Reduce heat, cover and simmer 5 minutes to blend flavors. Serve beans over rice and garnish with minced parsley.

Makes 4 servings.

PER SERVING: Cal 403 • Carbo 76 gm • Prot 12 gm • Total fat 6 gm • Sat fat 1 gm • Cal from fat 13% • Chol 0 mg

VARIATION
For faster meal preparation, use white rice and 2 (16-ounce) cans small red or pink beans. Add enough water to liquid with beans to make 1 cup, and heat through with onion mixture, as above.

EDUCATION: Find a relaxing spot to sit, then give yourself time to do so. Indoors or out, all you need is a comfortable chair and some peace and quiet. Choose a time when you're not likely to be interrupted, turn off the phone and unwind. Concentrate on slow, even breathing to help your mind unclutter.

INSPIRATION: *As long as I keep looking toward the past, I cannot see the doors of opportunity opening toward my future.*

Calf's Liver with Onions

❧ Calf's liver is much more delicate in flavor than beef liver, creating quite a tasty dish, garnished with onions.

2 onions, halved lengthwise and
    thinly sliced
$1/2$ tablespoon unsalted butter
8 slices (about 1 pound) calf's liver
$1/4$ cup unbleached all-purpose flour
$1/4$ teaspoon salt
$1/8$ teaspoon freshly ground
    black pepper
2 teaspoons olive oil
2 teaspoons chicken broth or water
1 teaspoon brown rice vinegar
Dash of dried thyme
Dash of ground cloves

Cook the onions in the butter in a large, nonstick skillet over medium heat, stirring frequently, until onions are golden brown and very soft, about 15 minutes. Remove onions to a bowl, cover and keep warm.

Dredge the liver in the flour, salt and pepper. Add oil to skillet over medium heat and brown liver slices, turning once, about 5 minutes or until cooked through, but still slightly pink on the inside. Remove liver from pan and keep warm.

Stir broth or water, vinegar, thyme and ground cloves into pan, loosening any browned bits. Add liver and onions and heat through. *Makes 4 servings.*

PER SERVING: Cal 456 • Carbo 26 gm • Prot 47 gm • Total fat 17 gm • Sat fat 6 gm • Cal from fat 34% • Chol 823 mg

EDUCATION: Include liver in your diet occasionally to take advantage of its storehouse of nutrients. Liver is especially rich in vitamin B_{12}, and is an excellent source of riboflavin, folacin, phosphorus, iron (of course), zinc, niacin and B_6. While low in fat, supplying 27 percent of its calories from this element, liver is high in cholesterol. For that reason it should be eaten infrequently.

INSPIRATION: *If I am courageous enough to see and accept my own mistakes and imperfections, my tolerance and compassion can extend to those around me.*

Oma's Dutch Split-Pea Soup

❧ Dutch winter weather is damp and chill. Oma and Opa handed down this delicious, comforting soup, good in cold weather anywhere in the world.

2 cups chopped carrots
1 cup chopped celery
1 cup chopped onion
1 tablespoon canola oil
3 garlic cloves, minced
1 bay leaf
$1/8$ teaspoon ground cloves
Dash of hot (cayenne) pepper
1 ham soup bone or $1/2$ cup diced baked ham
1 pound green split peas, picked over and rinsed
10 cups water
4 cups chicken broth
2 medium-size potatoes, peeled and cubed
$1/2$ teaspoon salt
$1/4$ teaspoon freshly ground black pepper
2 tablespoons finely chopped parsley

Cook the carrots, celery and onion in the oil in a nonstick Dutch oven over medium heat, stirring frequently, for 10 minutes or until vegetables just begin to brown. Add garlic, bay leaf, ground cloves and hot pepper and cook, stirring, 1 minute more. Add ham bone or ham, split peas, water, broth, potatoes, salt and pepper and bring to a boil. Reduce heat and simmer, uncovered, stirring occasionally, 1 hour or until split peas are tender. Remove bay leaf and soup bone.

Puree the soup in batches in a food processor or blender and return to the Dutch oven. Stir in parsley, heat through and serve.

Makes 10 servings.

PER SERVING: Cal 152 • Carbo 20 gm • Prot 8 gm • Total fat 5 gm • Sat fat 1 gm • Cal from fat 28% • Chol 8 mg

EDUCATION: Be prepared for unexpected company by freezing soups. Soups are easy to make in large quantity. Freezing extra in 1- or 2-serving–size containers provides maximum flexibility. Defrost as much—or as little—soup as needed for a quick meal or for entertaining. Many soups can be combined when extra quantities are needed. Don't be afraid to experiment.

D e c e m b e r   7

INSPIRATION: *When I feel low, I can reach out to do something for someone else. Offering encouragement to others rebounds to benefit me, as well.*

Best-Ever Gingersnaps

❧ Dusted with powdered sugar, these pretty cookies are made with whole-wheat pastry flour, resulting in the most delicious gingersnaps you'll find! They make a terrific holiday gift.

2 cups granulated sugar
³/₄ cup plus 2 tablespoons unsalted butter
2 eggs, beaten
¹/₂ cup medium, unsulfured molasses
2 teaspoons brown rice vinegar
3 cups whole-wheat pastry flour
¹/₂ cup unbleached all-purpose flour
1¹/₂ teaspoons baking soda
2¹/₂ teaspoons ground ginger
¹/₂ teaspoon ground cinnamon
¹/₄ teaspoon cloves
1 cup powdered sugar

Preheat oven to 325°F (165°C). Beat together granulated sugar and butter in a large bowl. Stir in the eggs, molasses and vinegar until well combined.

In a medium-size bowl, combine the flours, baking soda, ginger, cinnamon and cloves. Add the dry ingredients to the egg mixture and stir until combined.

Roll dough by hand into ³/₄-inch-diameter balls. Arrange the balls on a lightly buttered cookie sheet, about 2 inches apart. Bake about 12 minutes or until the cookies are lightly browned around the edges. With a pancake turner, remove the cookies to wire racks to cool. Place powdered sugar in a plastic bag, add 2 dozen cookies and shake until evenly coated. Shake off excess. Repeat with remaining cookies. Store cookies in a tightly covered container.

Makes 10 dozen.

PER COOKIE: Cal 40 • Carbo 8 gm • Prot trace • Total fat 1 gm • Sat fat trace • Cal from fat 22% • Chol 6 mg

EDUCATION: Set aside a weekend for baking, inviting a family member or friend to join in the fun. Make goodies for your own holiday entertaining, including unexpected drop-in guests, and enough to give to friends and neighbors. Hand out aprons, put on the holiday music albums and have fun!

INSPIRATION: *Taking risks through growing and changing means the possibility of more satisfaction from life than I ever thought possible.*

Kevin's Cinnamon Pecan Puffs

🌿 Kevin continues the tradition his mother started with these feathery-light, melt-in-the-mouth confections. Our blessing is that he makes enough to share with friends! These fabulous cookies are a once-a-year treat—too many fat calories for daily fare.

> 1/2 cup unsalted butter, at room
>   temperature
> 2 tablespoons granulated vanilla
>   sugar (see glossary)
> 1 cup pecan meats
> 1 cup cake flour
> 1/2 cup powdered sugar
> 1 teaspoon ground cinnamon

Preheat oven to 300°F (150°C). Cream together the butter and vanilla sugar, then beat until light. Grind pecans in a food processor or blender, with short bursts at high speed, until fine. Do not overblend to the point that pecan meal becomes sticky. Sift the flour or tap it through a sieve.

Lightly stir the ground pecans and flour into the butter mixture. Roll the dough into 1 1/2-inch balls and place them, without touching, on a lightly buttered baking sheet. Bake 30 minutes or until lightly golden.

Combine powdered sugar and cinnamon in a paper lunch bag. Shake a few of the cookies at a time, while still hot, in the cinnamon-sugar mixture.   *Makes about 3 dozen.*

PER COOKIE: Cal 62 • Carbo 5 gm • Prot trace
• Total fat 5 gm • Sat fat 2 gm • Cal from fat 66%
• Chol 7 mg

EDUCATION: To develop or maintain a sense of connection, keep up some of the holiday traditions of your childhood. A favorite food, for example, can bring pleasant memories just by the aroma of its cooking or baking. Sharing the tradition with others will add new life, and maybe even richer memories, to the tapestry of the past.

INSPIRATION: *Continuing the process of self-knowledge and awareness is one of my sustaining strengths.*

Broiled Salmon Steaks with Herbs

🌿 Having salmon steaks at room temperature as they marinate helps ensure even cooking. The tangy lime juice is a nice complement to salmon.

> 4 (1 1/4-inch-thick) salmon steaks
> 1/3 cup fresh lime juice
> Dash of paprika
> 1 tablespoon minced fresh parsley
> 1 tablespoon minced fresh basil or dill
> Lime slices for garnish
> Pomegranate seeds for garnish

Place the salmon steaks in a single layer in a shallow casserole dish and add lime juice. Marinate 30 minutes, at room temperature, turning steaks occasionally.

Preheat broiler. Drain and pat steaks dry with a paper towel. Broil salmon steaks 3 or 4 minutes per side, or just until opaque throughout. Serve sprinkled with minced herbs and garnished with lime slices and pomegranate seeds.   *Makes 4 servings.*

PER SERVING: Cal 127 • Carbo 2 gm • Prot 17 gm • Total fat 5 gm • Sat fat 1 gm • Cal from fat 35% • Chol 47 mg

EDUCATION: Eat salmon occasionally to keep your circulation healthy. Omega-3 fatty acids have demonstrated an ability to inhibit the formation of plaque inside blood vessels. This means lowering your risk of arteriosclerosis, heart disease and stroke.

December 10

INSPIRATION: *I can see darkness and sorrow as an inevitable part of life, and wait patiently for the return of joy and the light.*

Susan's Crisp Potato Latkes

Potato latkes are made with egg whites to reduce the cholesterol content. Using a nonstick skillet reduces the fat needed to produce a crisp, tasty pancake.

2 medium-size potatoes, peeled, shredded (about 2 cups)
1 1/2 teaspoons matzoh meal or unbleached all-purpose flour
6 egg whites
2 tablespoons grated onion
1/4 teaspoon salt
1/8 teaspoon fresh ground black pepper
1 cup applesauce (optional)
1/3 cup nonfat sour cream (optional)

Squeeze excess moisture from the potatoes and place in a large bowl. Sprinkle with flour and toss to combine. In a medium-size bowl, beat the egg whites just until frothy. Stir in onion, salt and pepper and stir mixture into potatoes until well-combined.

Drop the batter about 1/3 cup at a time, on a hot, lightly oiled or buttered nonstick skillet or griddle. Cook about 5 minutes per side, turning once or until lightly browned and crisp. Serve topped with applesauce or sour cream, if desired.   *Makes 6 servings.*

PER SERVING: Cal 115 • Carbo 19 gm • Prot 5 gm • Total fat 2 gm • Sat fat 2 gm • Cal from fat 18% • Chol 0 mg

EDUCATION: Cut down on cholesterol by using egg whites in place of whole eggs when making potato latkes or any other pancake. The cholesterol is contained in the yolk, which can be left out of the recipe with no significant change. Using a nonstick pan helps keep fat content low when making pancakes on top of the stove.

INSPIRATION: *As I go about discovering who I am, I can learn to treat myself with new respect. The more I respect myself, the more I can develop my individuality.*

Tender Braised Leeks & Fennel

❧ Slow braising develops a luscious flavor in vegetables. The leeks and fennel complement each other in flavor, though a variety of root vegetables could be used.

2 large leeks
2 fennel bulbs
2 teaspoons unsalted butter
¹/₄ to ¹/₂ cup chicken broth

Trim the leeks to within 2 inches of white part, halve leeks lengthwise and clean thoroughly. Trim tops from fennel bulbs and save a few feathery tops. Quarter fennel bulbs.

Cook the leeks and fennel in the butter in a nonstick, ovenproof Dutch oven over medium heat, stirring frequently, until the vegetables are lightly browned.

Add ¹/₄ cup broth and cover pan. Over very low heat, cook the vegetables until very soft and tender, about 45 minutes, adding additional broth, if needed, to keep ingredients moist. Garnish with fennel sprigs.   *Makes 4 servings.*

PER SERVING: Cal 65 • Carbo 10 gm • Prot 2 gm • Total fat 2 gm • Sat fat 1 gm • Cal from fat 28% • Chol 6 mg

EDUCATION: Braise vegetables to develop their rich flavors without adding a lot of fat. The slow cooking of the root vegetables above produces a melt-in-your-mouth texture and flavor unmatched by quicker cooking methods. Because there is no constant watching, braising can still be convenient. Read the paper, feed the pets, exercise, and then enjoy.

INSPIRATION: *Keeping a commitment made from the heart is effortless compared to trying to rely on willpower.*

Lamb Stew with Winter Vegetables

❧ Carrots and parsnips combine to lend a sweet flavor to this slowly simmered, easy stew. Beef cubes create just as appealing a dish.

3 pounds cubed lamb, trimmed of fat
4 teaspoons olive oil
*2 large onions, halved lengthwise
    and thinly sliced*
6 garlic cloves, sliced
2 cups beef broth or defatted chicken broth
*1 (28-ounce) can whole tomatoes, drained
    and chopped*
1¹/₂ teaspoons dried thyme
*4 carrots, peeled and cut into
    2-inch-thick slices*
*4 parsnips, peeled and cut into 2-inch-thick
    slices*
¹/₄ cup cold water
2 tablespoons unbleached all-purpose flour
2 tablespoons tomato paste
¹/₄ cup minced fresh parsley
¹/₂ teaspoon salt
¹/₄ teaspoon freshly ground black pepper
1 pound egg noodles, cooked

Brown half the meat in half the oil in a nonstick Dutch oven over medium heat, stirring frequently, about 5 minutes. Wipe out pan and repeat with remaining meat and oil.

Return all the meat to pan and cook with onions, stirring frequently, for about 5 minutes or until onions are translucent. Add garlic and cook, stirring, 1 minute.

Add broth, chopped tomatoes and thyme and bring to a boil. Reduce heat, cover and simmer 1¹/₂ hours. Stir in carrots and parsnips and return to a boil. Cover and simmer 45 minutes or until vegetables and meat are tender.

Place water and flour in a blender and process until smooth. Add tomato paste and $\frac{1}{2}$ cup of vegetables from the stew. Process until smooth and return to the Dutch oven. Add parsley, salt and pepper. Simmer 15 minutes or until the stew is slightly thickened. Serve over cooked noodles. *Makes 6 servings.*

PER SERVING: Cal 712 • Carbo 47 gm • Prot 61 gm • Total fat 30 gm • Sat fat 11 gm • Cal from fat 37% • Chol 210 mg

EDUCATION: Stay younger longer by eating antioxidant-rich vegetables, like the ones above, daily. Research suggests antioxidant vitamins C, E and beta-carotene work within our bodies to prevent cell damage, possibly offsetting the effects of aging. Antioxidants neutralize free-radical compounds—unstable particles that cause damage to cells.

December 13

INSPIRATION: *Beginning to reach for my dreams can reduce my fear of failure and release my energy.*

Shawn's Cream of Chicken Soup

Made with skinless chicken breast halves, this lean soup is easy to make, perfect for a working woman who likes relaxing at home with her cat, or anyone whose busy day calls for "feet up" in the evening.

2 boneless skinless chicken breast halves
1 tablespoon unsalted butter
1 teaspoon canola oil
$\frac{3}{4}$ cup finely chopped onion
4 medium-size potatoes, peeled and cubed
4 cups chicken broth

$\frac{1}{2}$ pound fresh spinach
1 cup low-fat (1%) milk
$\frac{1}{4}$ teaspoon salt
$\frac{1}{8}$ teaspoon freshly ground black pepper

Cut each breast half lengthwise in two, then cut crosswise into $\frac{1}{4}$-inch-thick strips. Cook the chicken strips in the butter in a nonstick Dutch oven, stirring frequently, just until they become opaque. Remove chicken with a slotted spoon to a medium-size bowl. Cover and keep warm.

Add oil to Dutch oven over medium heat and cook the onion, stirring frequently, until tender and lightly browned. Add the potatoes and broth and bring to a boil. Reduce heat, cover and simmer 15 minutes, or until potatoes are tender.

While potatoes are cooking, remove stems from spinach and wash carefully to remove any sand. Coarsely chop the leaves. Puree half the potato mixture in a blender or food processor just until smooth. Return puree to Dutch oven.

Add spinach and simmer 3 or 4 minutes, until spinach is tender. Stir in chicken, milk, salt and pepper and heat through serving.

Makes 4 servings.

PER SERVING: Cal 311 • Carbo 35 gm • Prot 25 gm • Total fat 8 gm • Sat fat 3 gm • Cal from fat 23% • Chol 47 mg

EDUCATION: Practice frequent hand-washing to avoid colds and flu. Cold weather brings everyone indoors—to share germs. When shopping or socializing, keep your hands away from your face. Germs picked up from handshakes or contaminated surfaces can find immediate access to the body by eye, nose and mouth.

December 14

INSPIRATION: *My experiences are dulled whenever I avoid being fully present in the moment.*

John's Applesauce Gingerbread

A moist gingerbread with no added fat creates a nice balance on a dessert buffet with holiday-rich offerings. The recipe can also be used to bake 4 mini-loaves for considerate, low-fat gift-giving (see below).

1/4 cup raisins
2 cups whole-wheat pastry flour
1 1/2 teaspoons baking soda
2 teaspoons ground ginger
1/4 teaspoon ground cinnamon
1/8 teaspoon ground cloves
1 egg
1 cup medium unsulfured molasses
3/4 cup buttermilk
1/2 cup applesauce
2 tablespoons grated gingerroot (optional)
Additional applesauce for garnish (optional)
Maple syrup for garnish (optional)

Place raisins in a small bowl, cover generously with water and set aside for 10 minutes. Combine the flour, baking soda, ginger, cinnamon and cloves in a large bowl.

Beat egg in a medium-size bowl and add the molasses, buttermilk and applesauce. Squeeze juice from grated gingerroot and add, if desired, stirring to combine ingredients. Drain raisins. Add raisins and egg mixture to dry ingredients and stir until combined. Pour into a lightly buttered 9-inch-square baking dish. Bake 35 to 40 minutes or until a wooden pick inserted in the center comes out clean. Cut into squares and serve warm, topped, if desired, with heated applesauce flavored with some maple syrup. *Makes 9 servings.*

PER SERVING: Cal 232 • Carbo 52 gm • Prot 5 gm • Total fat 1 gm • Sat fat trace • Cal from fat 4% • Chol 25 mg

NOTE: For mini-loaves, divide batter between 3 × 5 × 2-inch pans. Bake 20 to 25 minutes or until a wooden pick inserted in the center comes out clean.

EDUCATION: Put balance in your life by offsetting high-fat indulgences with low-fat enjoyments. Making a low-fat dessert does not have to mean major sacrificing. The gingerbread above is an example. Though it contains no added fats, it is moist and delicious. Add it to party buffets to allow guests the choice of indulging—or not.

December 15

INSPIRATION: *I can deal with anything, one day at a time.*

Irene's Easy Baked Papaya

Papaya makes an unusual, eye-catching dessert with little effort—a nice plus when days are busy, but you want to serve something different.

2 ripe papayas (see below)
1 tablespoon brown sugar
1/4 cup nonfat yogurt
1 tablespoon maple syrup
Mint sprigs for garnish

Preheat oven to 325°F (165°C). Halve papayas lengthwise and remove seeds. Arrange cut side up in a shallow 13 × 9-inch casserole dish. Add enough water to just cover the bottom of the dish. Sprinkle the papayas with the brown sugar. Bake 25 minutes or until tender.

Combine yogurt and maple syrup and drizzle over the papaya halves. Serve garnished with mint sprigs.   *Makes 4 servings.*

PER SERVING: Cal 60 • Carbo 15 gm • Prot 1 gm • Total fat trace • Sat fat trace • Cal from fat 0% • Chol 1 mg

NOTE: Choose fruits that are at least one-third yellow. They will ripen fully in 3 to 4 days at room temperature. If you plan to serve this dessert sooner, place the papayas in a paper bag with a banana to hasten ripening. Fruits that are all green will probably not ripen properly. Look for imported papayas from Hawaii during the holidays.

EDUCATION: Enjoy winter fruits, such as year-round papaya, to stock up on vitamin C. One-half of a papaya offers well over 100 percent of your daily allowance. Also high in vitamin A and potassium, nutrient-rich papayas pay back every cent of their purchase price. Unripe papayas can be cooked like squash, as a winter vegetable.

December 16

INSPIRATION: *I can trust my own truths. What is right for me is mine alone to decide and is not open for debate.*

Barb's Sweet Potato Casserole

❧ Minneapolis winters call for hearty, nutritious side dishes. A sweet potato version studded with luscious dates is gala enough for the holidays.

4 medium-size sweet potatoes, peeled
    and cubed
1/2 cup chopped, pitted dates
2 teaspoons butter
1 egg

1/2 cup evaporated low-fat
    (2%) milk
2 tablespoons maple syrup
1/4 teaspoon salt
Dash of freshly grated nutmeg

Preheat oven to 350°F (175°C). Boil the sweet potatoes in enough water to cover in a large saucepan 10 to 15 minutes or until very tender. Drain.

Meanwhile, cook dates in the butter in a small saucepan, stirring, for 2 minutes or until slightly softened.

Beat egg in a large bowl. Add milk, maple syrup, dates and sweet potatoes and stir until smooth.

Spoon sweet potato mixture into a medium-size casserole dish. Dust with nutmeg. Bake 20 to 25 minutes or until set.   *Makes 6 servings.*

PER SERVING: Cal 172 • Carbo 35 gm • Prot 3 gm • Total fat 3 gm • Sat fat 1 gm • Cal from fat 14% • Chol 41 mg

EDUCATION: Switch from canned to fresh sweet potatoes to maximize your consumption of their valuable store of beta-carotene, B vitamins and vitamin C. Canned sweet potatoes are substantially lower in all of these nutrients. A few minutes of extra cooking is all it takes and, as above, the flavor alone is worth it. The microwave is a valuable tool in making sweet potatoes more convenient. A large sweet potato in its skin (remember to pierce it) can be ready to eat in about 10 minutes. Top with some crushed pineapple for a satisfying low-fat treat.

INSPIRATION: *I will stop spreading my energy too thin by concentrating on things I do well and enjoy.*

Double-Corn Polenta Squares

❧ Stuffed with a layer of vegetables, these polenta squares are an elegant vegetarian main dish. Choose commercial pasta sauce or some of your homemade variety.

> 2 cups sliced portobello or white
>   mushrooms
> $^1/_2$ cup chopped onion
> 1 tablespoon olive oil
> 4 cups packed fresh spinach leaves,
>   stems removed
> $3^3/_4$ cups water
> $^1/_2$ teaspoon salt
> 1 cup stone-ground yellow cornmeal
> 1 cup frozen shoepeg or yellow corn,
>   thawed
> 1 tablespoon freshly grated Parmesan cheese
> Dash of freshly grated nutmeg
> $^1/_4$ cup shredded part-skim mozzarella
>   cheese
> $^1/_3$ cup low-fat (1%) cottage cheese
> 2 cups marinara sauce or other tomato pasta
>   sauce

Cook the mushrooms and onions in the oil in a large nonstick skillet over medium heat, stirring frequently, until liquid evaporates and onion is beginning to brown. Thinly slice spinach leaves and add to mushroom mixture, stirring until spinach wilts. Remove from heat.

Bring water and salt to a boil in a large saucepan. Reduce heat and, as water simmers, sprinkle in cornmeal, stirring constantly with a wire whisk to prevent lumping. Simmer over low heat, stirring frequently, until polenta is thick, about 10 minutes. Remove from heat and stir in corn, grated Parmesan and nutmeg.

Spoon half of the polenta into a lightly oiled 8-inch-square baking dish. Stir the cottage cheese and mozzarella into the vegetable mixture, and spoon vegetable and cheese mixture over the polenta in the baking dish. Spoon remaining polenta over vegetable mixture and put aside 10 minutes to set.

Preheat oven to 400°F (200°C). Bake polenta squares 10 to 15 minutes or until bubbly and heated through. Meanwhile, heat marinara or pasta sauce in a small saucepan. To serve, cut polenta into 4 squares and top each with pasta sauce.   *Makes 4 servings.*

PER SERVING: Cal 342 • Carbo 54 gm • Prot 14 gm • Total fat 10 gm • Sat fat 2 gm • Cal from fat 26% • Chol 6 mg

EDUCATION: To lower your risk of cancer, high blood pressure and heart disease, consume fewer animal products and more grains, legumes, fruits and vegetables high in vitamins A, C and E. Vegetarian dishes, like the one above, can offer a high-protein meal with a very minimum of low-fat dairy products. For a meal with no animal products, serve the polenta square above without the cheeses.

INSPIRATION: *By having the courage to change the things I can, it is more likely I will find work and relationships that give me joy and satisfaction.*

Jerusalem Artichokes in Lemon-Parsley Butter

❧ Also called "sun chokes," Jerusalem artichokes are the root of the beautiful sunflower. They make a delicious side dish for special, or simple, occasions.

3 cups water

3 pounds Jerusalem
   artichokes

2 tablespoons unsalted butter

2 tablespoons minced fresh parsley

$^1/_4$ teaspoon freshly grated
   lemon peel

Place the water in a large nonstick skillet. Peel the Jerusalem artichokes and cut into $^1/_4$-inch-thick slices. Immediately place slices in the water to avoid discoloration and bring to a boil. Reduce heat, cover and simmer 8 to 10 minutes or until firm-tender. Pour off water. Return to low heat and add the butter to the Jerusalem artichokes and stir until combined. Cook, stirring, until the artichokes begin to turn golden brown. Toss with parsley and lemon peel. *Makes 8 servings.*

PER SERVING: Cal 111 • Carbo 19 gm • Prot 6 gm • Total fat 3 gm • Sat fat 2 gm • Cal from fat 26% • Chol 8 mg

EDUCATION: Enjoy Jerusalem artichokes for their fabulous iron content. This root vegetable outshines fish, poultry and ham as a source of iron, with no fat. Eating Jerusalem artichokes with just a small amount of meat makes it easier for the body to absorb the iron. For vegetarians, choose a vitamin C–rich food such as citrus, cabbage, broccoli, bell peppers, strawberries or kale to help absorb the iron.

D e c e m b e r   1 9

INSPIRATION: *Recovery is not just giving up distractions and addictions, but a new way of living that encompasses my entire being.*

Virginia's Holiday Herbed Biscuits

✿ Biscuits are quick and easy but add a special touch to any meal. These feature a selection of fresh herbs for a more elaborate taste, but little extra effort.

1 cup unbleached all-purpose flour

1 cup whole-wheat pastry flour

1 teaspoon baking powder

$^1/_2$ teaspoon baking soda

$^1/_2$ teaspoon sugar

$^1/_2$ teaspoon salt

4 tablespoons unsalted butter

$^3/_4$ to 1 cup buttermilk

2 tablespoons minced fresh parsley

1 tablespoon minced fresh basil

2 teaspoons minced fresh thyme

2 teaspoons minced fresh marjoram

Preheat oven to 450°F (230°C). Combine flours, baking powder and soda, sugar and salt in a large bowl. Cut in butter with a pastry cutter until mixture resembles coarse meal. Add buttermilk and herbs. Stir until mixture holds together. Gently knead dough on a lightly floured surface, then roll out to $^1/_2$-inch thickness. Cut out biscuits with a 2-inch round cutter. Place biscuits on an unoiled baking sheet.

Gather scraps, roll and cut on a floured surface, as above, and add to baking sheet. Bake 12 to 15 minutes, until biscuits are golden and baked through. Transfer to a cooling rack for 5 minutes. Serve warm. *Makes 8 biscuits.*

PER BISCUIT: Cal 194 • Carbo 33 gm • Prot 5 gm • Total fat 4 gm • Sat fat 2 gm • Cal from fat 18% • Chol 11 mg

EDUCATION: If you're stressed out about a problem, figure out a plan to deal with it. Don't waste time blaming or fretting, but outline constructive steps toward a solution. Even if the solution fails, you'll gain self-esteem from having tried.

INSPIRATION: *It is the natural tendency of my body to strive for health, my emotions to strive for healing and my spirit to strive for renewal. I will do the groundwork and then let go.*

Red Cabbage Coleslaw

A pretty side dish for a buffet or family dinner, this coleslaw relies on nonfat sour cream to cut down on fats in the dressing.

1 small head red cabbage
1 small tart apple, peeled, cored and chopped
1 tablespoon grated onion
1/3 cup nonfat sour cream
1/3 cup sugar
3 tablespoons berry-flavored or cider vinegar (see glossary)
2 tablespoons reduced-fat mayonnaise
1/4 teaspoon salt

Shred the cabbage by thinly slicing with a sharp knife. Combine with the apple and grated onion. Combine the sour cream, sugar, vinegar, mayonnaise and salt. Toss with the cabbage mixture and chill until ready to serve.

Makes 6 servings.

PER SERVING: Cal 50 • Carbo 8 gm • Prot 1 gm • Total fat 2 gm • Sat fat 1 gm • Cal from fat 36% • Chol 2 mg

EDUCATION: To cut down on calories during the holidays, wait 20 minutes before reaching for seconds. That's how long it takes for the signal that you're full to reach the brain. When we socialize, we can become distracted and easily unaware of how much we're eating. By waiting for the "full-up" signal, we are much less likely to overindulge.

INSPIRATION: *The definition of who I am is written in my heart. I cannot look to others for its validity.*

Pumpkin Mousse Meringue Pie

A no-fat meringue crust helps create a light and unique pumpkin dessert.

3 egg whites
1 cup vanilla sugar (see glossary)
1 teaspoon white vinegar combined with 1 teaspoon water
1/2 teaspoon baking powder
1/8 teaspoon salt
3/4 cup canned evaporated low-fat (2%) milk
2/3 cup packed brown sugar
1 envelope unflavored gelatin
1 (16-ounce) can pumpkin
2 teaspoons medium unsulfured molasses
1 teaspoon ground cinnamon
1/2 teaspoon ground ginger
1/4 teaspoon freshly grated nutmeg
1/2 cup heavy cream
1 teaspoon sugar

Preheat oven to 275°F (135°C). Beat egg whites until stiff, then add vanilla sugar 1 teaspoon at a time, alternating with a few drops of the combined vinegar and water, beating continuously. Continue to beat for several minutes. Beat in baking powder and salt.

Spoon meringue into a lightly buttered 10-inch pie plate, shaping meringue flat across the bottom and bringing it up slightly above the sides of the pie plate. Bake 1 hour and 15 minutes, turn off oven and allow the crust to cool with the door propped slightly open.

Combine the evaporated milk and brown sugar in a saucepan. Sprinkle with the gelatin and let stand 10 minutes to soften. Set pan over medium heat and cook, stirring, until gelatin is dissolved and mixture begins to simmer. Remove from heat and let cool 10 minutes.

Combine the pumpkin, molasses, cinnamon, ginger and nutmeg in a large bowl. Stir in the cooled gelatin mixture, cover bowl and chill at least 1 hour or up to 3 hours.

Chill the cream, bowl and beaters 10 minutes in the freezer. Whip cream until very stiff, adding sugar gradually. Fold the whipped cream gently into the pumpkin mixture.

Spoon the pumpkin mixture into the cooled meringue pie shell, creating a rough surface to match the meringue. Cover well with plastic wrap and chill in the refrigerator at least 3 hours, until filling is set, or overnight. *Makes 8 servings.*

PER SERVING: Cal 264 • Carbo 51 gm • Prot 5 gm • Total fat 6 gm • Sat fat 4 gm • Cal from fat 20% • Chol 21 mg

EDUCATION: There's no need to totally eliminate higher-fat foods from your diet, as long as you indulge only occasionally, and keep portions small. The idea is to consume fat in moderation. That means balancing foods so that they average less than 30 percent of calories from fat overall. Selecting a nonfat meringue crust allows for a rich-tasting, creamy filling with a small amount of whipped cream.

December 22

INSPIRATION: *I can initiate activities and interactions with others, taking a positive lead in developing new relationships.*

New England Acorn Squash Soup

❧ Made easy with the microwave, this elegant soup is suitable for any entertaining. .

2 acorn squash (about 1¼ pounds each)
1 cup chopped onion
¼ cup thinly sliced celery
1 tablespoon unsalted butter
2 cups chicken broth

½ cup low-fat (1%) milk
⅛ teaspoon freshly grated nutmeg
2 tablespoons maple syrup
⅓ cup nonfat yogurt
¼ cup pomegranate seeds for garnish
6 mint leaves for garnish

Pierce each squash several times with a knife. Arrange on a large plate and microwave on HIGH 10 minutes. Turn the squash over, then microwave on HIGH 8 to 10 minutes or until tender. Halve, let cool, then remove and discard the seeds.

In a 3-quart casserole, combine the onion, celery, and butter. Microwave on HIGH 2 minutes or until the butter is melted. Stir, then microwave on HIGH 4 minutes or until the onion is tender.

Scoop the flesh from the squash shells and transfer to a food processor. Add the onion mixture and puree until smooth. Return to the casserole. Stir in the broth, milk, nutmeg, and 1 tablespoon of the maple syrup. Microwave on HIGH 5 to 7 minutes or until the mixture comes to a simmer. Ladle into bowls.

In a cup, combine the yogurt with the remaining tablespoon of maple syrup. Drizzle over each serving. Top with pomegranate seeds and a mint leaf for garnish. *Makes 6 servings.*

PER SERVING: Cal 149 • Carbo 26 gm • Prot 5 gm • Total fat 4 gm • Sat fat 2 gm • Cal from fat 24% • Chol 7 mg

EDUCATION: Enjoy acorn squash, with its substantial calcium bonus, to keep your bones strong in winter. Though lower in beta-carotene than the other winter squashes, acorn squash is rich in calcium. A cup of cooked acorn squash contains about 90 milligrams of calcium (just over 10 percent of the recommended daily allowance) with just 100 calories.

INSPIRATION: *Building relationships means allowing myself to communicate honestly and constructively with those I care about.*

Holiday Raisin Molasses Pancakes

🌿 When the family comes to visit, breakfast can become a special time. For some of us with dysfunctional families, it's especially reassuring to enjoy some good, hearty food. These pancakes will gird you for any eventualities of the season's visit.

3 cups whole-wheat pastry flour
$1/2$ cup unbleached all-purpose flour
$2^1/2$ teaspoons baking powder
$1/2$ teaspoon salt
$1/2$ teaspoon ground cinnamon
$1/8$ teaspoon freshly grated nutmeg
2 eggs
4 egg whites
$1/4$ cup medium unsulfured molasses
$3/4$ cup raisins
3 to $3^1/4$ cups skim milk

Place the flours, baking powder, salt, cinnamon and nutmeg in a large bowl. Beat the eggs with the egg whites in a small bowl and add to the flours along with the molasses, raisins and enough milk to achieve the desired consistency. Pour batter by $1/3$-cupfuls onto a hot, lightly oiled nonstick skillet or griddle. Turn when bottom is browned and bubbles cover top of pancake. Continue to cook until remaining side is browned and pancake is cooked through.   *Makes 8 servings.*

PER SERVING: Cal 326 • Carbo 64 gm • Prot 12 gm • Total fat 2 gm • Sat fat 1 gm • Cal from fat 6% • Chol 55 mg

VARIATION
Sprinkle unsalted, raw sunflower kernels over each of the pancakes before turning.

EDUCATION: Keep an ongoing list of things that make you happy. Some little thing that might have been forgotten may bring wonderful laughter years later. Also, as your list grows, you may gain a new perspective on the myriad gifts to be found in your life, despite the inevitable pain and losses.

INSPIRATION: *Being grateful to others for their caring actions, and telling them so from the heart, keeps my relationships alive.*

Three-Grain Pilaf with Dried Cranberries

🌿 Dried cranberries offer a refreshingly sweet-tart counterpoint to a blend of grains and savory vegetables in this holiday side dish. Brown and wild rice cook in the same amount of time, which saves you a pot to clean.

$1^1/2$ cups water
$1/2$ cup brown rice
$1/4$ cup wild rice
$1/2$ cup pearl barley, rinsed
1 cup finely chopped onion
$1/2$ cup finely diced celery
1 tablespoon unsalted butter
$1/3$ cup dried cranberries
1 cup chicken broth or water
$1/2$ teaspoon salt
$1/4$ teaspoon thyme
$1/4$ cup fresh minced parsley
Mint or parsley sprigs for garnish

Bring $1^1/2$ cups of lightly salted water to a boil in a medium-size saucepan. Add brown and wild rice and return to a boil. Reduce heat, cover and simmer 35 minutes, without stirring, until water is absorbed and grains are tender. Remove from heat and set aside, covered.

Fill another medium-size saucepan halfway with water and bring to a boil. Add barley, reduce heat, cover and simmer 25 minutes or until barley is tender. Drain and add to rice to keep warm.

Cook the onion and celery in the butter in a large, nonstick skillet over medium heat, stirring frequently, until tender, 4 or 5 minutes. Add the cranberries and cook, stirring, 1 minute. Add broth, salt, and thyme and bring to a boil. Reduce heat and simmer, uncovered, 3 minutes.

Stir in the barley, brown and wild rice, and heat through, stirring occasionally. Serve garnished with mint or parsley sprigs.

Makes 4 servings.

PER SERVING: Cal 268 • Carbo 50 gm • Prot 8 gm • Total fat 4 gm • Sat fat 2 gm • Cal from fat 15% • Chol 8 mg

EDUCATION: Remember to count beverages so you don't overdo the calories at holiday time. Eggnog, cider, juice and soda all add calories, even without alcohol. Even coffee, unless taken black, can add up. A cream and 2 sugars adds over 60 calories per cup. Multiply that by 5 or 6 cups a day, and you could have enjoyed a sensible lunch instead.

December 25

INSPIRATION: *"Having enough" is often a matter of appreciating the material, spiritual and emotional gifts I already possess.*

Christmas Day Cranberry Pudding

❧ Bill and Anne grew up delighting in this annual Christmastime treat. Now each of their families enjoys this splurge at the holidays. Actually, the pudding (more of an eggless cake) is quite reasonable in terms of fat. The sauce, however, is strictly a once-a-year indulgence.

> $^1/_2$ cup sugar
> $1^1/_2$ tablespoons unsalted butter, softened
> 1 cup unbleached all-purpose flour
> $1^1/_2$ teaspoons baking powder
> $^1/_4$ teaspoon salt
> $^1/_2$ cup milk
> 1 cup cranberries
>
> SAUCE:
> 3 tablespoons unsalted butter
> $^1/_2$ cup packed brown sugar
> 3 tablespoons half-and-half or low-fat
>   (1%) milk

Preheat oven to 325°F (165°C). Lightly oil a 9-inch-round cake pan. Cream together sugar and butter in a medium-size bowl. Combine the flour, baking powder and salt in a small bowl. Add to the sugar mixture with the milk and cranberries, stirring just until smooth. Spoon mixture into cake pan. Bake 40 to 45 minutes, until lightly browned and a toothpick inserted in the center comes out clean.

For sauce, combine the butter, brown sugar and half-and-half or milk in a small saucepan. Bring to a boil and cook, stirring, 2 to 3 minutes, until sauce is smooth. Cut pudding into 6 pieces and place on individual plates. Top with hot sauce. *Makes 6 servings.*

PER SERVING: Cal 309 • Carbo 54 gm • Prot 3 gm • Total fat 10 gm • Sat fat 6 gm • Cal from fat 29% • Chol 27 mg

VARIATION
This recipe can be easily doubled. Bake in 2 cake pans, double sauce and serve as above.

EDUCATION: Develop generosity of spirit. How we treat people is far more important than the material gifts we might give them. A kind word, a helping hand and a compassionate heart are the gold, frankincense and myrrh of human relationships.

INSPIRATION: *Fear of the future is more than I can handle. By staying in the moment, my life becomes more manageable.*

Black-eyed Peas with Creole Vegetables

Because this recipe makes a family–reunion–size amount, perhaps you'll have leftovers to freeze for New Year's Day, when some consider it lucky to eat black-eyed peas. If you've overdone it for the holidays, this can also serve as a low-fat vegetarian dinner.

> 1 1/4 cups dried black-eyed peas
> 2 pounds fresh green beans
> 3 cups peeled and cubed turnips
> 1 cup chopped onion
> 1/4 cup diced green bell pepper
> 1 tablespoon unsalted butter
> 1 teaspoon dried thyme
> 1/2 teaspoon salt
> 1/8 teaspoon freshly ground
>   black pepper
> 1 (14 1/2-ounce) can stewed
>   tomatoes

Pick over and rinse beans. Soak overnight in enough water to cover or use the quick-soak method (see glossary). Drain beans, add enough water to cover generously in a large saucepan and bring to a boil. Reduce heat, cover and simmer about 1 hour or until black-eyed peas are firm-tender. Drain.

Meanwhile, trim green beans and add with turnips to a nonstick Dutch oven. Cover with water and bring to a boil. Reduce heat, cover and simmer 18 to 20 minutes or until vegetables are tender. Drain and set vegetables aside, covered, in a bowl.

In the Dutch oven over medium heat, cook the onion and bell pepper in the butter until tender, 4 to 5 minutes. Add the thyme, salt and pepper and cook, stirring, 1 minute. Return the vegetables to the Dutch oven and add the black-eyed peas and the stewed tomatoes, breaking them up with a wooden spoon. Bring to a boil. Reduce heat, cover and simmer 15 to 20 minutes or until vegetables are tender and flavors are blended.   *Makes 12 servings.*

PER SERVING: Cal 65 • Carbo 15 gm • Prot 3 gm • Total fat trace • Sat fat 0 • Cal from fat 6% • Chol 0 mg

VARIATION
If you don't want to cook black-eyed peas from scratch, substitute two (16-ounce) cans black-eyed peas, rinsed and drained, for the final 15 to 20 minutes of cooking.

EDUCATION: Eat balanced meals following a big holiday instead of starving yourself to make up for overindulgences. Skipping meals just ensures you'll be hungrier when you do eat, and probably overeat as a result. Eat low-calorie snacks, such as raw vegetables, melba toast or plain popcorn or pretzels, to keep hunger pangs at bay while continuing your moderate eating plan.

INSPIRATION: *I may not be able to fix other people's problems, but by my presence and attention, I can share strength and hope.*

Bob's Roasted Root Vegetables

🌿 Half of a two-career couple, Bob finds the oven a great tool for making dinner while feeding horses and doing chores. Lucky Lydia reaps the benefit of his joy in cooking. The roasting renders the vegetables surprisingly sweet. You can vary the selection according to your taste.

> 4 medium-size red potatoes, scrubbed
>   and quartered
> 4 large carrots, peeled and cut into chunks
> 2 large sweet potatoes, peeled and
>   cut into thick slices
> 4 parsnips, peeled and cut into chunks
> 2 medium-size turnips, trimmed and quartered
> 2 medium-size red onions, peeled and quartered
> 1 small rutabaga, peeled and cut
>   into bite-size chunks
> 2 tablespoons olive oil
> 1 teaspoon dried thyme
> 1/2 teaspoon crushed, dried rosemary
> 1 teaspoon salt
> 1/2 teaspoon freshly ground black pepper

Preheat oven to 375°F (190°C). Place vegetables in the bottom half of a large roasting pan. Add the oil, thyme, rosemary, salt and pepper and toss until vegetables are coated. Bake 45 minutes, stirring and rearranging vegetables 2 or 3 times, until lightly browned and tender.   *Makes 8 servings.*

PER SERVING: Cal 308 • Carbo 66 gm • Prot 6 gm • Total fat 4 gm • Sat fat 1 gm • Cal from fat 12% • Chol 0 mg

EDUCATION: To save energy, use your hot oven for several chores at once. When preparing a meat roast, chose a dish like the vegetables above or even baked potatoes. You'll save your own energy, too, as there's less "hands-on" required by baking meats and vegetables.

INSPIRATION: *The more I am willing to admit that I cannot live my life in isolation, the more I realize that love and help are all around me.*

Golden Orange Carrot Soup

❧ The combination of citrus and sweet carrots yields a versatile soup that would be just as popular at brunch as at dinner. In summer, especially, this soup would be welcome chilled.

> *8 medium-size carrots, peeled and*
> *   thinly sliced*
> *1/4 cup finely chopped onion*
> *1/2 teaspoon minced gingerroot*
> *1 tablespoon unsalted butter*
> *3 cups defatted chicken broth*
> *1 1/2 cups fresh orange juice*
> *1/4 teaspoon salt*
> *1/8 teaspoon freshly grated nutmeg*
>
> GARNISHES
> *1 navel orange*
> *2 tablespoons nonfat yogurt*
> *1 tablespoon minced fresh cilantro*

Cook carrots, onion and gingerroot in the butter in a nonstick Dutch oven over low heat, stirring frequently, until onion is soft but not brown, about 10 minutes. Add half the broth and bring to a boil over medium heat. Reduce heat, cover and simmer 10 minutes, stirring occasionally or until carrots are tender.

Puree the carrot mixture in a blender or food processor and return to the pan. Add remaining broth, orange juice, salt and nutmeg. Heat soup through if serving warm, or chill. Peel orange and cut 4 thin slices for garnish. To serve, hot or cold, pour soup into 4 bowls. Garnish by floating an orange slice in each bowl, topping with a dollop of yogurt and sprinkling with minced cilantro.

Makes 4 servings.

PER SERVING: Cal 162 • Carbo 26 gm • Prot 6 gm • Total fat 4 gm • Sat fat 2 gm • Cal from fat 22% • Chol 8 mg

EDUCATION: Set aside a day to celebrate yourself. Sign up for a relaxing massage, have your hair washed at a salon, or create a mini-spa in your bathtub. Pick several things you like to do, then do them. You are as rare as the finest jewel, never to be duplicated. Now, that's something to celebrate!

INSPIRATION: *Today I will look for what's right in my life and the world in general.*

Papa Joe's Tamale Pie

❧ A skillet casserole combines peppers and cornmeal with ground turkey for a flavorful main dish. To turn down the heat, eliminate the jalapeño.

> *1/2 cup chopped onion*
> *1/2 cup diced green bell pepper*
> *2 teaspoons olive oil*
> *1 tablespoon minced fresh garlic*
> *1/2 jalapeño chile, minced (see glossary)*
> *1 tablespoon chili powder*
> *1/2 teaspoon ground coriander*
> *1/2 teaspoon ground cumin*
> *1/4 teaspoon dried oregano*
> *1/4 teaspoon salt*
> *1/8 teaspoon freshly ground black pepper*
> *1/2 pound ground skinless turkey breast*
> *1 (14 1/2-ounce) can whole tomatoes,*
> *   coarsely chopped, with juice*
> *1 cup frozen whole-kernel corn*
> *1/2 cup stone-ground yellow cornmeal*
> *1/2 cup nonfat yogurt*
> *1/2 cup chicken broth*
> *1 (4-ounce) can chopped mild chiles,*
> *   drained*

1/3 cup shredded sharp Cheddar cheese
1 tablespoon chopped pitted ripe olives
1 tablespoon chopped green olives
    with pimiento
Parsley sprigs for garnish

Cook onion and bell pepper in the oil in a large nonstick skillet, stirring frequently, until the onion is tender, 4 or 5 minutes. Add the garlic, jalapeño, chili powder, coriander, cumin, oregano, salt, and pepper and cook, stirring, 1 minute more.

Add turkey, breaking apart with a wooden spoon, and cook, stirring, until browned, 3 to 4 minutes. Add tomatoes and their juice, and corn and bring to a boil.

Combine the cornmeal, yogurt and broth. Reduce heat and as turkey mixture simmers, stir in 1 cup of the cornmeal mixture. Simmer (do not allow to boil) 3 minutes. Stir corn and chiles into remaining cornmeal mixture and drizzle over top and sprinkle with cheese. Cover and simmer over very low heat, without stirring, 15 to 20 minutes or until set. Sprinkle with olives. Remove from heat and let stand, covered, for 10 minutes. Spoon onto plates and garnish with parsley. *Makes 4 servings.*

PER SERVING: Cal 380 • Carbo 34 gm • Prot 24 gm • Total fat 17 gm • Sat fat 3 gm • Cal from fat 40% • Chol 44 mg

EDUCATION: Add whole grains when you serve meat to help your digestive tract. Meat, fish and poultry contain no fiber, giving your digestive tract little to work with in moving things along. High-fiber foods, such as the cornmeal above solve that problem while adding a tasty contribution to the meal.

INSPIRATION: *Sharing my journey of recovery with others helps me to remember where I've been and to see the progress I've made.*

Coriander-Spiced Sweet Potato Slices

❧ A definite change-of-pace taste for sweet potatoes, these slices go well with pork, but could spice up a vegetarian assortment of cooked vegetables.

2 large sweet potatoes
2 teaspoons olive oil
1/2 teaspoon ground cumin
1/4 teaspoon ground coriander
1/8 teaspoon salt
1/8 teaspoon freshly ground black pepper
Dash of hot (cayenne) pepper

Preheat oven to 450°F (230°C). Lightly oil two baking sheets. Peel sweet potatoes and cut into 1/4-inch-thick slices. Combine the oil, cumin, coriander, salt, black and cayenne pepper in a small bowl. Lightly brush both sides of the sweet potato slices with the mixture.

Arrange the potato slices on baking sheets. Bake 18 to 22 minutes, switching the baking sheets from upper and lower shelves and turning the slices once after 10 minutes. Remove from the oven when slices are golden brown. Pat with paper towels to remove excess oil and serve warm. *Makes 4 servings.*

PER SERVING: Cal 80 • Carbo 14 gm • Prot 1 gm • Total fat 2 gm • Sat fat trace • Cal from fat 27% • Chol 0 mg

EDUCATION: Count on potatoes and sweet potatoes to fill you up so you are less tempted by higher-fat foods. The myth that carbohydrates are fattening is just that. Prepared in a low-fat way, without rich sauces or toppings, potatoes and sweet potatoes are a dieter's friend.

INSPIRATION: *Ingredient by ingredient, I am putting my world together: finding right work, right relationships and creating my personal recipe for life.*

Lemon Wild Rice with Green Onions

 Whatever your favorite main dish for New Year's Eve, wild rice makes an impressive and delicious side dish.

> ³/₄ cup wild rice
> ¹/₄ cup long- or short-grain
>   brown rice
> 2 cups chicken broth
> 1 lemon
> ¹/₄ cup minced green onions
> 1 teaspoon unsalted butter or
>   margarine
> 2 tablespoons minced fresh parsley
> Twist of lemon peel for garnish
>   (optional)
> Parsley sprigs for garnish (optional)

Rinse and drain wild rice and place in a medium-size saucepan with brown rice and broth. Bring to a boil over medium heat. Meanwhile, grate the lemon peel. (Only grate the yellow part; the white part is bitter.) Squeeze juice from lemon. When rice comes to a boil, stir in grated lemon peel and 2 tablespoons lemon juice.

Reduce heat to low, cover and simmer 50 minutes or just until liquid is absorbed and rice is tender. Check for doneness toward the end of cooking time. Stir in a little extra liquid if rice seems dry.

In a small, nonstick skillet, cook green onions in the butter over medium heat just until they begin to turn translucent, about 2 minutes. Stir in parsley and cook, stirring, just until wilted, about 30 seconds. Stir green onions and parsley mixture into brown rice. Turn brown rice out into a serving bowl. Garnish, if desired, with a twist of lemon peel atop several parsley sprigs.   *Makes 4 servings.*

PER SERVING: Cal 136 • Carbo 23 gm • Prot 6 gm • Total fat 2 gm • Sat fat 1 gm • Cal from fat 13% • Chol 2 mg

EDUCATION: Be good to yourself so you can enjoy every day. Part of being good to yourself means finding balance in your life: avoiding rigid diets or mindless overeating; finding time for yourself, as well as for work, friends and family; weighing the spiritual and material to find the life-style that's comfortable for you.

Glossary

Acid foods

Acid foods, such as tomatoes and lemon marinades, are valuable aids in tenderizing meats or poultry. This is an advantage when serving lean, inexpensive cuts of meat. Cooked with vegetables, however, acid foods have the opposite effect. Remember when you're cooking vegetables to add any large amounts of acid foods toward the end of cooking to ensure the vegetables' tenderness.

Alcohol

Because many of us, or guests at our tables, may have a problem with alcohol, this ingredient is avoided in all of these recipes. Cooks may assume that the alcohol burns off during cooking. However, studies at Washington State University indicate it does not. Chicken breast in white wine retained 40 percent of its alcohol after 10 minutes of simmering, while even a pot roast cooked in red wine 2½ hours had 5 percent of its original alcohol content. If you are a recovering alcoholic, or cooking for friends who may be, avoid all foods cooked with wine, spirits or beer. Alcoholics Anonymous also suggests avoiding small sources of alcohol, such as vanilla extract (which has an alcohol content equal to that of most spirits), tamari soy sauce, which is often preserved with alcohol, and cooking oil sprays, which most often contain grain alcohol. These are also avoided throughout this book.

Alfalfa sprouts

To become an alfalfa seed farmer, all you need is a quart jar, a piece of cheesecloth and a rubber band. Start with 1 tablespoon of alfalfa seeds. Soak overnight in water to cover. Cover the mouth of the jar with cheesecloth and secure with a strong rubber band. Drain the sprouts well, then shake the jar to distribute the seeds. Place the jar on a windowsill or countertop on its side. Rinse, drain and distribute the seeds around the inside of the jar about four times a day.

After three to four days, when the sprouts are about 2 inches long, they are ready to harvest. Keep them in the sun the last day to develop valuable chlorophyll. Store them in the refrigerator. If you want to raise sprouts on a larger scale, get a gallon-size jar. Experiment with radish, sunflower or mustard seeds, lentils, soybeans, mung beans or whole, dried peas.

Make certain the beans, peas and seeds were intended for human consumption and not for planting in your garden. Harvest larger bean and seed sprouts within a few days of sprouting.

Artichokes

Unlike their large, fresh counterparts, the baby artichokes used for canning are tiny. They have not developed the thistlelike choke. Canned artichokes include the tender bottom portion, along with some of the inner leaves. Remember to drain and rinse artichoke hearts before incorporating them in recipes to reduce their sodium content.

When eating fresh artichokes, provide a separate bowl for each person to use for discarding leaves. To eat, turn artichokes stem side down and remove leaves, one at a time, dipping the meaty end into sauce and pulling the inverted leaf over your bottom teeth to nibble off the artichoke flesh. Continue until leaves are removed and you have reached the "choke" or thistle. Carefully cut out the choke with a sharp knife and discard it. Cut artichoke bottom into pieces, dip in sauce and enjoy!

Baking powder, aluminum free

If you cannot find an aluminum-free baking powder in your area, make your own. Combine 2 tablespoons cream of tartar, 2 tablespoons arrowroot and 1 tablespoon baking soda to make approximately 1/4 cup of baking powder. Store, tightly covered, in a cool, dry place.

Beans, soaking

Cover dried beans generously with cold water. Let stand 3 hours or overnight, or use this quick-soak method: bring beans to a boil, remove from heat and allow beans to stand 1 hour. Drain beans and discard water. Cover

with fresh cold water. Bring to a boil, reduce heat and simmer, partially covered, 30 minutes. Discard water. Add fresh water and continue cooking beans until tender. This method will remove the oligosaccharides, which are responsible for intestinal discomforts.

Brown rice

Brown rice takes longer to cook than white rice. Unless you buy the quick-cooking variety, you may have to plan ahead a little to conveniently add whole-grain rice to your diet. One way is to begin cooking the rice before assembling and preparing the rest of your meal. Or, cook up large batches of brown rice, then refrigerate or freeze in serving-size portions. To cook, place 2 cups of brown rice in a large saucepan with 4 cups of water and bring to a boil. Boil 2 minutes, then reduce heat to low, cover and let rice steam 35 to 45 minutes or until water is absorbed and grains are tender. Never stir rice as it cooks, or it will clump together. Reheat refrigerated or frozen rice in the microwave or by placing in a colander over boiling water.

Butter

Because many cooking oil sprays contain grain alcohol, the recipes here are generally cooked in nonstick utensils. For even greater ease in cooking, a small amount of butter held in the wrapper can be glided quickly across the bottom of a heated pan. The amount of butter added in this way should generally be 1/4 teaspoon or less.

Chestnuts

To roast chestnuts, cut an X in the flat side of the shell, put the chestnuts in a pan and cover with foil. Bake in a 450°F (230°C) oven for 30 minutes. Wrap chestnuts in a towel and seal in a plastic bag until cool enough to handle. Peel while still warm, removing the papery inner shell. One pound of chestnuts equals approximately 1 cup cooked and peeled. Enjoy them as a snack or use in recipes.

Clams

Clams, because of their burrowing nature, may be protected in part from any pollutants in coastal waters through the natural filtering qualities of sand. To clean hard-shelled clams, scrub them thoroughly with a stiff vegetable brush under cold running water. Discard any clams with cracked or broken shells or shells that are not shut tightly. Likewise, discard any clams that do not open upon cooking. Clams are very low in calories, low in fat, high in protein and a modest source of calcium.

Coconut milk

To make coconut milk, select a whole coconut, shaking it first to be sure it is filled with liquid. Avoid coconuts with wet or moldy "eyes."

Using an ice pick, drill into two of the "eyes" and drain out the coconut water. This liquid is not used in cooking. Place the coconut in a preheated 400°F (200°C) oven 20 minutes or until it cracks. Pry it open. Place the coconut halves in a heavy, self-sealing plastic bag. On a firm, nonmarring surface, hit the coconut with a hammer to break it into pieces. Remove the shell and shave off brown skin with a vegetable peeler or paring knife. Rinse, drain and place coconut meat in a blender.

Pour 2 cups hot water into the blender and process until smooth, scraping down the sides of the container as needed. Line a medium-size bowl with 2 layers of cheesecloth. Pour in the blended coconut mixture, gather up the cheesecloth to make a "bag" and squeeze into the bowl until the coconut meat is dry. Let liquid stand about 1 hour while preparing soup.

Skim off and discard the top layer of high-fat coconut cream that rises to the surface, reserving 1½ cups of coconut milk.

Flours

As you switch to whole-grain flours, you may notice that recipes often call for a "sliding scale" of liquids. Depending on where and when a grain has grown, ripened and matured and how it's been stored, flours will absorb varying amounts of liquid. When a recipe calls for 1 to 1½ cups of liquid, always begin with the smaller amount. Then, if the batter is too thick, add additional liquid gradually, stirring it well into the batter, until the desired consistency is reached.

Like regular whole-wheat flour, whole-wheat pastry flour is made from the whole-wheat berry. It includes the germ, rich in vitamin E as well as B vitamins and trace minerals, and the bran, which is high in fiber. Regular whole-wheat flour is made from hard, winter wheat, which is high in gluten. Gluten is the "stretchy" component of yeast dough that holds onto expanding gases and allows yeast breads to rise. Whole-wheat pastry flour, available in health food stores, is made from soft, spring wheat. Low in gluten, whole-wheat pastry flour is perfect for quick breads, pie crusts and other baked goods, where it gives a finely textured, light and flaky crumb. Whole-wheat pastry flour can be used to thicken sauces, and can even be used to provide fiber and flavor to yeast breads, as long as it is combined with high-gluten bread flour or all-purpose flour.

Gingerroot

If you like the flavor of fresh ginger, but want to avoid the pungency of biting into a piece of the flavorful root, grate the ginger. Place grated ginger in a square of cheesecloth and squeeze out flavorful liquid. Discard gratings. One-quarter cup grated ginger yields about one teaspoon ginger juice.

Greens

You may be surprised at the variety: mustard greens, chicory, collard greens, kale, spinach, turnip greens, beet greens and Swiss chard. What they contain in common is: impressive levels of carotene, the plant form of vitamin A; high vitamin C and fiber; valuable chlorophyll; low fat content and few calories, as little as 20 calories per cup of cooked greens. Some tips for adding greens to your diet: Cook them just until tender; overcooking will unfavorably alter their flavor. Begin with delicately flavored greens, such as Swiss chard, spinach or beet greens. Add chopped greens in the last minutes of cooking to soups or stews. Add dark greens, thinly sliced, to salads.

Jalapeño Chiles

Jalapeño chiles contain volatile oils that can cause intense stinging, especially of eyes and mucous membranes. When you chop jalapeños, wear rubber gloves. When finished, wash gloves well in hot soapy water. Do not touch your face or eyes when handling jalapeños or other hot chiles. The seeds are the hottest part of the chiles, so discard them if you want a slightly milder dish.

Leeks

Leeks are grown in sandy soil and require some special attention when cleaning. Trim root ends. Insert a knife into the white part of the leek about an inch below the green tops, and slice the leek in half from that point to the tips of the leaves. Turn leek one-quarter turn, insert knife and slice again to leaf tips. Fan out the green tops and rinse leeks under lukewarm water to remove sand and grit. Slice or chop leeks as needed.

Lentils

Among dried beans, red lentils are a real convenience food. Compared to an hour or more of cooking for most dried beans, even after overnight soaking, red lentils are ready in one-fourth the time. And there's no presoaking. Cooked red lentils can be a protein-rich, high-fiber addition to spaghetti sauces, soups, stews and casseroles. Add them to taco and burrito fillings and reduce the amount of ground meat. Their mild flavor make them welcome in a variety of dishes.

Pancake mix

In a self-sealing plastic bag, combine 2 cups unbleached all-purpose flour, 1 cup whole-wheat flour, 1/2 cup rolled oats, 2 tablespoons sugar, 1 tablespoon baking powder and 1/2 teaspoon salt. Shake it up until all the ingredients are combined. You will have 3 cups mix. For 6 pancakes, combine 1 cup of the dry mix with 1 beaten egg, 2/3 cup milk and 1 tablespoon oil.

Parsley

Parsley loses much of its vitamin content when it is dried, so keep fresh on hand in the refrigerator. Place stems in a glass of water and cover tops loosely with a plastic bag to prevent drying. Change the water daily. Or, rinse parsley briefly and place in a perforated plastic bag in the refrigerator.

Pumpkin

If you have canned pumpkin left over when making a recipe, you don't have to let it go to waste. Make one of the easiest soups ever. For each ½ cup pumpkin puree, add 1 cup skim milk, 2 teaspoons brown sugar and a dash of cinnamon and ginger. Heat through, but do not boil. Serve the soup hot. Leftover soup can be frozen for later use.

Quinoa

To prepare quinoa, rinse well in a fine strainer under cold running water. Drain well. Brown the grain in an ungreased iron skillet 5 minutes before cooking to develop a roasted flavor. In a small pan, combine ½ cup rinsed, roasted quinoa with 1 cup apple juice (for muffins, breakfast or dessert), chicken stock (for pilafs or casseroles) or water. Bring to a boil, reduce heat, cover and simmer 15 minutes, or until grains are translucent and have expanded. Stir into rice pudding, cooked breakfast cereals, casseroles, soups or salads.

Saffron

Because saffron is so expensive, substitutes abound. Flowers of marigold or safflower are sometimes mixed in with powdered saffron to reduce its cost. Safflower is sometimes marketed as "Mexican saffron," but it lacks the pungent and distinctive aroma and flavor of saffron. Turmeric will add a saffron color to dishes, but has a different flavor. Here, as in other areas of our lives, we learn there are no true substitutes for what's real.

Shrimp

Peel shrimp, leaving the tail intact, if you desire. With a knife, cut a shallow slit down the back, or outside curve, of each shrimp. Remove the vein from the entire length of the shrimp.

Stock

Perk up low-fat stocks to make flavorful soups from scratch. It's easy to make your own stock (so many cookbooks tell you that), but if it's easier to open a can (and it almost always is) enrich the flavor with the following: Place 2 or more cups of canned stock in a saucepan with ½ onion, 1 carrot, ½ stalk of celery, ½ bay leaf and 2 peppercorns. Bring to a boil, reduce heat and simmer 10 minutes. Pour through a strainer before using. Also, a convenient stock base, to which you just add water, is available from Redi-Base, P.O. Box 846, Whitehall, PA 18052 (1-800-820-5121). The stock is tasty, requires little storage space, and is available in chicken, beef, ham, seafood and vegetable flavors.

Stuffing

Always cool stuffings before inserting into poultry, fish or meats to prevent the growth of bacteria. Hot stuffing can raise the temperature of surrounding meats to the point where bacteria can rapidly multiply. Adding cool stuffing to cool poultry maintains the even, low temperature necessary for food safety.

Toasting nuts

Toast nuts in a small cast-iron pan, stirring constantly, until fragrant and lightly browned.

Tofu

Tofu, also called bean curd, is very like cheese, except that it is made from soybeans instead of dairy milk. High in protein, low in sodium and fat, with no cholesterol, tofu is an excellent meat substitute, especially when served with brown rice. One of the advantages of tofu is its bland flavor, which makes it right at home in a variety of dishes. It can be mashed and substituted for cottage or ricotta cheese in Italian dishes, or sliced, marinated and added to stir-frys. Store refrigerated, with water to cover the tofu, and change the water daily. If you can't use the tofu within a week, freeze it. Defrost and press out excess water before using.

Vanilla sugar

Widely available in Europe, vanilla sugar is not as popular in the United States. However, if you are not using vanilla extract because of its alcohol content, vanilla sugar is an easy alternative. Simply cut up a vanilla bean, place it in a jar with a lid, and pour in granulated sugar. (This also works with powdered sugar—just slip a whole bean in the package.) Put on the lid and shake the jar to distribute the bean. Remove vanilla bean pieces when you measure out the sugar. Pop the pieces back in the jar and add fresh sugar. That way you'll always have vanilla sugar on hand.

Vinegar, flavored

Buy white vinegar, as many pints as you plan to use. Heat the vinegar in a stainless steel pan. For berry vinegars, add 1 tablespoon honey, $1/2$ cup rinsed, dried berries and a twist of lemon or orange peel. When the vinegar begins to simmer, remove from heat. Cool and allow vinegar and fruit to steep for 2 days in a cool place. Pour flavored vinegar into a pint bottle, straining out berries and peel.

For herb vinegars, add $1/4$ cup fresh herbs and a halved garlic clove, if desired, to vinegar as it simmers. Let steep, as above. Place a sprig of herb into pint jar and add strained vinegar.

The herb will identify the flavored vinegar. You can find decorative bottles, or remove labels from the purchased vinegar bottles and tie with ribbon and add an ornament or a few sprigs of decorative eucalyptus for fancy touch.

Wheat berries

Plan ahead with wheat berries to shorten the actual cooking time. Bring grain and water to a boil and boil 10 minutes. This can be done in the morning. Cover pan and set aside for 8 to 12 hours. Return pan to stove and cook grain 15 to 20 minutes, until tender. Grains can also be cooked by the Thermos® method. Place 1 cup grain in a wide-mouthed quart Thermos container. Add boiling water, leaving an inch of space between water and bottom of stopper. Close the Thermos and shake to distribute the grain and water evenly. Let stand 8 to 12 hours. When you're doing other baking, cook grains generously covered with water in an ovenproof casserole dish in the oven until tender.

Yogurt cheese

Line a colander with cheesecloth and set the colander over a large bowl. Spoon 4 cups of plain nonfat yogurt (made without gelatin or stabilizers) into the lined colander and refrigerate. By morning you'll have about $1^3/4$ cups of yogurt cheese. You can discard the drained whey or use in baking. For desserts, try draining nonfat vanilla yogurt and serve with fruits.

Metric Conversion Chart

Comparison to Metric Measure				
When You Know	Symbol	Multiply By	To Find	Symbol
teaspoons	tsp	5.0	milliliters	ml
tablespoons	tbsp	15.0	milliliters	ml
fluid ounces	fl. oz.	30.0	milliliters	ml
cups	c	0.24	liters	l
pints	pt.	0.47	liters	l
quarts	qt.	0.95	liters	l
ounces	oz.	28.0	grams	g
pounds	lb.	0.45	kilograms	kg
Fahrenheit	F	5/9 (after subtracting 32)	Celsius	C

Liquid Measure to Milliliters		
1/4 teaspoon	=	1.25 milliliters
1/2 teaspoon	=	2.5 milliliters
3/4 teaspoon	=	3.75 milliliters
1 teaspoon	=	5.0 milliliters
1-1/4 teaspoons	=	6.25 milliliters
1-1/2 teaspoons	=	7.5 milliliters
1-3/4 teaspoons	=	8.75 milliliters
2 teaspoons	=	10.0 milliliters
1 tablespoon	=	15.0 milliliters
2 tablespoons	=	30.0 milliliters

Fahrenheit to Celsius	
F	C
200–205	95
220–225	105
245–250	120
275	135
300–305	150
325–330	165
345–350	175
370–375	190
400–405	205
425–430	220
445–450	230
470–475	245
500	260

Liquid Measure to Liters		
1/4 cup	=	0.06 liters
1/2 cup	=	0.12 liters
3/4 cup	=	0.18 liters
1 cup	=	0.24 liters
1-1/4 cups	=	0.3 liters
1-1/2 cups	=	0.36 liters
2 cups	=	0.48 liters
2-1/2 cups	=	0.6 liters
3 cups	=	0.72 liters
3-1/2 cups	=	0.84 liters
4 cups	=	0.96 liters
4-1/2 cups	=	1.08 liters
5 cups	=	1.2 liters
5-1/2 cups	=	1.32 liters

Index

ABOUT THE AUTHOR

Sharon Sassaman Claessens, a former daily newspaper food editor, has written five previous health-oriented cookbooks. Her 20 *Minute Natural Foods Cookbook* won a National Tastemaker Award for Excellence in 1982. She has written articles for *Organic Gardening, Prevention* and *Quick and Healthy Cooking Magazine.*

A graduate of Hood College, Frederick, Maryland, she also studied at Trinity College, Oxford, and at the Cordon Bleu School of Cookery in London. She has lived in England, Belgium and the Netherlands, and has traveled throughout Europe, the Caribbean, Central Asia and parts of Africa exploring indigenous cuisines. She is a member of the International Association of Cooking Professionals. Best of all, she has a 15-year-old son, Adam, who loves to eat and who also is a terrific baker.

Her recovery process has included participation in several 12-step groups, cancer support groups and individual and group therapy. She spent several years facilitating women's groups developing communication skills, relaxation techniques and self-esteem. She is currently involved in the ongoing discovery of what it is to live one day at a time with cancer and to savor each day.